Experiential Legal Research

Aspen Coursebook Series

Experiential Legal Research

Sources, Strategies, and Citation

Diana R. Donahoe

Professor of Legal Research and Writing
Georgetown Law Center

Wolters Kluwer
Law & Business

Published by Wolters Kluwer Law & Business in New York.

Wolters Kluwer Law & Business serves customers worldwide with CCH, Aspen Publishers, and Kluwer Law International products. (www.wolterskluwerlb.com)

To contact Customer Service, e-mail customer.service@wolterskluwer.com, call 1-800-234-1660, fax 1-800-901-9075, or mail correspondence to:

Wolters Kluwer Law & Business
Attn: Order Department
PO Box 990
Frederick, MD 21705

Printed in the United States of America.

1 2 3 4 5 6 7 8 9 0

ISBN 978-0-7355-9835-5

Library of Congress Cataloging-in-Publication Data

Donahoe, Diana R., 1964-
 Experiential legal research : sources, strategies, and citation / Diana R. Donahoe.
   p. cm. — (Aspen coursebook series)
 ISBN 978-0-7355-9835-5
 1. Legal research—United States. 2. Citation of legal authorities. I. Title.
 KF240.D66 2011
 340.072'073—dc23

                                                                2011026040

About Wolters Kluwer Law & Business

Wolters Kluwer Law & Business is a leading global provider of intelligent information and digital solutions for legal and business professionals in key specialty areas, and respected educational resources for professors and law students. Wolters Kluwer Law & Business connects legal and business professionals as well as those in the education market with timely, specialized authoritative content and information-enabled solutions to support success through productivity, accuracy and mobility.

Serving customers worldwide, Wolters Kluwer Law & Business products include those under the Aspen Publishers, CCH, Kluwer Law International, Loislaw, Best Case, ftwilliam.com and MediRegs family of products.

CCH products have been a trusted resource since 1913, and are highly regarded resources for legal, securities, antitrust and trade regulation, government contracting, banking, pension, payroll, employment and labor, and healthcare reimbursement and compliance professionals.

Aspen Publishers products provide essential information to attorneys, business professionals and law students. Written by preeminent authorities, the product line offers analytical and practical information in a range of specialty practice areas from securities law and intellectual property to mergers and acquisitions and pension/benefits. Aspen's trusted legal education resources provide professors and students with high-quality, up-to-date and effective resources for successful instruction and study in all areas of the law.

Kluwer Law International products provide the global business community with reliable international legal information in English. Legal practitioners, corporate counsel and business executives around the world rely on Kluwer Law journals, looseleafs, books, and electronic products for comprehensive information in many areas of international legal practice.

Loislaw is a comprehensive online legal research product providing legal content to law firm practitioners of various specializations. Loislaw provides attorneys with the ability to quickly and efficiently find the necessary legal information they need, when and where they need it, by facilitating access to primary law as well as state-specific law, records, forms and treatises.

Best Case Solutions is the leading bankruptcy software product to the bankruptcy industry. It provides software and workflow tools to flawlessly streamline petition preparation and the electronic filing process, while timely incorporating ever-changing court requirements.

ftwilliam.com offers employee benefits professionals the highest quality plan documents (retirement, welfare and non-qualified) and government forms (5500/PBGC, 1099 and IRS) software at highly competitive prices.

MediRegs products provide integrated health care compliance content and software solutions for professionals in healthcare, higher education and life sciences, including professionals in accounting, law and consulting.

Wolters Kluwer Law & Business, a division of Wolters Kluwer, is headquartered in New York. Wolters Kluwer is a market-leading global information services company focused on professionals.

SUMMARY OF CONTENTS

CONTENTS

ACKNOWLEDGMENTS

Many people contributed to this book. Special thanks to: Noelle Adgerson for her continuous support in helping to produce the manuscript; my research assistants over the last few years for their many contributions, including: Daniel Solomon, Robyn English, Life Marshall, Stephen Winslow, Jackie Bean, Hanna Hickman; faculty and librarians for their input into the content and design, including Sara Sampson, Susan Sloane, Andrea Funk and the faculty at Whittier Law School, Dave Simon, Mitch Fleischmann, Michael Cedrone, Julie Ross, Michael Golden, David Wolitz, Sonya Bonneau, and Rima Sirota; the people at Aspen, including Barbara Roth, Emily Bender, Susan Boulanger, John Chatelaine, Carol McGeehan, and Richard Mixter. Thanks also to the support of Georgetown University Law Center.

A special thanks to: my family for their support, including my husband, Keith Donahoe, and my children Allie and Peter Donahoe, who have put up with my constant work during evenings and weekends; to my parents, Robert and Norma Roberto, for their support through the years; and to my family of Law Fellows, too numerous to name, who have been an integral part of my development of innovative material to engage students in the classroom.

I would also like to acknowledge the publishers and organizations that permitted me to reprint copyrighted material in this text:

United States Code Annotated
Reprinted with permission of Thomas Reuters, *United States Code Annotated*, Title 20 § 1079 (2010), pp. 350, 353

USCA Popular Names Table,
Reprinted with permission of Thomas Reuters, *United States Code Annotated*, Popular Names Table (2010), p. 887

The Supreme Court Website Screen Shot
Permission of supremecourt.gov

The Oyez.org Website Screen Shot
Permission of Oyez.org

The Lawprose.org Website
Permission of Lawprose.org

The Scotusblog Website Screen Shot
Permission of Scotusblog

Anatomy of a Federal Case
Reprinted with permission of Thomas Reuters, *Barron v. Runyon*, 11 F. Supp. 2d. 676, 677 (1998)

Federal Digest
Reprinted with permission of Thomas Reuters, *West's Federal Practice Digest* 4, Vol. 81E (2009) p. 481

Table of Cases By Name
Reprinted with permission of Thomas Reuters, *West's Federal Practice Digest* 4, Vol. 103A, Table of Cases (2009) p. 184

Annotated State Statute
Reprinted with permission of Thomas Reuters. *Vernon's Texas Codes Annotated, Civil Practice and Remedies* 4, §§96.001-002, p. 343 (2005)

Anatomy of a State Court Case
Reprinted with permission of Thomas Reuters, 831 *Garcia v. Stickel*, 831 N.Y.S. 2d 380 (2007)

The New York Digest
Reprinted with permission of Thomas Reuters, *The New York Digest* 4, Vol. 30 (2010) p. 847

C.J.S.
Reprinted with permission of Thomas Reuters, *Corpus Juris Secundum* Vol. 35, pp. 627-28 (2007)

American Jurisprudence
Reprinted with permission of Thomas Reuters, *American Jurisprudence 2d*, Vol. 31, pp. 193, 196 (2007)

Maryland State Encyclopedia
Reprinted with permission of Thomas Reuters, *Maryland Law Encyclopedia*, Vol. 16 pp. 327-28 (1999)

American Law Reports
Reprinted with permission of Thomas Reuters, *American Law Reports*, Fed. Ser., Vol. 125 (1995) pp. 273-77

HeinOnline Screen Shot
HeinOnline database screenshot reprinted with permission from William S. Hein & Co., Inc.

Law Review Article
Reprinted with permission of the Journal of Legal Education, Diana R. Donahoe, *An Autobiography of a Digital Idea: From Waging War Against Laptops to Engaging Students with Laptops,* 59 J. Legal Educ. 1 (May, 2010)

Restatement of Torts
Copyright 1965 by The American Law Institute. Reprinted with permission. All rights reserved. *Restatement, Second, of the Law of Torts,* §166 (1965) p. 304

Westlaw Key Numbers Screen Shot
Permission of Thomas Reuters

Key Numbers in Digests
Reprinted with permission of Thomas Reuters, West's *Federal Practice Digest* 4, Vol. 81E (2009) p. 491

Key Numbers in Cases
Reprinted with permission of Thomas Reuters, *Barron v. Runyon*, 11 F. Supp. 2d 676 (1998)

Traditional Westlaw Screen Shot
Permission of Thomas Reuters

WestlawNext Screen Shots
Permission of Thomas Reuters

Traditional Lexis Screen Shot
Permission of LexisNexis

Lexis Advance Screen Shots
Permission of LexisNexis

New York Code Index
Reprinted with permission of Thomas Reuters, *McKinney's Consolidated Laws of New York Annotated*, General Index E to L (2010), p. 1331

New York Code Annotated
Reprinted with permission of Thomas Reuters, *McKinney's Consolidated Laws of New York Annotated*, Book 30, § 740 (2002) pp 108, 111, 112

Index to New York Digest
Reprinted with permission of Thomas Reuters, *The New York Digest* 4, Vol. 48A (2010) p. 491

New York Digest
Reprinted with permission of Thomas Reuters, *The New York Digest* 4, Vol. 30 § 367 (2010) p. 846

USCCAN Index
Reprinted with permission of Thomas Reuters, *United States Code Congressional and Administrative News*, 110th Congress-Second Session 2008, Vol. 6 (2008) Index, p. I-24

USCCAN
Reprinted with permission of Thomas Reuters, *United States Code Congressional and Administrative News*, 110th Congress-Second Session 2008, Vol. 1 (2008) Public Law 110-233, (122 Stat. 881)

CIS Index

Reprinted with permission from LexisNexis, *CIS/Annual 2008,* Index to Congressional Publications and Legislative Histories (2008), p. 280

CIS Abstract

Reprinted with permission from LexisNexis, *CIS/Annual 2008,* Abstract from Congressional Publications and Legislative Histories (2008), p. 131

KeyCite Westlaw Screen Shot

Reprinted with permission of Thomas Reuters

KeyCite Flags and Symbols for Westlaw and WestlawNext

Reprinted with permission of Thomas Reuters

Shepard's Lexis Screen Shot

Reprinted with permission of LexisNexis

Shepard's Symbols

Reprinted with permission of LexisNexis

ALWD Manual Front Cover

Reprinted from ALWD Citation Manual: A Professional System of Citation, 4th edition (ISBN 07355-8930-8) by the Association of Legal Writing Directors, with the permission of Wolters Kluwer Law and Business.

Bluebook Front Cover

Reprinted by permission of The Harvard Law Review Association. *The Bluebook A Uniform System of Citation* (19th Edition, The Harvard Law Review Association 2010)

PREFACE

"One can't become skilled simply by reading about skills."[1]

This book is designed to teach today's law students using experiential learning pedagogy. Instead of simply reading about research techniques, students using this book become actively engaged in their learning process through problem-based simulations, interactive exercises, immediate feedback, and thoughtful reflection. Through active engagement, students retain the material, understand the relevance and importance of what they are learning, and become effective and efficient with their new skills. This unique book is a powerful tool to help students form long-term professional habits, become efficient problem-solvers, and think and behave like lawyers.

The content of the book focuses the students on both sources and strategies for researching in today's legal practice. It highlights up-to-date platforms such as WestlawNext and Lexis Advance. In addition, it provides a historical perspective of legal research so that students can research effectively and efficiently by making thoughtful choices about print and electronic sources as well as cost-effective choices. Some of the highlights of this book include the following:

- **Research Sources:** begins with an introduction to research, including an example of a research problem from start to finish; then focuses on primary law, including finding federal and state statutes, cases, administrative law and legislative history; then focuses on using secondary sources.
- **Research Strategies:** discusses strategies for the research process by (1) focusing on the U.S. legal system and stare decisis; (2) presenting strategies for both book research and online research (including traditional Westlaw and Lexis, WestlawNext, Lexis Advance, and free legal sources); (3) discussing strategies for practicing lawyers; and (4) presenting specific strategies for each legal source including specifics on updating the law.
- **Grammar and Citation:** covers citation rules in both the Bluebook and ALWD as well as grammar rules with quizzes and self-assessments for the students.
- **Scanned Pages and Screen Shots:** illustrates and annotates research sources in print and online for the students so they can see the research come to life instead of merely reading about it.
- **Quick References and Checklists:** acts as study aid material for the students to reinforce and test their understanding of the material.
- **Quizzes and Self-Assessments:** provides interactive tools and immediate feedback for students and teachers to test the students' understanding of the materials.

---

1. Roy Stucky et al., Best Practices for Legal Education, p. 170-71 (Clinical Legal Education Association 2007).

- **Class Exercises:** used by teachers as in-class problem sets, out-of-class research projects, or memo and brief assignments for the semester's projects. These exercises range from state-specific material to federal material and cover finding statutes, cases, or both.
- **Answer Keys:** available for professors online and in Teacher's Manual.

This research book can be used in conjunction with its writing book counterpart, *Experiential Legal Writing: Analysis, Process, and Documents.* When used together, the two books provide all the required reading material in a typical modern legal research and writing course:

- Research (including Westlaw, WestlawNext, Lexis, Lexis Advance);
- Writing (memos, briefs, client letters, motions, pleadings, and scholarly documents);
- Analysis (statutory interpretation, common law analysis, policy, etc.);
- Citation (ALWD 4th Edition and the Bluebook 19th Edition); and
- Grammar (included self-assessments and quizzes).

This book is designed as a standalone print book. However, it can also be used, if desired, in conjunction with its online version, *TeachingLaw.com.* The online version provides extra functionality such as (1) a courseware program that links directly with the content, (2) idea banks for professors to share information, assignments, and projects, (3) direct links to other useful web sites so students can research while they learn about sources, (4) self-assessments that report to the professors, and (5) more interactive features for students. Professors may choose to offer the print book, the online version, or both for their students. Appendix B at the end of this book provides a table of contents with both page numbers and screen numbers so that students can be "on the same page" regardless of which version they choose.

A Teacher's Manual accompanies this book. It provides both pedagogical theories and substantive techniques for teaching an experiential learning course, including:

1. Experiential learning pedagogy techniques, including preparing research and writing assignments, designing simulations and class exercises, and crafting the syllabus for both objective and persuasive semesters.
2. Specific assignments with accompanying research in multiple jurisdictions, similar to an idea bank or shared bank for professors;
3. Ready-made research projects and accompanying answer keys;
4. In-class exercises for experiential learning pedagogy and accompanying answer keys;
5. Detailed lesson plans that highlight experiential learning pedagogy to actively engage students in and out of the classroom;
6. Techniques for providing effective and efficient professor feedback and student reflection on draft and final papers.

Reading about legal research is not enough. Students need to be actively engaged in the process to understand the plethora of sources and strategies available in today's legal world. By using experiential learning pedagogy, professors can help their students attain and retain the material and skills needed so that they can become professional, effective, and efficient researchers in any legal field. When these students become practicing lawyers, they will be able to learn new sources and strategies on their own because they have been actively engaged in the learning process throughout their academic lives.

Diana R. Donahoe

Experiential Legal Research

CHAPTER 1

Introduction to Legal Research

This chapter is designed to introduce you to legal research. It gives an overview of the various types of legal authority you may research as a lawyer, explains the importance of accurately citing to each authority, and provides an overview and example of the research process. It also covers briefing cases as a student for class and as a lawyer for research. This chapter is simply an overview; each subject—sources, strategies, and citation—is discussed in separate chapters.

I. THE IMPORTANCE OF EFFECTIVE LEGAL RESEARCH

All lawyers must know how to research the law. Good lawyers know how to research efficiently and thoroughly. This text provides you with research knowledge as well as research strategies and interactive practice to help you become an efficient and a thorough legal researcher, whether you are using print or online sources.

You will need strong legal research skills no matter what type of legal profession you choose. If you become a practicing attorney, clients will ask you for advice. They might ask whether they can perform some action such as purchase another company or build on a particular piece of land. In these situations, you will need to find the law to answer their questions and provide advice. Clients will also come to you with preexisting legal problems. They might want to sue someone, for instance, or they might be defendants in a lawsuit themselves. Here, you will need to research the applicable law to argue the case on behalf of your clients. Other clients will ask you to draft documents such as contracts or wills. For these clients, you will need to know the applicable law in order to bind the parties to the contract or to distribute your client's estate according to his or her wishes. If you choose a legal profession in which you do not practice the law directly (for instance, teaching), you will need to research the law to prepare for your classes or to publish scholarly articles in your field.

Regardless of the type of profession you choose in the law, remember that the legal audience is a doubting audience. A judge will not believe your argument unless you cite to precedent. The opposing side will look for sources to prove the opposing point. A lawyer will argue that your contract provisions are not legal. Another scholar will argue that your theories are irreconcilable with other legal positions. Therefore, to be effective, you will need to prove every argument you make. To do so, you will need to ground your arguments in the law by citing to legal sources. Of course, you need to know how to find those sources first and to make sure that you have found all the applicable law on point.

II. OVERVIEW OF TYPES OF LEGAL AUTHORITY

Legal researchers find the law they need in a variety of places. The research process will become more manageable if you first understand the various legal sources and how they function together. The broadest categories of legal authority are (1) primary law and (2) secondary sources.

A. Primary Law

Primary law refers to those legal sources that are the law itself. Primary law is created by different branches of the government, both federal and state.

The three main categories of primary law are (1) constitutions and statutes, (2) cases, and (3) administrative law.

1. Constitutions and Statutes: Federal and State

Constitutions are created on federal and state levels; they establish the form of government and define individual rights. The United States Constitution provides the framework for our laws, and no other law created can violate the United States Constitution. States create their own constitutions, which can grant further protections for individuals but cannot lessen the rights granted by the federal constitution.

Statutes are also created on federal and state levels. They are written by the legislative branch (and approved by the executive) and published as statutory codes. Statutes cover a broad range of topics, from criminal to civil, and apply to all citizens, whether individual or corporate. They are usually written in general terms to cover a wide range of circumstances. Often they contain definition sections, purpose clauses, specific penalties, and other provisions. The intent of the legislature in creating statutes becomes important when courts are asked to interpret the statutory language on a case-by-case basis.

For more information on the federal Congress and federal statutes, see pages 27-31. For more information on state legislatures and state statutes, see pages 54-58.

2. Cases: Federal and State

Federal and state judges interpret the law when they hear cases between specific parties. The case opinions judges write to resolve these disputes not only bind the particular litigants, but also provide precedent for future cases. In writing cases, judges can decide that a particular law is unconstitutional. Otherwise, judges apply the laws to the particular facts of the case according to the legislative intent of the statute. If there is no statute on point, judges use legal principles to create rules to apply to the factual situation; this body of law from case opinions is called common law.

For more information on federal courts and cases, see pages 32-44. For more information on state courts and cases, see pages 59-64.

3. Administrative Law: Federal and State

Regulations are created by the executive branch. The executive branch has the power to create agencies, such as the Federal Trade Commission (FTC) or the Federal Communication Commission (FCC). These agencies create regulations and decisions for the particular industry covered. There are both federal and state regulations and decisions.

For more information on federal agencies and administrative law, see pages 44-53. For more information on state agencies and administrative law, see page 65.

Statutes, rules, cases, and regulations are all primary law. Statutes are usually the starting point in analyzing primary law. Cases interpret the meaning of a statute or deal with areas of law not addressed by statutes. (This is called common law.) Often legislatures will codify common law by creating a statute that synthesizes the prior law into an enacted code. In addition, when courts interpret statutes incorrectly, the legislature can rewrite the statute. But this primary law is not always persuasive in all jurisdictions. It is therefore important to understand that primary law itself falls into two separate categories: (1) law that is binding or mandatory, and (2) law that is merely persuasive.

Mandatory or binding law is law that is binding in that jurisdiction; it must be followed under the principle of stare decisis. For example, a trial court in Maryland must follow Maryland state codes and decisions from higher Maryland courts because they are binding authorities.

Persuasive law is law from a lower court or a different jurisdiction that that gives guidance but does not have to be followed. For example, a New York court does not have to follow a California court's decision. Likewise, a justice who sits on the Supreme Court of California, that state's highest court, is not required to follow a California trial judge's opinion.

The distinction between mandatory and persuasive law is important when deciding the best cases to rely on when writing a legal document. Usually, you want to show the judge that she is bound by certain law. However, at times, you will need to rely on persuasive authority. For example, although an opinion from the same level court is not binding on that court (one trial court judge is not bound by his colleague's opinion) because it is technically only persuasive authority, an opinion from the same level court would be extremely relevant to the judge making the decision. In addition, when no binding authority exists on an issue, you will need to use persuasive authority to make your argument.

B.   *Secondary Sources*

Secondary sources are materials that discuss and comment on primary law. They are written by scholars, judges, and others to provide commentary and background materials on the law. Although they are not the law itself, secondary sources can help a legal researcher understand a particular body of law as well as find primary law on a subject. They are especially helpful for first-year students, who tend to know very little about most legal subjects, as well as for experts in a particular field, who refer to these sources when developing law in their areas.

Secondary sources are considered persuasive authority. However, at times, a secondary source, such as a restatement, might be adopted by a specific jurisdiction—at which time it becomes binding law on that jurisdiction.

Secondary sources come in a variety of forms. Regardless of the secondary source you choose, finding information within it usually entails referencing a table of contents or index, finding the material itself within the main volumes, and updating that information by locating the primary law or making sure you have the most recent secondary source on point.

See the following pages for additional information on the various types of secondary sources:

- Legal Encyclopedias, page 66.
- American Law Reports, page 74.
- Hornbooks and Treatises, page 80.
- Law Reviews, page 80.
- Restatements, page 84.

1. Deciding to Use a Secondary Source

Secondary sources are handy in certain situations and can help you research primary law efficiently. However, a secondary source is not always the best starting place in your research strategy. Consider using a secondary source in the following circumstances:

- **If you are asked to research a subject area that you do not understand:** Often, you will be asked to research an area of law that you have never studied. In these circumstances, referencing a secondary source, such as a legal encyclopedia, will help you understand the general law in its basic form.
- **If you are asked to compare the law in different jurisdictions:** You might be asked to write a comparative piece in which you contrast a particular law in different jurisdictions. Instead of tediously researching each state's law on point, consider using a secondary source, such as American Law Reports, which compiles trends on the law in different states, explains those trends, and provides citations to the law in each jurisdiction. If you find a secondary source on point, you might save days of research on your issue.
- **If you are asked to criticize the law or develop a new theory:** There might be times when you are asked to criticize existing law or create a new theory. Chances are that scholars have already written about the subject area. Referencing law reviews will help you find legal theories and criticisms about the area as well as references and citations to other legal sources on point.
- **If your initial research of primary law yields poor results:** There may be times when you start your research in primary law but find too little or too much law on point. In these circumstances, consider using a restatement or treatise to help you learn more about the general subject area, to help formulate search terms, and to find primary law to act as a starting point.

2. Deciding Not to Use a Secondary Source

Often, it will not be useful to use a secondary source at all in your legal research. For example, if you are asked to research a statute in a certain jurisdiction, it makes the most sense to look in that state's code directly instead of finding information about the code first in a secondary source. In addition, if you are very familiar with an area of law, you probably do not need to learn more about it in a secondary source. You want to find the most streamlined research strategy to help you locate primary law. Therefore, secondary sources are not always the best starting point.

Remember that secondary sources are not binding on courts, so you should cite to them only sparingly in court documents. (On the other hand, scholarly articles are replete with secondary source citations.) In addition, if you use a secondary source to find primary law, you should always find that primary law as well to make sure that it is accurate and up to date.

III. CITING TO SOURCES

Because the legal audience is a doubting audience, you will need to prove all your legal assertions by grounding them in the law. To do so, you will first need to find the law, and then you will need to cite to it in your documents. These citations are important to the legal reader because they reference your supporting law and allow the reader to find that law. In addition, they tell your reader important information about the law, such as whether it is binding or persuasive and how old it may be.

Citations are governed by strict formatting rules so that lawyers have a uniform system for finding authority. If you fail to follow those rules, your reader might not be able to find your legal authority and you might lose credibility with the reader. (If you cannot cite correctly, how does the reader know that your research is accurate or thorough?)

There are two main manuals that currently provide the formatting rules for legal citation:

1. *The Bluebook: A Uniform System of Citation* (known simply as the Bluebook), available both in print and online.[1]
2. *ALWD Citation Manual: A Professional System of Citation* (ALWD is pronounced "allwood").

For more on citing sources, see chapter 4, Citation.

IV. OVERVIEW OF RESEARCH PROCESS AND STRATEGY

A. *Develop a Cohesive Research Strategy*

Many students fail to recognize the importance of a cohesive research strategy. Instead, when they are given an assignment, they often log onto Westlaw and Lexis and begin searching. As a result, the students waste time and become

---

1. See http://www.legalbluebook.com.

frustrated or they find too many "hits" and have a hard time wading through the sea of authority. To avoid this pitfall, you should begin to think like a lawyer by following some basic research strategies. For more on organizing your research strategy, see chapter 3.

B. Think First

Before launching into your research, think about a plan of action. You should ask yourself or the supervisor important questions, brainstorm ideas for search terms, write an issue statement and a cohesive plan, and take notes. In addition, questions about cost and time might not seem relevant as a student, but they are very important when you begin billing clients.

C. Identify Appropriate Legal Sources

Once you have brainstormed ideas and focused on your issue, you should consider which authorities will be most relevant. Your thought process should include the following factors:

1. **Jurisdiction.** First, you should be sure what jurisdiction's law applies. Usually, the supervisor giving you the assignment will tell you the jurisdiction, such as New York State law or federal law in the Second Circuit. However, sometimes you will need to figure out the appropriate jurisdiction. If so, you might need to research civil procedure rules or conflict of laws materials. Once you know your jurisdiction, focus your initial research within the law of that jurisdiction.
2. **Primary Law vs. Secondary Sources.** While your ultimate goal will usually be to find primary law, sometimes you will find it more easily by looking first in secondary sources, especially if you know nothing about the issue. A secondary source will provide you with background information, context about the issue, and oftentimes citations to get you started. However, if you know something about your issue or have an idea about what category of law applies (contracts, torts, property), it makes more sense to begin with primary law—statutes, cases, and regulations.
3. **Statutes, Cases, and Regulations.** It is often helpful to figure out which sources are most likely to address your issue. Statutes are often a good starting point because much of today's law is codified. However, there are still pockets of legal issues that are addressed only by common law, such as privacy torts. Therefore, if you are unable to find a statute on point in your jurisdiction, consider searching for cases. If your topic is covered by an administrative agency, such as food and drug law, consider beginning your research in regulations.
4. **Binding vs. Persuasive Law.** In general, you want to rely on binding law. However, you may also find (and rely on) persuasive law that will be quite helpful. Therefore, do not limit your research to binding law.

Consider starting with binding law but branching out to persuasive authority as well. At times, when you find no binding law, you will need to rely on persuasive authority alone.

5. **Dates.** The dates of applicable statutes, regulations, and cases are important. For example, if you find a relevant statute, be sure to check the date of enactment; cases that were decided before the statute may no longer be applicable. In addition, older cases, even if they are still good law, may not seem very persuasive to your audience, especially when there are more recent cases on point.

D. *Consider Print vs. Electronic Sources*

As a legal researcher, you will need to make choices. You can search for many (but not all) legal sources in both print and online sources. Although your natural tendency may be to look online for materials, you might discover that using the books in certain circumstances can save you time and lead to finding more relevant primary law on point.

1. Print Sources

Print sources are usually organized alphabetically by jurisdiction and then by type of authority. For example, the primary law in your school's library might start with Alabama and end with Wyoming. Within each state, you will find that state's code, encyclopedia, reporters, and possible print digests. The federal law is usually located separately. Each book will provide citations to other sources, and you will need to uses multiple books before you locate all your sources. Once you find those sources, you might want to copy them so that you have them for your files. In addition, you will want to update the law by looking in separate "pocket parts" and supplements stored either at the back of a volume or at the end of a volume set.

Although the process of using multiple sources and making copies might seem tedious, often the research process in print sources takes less time because you can quickly page through, skim irrelevant material, and grasp the context of a subject area due to its relative location within the law. In addition, the index and table of contents are good tools to learn the context and organization of particular bodies of law. Most researchers prefer finding statutes in the print sources because their indexes and categorical organization of the codes make them easier to use than online sources.

For more on conducting research using print sources, see "Strategies for Book Research," page 117, in chapter 3.

2. Electronic Sources

Online searching is often more convenient, and the law is updated more frequently than print sources; however, it is usually not free. The main commercial legal services are Lexis and Westlaw. Recently, each service added a new, advanced platform—WestlawNext and Lexis Advance. This book covers both the traditional versions and the new platforms of each service but often refers in general to Lexis and Westlaw. Although these commercial services are usually free for law students (because law schools often pay the fee), they cost practicing lawyers quite a bit of money. Therefore, legal researchers should consider free databases—such as those mentioned throughout this book—before researching on a pay-for-use site.

Accessing electronic sources can be accomplished by a variety of methods. Often, a lawyer can choose between researching online by jurisdiction, subject matter, or word searches. Some online services provide a list of authorities but require you to actually find those authorities in print. Most services provide direct links to authority, which you can then download, print, or send to your e-reader. While most services have indexes and table of contents, often researchers focus on word searches instead. As a result, the search terms chosen are extremely important.

For more on conducting research using electronic sources, see "Strategies for Online Research," page 118, in chapter 3.

E.   *Create Effective Search Terms*

Many Internet-savvy students think that legal research is similar to using a search engine. However, legal research is more complicated. Instead of typing a word or two as if performing a general search, the legal researcher should think in terms of the following:

1. **Courses as Categories.** Often, a problem can be categorized into one of the typical first-year courses in law school: torts, contracts, property, criminal procedure, and civil procedure. As you move on in law school, you will be exposed to other broad topics such as corporations, tax, evidence, and family law. While there is quite a bit of overlap (consider contracts and torts alone), you can often think of legal problems in terms of typical legal courses. If you are able to break down the issue into these easily manageable categories, you can generate search terms using the language you learned in each class (offer and acceptance, intentional torts, etc.).

2. **Who, What, Where, When, Why.** Many legal editors break down the categories of legal research into who, what, where, when, and why. If you can do the same thing, you will more easily find search terms that will lead to applicable law:

   - **Who:** Think in terms of parties such as employer or employee.
   - **What:** Think of the legal action (joint custody) or tangible objects (a defective product).
   - **Where:** Think beyond jurisdiction to a more specific location (at a school, in a workplace).
   - **When:** Think about the timing. It will matter in terms of applicable law.

- **Why:** Think about possible motives (intent) and defenses (self-defense).

3. **Expanding or Narrowing Search Terms.** If your initial search term does not yield enough results, consider adding a synonym (use "house or home") or making your term searchable by the root instead of the whole word (using "employ!" will find employment, employer, employee, employed, etc.). If your search terms yield too many results, consider restricting the terms by limiting the search within a sentence, a paragraph, or a number of words. Also, consider adding more search terms to narrow a topic. You can also narrow your search by date, headnote number, judge's name, etc.

F. Use Helpful Finding Tools

Indexes, tables of contents, and other research tools (such as popular names tables) are very helpful when performing legal research. Both online and print sources now usually have both, and they will help you locate terms either categorically (table of contents) or alphabetically (indexes). By skimming these sources, you will glean a sense of legal terms of art, context, and organization of the law. In addition, it will be easier to find your terms of art when conducting word searches if you have first availed yourself of these tools.

For more information on finding and using helpful tools, see "Strategies for Particular Sources," page 129, in chapter 3.

G. Update the Law

Once you have found a statute, case, or regulation on point, you will need to ensure that it is still good law. Statutes and regulations may be repealed or revoked, and cases may be reversed. Be certain to update the law for your particular source to verify its status.

For more information on updating, see "Updating the Law," page 156, in chapter 3.

H. Use Sources to Find Other Sources and Know When to Stop Researching

The sources you find will cite to other authorities. You should read those authorities; they might also lead to other sources. As you can imagine, the loop can become endless. So when do you stop researching? The best time to stop researching is when authorities start to repeat themselves. However, there will be times when stopping will be determined by pure economics (you have already spent too much money on the client's issue) or timing (you have to go to court or meet with your client in ten minutes).

For more information, see "Deciding When to Stop," page 111, in chapter 3.

V.   A RESEARCH PLAN EXAMPLE: FROM START TO FINISH

It is helpful to illustrate a research strategy on a client's issue from start to finish. In this section, you will read about a client's particular problem and follow some basic research strategies. While this example is not exhaustive, it will provide you with a starting point for developing your own research strategy.

The Client's Problem

Keep in mind that clients do not have fact patterns; they have very real problems. While you might receive your information from a professor in written form like the example provided below, most real-world clients walk through the door and are interviewed—either by you or a supervising attorney. You might also receive information from a case file; however, the file will rarely be a neatly arranged, chronological story such as a fact pattern. Usually, you will need to fit the multiple pieces together to develop a clear and concise story. More often than not, you will find holes in the story and will need to investigate more facts—by meeting with the client or witnesses, going to the scene, or poring through documents. Below is a neatly arranged, abbreviated fact pattern for convenience in discussing a basic research strategy.

Sally Meets Harry:

On the first day of class, Sally was unable to log onto *TeachingLaw.com*, her interactive ebook for legal research and writing. In a panic, Sally asked Harry, a student sitting next to her in class, for permission to use his email and password in order to access the first assignment in the ebook. Harry agreed and gave Sally this information. As a result, Sally was able to log onto the ebook and download the assignment.

The next day, Sally told Harry she was now able to log in using her own email and password and asked Harry if he wanted to work on the assignment together. This time, Harry declined and said he preferred to work independently so he could learn all the material himself. Sally felt somewhat slighted and disappointed. Sally worked on the assignment herself and uploaded it that night using her own password. As she was uploading her own assignment, she decided to play a trick on Harry. She logged out of the ebook and logged back in, but this time using Harry's password. When she entered the uploading feature, she noticed that Harry already had a green check mark on his first assignment (indicating he had uploaded successfully). Sally crafted answers for the assignment that did not make any sense and included sensitive and intimate language purportedly regarding Harry's personal life. Sally then uploaded this document into Harry's uploaded documents. (As long as the new upload occurred before the time period for the assignment ended, the new document replaced the old upload.)

> After the professor downloaded and read Harry's document, she called Harry to her office and showed him the document. Harry was extremely upset and wound up having a nervous breakdown. He had to withdraw from law school.
>
> Harry has hired you to pursue a claim against Sally.

Step 1: Find the Facts

Your first job is to make sure you have all the facts. In a real situation, you would ask the client specific questions, take a look at the document in question so you could examine the language that Sally used, and talk to Harry's doctors. You would also want to investigate the damages by copying all medical bills, accessing any lost wages, and discovering any other expenses Harry might have incurred. Keep in mind that being able to prove liability is not, by itself, a reason to accept this case. If Harry cannot collect any real damages, accepting the case makes no economic sense for either the client or for you. In the real world, finding the facts and deciding whether to take a case are often very difficult.

·Take Notes

Step 2: Spot the Issues *Might Research to find*

As in any law school exam, you want to determine what potential claims (and possible defenses) are available to the client (and to the other side). You can break the claims into categories, such as criminal charges and civil causes of action. Any of the following would be reasonable:

·Treatises
·overview of Law
·not clear of elements
·Take Notes & Highlight

- **Potential Civil Claim 1:** Intentional infliction of emotional distress
- **Potential Civil Claim 2:** Identity theft (civil liability)
- **Potential Civil Claim 3:** Slander and libel
- **Potential Criminal Charge:** Identity theft (criminal charge)

Step 3: Choose a Starting Point

First, begin taking notes. Consider writing down all possible claims and starting a separate file (either a hard copy or on your computer) for each claim. Then, attack each claim separately so that you do not become overwhelmed with sources and strategies. You will want to keep notes on each claim as you progress throughout your strategy. For more information, see "Taking Notes," on page 110, chapter 3.

Let's start with the potential civil claim of intentional infliction of emotional distress.

Step 4: Think First

Before logging on to Lexis or Westlaw or running off to the library, begin by thinking about your issue. This might take you five minutes or an hour, but it will save you time in the long run. First, write an issue statement so that you remain focused throughout your research. (Your issue statement need not be perfect.)

Sample Issue Statement

Does Harry have a claim against Sally for intentional infliction of emotional distress when she uploaded a document under his name into an electronic book and that document included sensitive language, was read by the teacher, and caused Harry to have a mental breakdown?

Next, brainstorm ideas for search terms. Use the issue statement as a starting point. Keep notes so that you don't repeat a failed search. Ask your supervisor questions. For more information on asking the right questions, see page 109 in chapter 3.

Step 5: Identify Appropriate Legal Sources

To streamline your research, consider what jurisdiction applies, whether you will need to research beyond primary authority, and what possible sources will be most useful.

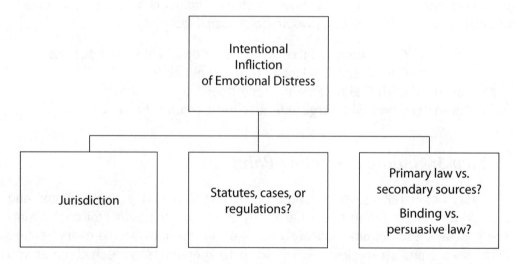

- **Jurisdiction:** Where do Sally and Harry attend law school? If they are in Chicago, then the law of Illinois applies because the action that led to this possible claim took place in Illinois. (This is very simplified; other rules might apply that would make your claim a federal one or one of another state jurisdiction.)
- **Statutes, Cases, or Regulations:** Start by looking in the Illinois state code. If there is nothing in the code on intentional infliction, consider moving on to cases. (You might remember from torts that many intentional torts are governed by common law.)

- **Primary Law vs. Secondary Sources:** If you cannot remember anything about intentional infliction of emotional distress, you might pick up your first-year torts book, research the issue in a legal encyclopedia, or look at the Restatement on Torts to get some background information on the law. However, if you already have some general knowledge of intentional torts, this step might not be necessary.
- **Binding vs. Persuasive Law:** Most (if not all) jurisdictions will have law on intentional infliction of emotional distress. However, if you find yourself in a new area of law or one in which your jurisdiction has little law on point, you might decide to expand into the law of other jurisdictions. Perhaps your jurisdiction has not yet addressed the issue of using the Internet to intentionally inflict emotional distress. Consider expanding your research to other jurisdictions to see if another court has addressed this issue.

Step 6: Create Effective Search Terms

1. **Courses as Categories:** You have probably already identified torts as the overall category for intentional infliction of emotional distress. From here, you want to identify some of the issues and subcategories you discussed in torts, such as emotional distress, mental suffering, or damages. So now you have a few potential categorical search terms from your torts class.
2. **Who, What, Where, When, Why:** Here, you can try to come up with other terms that might help you narrow your search.
   - **Who:** student; peer
   - **What:** caused emotional or mental injury; uploaded document
   - **Where:** Chicago, Illinois; at school; online
   - **When:** when given permission at first; on September 1, 2011
   - **Why:** to offend; intentionally, to harm, to trick
3. **Expanding or Narrowing Your Search Terms:** Choose some of the broadest search terms first and consider making them expandable.

> *Intentionally ? Intent!*
> *Emotional ? Emotion!*

If your search terms are too narrow, consider creating a broader, more categorical term:

> *Torts ? Civil liability*

Consider using a combination of both categorical terms and specific search terms:

> *Torts or Civil liability and intent! or emotion!*

Narrow the number of hits you might get by making sure that the main terms are only within a few words of each other:

> *intent! w/3 emotion! w/3 distress*

To quickly find elements of intentional infliction of emotional distress, try:

> *elements /s intent! w/3 emotion! w/3 distress*

4. **Print vs. Electronic Research:** Do not assume that researching on your computer is always the most efficient strategy. Many researchers prefer finding statutes in print. It might make the most sense to head to the library first and find the Illinois code section on intentional infliction of emotional distress. You might also skim through the table of contents or index of the Illinois code for intentional torts. If there is nothing in the code (or even if there is), you could begin to research cases using the digests, which are located in the same section of the library.

   If you are not near the library or are more comfortable with the computer, start with online searching. Ask yourself first whether a free source is available. Try finding the Illinois statutes to search the state code. You can try a word search or search through the table of contents or online index. Instead of finding intentional infliction, you might notice there is a statute on slander and libel (in civil liabilities). Take note of this provision; it might be another claim you could file against Sally.

   In addition, log on to either platform in Lexis or Westlaw. Here, you will want to decide your best strategy. Because you know you are looking for an Illinois statute, it makes sense to narrow your search by jurisdiction. If you have already determined that there is no statute on point, you would want to narrow the database in Illinois for cases. Here, you would try the word search you have already created and work on expanding or narrowing the search depending on your number of hits.

   If you find only a few sources, consider printing them to read. However, if you find a lot of law, you might want to read on screen first to cull out irrelevant materials before printing. Annotations will give you synopses of the cases or articles, which will assist your decision-making process. The folders feature in Lexis Advance and WestlawNext will help organize your research.

   For more information on using print and electronic sources, see chapter 3, page 111.

Step 7: Use Helpful Finding Tools

For this problem, there are many useful tools that would help expedite your research:

- **Indexes:** The index to the state code might be a useful starting point (if there is a statute on point). The digests will also have indexes for searching cases.
- **Table of Contents:** Each state code will have a table of contents. You could use either the table of contents in the print books or the table of contents provided by Lexis and Westlaw to search categorically. Online, these expand as you get deeper into a subject area. You will find as you search the Illinois code that there is no statute on intentional infliction of emotional distress. However, you might note that there is a slander and libel act under the general civil liabilities section. You would want to look in this section to see if Sally's actions fit within this statute.
- **Key Number System:** This system is particular to West (Westlaw online and West published books) and categorizes issues into a uniform numbered system. These also expand online as you click deeper within each subject. Here, you would find the Damages key number 57 section helpful for intentional infliction of emotional distress. For more on the key number system, see chapter 3, page 113.
- **Pages or Screens in Same Area:** Because codes and digests are arranged by subject, it is often helpful to browse in the same general area to look for additional relevant law.

Step 8: Use Sources to Find Other Sources

The sources you find will help you find other sources. For example, if there is a statute on intentional infliction of emotional distress, the annotations in the statute will lead you to cases and secondary sources regarding your issue. Cases you read will cite to other cases (or statutes or secondary sources) that are relevant to intentional infliction as well. When you update these cases, you will also find citations to cases that have referenced that case. (See chapter 3, page 156, for more information on updating your sources.)

Step 9: Know When to Stop

The worst feeling when you walk into court is wondering whether you found all the relevant law for your argument. Therefore, you want to be thorough in your research. A good time to stop your research is when you keep finding the same law. For example, you might update a case and find references to three cases you have already read. You might find annotations in a statute and then cases in a digest that are almost all identical. You might read a secondary source that covers all the issues you have covered in your research.

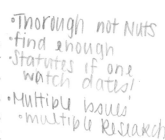
- Thorough not Nuts
- find enough Statutes if one
  watch dates!
- Multiple Issues
- multiple Research

If you find no statute on point (such as in this intentional infliction example), then the cases you find should not reference a relevant statute. If they do, make sure to read that statute to determine if it applies.

To be thorough, however, consider using a variety of sources—print and electronic, Lexis and Westlaw, indexes and tables of contents—to ensure you are not missing a major piece of law on point. Keep in mind that research is not a linear process; just because you have followed one research strategy from start to finish does not mean you are done with your research. Often, you will find holes in your argument as you are writing a document; at that point, do more research so you can be thorough when citing to authority.

Once you have finished researching for one claim, repeat the process for each potential claim. In fact, you might have found more potential claims during your research on the first one. You also need to ask Harry how much money he wants to spend on his case. The amount of time you research this issue might be limited in terms of economics. For more information on deciding when to stop, see chapter 3, page 111.

VI. BRIEFING CASES

You will brief a case for two different purposes. First, as a student, you will brief cases for your classes to prepare for questions posed by your professors. Second, as a legal researcher, you will brief cases to prepare to write a legal document and analyze a particular legal issue. Although both are often called case briefs, they are very different in product, process, and purpose.

A. Briefing Cases as a Student for Class

As a student, you will probably brief assigned cases for class. The purpose of this case brief is to prepare to answer the professor's questions and to begin to digest the law for the course. In essence, a case brief is a summary of the judge's opinion. Therefore, a good case brief will summarize each step of the judge's reasoning by diagramming the various parts of the case and analyzing the legal reasoning. You will need to find the method of case briefing that works best for your learning style. Some students write lengthy briefs while others simply take notes within the case books. Below, you will find the various parts of a case that are often worth diagramming and analyzing in a case brief.

1. <u>Case Name</u>: <u>Smith v. Jones</u>, 310 U.S. 200 (2000). It is a good idea to include the full citation, including the date of the opinion, for future reference.

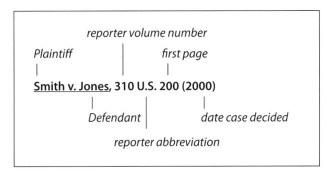

2. <u>Facts</u>: Usually a judge will have paragraphs of the opinion dedicated to a description of the facts. You need not include all the facts in your case brief; however, try to include facts that are most relevant to the court's reasoning. Important facts usually include the cause of action or claim and possible defenses.

3. <u>Procedural History</u>: Most cases you will read for class are appellate opinions in which an appellate judge reviews a trial judge's opinion. Therefore, the appellate judge will explain what happened to the case below in the trial court. These facts are helpful to understand the posture of the case when it came before this particular court.

4. <u>Issue</u>: The issue is the particular question the court had to decide in this case. It usually includes specific facts as well as a legal question.

5. <u>Holding</u>: The holding is the way in which the court decided the issue.

6. <u>Reasoning</u>: The judge should explain the holding using legal reasoning. Here the judge should cite to other cases as well as any particular statute, constitutional provision, or regulation that supports the holding. In briefing the case for class, you usually need not cite to these authorities. However, you should be able to summarize the legal reasoning of the court. Oftentimes a professor will ask questions relating to the basis of this legal reasoning and try to poke holes in the judge's logic. In addition, professors will often ask you how far you think this legal reasoning should be applied by asking hypothetical problems and asking you to employ the same reasoning.

7. <u>Dissent</u>: The dissent is an opinion written by another judge sitting on the same panel as the writing judge. Although this opinion is not considered law, the professor might ask questions about this judge's legal reasoning or use some of the dissenting judge's arguments to discuss the issue.

Three Sample Student Case Briefs for <u>Garratt v. Dailey</u>

Garratt v. Dailey

46 Wash. 2d 197, 279 P.2d 1091 (1955)

FACTS: Defendant Brian Dailey, five years old, was visiting the home of the sister of the plaintiff, Ruth Garratt. Plaintiff was in the process of seating herself on a lawn chair when Defendant pulled the chair out from underneath her and sat upon it himself. Defendant alleges that when he realized the plaintiff was about to sit where the chair had been, he attempted to return it to its site but was unable to do so. Plaintiff fell on the ground, fracturing her hip.

ISSUE: Whether a child committed a battery on another party through a volitional act but absent a desire to do harm.

HOLDING: Remanded for clarification. A child can be found liable for battery absent desire to do harm if he knew with substantial certainty the consequences of his action.

REASONING: When a minor has committed a tort with force, he is liable to be pro-ceeded against as any other person. Battery is the intentional infliction of harmful bodily contact upon another. For an act to be intentional, it must be done for the purpose of causing contact or apprehension or with the knowledge on the part of the actor that such contact is substantially certain to be produced. A battery would be established if Brian knew, with substantial certainty, that Ruth Garratt would attempt to sit where the chair had been. Absence of intent to injure is insufficient to absolve him from liability.

Garratt v. Dailey

46 Wash. 2d 197, 279 P.2d 1091 (1955)

FACTS: Plaintiff alleges that five-year-old defendant deliberately pulled the chair out from under her as she attempted to sit down in her backyard, causing her to sustain a hip fracture and other injuries. The trial court found that, where the defendant Brian did move the chair, he did not have any willful or unlawful purpose in doing so, that he did not have any intent to injure the plaintiff or bring about any unauthorized or offensive contact with her. Plaintiff appeals from a judgment dismissing the action and asks for the entry of a judgment in the amount of $11,000 (the amount of damages determined by the trial court) or a new trial.

ISSUE: Is Brian Dailey liable for the appellant's injuries?

HOLDING: Case remanded for a clarification of the findings with regard to whether Brian had substantially certain knowledge that the plaintiff would attempt to sit where the chair had been. If he did, then he would be liable for battery.

REASONING: The court looks at the question of intent and its place in the law of battery. The court (citing the First Restatement) holds that it is not required that the defendant intend to injure or embarrass the plaintiff. For battery, the defendant may still be held liable if he knew with substantial certainty that contact or apprehension of contact would result. If he had no knowledge that contact would result from his action, there was no wrongful act by him, and the basic principle of liability for battery would not be established.

Sample Student Case Briefs for <u>Garratt v. Dailey</u> (continued)

<u>Garratt v. Dailey</u>

46 Wash. 2d 197, 279 P.2d 1091 (1955)

FACTS: Brian Dailey, a minor, was a guest at Naomi Garratt's house. When Ruth Garratt attempted to sit in a lawn chair, Brian moved the chair out from under her and, as a result, Garratt's hip was broken. Garratt asserts that Brian acted deliberately to injure her. Brian asserts that he was attempting to sit in the chair and was unable to move the chair back under Garratt in time to prevent her fall. The trial court adopted Brian's version of the story. The trial court found that he did not have any intent to injure Garratt in any way and dismissed Garratt's lawsuit.

ISSUE: Should Garratt's lawsuit for battery have been dismissed due to lack of intent?

HOLDING: No. It cannot be established that Brian did not know that Garratt would attempt to sit where the chair had been prior to his moving it.

REASONING: A battery is the intentional infliction of a harmful bodily contact upon another. Liability for a battery exists when an actor has acted with the intent to bring about a harmful or offensive contact to another in the absence of consent or privilege. Intent for a battery exists if the action is done for the purpose of causing the contact or with knowledge on the part of the actor that the contact is substantially certain to occur. If the actor did not act for the purpose of causing the harmful or offensive contact and had no knowledge that such a contact might be the result of the action, liability cannot exist. Applied to the present facts, liability, therefore, would exist if:

1. Garratt could prove that Brian moved the chair with the intent of causing Garratt to hit the ground (Garratt was unable to prove this).
2. Garratt could prove that when Brian moved the chair, he knew with substantial certainty that Garratt would attempt to sit down where the chair had been (the trial court failed to consider this before dismissing Garratt's suit).

The lack of intent to cause an offensive contact or injury will not prevent liability if Brian did know with substantial certainty that Garratt would attempt to sit where the chair had been. When a minor has committed a tort with force, he is liable to be prosecuted as an adult. Brian's age is relevant only in determining what he could have known with substantial certainty.

B. Briefing Cases as a Lawyer for Research

As a lawyer or law student, you will need to research cases to provide support and analysis in your legal documents. Therefore, when researching the law for a particular document, you will need to brief cases for research. Essentially, this means you will take notes on each relevant case that you find. A good case brief for researching includes a summary of the facts, holding, and reasoning of the court as well as a list of other relevant sources for future research.

1. <u>Case Name</u>: <u>Smith v. Jones</u>, 310 U.S. 200 (2000). It is a good idea to include the full citation, including the date of the opinion, for future reference and citation. Be sure to include pinpoint cites (cites to a particular page) so you can cite specifically in your legal document.

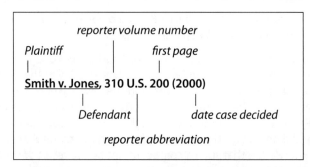

2. <u>Facts</u>: An outline of the facts is often helpful. However, concentrate on the facts that are used by the judge in his legal reasoning. These facts are called legally significant facts.
3. <u>Procedural History</u>: As a legal researcher, the legal history is important only to understand what "reversed" or "affirmed" means for your particular case.
4. <u>Issue</u>: The issue is the particular question the court had to decide in this case. It usually includes specific facts as well as a legal question. Oftentimes, you will not need to note the issue in your brief as long as it is clear from your notes on the holding.
5. <u>Holding</u>: The holding is the way in which the court decided the issue. It is especially important in case briefing for research as it lays out the answer to the issue as well as the most legally significant facts that led the court to that answer.
6. <u>Reasoning</u>: The judge should explain the holding using legal reasoning. Here the judge should cite to other cases as well as any particular statute, constitutional provision, or regulation that supports the holding. In briefing a case for research, you should note these other authorities as potential supplemental sources. If you are reading the case online, consider clicking on the other authorities to see if they are relevant for your issue. If you are reading the case in print, write down these authorities and their full citations so that you can research them later.
7. <u>Dissent</u>: The dissent is an opinion written by another judge sitting on the same panel as the writing judge. Although this opinion is not considered law, you might garner some information about the legal reasoning and jurisprudence on your particular legal issue. At times, though not often, you might cite to a dissent in your legal document.

Sample Lawyer's Case Brief for <u>*Garratt v. Dailey*</u>

<u>Garratt v. Dailey</u>, 46 Wash. 2d 197, 279 P.2d 1091 (Wash. 1955)

<u>Facts</u>: P fractured her hip when attempting to sit on lawn chair. D, five-year-old boy, pulled chair out from under her when P was about to sit.

<u>PH</u>: Case dismissed.

<u>Issue</u>: Did boy's action = battery?

<u>Holding</u>: Only if P can establish that when D moved chair, he knew with substantial certainty that P would attempt to sit where chair had been. Remanded for factual finding by trial court.

<u>Reasoning</u>: When minor commits tort, he is liable as an adult.

Prosser on Torts 1085

27 Am. Jur. 812, Infants 90

<u>Briese v. Baechtle</u>, 130 N.W. 893 (1911)

Battery = intentional infliction of a harmful bodily contact upon another.

1 Restatement, Torts, 29, 13

Prosser on Torts 41, 8.

Battery will be proven if P establishes that when D moved chair, he knew with substantial certainty that P would attempt to sit down where chair had been. <u>Mercer v. Corgin</u>, 20 N.E. 132 (1889)

C H A P T E R 2

Research Sources

This chapter focuses on primary law, the actual law on the books; and secondary sources, materials that discuss and comment on primary law. The primary law section is divided into federal law and state law materials and explains the various legal sources and structure within each. The secondary sources section describes these sources, when you would use them, and how to find them both online and in print. Sample pages and screen shots are provided to illustrate the various sources.

I. Primary Law
   A. Federal Law
      1. Federal Congress and Federal Statutes
         a. Federal Congress
         b. Federal Constitutions
         c. Federal Statutes
      2. Federal Courts and Cases
         a. United States Supreme Court
         b. Federal Courts of Appeals
         c. Federal District Courts
         d. Federal Cases
      3. Federal Agencies and Administrative Law
   B. State Law
      1. State Legislatures and State Statutes
      2. State Courts and State Cases
         a. State Courts
         b. State Cases
      3. State Agencies and State Administrative Law
II. Secondary Sources
   A. Legal Encyclopedias
   B. American Law Reports (A.L.R.)
   C. Hornbooks and Treatises
      1. Hornbooks
      2. Treatises
   D. Law Reviews
   E. Restatements
III. Study Aids—Research Sources
   A. Quick References and Checklists
      1. Statutes: Quick Reference
      2. Courts and Cases: Quick Reference

25

I. PRIMARY LAW

A. *Federal Law*

There are three branches of the federal government that create federal law: the legislature, the judiciary, and the executive. The federal legislative branch consists of both houses of Congress, which enact codes. The federal courts of the judiciary interpret and create laws through case opinions. The executive branch, in addition to the presidency, consists of administrative agencies that regulate specific areas of the law, such as food, transportation, and drugs.

1. Federal Congress and Federal Statutes

a. *Federal Congress*

The United States Congress is divided into two chambers: the House of Representatives and the Senate. To become law, a bill must pass each chamber.[1] For legislative information on the Web, see Thomas, the Library of Congress site named for Thomas Jefferson.[2] Additional information on both the House and the Senate is also available online.[3]

b. *Federal Constitutions*

- **What:** Constitutions are the highest primary authority. The United States Constitution[4] creates the broad governmental framework, describes governmental powers and restraints, defines political relationships, and enumerates individual rights and liberties.
- **Where:** The United States Constitution is found in print version in the first volume of the federal code (U.S.C., U.S.C.A., U.S.C.S.).
- **Why:** You are more likely to reach for the U.S.C.A. or U.S.C.S. to research constitutional issues because these sources are published more frequently than the U.S.C. and they are annotated, meaning they provide references to cases, statutes, regulations, and secondary sources that discuss each constitutional provision.
- **How:** For information on finding constitutions and statutes, see chapter 3, page 129.[5]

---

1. For information on how a federal bill becomes a law, see How a Bill Becomes a Law on page 133.

2. See http://thomas.gov.

3. See http://www.house.gov for information on the House and http://www.senate.gov for information on the Senate.

4. For the text of the United States Constitution, see http://www.archives.gov/exhibits/charters/charters.html.

5. To access a tutorial on finding constitutions and statutes, see http://www.ll.georgetown.edu/tutorials/stat/index.cfm.

c. *Federal Statutes*

- **What:** Federal statutes are laws passed by the United States Congress. They are codified in the United States Code, which is organized into 50 titles or subject areas. The titles are then subdivided into chapters, and the chapters are subdivided into sections.
- **Where:** Federal statutes can be found in chronological and subject-matter sources:
  - The **chronological** form is a session law, which is published in a volume that contains all the laws passed by a legislative body during each year or session. Session laws are published (very slowly) in the Statutes at Large (Stat.). For a citation to 109 Stat. 2213, you would look in the 109th volume of the Statutes at Large on page 2213.
  - The **subject-matter** form of publication is in either the **official** or **annotated codes.** They are the preferred citations and most often used by lawyers because they are easy to access by way of topical or popular name index. The volumes contain collections of all statutes in that particular jurisdiction and are arranged in broad topics called "titles." The official code is the United States Code (U.S.C.). The annotated codes are the United States Code Annotated (U.S.C.A.) (see pages 29-30) and the United States Code Service. Each has its own index, usually located at the end of the set of volumes. You can find these annotated versions in book form and on Lexis or Westlaw. These annotated codes also have **popular names tables** (see page 31) and **conversion tables.** The popular names tables allow you to search for a statute if you know its name but not its citation—for example, the Americans with Disabilities Act. The conversion tables allow you to search if you know the public law number of your statute. The annotated versions also contain many helpful resources, including Notes of Decisions, which provide references to cases applying that statute. The **table of contents** can help when you are searching for a statute in a general area of law such as Bankruptcy.
- **Why:** The Statutes at Large are rarely used for research because the chronological arrangement makes them difficult to access. The U.S.C., U.S.C.A., and U.S.C.S., however, are arranged by subject matter and are heavily indexed so that the legal researcher can easily find a particular code provision. The U.S.C.A. and U.S.C.S., both published by commercial publishers, are updated more frequently than the official U.S.C., which is published by the government. Code provisions, once written by the Congress, are often litigated by lawyers, interpreted by the courts, and criticized by scholars. The annotated codes are therefore the most helpful tools for lawyers to find statutes because they also provide annotations to the various interpretations of each code provision.
- **How:** For information on finding constitutions and statutes, see chapter 3, page 129.[6] For information on citations to federal constitutions, see chapter 4, pages 252 (Bluebook) and 198 (ALWD).

---

6. To access a tutorial on finding constitutions and statutes, see http://www.ll.georgetown. edu/tutorials/stat/index.cfm.

United States Code Annotated (U.S.C.A.)

---

§ 1079. Certificate of Federal loan insurance—effective date of insurance

(a) Loan-by-loan insurance

(1) Authority to issue certificates on application

If, upon application by an eligible lender, made upon such form, containing such information, and supported by such evidence as the Secretary may require, and otherwise in conformity with this section, the Secretary finds that the applicant has made a loan to an eligible student which is insurable under the provisions of this part, he may issue to the applicant a certificate of insurance covering the loan and setting forth the amount and terms of the insurance.

(2) Effectiveness of certificate

Insurance evidenced by a certificate of insurance pursuant to subsection (a)(1) of this section shall become effective upon the date of issuance of the certificate, except that the Secretary is authorized, in accordance with regulations, to issue commitments with respect to proposed loans, or with respect to lines (or proposed lines) of credit, submitted by eligible lenders, and in that event, upon compliance with subsection (a)(1) of this section by the lender, the certificate of insurance may be issued effective as of the date when any loan, or any payment by the lender pursuant to a line of credit, to be covered by such insurance was made. Such insurance shall cease to be effective upon 60 days' default by the lender in the payment of any installment of the premiums payable pursuant to subsection (c) of this section.

350

Code number and title

The statute itself, divided into sections

United States Code Annotated (U.S.C.A.) *(continued)*

Historical and Statutory Notes—references for revision notes, legislative reports, and provisions

Cross References—list of other statutes that refer to this one

Library References— other references to this statute

Westlaw Electronic Research—ways to find more information via Westlaw

Notes of Decisions— cases that have interpreted the statute or used it in a decision, grouped by subtopic

Ch. 28   HIGHER EDUCATION ASSISTANCE   20 § 1079
Note 2

HISTORICAL AND STATUTORY NOTES

Revision Notes and Legislative Reports
1986 Acts. House Reports Nos. 99–383, 99–598, House Conference Report No. 99–861, and Statement by President, see 1986 U.S.Code Cong. and Adm. News, p. 2572.

Prior Provisions
A prior section 1079, Pub.L. 89–329, Title IV, § 429, Nov. 8, 1965, 79 Stat. 1243; Pub.L. 94–482, Title I, § 127(a), Oct. 12, 1976, 90 Stat. 2123; Pub.L. 96–374, Title XIII, § 1391(a)(1), (2), Oct. 3, 1980, 94 Stat. 1503, related to certificates of Federal loan insurance, prior to the general revision of this part by Pub.L. 99–498.

CROSS REFERENCES

Delegable functions of Secretary of Education, see 20 USCA § 1082.
Federal insurance barred where State or private insurance available, see 20 USCA § 1073.
Insurance beneficiary defined, see 20 USCA § 1085.
Insured consolidation loans, see 20 USCA § 1078–3.
Sale of debt to Federal Financing Bank, see 20 USCA § 1087–2.

LIBRARY REFERENCES

American Digest System
Colleges and Universities ⬤➡9.25(2).
Key Number System Topic No. 81.

Research References

ALR Library
73 ALR, Fed. 303, Rights and Obligations of Federal Government, Under 20 U.S.C.A. § 1080, When Student Borrower Defaults on Federally Insured Loan.

WESTLAW ELECTRONIC RESEARCH

See Westlaw guide following the Explanation pages of this volume.

Notes of Decisions

Agreement between lender and government   2
Monitoring of eligibility status   3
Rules and regulations   1
Terms and conditions of participation   4
Time of issuance of insurance   5

_____

1.   Rules and regulations

Regulation requiring prior federal approval of insurance on higher education student loan before disbursal of funds by lender unless expressly provided for otherwise, is not satisfied by proof of conduct on part of Commissioner or agents from which it might be reasonably assumed that a waiver was made, and only an express statement by Commissioner that regulation was being waived would satisfy regulation language. Hicks v. Califano, N.D.Ga.1977, 450 F.Supp. 278, af-firmed 606 F.2d 65. Colleges And Universities ⬤➡ 9.25(2)

2.   Agreement between lender and government

Agreement between lender and government with respect to the federal student loan program merely recognized that the lender was eligible under this subchapter and that if in the future Commissioner should approve and issue insurance for any particular loan application submitted by lender then lender would abide by all the appropriate regulations; agreement was not a contract of insurance on the date of execution thereof for future loans which, in overwhelming majority of cases, were insured on an individual loan by loan basis. Hicks v. Califano, N.D.Ga. 1977, 450 F.Supp. 278, affirmed 606 F.2d 65. Colleges And Universities ⬤➡ 9.25(2)

353

887 POPULAR NAME TABLE

Retired Federal Employees Health Benefits Act
Pub.L. 86–724, Sept. 8, 1960, 74 Stat. 849
This Public Law enacted no currently effective sections. For sections affected by this law, see Pub.L. 86–724 in the USCA-TABLES database and the enacting credit set out below.
Enacting law:
Pub.L. 86–724, Sept. 8, 1960, 74 Stat. 849
Amending laws:
Pub.L. 89–45, June 22, 1965, 79 Stat. 170
Pub.L. 94–310, § 3(b), June 15, 1976, 90 Stat. 687
Pub.L. 96–156, Dec. 27, 1979, 93 Stat. 1166

Retiree Benefits Bankruptcy Protection Act of 1988
Pub.L. 100–334, June 16, 1988, 102 Stat. 610
Short title, see 11 USCA § 101 note
Current USCA classifications:

Section of Pub.L. 100–334	USCA Classification
2(a)	11 USCA § 1114

This list contains only sections enacted by this Public Law. For all sections affected by this law, see Pub.L. 100–334 in the USCA-TABLES database and the enacting credit set out below.
Table of Contents for current USCA classifications:
11 USCA § 1114
Enacting law:
Pub.L. 100–334, June 16, 1988, 102 Stat. 610 (11 §§ 101 note, 1101, 1106 notes, 1114, 1114 note, 1129)

Retirement Act
See Civil Service Retirement Acts

Retirement and Survivors' Annuities for Bankruptcy Judges and Magistrates Act of 1988
Pub.L. 100–659, Nov. 15, 1988, 102 Stat. 3910
Short title, see 28 USCA § 1 note
Current USCA classifications:

Section of Pub.L. 100–659	USCA Classification
2(a)	28 USCA § 377
7(a)	5 USCA 8440b

This list contains only sections enacted by this Public Law. For all sections affected by this law, see Pub.L. 100–659 in the USCA-TABLES database and the enacting credit set out below.
Table of Contents for current USCA classifications:
5 USCA § 8440b; 28 USCA § 377
Enacting law:
Pub.L. 100–659, Nov. 15, 1988, 102 Stat. 3910 (5 §§ 8334, 8401, 8402, 8440a; 28 §§ 155, 375 to 377, 604, 631, 636)

Retirement Equity Act of 1984 (REA)
Pub.L. 98–397, Aug. 23, 1984, 98 Stat. 1426
Short title, see 29 USCA § 1001 note
Current USCA classifications:

Section of Pub.L. 98–397	USCA Classification
203(b)	26 USCA § 417

This list contains only sections enacted by this Public Law. For all sections affected by this law, see Pub.L. 98–397 in the USCA-TABLES database and the enacting credit set out below.
Table of Contents for current USCA classifications:
26 USCA § 417
Enacting law:
Pub.L. 98–397, Aug. 23, 1984, 98 Stat. 1426 (26 §§ 72, 401, 402, 410, 411, 414, 417, 6057, 6652; 29 §§ 1001 note, 1025, 1052 to 1056, 1144)
Amending laws:
Pub.L. 99–514, §§ 1145(c), 1898(a)(1)(A), (a)(2), (3), (a)(4)(A), (b)(1)(A) to (14)(A), (b)(15)(A), (B), (c)(1)(A), (B), (c)(2)(A), (c)(3), (c)(4)(A), (c)(6)(A), (c)(7)(A), (d)(1)(A), (d)(2)(A), (e), (f)(1)(A), (g), (h)(1)(A), (B), (h)(2), (3), Oct. 22, 1986, 100 Stat. 2491, 2941, 2943 to 2945, 2947 to 2951, 2953 to 2957 (26 §§ 72, 401, 402, 411, 414, 415, 417, 2503; 29 § 1001 notes)

2.   Federal Courts and Cases

The federal court system is hierarchical. At the lowest level, trials are held in the **United States district courts.** The first level of appeal is in the **courts of appeals** or **circuit courts.** The highest appeal is held in the **United States Supreme Court.** The district courts and the courts of appeals are broken down geographically into circuits.

There are eleven numbered circuits as well as the D.C. Circuit and the Federal Circuit. Each circuit has its own district court and appellate court judges. (See the map and tables on pages 35-38.)

```
┌────────────────────────────────────────┐
│      United States Supreme Court        │
│                   ↑                     │
│      Court of Appeals (Circuit Court)   │
│                   ↑                     │
│             District Court              │
└────────────────────────────────────────┘
```

a.   *United States Supreme Court*

Supreme Court cases are cited in the United States Reports (U.S.), which is the Court's official reporter, as well as in the Supreme Court Reporter (S. Ct.) and the United States Supreme Court Reports, Lawyers' Edition (L. Ed., L. Ed. 2d). You can also find Supreme Court Cases on Lexis and Westlaw. The Supreme Court sits as the final appellate court for each circuit, but the Supreme Court hears only the cases it decides warrant further appellate review by "granting certiorari."

The web offers numerous sites for learning more about the Supreme Court. The Court's own site should be your first stop.[7] You can listen to oral arguments before the Supreme Court at Oyez (see page 33).[8] Supreme Court Justices discuss legal writing on Law Prose (see page 34).[9] Finally, you can follow Supreme Court cases on SCOTUSblog (see page 34).[10]

b.   *Federal Courts of Appeals*

The courts of appeals are divided into thirteen circuits: Circuits 1 through 11, the D.C. Circuit, and the Federal Circuit. Courts of appeals are cited in the Federal Reporter (F., F.2d, F.3d). Consult each circuit's web home page for docket or court information or to search for recent court decisions. Published circuit cases can be researched on Lexis and Westlaw.

---

7. http://www.supremecourtus.gov/.

8. http://www.oyez.org/.

9. http://www.lawprose.org/interviews/.

10. http://www.scotuswiki.com/index.php?title=Main_Page.

The Supreme Court Website

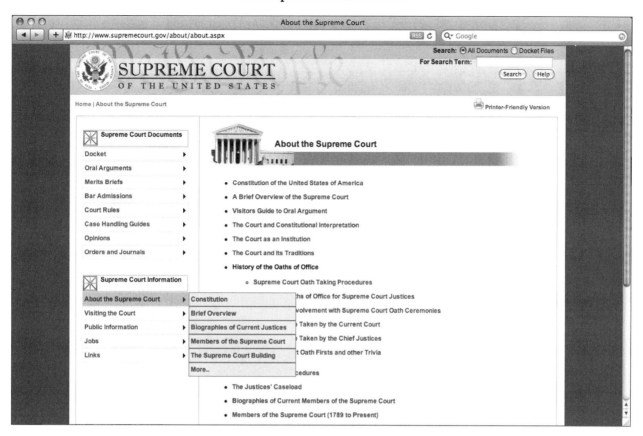

The Oyez.org Website

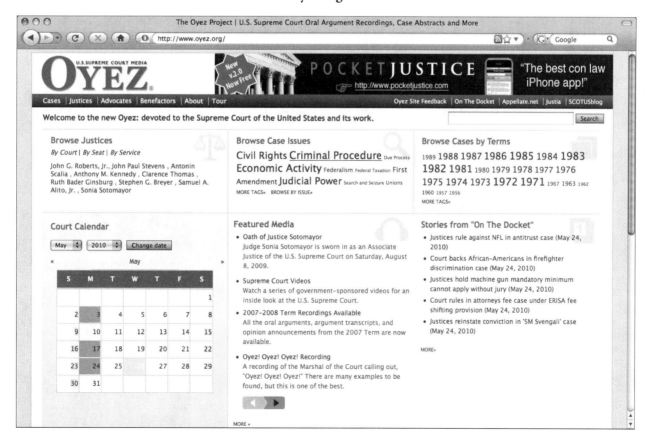

The Lawprose.org Website

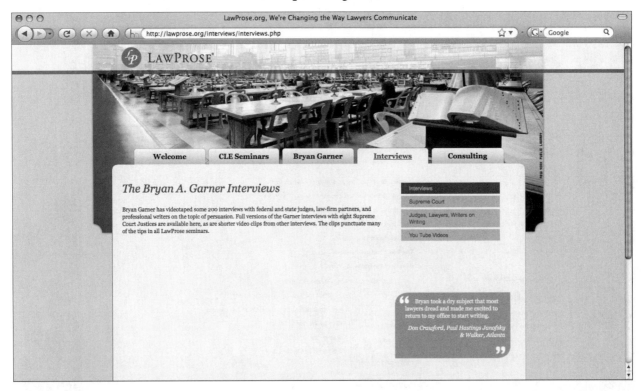

The SCOTUSblog

c. Federal District Courts

The district courts serve as the trial courts within each circuit. Some circuits have many district courts, which are divided according to their regions. District court cases are most often cited in the Federal Supplement (F. Supp., F. Supp. 2d). Consult the individual circuit websites for particular district court dockets, information, and recent cases (see Table 2.1). For all published district court cases, you can also search on Lexis or Westlaw.

U.S. Circuit Courts Map

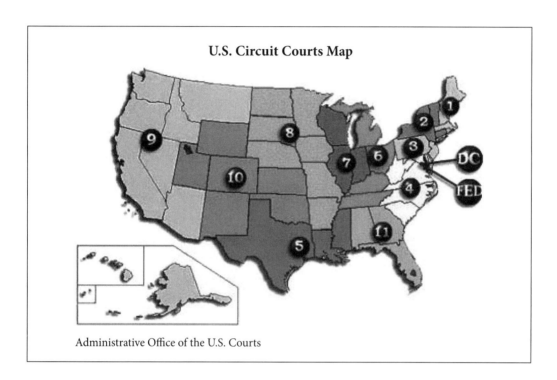

Administrative Office of the U.S. Courts

U.S. Circuits

Circuit 1: Maine, New Hampshire, Massachusetts, Rhode Island, Puerto Rico
Circuit 2: New York, Vermont, Connecticut
Circuit 3: Pennsylvania, New Jersey, Delaware
Circuit 4: West Virginia, Virginia, Maryland, North Carolina, South Carolina
Circuit 5: Texas, Louisiana, Mississippi
Circuit 6: Michigan, Ohio, Kentucky, Tennessee
Circuit 7: Wisconsin, Illinois, Indiana
Circuit 8: North Dakota, South Dakota, Minnesota, Nebraska, Iowa, Missouri, Arkansas
Circuit 9: Washington, Montana, Oregon, Idaho, California, Nevada, Arizona, Alaska, Hawaii, Northern Mariana Islands, Guam
Circuit 10: Wyoming, Utah, Colorado, Kansas, New Mexico, Oklahoma
Circuit 11: Alabama, Georgia, Florida
D.C. Circuit: District of Columbia
Federal Circuit: Within District of Columbia—hears specialized federal cases

Table 2.1. Websites for the Circuit Courts and District Courts of the United States

First Circuit
Court of Appeals: http://www.ca1.uscourts.gov
Maine District Court: http://www.med.uscourts.gov
Massachusetts District Court: http://www.mad.uscourts.gov
New Hampshire District Court: http://www.nhd.uscourts.gov
Rhode Island District Court: http://www.rid.uscourts.gov
Puerto Rico District Court: http://www.prd.uscourts.gov

Second Circuit
Court of Appeals: http://www.ca2.uscourts.gov
Connecticut District Court: http://www.ctd.uscourts.gov
New York Eastern District Court: http://www.nyed.uscourts.gov
New York Northern District Court: http://www.nynd.uscourts.gov
New York Southern District Court: http://www.nysd.uscourts.gov
New York Western District Court: http://www.nywd.uscourts.gov
Vermont District Court: http://www.vtd.uscourts.gov

Third Circuit
Court of Appeals: http://www.ca3.uscourts.gov
Delaware District Court: http://www.ded.uscourts.gov
New Jersey District Court: http://www.njd.uscourts.gov
Pennsylvania Eastern District Court: http://www.paed.uscourts.gov
Pennsylvania Middle District Court: http://www.pamd.uscourts.gov
Pennsylvania Western District Court: http://www.pawd.uscourts.gov
Virgin Islands District Court: http://www.vid.uscourts.gov

Fourth Circuit
Court of Appeals: http://www.ca4.uscourts.gov
Maryland District Court: http://www.mdd.uscourts.gov
North Carolina Eastern District Court: http://www.nced.uscourts.gov
North Carolina Middle District Court: http://www.ncmd.uscourts.gov
North Carolina Western District Court: http://www.ncwd.uscourts.gov
South Carolina District Court: http://www.scd.uscourts.gov
Virginia Eastern District Court: http://www.vaed.uscourts.gov
Virginia Western District Court: http://www.vawd.uscourts.gov
West Virginia Northern District Court: http://www.wvnd.uscourts.gov
West Virginia Southern District Court: http://www.wvsd.uscourts.gov

Fifth Circuit
Court of Appeals: http://www.ca5.uscourts.gov
Louisiana Eastern District Court: http://www.laed.uscourts.gov
Louisiana Middle District Court: http://www.lamd.uscourts.gov
Louisiana Western District Court: http://www.lawd.uscourts.gov
Mississippi Northern District Court: http://www.msnd.uscourts.gov
Mississippi Southern District Court: http://www.mssd.uscourts.gov
Texas Eastern District Court: http://www.txed.uscourts.gov
Texas Northern District Court: http://www.txnd.uscourts.gov
Texas Southern District/Bankruptcy Courts: http://www.txsd.uscourts.gov
Texas Western District Court: http://www.txwd.uscourts.gov

Table 2.1. Websites for the Circuit Courts and District Courts of the
United States *(continued)*

Sixth Circuit
Court of Appeals: http://www.ca6.uscourts.gov
Kentucky Eastern District Court: http://www.kyed.uscourts.gov
Kentucky Western District Court: http://www.kywd.uscourts.gov
Michigan Eastern District Court: http://www.mied.uscourts.gov
Michigan Western District Court: http://www.miwd.uscourts.gov
Ohio Northern District Court: http://www.ohnd.uscourts.gov
Ohio Southern District Court: http://www.ohsd.uscourts.gov
Tennessee Eastern District Court: http://www.tned.uscourts.gov
Tennessee Middle District Court: http://www.tnmd.uscourts.gov
Tennessee Western District Court: http://www.tnwd.uscourts.gov

Seventh Circuit
Court of Appeals: http://www.ca7.uscourts.gov
Illinois Central District Court: http://www.ilcd.uscourts.gov
Illinois Northern District Court: http://www.ilnd.uscourts.gov
Illinois Southern District Court: http://www.ilsd.uscourts.gov
Indiana Northern District Court: http://www.innd.uscourts.gov
Indiana Southern District Court: http://www.insd.uscourts.gov
Wisconsin Eastern District Court: http://www.wied.uscourts.gov
Wisconsin Western District Court: http://www.wiwd.uscourts.gov

Eighth Circuit
Court of Appeals: http://www.ca8.uscourts.gov
Arkansas Eastern District Court: http://www.ared.uscourts.gov
Arkansas Western District Court: http://www.arwd.uscourts.gov
Iowa Northern District Court: http://www.iand.uscourts.gov
Iowa Southern District Court: http://www.iasd.uscourts.gov
Minnesota District Court: http://www.mnd.uscourts.gov
Missouri Eastern District Court: http://www.moed.uscourts.gov
Missouri Western District Court: http://www.mowd.uscourts.gov
Nebraska District Court: http://www.ned.uscourts.gov
North Dakota District Court: http://www.ndd.uscourts.gov
South Dakota District Court: http://www.sdd.uscourts.gov

Ninth Circuit
Court of Appeals: http://www.ca9.uscourts.gov
Alaska District Court: http://www.akd.uscourts.gov
Arizona District Court: http://www.azd.uscourts.gov
California Central District Court: http://www.cacd.uscourts.gov
California Eastern District Court: http://www.caed.uscourts.gov
California Northern District Court: http://www.cand.uscourts.gov
California Southern District Court: http://www.casd.uscourts.gov
Guam District Court: http://www.gud.uscourts.gov
Hawaii District Court: http://www.hid.uscourts.gov
Idaho Bankruptcy/District Court: http://www.id.uscourts.gov
Montana District Court: http://www.mtd.uscourts.gov
Nevada District Court: http://www.nvd.uscourts.gov
Northern Mariana Islands District Court: http://www.nmid.uscourts.gov
Oregon District Court: http://www.ord.uscourts.gov
Washington Eastern District Court: http://www.waed.uscourts.gov
Washington Western District Court: http://www.wawd.uscourts.gov

Table 2.1. Websites for the Circuit Courts and District Courts of the
United States *(continued)*

Tenth Circuit
Court of Appeals: http://www.ca10.uscourts.gov
Colorado District Court: http://www.cod.uscourts.gov
Kansas District Court: http://www.ksd.uscourts.gov
New Mexico District Court: http://www.nmd.uscourts.gov
Oklahoma Eastern District Court: http://www.oked.uscourts.gov
Oklahoma Northern District Court: http://www.oknd.uscourts.gov
Oklahoma Western District Court: http://www.okwd.uscourts.gov
Utah District Court: http://www.utd.uscourts.gov
Wyoming District Court: http://www.wyd.uscourts.gov

Eleventh Circuit
Court of Appeals: http://www.ca11.uscourts.gov
Alabama Middle District Court: http://www.almd.uscourts.gov
Alabama Northern District Court: http://www.alnd.uscourts.gov
Alabama Southern District Court: http://www.alsd.uscourts.gov
Florida Middle District Court: http://www.flmd.uscourts.gov
Florida Northern District Court: http://www.flnd.uscourts.gov
Florida Southern District Court: http://www.flsd.uscourts.gov
Georgia Middle District Court: http://www.gamd.uscourts.gov
Georgia Northern District Court: http://www.gand.uscourts.gov
Georgia Southern District Court: http://www.gasd.uscourts.gov

D.C. Circuit
Court of Appeals: http://www.cadc.uscourts.gov
District Court for the District of Columbia: http://www.dcd.uscourts.gov/dcd
D.C. Bankruptcy Court: http://www.dcb.uscourts.gov
Federal Public Defender: http://www. www.dcfpd.org

Federal Circuit Court
U.S. Court of Appeals for the Federal Circuit: http://www.cafc.uscourts.gov

---

d. Federal Cases

- **What:** Federal cases are written by federal judges. These judges inter-pret the United States Constitution and federal statutes and create federal common law by deciding on specific cases and writing opinions. Only the written opinion of the court is considered case precedent. However, when published, editors include other helpful information such as the following.
  - **Citation and Heading:** The citation includes the case name, reporter (sometimes there is an official and an unofficial reporter provided in a parallel citation), and the year of the decision. The heading con-tains a bit more detail by providing the name of the court as well as the actual date of the decision.
  - **Case synopsis:** The editors usually provide a summary of the opinion. This summary is identified as the syllabus in a Supreme Court opinion. Remember that a case synopsis is not part of the official opinion.
  - **Headnotes:** These are short paragraphs that summarize key points of the opinion. Usually, editors will provide corresponding numbers

to the text of the opinion, or, in online materials, headnotes may be hyperlinked to the text of the opinion. West also provides key numbers to these headnotes. (For more information on key numbers, see chapter 3, page 113.)

- **Names:** Here, the editor provides the names of the attorneys as well as the name of the judge who wrote the opinion. *Per curiam* means that no one particular judge is taking credit for the opinion; it is an anonymous opinion. *En banc* means that the full appellate court has heard the argument and rendered a decision (as opposed to a three-judge panel).
- **Written Opinion:** The actual opinion appears next in the text and is the only part of the published decision you should cite.

These published opinions become binding precedent. However, only the cases chosen by the courts for publication are considered "published." As a result, only the published opinions are ultimately placed in the reporters. Although many unpublished decisions are available through services such as Westlaw and Lexis, most jurisdictions do not rely on unpublished decisions as binding precedent, so lawyers are wary of citing them in court documents. Check with your local rules regarding reliance on unpublished opinions.

- **Where:** Federal cases are published in chronological and subject-matter form.
  - The **chronological** publication is through a variety of books called federal reporters, which are found in the following volumes:
    - **Supreme Court**
      - The United States Reports (U.S.), the official reporter for the Supreme Court, published by the federal government
      - The Supreme Court Reporter (S. Ct.), published by West Group
      - The United States Supreme Court Reports (L. Ed., L. Ed. 2d), published by Lawyers Cooperative
    - **Courts of Appeals**
      - The Federal Reporter (F., F.2d, F.3d), published by West Group
    - **District Court Cases**
      - The Federal Supplement (F. Supp., F. Supp. 2d), published by West Group
      - The Federal Rules Decisions (F.R.D.)
      - The Federal Reporter (F., F.2d), for cases decided between 1880 and 1932
  - The **subject-matter form** of publication is in federal digests. However, the cases in the digests are not printed in full; instead, they are summaries of cases grouped by subject matter and function as an index to the reporters. Each reporter has its own digest.
- **Why:** Your ultimate goal is to find a case within the chronological reporter. However, you would start with the chronological reporter only if you had a citation or the plaintiff's or defendant's name (to check the table of

cases by name; see page 44). Most of the time, you will be searching for cases based on subject matter. Most researchers begin on Lexis or Westlaw with word searches based on specific terms to narrow the issue. For print research, the best place to begin your common law research is through the digests. Each digest contains an index and then volumes arranged alphabetically by subject matter. These subjects have been created and maintained by publishers who act as the researchers' first set of eyes to cull and sort case law. Once you find your subject matter, the digest (see page 43) will provide citations to the reporters as well as a short annotation summarizing the case. You should never cite directly to the digest.

- **How:** For more on researching case law, see "Finding Cases," chapter 3, page 136.[11] For information on citations to federal case law, see chapter 4, pages 251 (Bluebook) and 197 (ALWD).

---

11. For a case law research tutorial, see http://www.ll.georgetown.edu/tutorials/cases/index.cfm.

Anatomy of a Federal Case

676   **11 FEDERAL SUPPLEMENT, 2d SERIES**

their May 8, 1998 "Order on Rule to Show Cause" against the plaintiffs.

It is so ORDERED

Willie BARRON, Jr., Plaintiff, ——— Name of case

v.

Marvin T. RUNYON, Defendant.

No. CIV. A. 98–100–A.

United States District Court,
E.D. Virginia,
Alexandria Division. ——— Court

July 7, 1998. ——— Date case decided

Employee brought action against employer, alleging that he was unlawfully terminated for absences protected by the Family Medical Leave Act (FMLA). Employer moved for summary judgment. The District Court, Ellis, J., held that: (1) as applied to employee, effective date of FMLA was one year after the date of enactment; (2) employee, who sought intermittent leave under the FMLA to care for his wife, was only required to establish his eligibility for the first absence related to that leave; and (3) triable issues existed regarding whether employee was terminated for taking leave protected by the FMLA.

Motion denied.

——— Editor's synopsis (not part of judge's opinion)

1. Civil Rights ⚷102.1

For purposes of employee's action under the Family Medical Leave Act (FMLA) where a collective bargaining agreement (CBA) covering the employee was in effect on the date of enactment of the Act, effective date of FMLA was one year after the date of enactment, though both employer and employee's union voluntarily adopted terms of FMLA and explicitly made them effective with respect to their employees on an earlier

date. Family and Medical Leave Act of 1993, § 2 et seq., 29 U.S.C.A. § 2601 et seq.

2. Statutes ⚷250

Private parties have no power to change or vary, by fiat or agreement, the effective date of a legislative enactment; only Congress can set a law's effective date.

3. Civil Rights ⚷173.1

Employee who sought intermittent leave under the Family Medical Leave Act (FMLA) to care for his wife was only required to establish his eligibility for the first absence related to that leave, and was not required to reestablish eligibility for each subsequent absence taken for the same reason during the following 12 months. Family and Medical Leave Act of 1993, §§ 101(2)(A), 102(a)(1), (b)(1), 29 U.S.C.A. §§ 2611(2)(A), 2612(a)(1), (b)(1); 29 C.F.R. §§ 825.100(a), 825.110(a)(2), 825.203(a), (c)(1).

4. Civil Rights ⚷173.1

An employee who is eligible for intermittent leave under the Family Medical Leave Act (FMLA) need only establish his eligibility on the occasion of the first absence, and not on the occasion of each subsequent absence. Family and Medical Leave Act of 1993, §§ 101(2)(A), 102(a)(1), 29 U.S.C.A. §§ 2611(2)(A), 2612(a)(1); 29 C.F.R. §§ 825.100(a), 825.110(a)(2), 825.203(a), (c)(1).

5. | **Civil Rights** ⚷173.1

——— Headnote number— references part of case where this legal issue is discussed

——— West key number

For purposes of the Family Medical Leave Act (FMLA), a series of absences, separated by days during which the employee is at work, but all of which are taken for the same medical reason, subject to the same notice, and taken during the same 12–month period, comprises one period of intermittent leave. Family and Medical Leave Act of 1993, §§ 101(2)(A), 102(a)(1), (b)(1), 29 U.S.C.A. §§ 2611(2)(A), 2612(a)(1), (b)(1); 29 C.F.R. §§ 825.100(a), 825.110(a)(2), 825.203(a), (c)(1).

——— Headnote—editor's summary of key points of law in opinion

6. Federal Civil Procedure ⚷2497.1

Genuine issues of material fact regarding whether employee was terminated for taking leave that was covered by the Family Medical Leave Act (FMLA) or for taking leave that was not protected under such Act

Anatomy of a Case (continued)

BARRON v. RUNYON   **677**

Cite as 11 F.Supp.2d 676 (E.D.Va. 1998)

precluded summary judgment on employee's FMLA claim against employer. Family and Medical Leave Act of 1993, § 105(a)(2), 29 U.S.C.A. § 2615(a)(2); Fed.Rules Civ.Proc. Rule 56(c), 28 U.S.C.A.

———

Declan C. Leonard, Martin, Arif & Petrovich, Burke, VA, for Plaintiff.

Attorneys ——— Helen F. Fahey, U.S. Atty., Richard Parker, Asst. U.S. Atty., Alexandria, VA, Roderick Eves, U.S. Postal Service, Mid–Atlantic Law Office, Washington, DC, for Defendant.

MEMORANDUM OPINION

Judge who wrote decision ——— ELLIS, District Judge.

Beginning of decision ——— This Family Medical Leave Act ("FMLA" or "the Act")[1] action presents two issues of statutory interpretation not yet resolved in this circuit. The first issue requires determination of the FMLA's effective date in circumstances in which an employer voluntarily adopted the terms of the Act as part of its internal policies prior to the effective date specified in the statute. The second, and central, issue is whether an employee who takes intermittent leave under the Act for a valid medical reason must qualify as an "eligible employee" each time he is absent from work for that reason, or whether his eligibility must be established only the first time he is absent for that reason. Apart from these statutory questions, there is also presented the question whether the existing summary judgment record supports plaintiff's allegation that there was a causal connection between his termination and his use of FMLA-protected leave.

I

Plaintiff was employed as a processing clerk for the U.S. Postal Service in Merrifield, Virginia, where he was a member of the American Postal Workers Union ("APWU"). Plaintiff worked 1,394 hours in the Postal Service's 1993 leave year[2] and 1,192 hours in the 1994 leave year. In the twelve months immediately preceding February 25, 1994, plaintiff worked a total of 1,244 hours. There is no twelve-month period ending after that date during which he worked at least 1,250 hours.[3]

Labor relations between the Postal Service and the APWU were governed by a collective bargaining agreement ("CBA") that was in effect from June 12, 1991, until November 20, 1994. Pursuant to the terms of the CBA, on November 9, 1993, plaintiff was issued a Notice of Removal for "unsatisfactory attendance/repeated failure to maintain regular schedule/AWOL." Thereafter, on December 23, 1993, plaintiff and the Postal Service entered into a Last Chance/Firm Choice Agreement, under which plaintiff's Notice of Removal would be held in abeyance for one year provided certain conditions were met. Specifically, plaintiff agreed to enroll in a structured Employee Assistance Program and to maintain satisfactory attendance at work. Under this Agreement, whether plaintiff's attendance was satisfactory was committed to the discretion of his immediate supervisor, Karen Robinson. Moreover, the Agreement provided that "any unscheduled absences may result in the issuance of a Notice of Removal."

According to Robinson, plaintiff's attendance over the next year was not satisfactory, and so on December 20, 1994, plaintiff was issued a second Notice of Removal for "unsatisfactory attendance/repeated failure to maintain regular schedule/AWOL/violation of settlement agreement," and he was terminated. This second notice listed the following fourteen periods over the one-year duration of the Agreement in which plaintiff's attendance was allegedly unsatisfactory:

Unscheduled LWOP

December 30, 1993–January 7, 1994	56 hours

———

1. The FMLA is codified at 29 U.S.C. §§ 2601–2654.

2. It appears from the existing record that, at times relevant here, the Postal Service's leave year began and ended in the last week of December.

3. As becomes evident below, this information is relevant because the FMLA requires that an employee work at least 1,250 hours in the twelve months preceding the leave to be eligible for protected leave under the Act.

Federal Digest

PRODUCTS LIABILITY ⚷417 — Key number

For references to other topics, see Descriptive-Word Index

scription drug to her physicians constituted negligence on patient's part was question of comparative negligence to be determined by jury.

Nichols v. McNeilab, Inc., 850 F.Supp. 562.

D.N.H. 2005. Under New Hampshire law, whether a plaintiff's injuries are indivisible, for purposes of contribution and apportionment between joint tortfeasors, is a question of law for the trial judge in a crashworthiness case.

McNeil v. Nissan Motor Co., Ltd., 365 F.Supp.2d 206.

D.N.M. 2005. City's negligence was not so extraordinary as to be independent intervening cause of accident involving asphalt emulsion distributor used in road resurfacing work, but evidence of city's negligence was sufficient to go to jury on issue of comparative fault in operator's products liability action.

Morales v. E.D. Etnyre & Co., 382 F.Supp.2d 1278.

E.D.N.Y. 1989. Evidence that plaintiff in asbestos-related personal injury action continued smoking despite knowing of health hazards and that smoking aggravates effects of asbestosis was sufficient to create jury issue as to whether plaintiff was contributorily negligent. Fed.Rules Civ.Proc.Rule 50(b), 28 U.S.C.A.

In re Joint Eastern and Southern Districts Asbestos Litigation, 124 F.R.D. 538, affirmed Johnson v. Celotex Corp., 899 F.2d 1281, certiorari denied 111 S.Ct. 297, 498 U.S. 920, 112 L.Ed.2d 250.

M.D.Pa. 1992. Even if apportionment of liability was appropriate in asbestos case, issue should have been raised before case was submitted to jury.

Sealover v. Carey Canada, 791 F.Supp. 1059, reversed 996 F.2d 42.

E.D.Tenn. 2000. Under Tennessee law, the comparative fault of a plaintiff in a products liability action is a matter ordinarily left to the jury.

Martin v. Michelin North America, Inc., 92 F.Supp.2d 745.

⚷416. —— Misuse of product.

C.A.7 (Ind.) 1987. Evidence that heart catheter was designed for general and variable therapeutic purposes, but not specifically for kind of use to which operating surgeon put catheter in open-heart surgery, and evidence that operating surgeon sutured catheter in manner not intended by manufacturers, raised jury question on defense of misuse in strict products liability suit against manufacturers to recover damages sustained when catheter broke and

portion remained inside patient's heart. IC 33–1–1.5–4 (1982 Ed.).

Phelps v. Sherwood Medical Industries, 836 F.2d 296.

C.A.10 (Okla.) 2004. Under Oklahoma law, issue of whether injuries sustained by passenger involved in motor vehicle accident resulted from passenger's misuse of vehicle's front seat by riding in a reclined position was for jury in personal injury suit brought by passenger against automobile manufacturer alleging that passenger's injuries resulted from a flawed seat belt system and seat design.

Cummings v. General Motors Corp., 365 F.3d 944, as modified on denial of rehearing.

M.D.Ala. 1995. In action brought under Alabama Extended Manufacturer's Liability Doctrine (AEMLD), ordinarily, whether someone misused allegedly defective product is factual issue for jury.

Dickerson v. Cushman, Inc., 909 F.Supp. 1467.

— Court

D.Colo. 1988. Injured worker's failure to follow warning supplied with machine causing injury did not as matter of Colorado law, bar his products liability claim alleging design defect; question of misuse of product was properly submitted to jury, presence or absence of warning is merely one factor of several to consider in determining whether product is defective or unreasonably dangerous, and warnings and instructions, even when they are adequate, are not substitute for safe design.

— Summary of this issue in the case

McHargue v. Stokes Div. of Pennwalt, 686 F.Supp. 1428.

— Case citation

S.D.Fla. 1990. Plaintiff did not misuse motorcycle as a matter of law by riding it at high speed along dirt trails.

Mendez v. Honda Motor Co., 738 F.Supp. 481.

⚷417. —— Assumption of risk. — Key number

C.A.11 (Ala.) 1992. Contributory negligence questions in actions under Alabama Extended Manufacturer's Liability Doctrine are normally for jury, and trial court must be careful not to construe the phrase "intended use" so strictly as to actually resolve questions of contributory negligence or assumption of risk without submitting those issues to jury.

Goree v. Winnebago Industries, Inc., 958 F.2d 1537.

C.A.11 (Ala.) 1986. Whether wood cutter appreciated danger of using chain saw without a chain brake due to illiteracy and a low level of intelligence, thereby rendering defense of assumption of risk unavailable to chain saw manufacturer under Alabama Extended Manufacturer's Liability Doctrine, was for jury in products

† This Case was not selected for publication in the National Reporter System
For cited U.S.C.A. sections and legislative history, see United States Code Annotated

Table of Cases, By Name

3. Federal Agencies and Administrative Law

Federal agencies fall under the executive branch. They are created through congressional legislation that defines the specialized topic and mission of the agency. Once established, an agency may issue rules and regulations pertaining to its mission and hear and settle disputes arising from them. Law produced by agencies is called administrative law.

Examples of well-known agencies include the Environmental Protection Agency, the Federal Communications Commission, and the Federal Trade Commission. All federal agencies have websites; these three examples can be found at www.epa.gov, www.fcc.gov, and www.ftc.gov.

To find a particular agency, consult the following references:

- Agency Index[12]
- Federal Web Locator[13]
- FirstGov[14]

Before 1936, there was no official publication of rules and regulations. As a result, there was no way to determine whether an act was prohibited by a particular agency. Roosevelt's New Deal created a growth of agencies, which produced thousands of regulations, but there was no method to publish them.

---

12. www.washlaw.edu/doclaw/executive5m.html.

13. www.infoctr.edu/fwl or www.loc.gov/rr/news/fedgov.

14. www.usa.gov/Agencies/Federal/All_Agencies/index.shtml.

In *Panama Refining Co. v. Ryan*, 293 U.S. 388 (1935), a corporation was prosecuted for violations of a regulation that had been revoked before the lawsuit was filed. Therefore, in 1935, Congress passed the Federal Register Act, which required any administrative rule or regulation to be published in the Federal Register. Since 1936, the Federal Register has published, in chronological order, every regulation having "general applicability and legal effect."

In 1937, Congress provided for a method of subject codification of the regulations into the **Code of Federal Regulations (C.F.R.),** which was first published in 1939. Since 1968, the C.F.R. has been published yearly, in quarterly installments.

In 1946, Congress passed the Administrative Procedure Act, which required the agencies to publish proposed rules and allowed the public to comment on those proposed rules in the Federal Register. Subsequent legislation requires agencies to publish descriptions of the agencies, rules of procedure, policy statements, and notices of most meetings (the latter from the Sunshine Act of 1976).

- **What:** Each executive agency creates administrative law, which includes rules and regulations, decisions, and a variety of other documents particular to that agency.
  - **Administrative Rules and Regulations:** Agencies create rules and regulations, which implement statutes that have already been passed by Congress. These statutes give the agencies the power to enforce the statute by promulgating specific regulations and rules that must be followed. Regulations (sometimes called rules) look very similar to statutes. When an agency promulgates a rule or regulation, it must notify the public by publishing the proposed regulation in the Federal Register, solicit comments regarding the regulation, and publish the regulation before it becomes effective.
  - **Administrative Agency Decisions:** Agency decisions are similar in form to judicial decisions. Administrative agencies exercise a quasi-judicial power in that they make decisions involving issues arising under their regulations. Under the Administrative Procedure Act, agency hearings are conducted by an administrative judge, who acts as a trial judge making decisions of the agency. A party can appeal the agency decision to the federal district court.
- **Where:** Similar to statutes, administrative regulations are published chronologically and by subject matter.
  - **Chronologically:** The Federal Register. The Federal Register is published daily (based on workdays), and all issues within a year constitute a single volume. A table of contents page lists all executive agencies and documents produced by each agency. A daily issue publishes material in the following order:
    - Presidential documents
    - Rules and regulations
    - Proposed rules
    - Explanations and justifications for new or amended regulations
    - Notices
    - Notices of Sunshine Act meetings

The Federal Register also contains helpful finding aides, such as:
- An Index by Subject and Name (see page 49)
- A List of C.F.R. parts affected in that issue
- Telephone numbers
- A parallel table of Federal Register pages for the month
- A cumulative table of C.F.R. Parts affected during the month
- A list of Public Laws

- **Subject Matter:** The C.F.R. (see pages 50-53) arranges administrative rules and regulations topically. It is arranged in a format similar to the United States Code. The regulations are arranged in 50 titles, some of which match the titles of the U.S.C. The titles are then divided into chapters, which regulate a particular agency.

    Administrative Agency decisions are similar in form to judicial decisions. However, there is no comprehensive system for publishing these cases. To find administrative decisions you can try several sources.

    - **Agency Reporters and Web Sites.** Many agencies publish their opinions in their own reporters, such as the Federal Trade Commission Reports or Agriculture Decisions.[15]
    - **Lexis.** On Lexis, click on Area of Law by Topic; then within each topic, look for Administrative Materials (see page 122).
    - **Lexis Advance.** On Lexis Advance, click on Content Type; then look within Analytical Materials.
    - **Westlaw.** On Westlaw, click on Directory; Topic Practice Areas; a specific topic; Federal Administrative Materials.
    - **WestlawNext.** On WestlawNext, click Regulations on the All Content tab in the Browse section.

- **Why:** If you work in a particular area of law, such as food and drug law, you will need to become very familiar with the applicable regulations and agency.

- **How:** The best place to find regulation is through the C.F.R., which is a set of soft-cover volumes. To find regulations in the C.F.R., you can search by subject or by citation to the regulation or to the statute. There are a number of sources to find regulations:

    - **Online.** The C.F.R. is available online through a number of sources:
        - **Government Printing Office.**[16] There are two version on GPO Access:
            - the PDF version, which is the "official" version and is as up-to-date as the print version; and
            - the e-CFR which is more current but not "official."

        In addition, GPO Access has a Parallel Table of Authorities and Rules so that you can find a regulation from a statute citation.

---

15. To find a particular agency online, go to www.usa.gov/Agencies/Federal/All_Agencies/ index.shtml.

16. http://origin.www.gpoaccess.gov/cfr/.

- **Agency Web Sites.** Agencies will post their specific regulations.
- **Westlaw.** When you have a citation to the C.F.R., use Find. Otherwise go to Administrative Code. You can use the C.F.R. index or do a search.
- **WestlawNext.** When you have a citation to the C.F.R., type it into the text box at the top of the page and click Search.
- **Lexis.** When you have a citation to the C.F.R., use Find a Document. Otherwise, go to Code of Federal Regulations. Lexis does not have a C.F.R. index.
- **Lexis Advance.** When you have a citation to the C.F.R., type it into the text box at the top of the page and click Search.
- **Regulations.gov.**[17] This is a government website where you can find proposed regulations.

- **Book Research.** To find regulations in the print C.F.R.:
  - **The index to the C.F.R.** There are three print indexes: the Index and Finding Aids volume of the C.F.R. (see page 50), a special volume of U.S.C.S.; and one published by West.
  - **Annotated Codes.** U.S.C.A. and U.S.C.S. frequently cross reference regulations from the specific statutes.
  - **Updating Regulations:** Once you find the applicable regulation, you will need to make sure it is up to date. The C.F.R. is updated quarterly each year.
    - Titles 1-16 contain regulations in force as of January 1 of that year.
    - Titles 17-27 contain regulations in force as of April 1 of that year.
    - Titles 28-41 contain regulations in force as of July 1 of that year.
    - Titles 42-50 contain regulations in force as of October 1 that year.

    Each year's volumes are a particular color. Thus, in June, half the set will be one color and the other half will be a different color. By the end of the year, the whole set is the same color. The cover of each volume states the dates of coverage. Because the C.F.R. is updated so frequently, there are no pocket parts. However, because a regulation can be changed after the particular title has been published, you will need to update your regulations carefully using the List of Sections Affected or online resources.
  - **The List of Sections Affected (L.S.A.).** The L.S.A. (see page 53) is published monthly and contains the finalized and proposed changes made since the latest publication of the C.F.R. The

---

17. http://www.regulations.gov/search/Regs/home.html#home.

L.S.A. arranges final regulations by C.F.R. title and section and provides page references to the Federal Register. The L.S.A. arranges proposed changes by title and part and references pages in the Federal Register. To update a regulation you need to find the most recent issue of the L.S.A. Look on the inside cover to determine the time period covered. Next, look up your regulation by title number and then specifically by part or section. If your number is not listed, the regulation has not been updated. If it has been listed, you will find a reference to the Federal Register where the information on the regulation will be posted. Next, you will need to update further to make sure that no further action has been taken on that regulation since the publication of the most recent L.S.A. To do so, use the table on the back cover of the most current issue of the Federal Register (C.F.R. Parts Affected).

- **Updating Online.** To update online, you can use these sources:
  - **GPO Access.** The e-CFR provides updating through the Federal Register.
  - **Westlaw and WestlawNext.** Use Keycite flags.
  - **Lexis and Lexis Advance.** Shepardizing a regulation will only provide you with cases or law review articles citing the regulation. It will not tell you about any changes in a regulation.
  - **Regulations.gov.** Here, you can find proposed regulations.

For more information on researching administrative law, see chapter 3, page 151.[18] For information on citations to administrative materials, see chapter 4, pages 253 (Bluebook) and 199 (ALWD).

---

18. For an online tutorial on finding administrative law, see http://www.ll.georgetown.edu/tutorials/admin/index.cfm.

Index by Subjects and Names

Abadi, Sam
Shipping Act violation complaint: FMC
(7/23/N) 39569

Abandoned Barge Act
Barges (undocumented) over 100 gross tons,
numbering regs estab: USCG–
Advance NPRM *(7/6/PR) 36384*

Abandoned Mine Land Reclamation Act
Abandoned mine land reclamation program of IL,
regs revision: OSM *(11/16/PR) 63630*

Abandoned mine land reclamation program
Financing of abandoned mine land reclamation
project involving incidental coal extraction, regs
revision: OSM–
Comment period reopening *(9/3/PR) 46951*
OSM abandoned mine land reclamation program
expansion, regs estab: OSM–
Comment period reopening *(7/31/PR) 40871*
–Illinois
Regs revision: OSM *(11/16/PR) 63630*
–Pennsylvania
Govt construction contract regs, estab: OSM–
Comment period reopening *(7/28/PR) 40237;
(11/3/PR) 59259*
–Texas
Revision: OSM *(11/25/R) 65068*
Comment period reopening *(10/2/PR) 53003*

Abandoned property
Barges (undocumented) over 100 gross tons,
numbering regs estab: USCG–
Advance NPRM *(7/6/PR) 36384*
see also Abandoned mine land reclamation program

ABB Combustion Engineering
Locomotive (steam) inspection and maintenance
stds revision: FRA *(9/25/PR) 51404*
Nuclear plant safety design certification filings and
actions: NRC *(7/2/N) 36271*

Abbott Laboratories
Bacillus sphaericus residue tolerance rqmt
exemption for foods: EPA *(9/11/R) 48594*
Foreign trade zone appls and actions: FTZB–
Chicago IL *(12/29/N) 71617*
Lake Cty IL *(12/29/N) 71617*
New drug appl approval withdrawals: FDA
*(9/25/N) 51359; (12/2/N) 66549;
(12/17/N) 69631*

Abrishami, Elham
Export privileges temporary denial orders filings
and actions: BXA *(8/13/N) 43370*

Absecon Bay
Flood ins base elevation determinations: FEMA
(10/14/PR) 55072

ABT Associates
EPA confidential info transfer to contractors: EPA
(7/13/N) 37564; (11/24/N) 64962

Abu Dhabi
see United Arab Emirates

Academy of Motion Picture Arts and Sciences
Cultural objects exhibition imports significance
determinations: USIA–
UFA Film Posters, 1918-1943 *(8/21/N) 44958*

Acadiana Treatment Systems
Clean Water Act violation: DOJ *(8/11/N) 42874*

Accelerators
see Motor vehicle parts and supplies

Accidental deaths
Medical device distributor and importer adverse
incident rptg, facility registration, and device list
rqmts, revision: FDA–
Withdrawal *(8/27/N) 45716*
Vet disability and death from Vets Affairs medical
and surgical exam, rehabilitation, training, and

treatment svcs, compensation eligibility
adjudication regs revision: Vets Affairs
(8/24/R) 45004

Accidents and accident prevention
Alcohol and drug abuse by transport workers,
random testing rates revision: FTA
(12/14/N) 68818
Disability and rehabilitation research and training
grants, appls solicitation: Educ Dept
(7/2/N) 36298
Disability and rehabilitation research and training
grants, funding priorities: Educ Dept
(7/27/N) 40156
Hazardous substance environ release rptg rqmts:
EPA–
Caprolactam hazardous wastes, reportable
quantity revision *(12/15/PR) 69169;
(12/15/R) 69166*
2,4,6-tribromophenol, reportable quantity
revision, effective date revision
(8/10/R-cx) 42580
Injury control research center grants, availability:
CDC *(9/2/N) 46793*
Injury Prevention and Control Adv Cmtee, renewal:
CDC *(11/12/N) 63319*
Manufactured housing construction and safety stds
inc by reference, revision: HUD
(10/30/PR) 58570
Natural gas (liquefied) pipeline safety stds,
incorporation by reference: RSPA
(12/22/PR) 70735
Natural gas and hazardous liquid pipeline owners
and operators Year 2000 computer problems,
industry guidelines availability: RSPA
(8/7/N) 42478
NTSB accident investigations and claims ops,
authority delegation and regs revision: NTSB
(12/29/R) 71605
Steel erection and fall protection, safety stds
revision: OSHA–
Hearing *(8/13/PR) 43452*
see also Accidental deaths
see also Agricultural accidents and safety
see also Aviation safety and standards
see also Fires and fire prevention
see also Marine accidents and safety
see also Mine safety standards, general
see also Mine safety standards, specific
modifications
see also Motor vehicle safety and standards
see also Nuclear accidents and safety
see also Nuclear radiation
see also Occupational health and safety standards
see also Poisoning and drug reaction
see also Product safety standards
see also Railroad accidents and safety
see also Safety inspections
see also Safety regulation
see also Traffic accidents and safety
see also Traffic engineering

Accomack County Farm Bureau
Tomatoes (fresh) from Mexico, antidumping
proceeding: ITA *(8/14/N) 43674*

**Accountable Pipeline Safety and Partnership
Act**
Pipeline operator (carbon dioxide, gas, and
hazardous liquid) personnel qualification and
training stds, estab: RSPA *(10/27/PR) 57269*

Accounting and auditing
Acctg Stds Fed Adv Bd guidelines availability:
GAO *(11/9/N) 60350*
Acq and procurement by Fed agencies, FAR regs
revision: DOD, GSA, and NASA–
Fed Acq Circular 97-10 *(12/18/R) 70292*

Actuarial Examinations Adv Cmtee, renewal:
Actuaries Enrollment Jt Bd *(10/19/N) 55844*
Air carrier uniform system of accounts and
financial data rptg rqmts, review: DOT–
Advance NPRM *(7/15/PR) 38128*
Automobile business mileage allowance
substantiation, income tax regs revision: IRS
*(10/1/IR) 52600; (10/1/PR) 52660;
(10/1/R) 52600*
Bank (natl) and foreign bank US branch intl loan
fee acctg regs, revision: OCC *(10/26/R) 57047*
Bank, holding co, and savings assn capital
adequacy, equity securities unrealized holding
gains risk-based capital stds revision: FDIC, FRS,
OCC, and OTS *(9/1/R) 46518*
Bank, holding co, and savings assn capital
adequacy, servicing assets treatment stds revision:
FDIC, FRS, OCC, and OTS *(8/10/R) 42668*
Broker-dealer Year 2000 computer program
compliance rptg, independent public accountant
attestation regs estab: SEC–
Comment period reopening *(7/13/PR) 37709*
Child poverty rate determination re needy family
temporary aid to States and tribes, methodology
estab: ACF *(9/23/PR) 50837*
Commodity pool operator and trading adviser
performance rate of return computation method
and disclosure, regs review: CFTC–
Comment period extension *(8/6/PR) 41982*
Conduct (improper professional) of accountants,
determination std revision: SEC
(10/26/R) 57164
Coop research agmt filings: DOJ *(11/2/N) 58787*
Corp group consolidated income tax return member
overall foreign loss account regs, revision: IRS
(12/29/R) 71609
Effective dates revision *(12/29/IR) 71589;
(12/29/R) 71589*
Corp start-up expenditure amortization, income tax
regs revision: IRS *(12/17/R) 69554*
Cost acctg principles for higher educ instns
receiving Fed aid, revision: OMB–
Trustee travel expense authorization
(10/27/N) 57332
Cost Acctg Stds Fed Adv Bd, revenue-related
transaction disclosure stds policy statement: GAO
(11/23/N) 64717
Cost effectiveness analysis of Fed regs,
Congressional rpt availability: OMB
(8/17/N) 44034
Comment period extension *(9/18/N) 49935*
Customs duty, internal revenue tax, and fee
drawbacks and false claims penalties, automated
selectivity program estab: Customs Svc
(12/8/N) 67722
Depository instn (insured) safety and soundness
stds, revision: FDIC, FRS, OCC, and OTS–
Interagency guidelines *(10/15/IR) 55486*
Year 2000 interagency guidelines
(10/15/IR) 55480
Electric and telephone borrower (rural) audit regs,
revision: RUS *(7/17/R) 38720*
Electric utility (public) non-discriminatory open
access transmission svc info network rqmts,
estab: FERC–
Next-hour transactions experimental procedures
authorization *(7/17/N) 38638*
OASIS Phase 1-A business practices rpt filing
(7/17/N) 38638
OASIS transmission customer "source and
sink" info disclosure rqmts *(7/20/R) 38884;
(10/8/R) 54258*
Electric utility (public) open access same-time info
system transmission path naming stds, review:
FERC *(10/20/N) 56022; (10/26/N-cx) 57161;
(10/29/N) 58031*

C.F.R. Index

Access to or control over, criteria and procedures for determining eligibility, 10 CFR 11

Domestic licensing, 10 CFR 70

Spent nuclear fuel, high-level radioactive waste, and reactor-related Greater than Class C waste, licensing requirements for independent storage, 10 CFR 72

Supplemental standards of ethical conduct for agency employees, 5 CFR 5801

Trespassing on NRC property, 10 CFR 160

Well logging, licenses and radiation safety requirements for, 10 CFR 39

Reference to C.F.R. title and part on food labeling

Nuclear safety

See Radiation protection

Nuclear vessels

Marine casualties and investigation, 46 CFR 4

Nuclear Waste Technical Review Board

Privacy Act, 10 CFR 1304

Nursery stock

See also Plants

Emergency agricultural disaster assistance programs (2006), 7 CFR 1416

Nursery industry guides, 16 CFR 18

Plant protection and quarantine, foreign quarantine notices, 7 CFR 319

Nursing homes

See also Health facilities

Medicaid and Medicare, States and long term care facilities, requirements, 42 CFR 483

Medicaid, nursing facilities and intermediate care facilities for mentally retarded, payment standards, 42 CFR 442

Nursing homes, intermediate care facilities, and board and care homes, mortgage coinsurance, 24 CFR 252

Nursing homes, intermediate care facilities, board and care homes, and assisted living facilities, mortgage insurance, 24 CFR 232

Veterans

Medical care, 38 CFR 17

State homes—

Grants to States for construction or acquisition, 38 CFR 59

Payments to States for programs to promote the hiring and retention of nurses, 38 CFR 53

Per diem for adult day health care, 38 CFR 52

Per diem for nursing home care, 38 CFR 51

Per diem for nursing home care, forms, 38 CFR 58

Nursing schools

See Medical and dental schools

Nutrition

See also Food assistance programs; Foods

Food labeling, 21 CFR 101

Meat inspection, nutrition labeling, 9 CFR 317

Poultry products inspection, nutrition labeling, 9 CFR 381

Foods, nutritional quality guidelines, 21 CFR 104

Hawaiian Natives, grants for supportive and nutritional services for aged, 45 CFR 1328

Head Start program

Performance standards—

Grantee and delegate agencies, 45 CFR 1304

Services for children with disabilities, 45 CFR 1308

Indian tribes, grants for supportive and nutritional services for aged, 45 CFR 1326

Infant formula

Quality control procedures, 21 CFR 106, 21 CFR 107

Medicare and Medicaid, long term care facilities, requirements, 42 CFR 483

National school lunch program, 7 CFR 210

Nutrition education and training program, 7 CFR 227

School breakfast program, 7 CFR 220

Senior farmers' market nutrition program, 7 CFR 249

Special supplemental food program for women, infants, and children, 7 CFR 246

State and community program grants on aging, 45 CFR 1321

WIC farmers' market nutrition program (FMNP), 7 CFR 248

Nuts

Commodity laboratory testing programs, processed fruits and vegetables, 7 CFR 93

Entries in the C.F.R.

of a food described in this section shall be exempt from declaration of the statements which paragraphs (a) and (b) of this section require immediately following the name of the food. Such exemption shall not apply to the outer container or wrapper of a multiunit retail package.

(e) All salt, table salt, iodized salt, or iodized table salt in packages intended for retail sale shipped in interstate commerce 18 months after the date of publication of this statement of policy in the FEDERAL REGISTER, shall be labeled as prescribed by this section; and if not so labeled, the Food and Drug Administration will regard them as misbranded within the meaning of sections 403 (a) and (f) of the Federal Food, Drug, and Cosmetic Act.

[42 FR 14306, Mar. 15, 1977, as amended at 48 FR 10811, Mar. 15, 1983; 49 FR 24119, June 12, 1984]

PART 101—FOOD LABELING

Subpart A—General Provisions

Sec.
101.1 Principal display panel of package form food.
101.2 Information panel of package form food.
101.3 Identity labeling of food in packaged form.
101.4 Food; designation of ingredients.
101.5 Food; name and place of business of manufacturer, packer, or distributor.
101.9 Nutrition labeling of food.
101.10 Nutrition labeling of restaurant foods.
101.12 Reference amounts customarily consumed per eating occasion.
101.13 Nutrient content claims—general principles.
101.14 Health claims: general requirements.
101.15 Food; prominence of required statements.
101.17 Food labeling warning, notice, and safe handling statements.
101.18 Misbranding of food.

Subpart B—Specific Food Labeling Requirements

101.22 Foods; labeling of spices, flavorings, colorings and chemical preservatives.
101.30 Percentage juice declaration for foods purporting to be beverages that contain fruit or vegetable juice.

Subpart C—Specific Nutrition Labeling Requirements and Guidelines

101.36 Nutrition labeling of dietary supplements.
101.42 Nutrition labeling of raw fruit, vegetables, and fish.
101.43 Substantial compliance of food retailers with the guidelines for the voluntary nutrition labeling of raw fruit, vegetables, and fish.
101.44 Identification of the 20 most frequently consumed raw fruit, vegetables, and fish in the United States.
101.45 Guidelines for the voluntary nutrition labeling of raw fruit, vegetables, and fish.

Subpart D—Specific Requirements for Nutrient Content Claims

101.54 Nutrient content claims for "good source," "high," "more," and "high potency."
101.56 Nutrient content claims for "light" or "lite."
101.60 Nutrient content claims for the calorie content of foods.
101.61 Nutrient content claims for the sodium content of foods.
101.62 Nutrient content claims for fat, fatty acid, and cholesterol content of foods.
101.65 Implied nutrient content claims and related label statements.
101.67 Use of nutrient content claims for butter.
101.69 Petitions for nutrient content claims.

Subpart E—Specific Requirements for Health Claims

101.70 Petitions for health claims.
101.71 Health claims: claims not authorized.
101.72 Health claims: calcium and osteoporosis.
101.73 Health claims: dietary lipids and cancer.
101.74 Health claims: sodium and hypertension.
101.75 Health claims: dietary saturated fat and cholesterol and risk of coronary heart disease.
101.76 Health claims: fiber-containing grain products, fruits, and vegetables and cancer.
101.77 Health claims: fruits, vegetables, and grain products that contain fiber, particularly soluble fiber, and risk of coronary heart disease.
101.78 Health claims: fruits and vegetables and cancer.
101.79 Health claims: Folate and neural tube defects.
101.80 Health claims: dietary noncariogenic carbohydrate sweeteners and dental caries.

10

Entries in the C.F.R. *(continued)*

Food and Drug Administration, HHS   **§ 101.2**

101.81   Health claims: Soluble fiber from certain foods and risk of coronary heart disease (CHD).
101.82   Health claims: Soy protein and risk of coronary heart disease (CHD).
101.83   Health claims: plant sterol/stanol esters and risk of coronary heart disease (CHD).

Subpart F—Specific Requirements for Descriptive Claims That Are Neither Nutrient Content Claims nor Health Claims

101.93   Certain types of statements for dietary supplements.
101.95   ''Fresh,'' ''freshly frozen,'' ''fresh frozen,'' ''frozen fresh.''

Subpart G—Exemptions From Food Labeling Requirements

101.100   Food; exemptions from labeling.
101.105   Declaration of net quantity of contents when exempt.
101.108   Temporary exemptions for purposes of conducting authorized food labeling experiments.
APPENDIX A TO PART 101—MONIER-WILLIAMS PROCEDURE (WITH MODIFICATIONS) FOR SULFITES IN FOOD, CENTER FOR FOOD SAFETY AND APPLIED NUTRITION, FOOD AND DRUG ADMINISTRATION (NOVEMBER 1985)
APPENDIX B TO PART 101—GRAPHIC ENHANCEMENTS USED BY THE FDA
APPENDIX C TO PART 101—NUTRITION FACTS FOR RAW FRUITS AND VEGETABLES
APPENDIX D TO PART 101—NUTRITION FACTS FOR COOKED FISH

AUTHORITY: 15 U.S.C. 1453, 1454, 1455; 21 U.S.C. 321, 331, 342, 343, 348, 371; 42 U.S.C. 243, 264, 271.

SOURCE: 42 FR 14308, Mar. 15, 1977, unless otherwise noted.

EDITORIAL NOTE: Nomenclature changes to part 101 appear at 63 FR 14035, Mar. 24, 1998, 66 FR 17358, Mar. 30, 2001, and 66 FR 56035, Nov. 6, 2001.

Subpart A—General Provisions

§ 101.1   Principal display panel of package form food.

The term *principal display panel* as it applies to food in package form and as used in this part, means the part of a label that is most likely to be displayed, presented, shown, or examined under customary conditions of display for retail sale. The principal display panel shall be large enough to accommodate all the mandatory label information required to be placed thereon by this part with clarity and conspicuousness and without obscuring design, vignettes, or crowding. Where packages bear alternate principal display panels, information required to be placed on the principal display panel shall be duplicated on each principal display panel. For the purpose of obtaining uniform type size in declaring the quantity of contents for all packages of substantially the same size, the term *area of the principal display panel* means the area of the side or surface that bears the principal display panel, which area shall be:

(a) In the case of a rectangular package where one entire side properly can be considered to be the principal display panel side, the product of the height times the width of that side;

(b) In the case of a cylindrical or nearly cylindrical container, 40 percent of the product of the height of the container times the circumference;

(c) In the case of any otherwise shaped container, 40 percent of the total surface of the container: *Provided, however,* That where such container presents an obvious ''principal display panel'' such as the top of a triangular or circular package of cheese, the area shall consist of the entire top surface. In determining the area of the principal display panel, exclude tops, bottoms, flanges at tops and bottoms of cans, and shoulders and necks of bottles or jars. In the case of cylindrical or nearly cylindrical containers, information required by this part to appear on the principal display panel shall appear within that 40 percent of the circumference which is most likely to be displayed, presented, shown, or examined under customary conditions of display for retail sale.

§ 101.2   Information panel of package form food.

(a) The term *information panel* as it applies to packaged food means that part of the label immediately contiguous and to the right of the principal display panel as observed by an individual facing the principal display panel with the following exceptions:

(1) If the part of the label immediately contiguous and to the right of the principal display panel is too small

11

Statutory authority for regulation ——

Federal Register citation where regulation is published chronologically

C.F.R. L.S.A.

26	LSA—LIST OF CFR SECTIONS AFFECTED

CHANGES APRIL 1, 2008 THROUGH JANUARY 30, 2009

TITLE 21 Chapter I—Con.

17.1 (c) through (g) redesignated as (e) through (i); new (c) and (d) added **66752**
17.2 Revised **66752**
56.102 (b)(12) amended; eff. 7–14–09 2368
56.106 Added; eff, 7–14–09 2368
73.100 (d) revised; eff. 1–5–11 216
73.2087 (c) revised; eff. 1–5–11 216
101 Technical correction **66754**
  Uniform compliance date **74349**
101.22 (k)(2) revised; eff. 1–5–11 216
101.72 Revised; eff. 1–1–10 ....**56486**
101.80 Regulation at 72 FR 52789 confirmed **30301**
101.81 (c)(2)(iii)(C) revised; (c)(2)(iii)(D) added **23953**
  Regulation at 73 FR 9947 confirmed **47829**
111.75 (c)(3) correctly revised..........**27727**
179.26 (b) table amended **49603**
189.5 (a)(1) revised; (e) added; interim **20793**
201.66 Regulation at 73 FR 403 confirmed **63897**
203.3 (q) revised **59500**
203.22 (h) and (i) added **59500**
205.3 (h) revised................................**59501**
208.20 Regulation at 73 FR 404 confirmed **63897**
209 Regulation at 73 FR 404 confirmed **63897**
210 Technical correction **63361**
210.2 (c) added **40462**
210.3 Regulation at 72 FR 68068 withdrawn...................................**18440**
  (b)(6) revised **51931**
211 Technical correction....................**63361**
211.48 Regulation at 72 FR 68068 withdrawn...................................**18440**
211.67 Regulation at 72 FR 68068 withdrawn...................................**18440**
  (a) revised.....................................**51931**
211.68 Regulation at 72 FR 68068 withdrawn...................................**18440**
  (c) added..**51932**
211.72 Regulation at 72 FR 68068 withdrawn...................................**18440**
  Revised...**51932**
211.82 Regulation at 72 FR 68069 withdrawn...................................**18440**
  (b) revised......................................**51932**
211.84 Regulation at 72 FR 68069 withdrawn...................................**18440**
  (c)(1), (d)(3) and (6) revised **51932**

211.94 Regulation at 72 FR 68069 withdrawn...................................**18440**
  (c) revised......................................**51932**
211.101 Regulation at 72 FR 68069 withdrawn...................................**18440**
  (c) and (d) revised **51932**
211.103 Regulation at 72 FR 68069 withdrawn...................................**18440**
  Revised...**51932**
211.110 Regulation at 72 FR 68069 withdrawn...................................**18440**
  (a) introductory text revised; (a)(6) added **51932**
211.113 Regulation at 72 FR 68069 withdrawn...................................**18440**
  (b) revised......................................**51932**
211.160 Regulation at 72 FR 68069 withdrawn...................................**18440**
  (b)(1) revised **51932**
211.182 Regulation at 72 FR 68069 withdrawn...................................**18440**
  Revised...**51933**
211.188 Regulation at 72 FR 68070 withdrawn...................................**18440**
  (b)(11) revised **51933**
312.3 (b) amended...............................**22815**
312.84 (c) amended.............................**39607**
312.120 Revised **22815**
314.3 (b) amended........**39607, 49609, 56491**
314.50 (d)(5)(vi)(b) amended..............**39608**
314.60 (b) and (c) redesignated as new (c) and (d); new (b) added; heading, (a), new (c)(1)(iii) and (iv) revised; new (c)(2) amended...................**39608**
314.65 Amended **39609**
314.70 (c)(6)(iii) introductory text and (A) revised **49609**
314.71 (c) amended............................**39609**
314.81 (b)(2)(ii) redesignated as (b)(2)(ii)(a); (b)(2)(ii)(b) added **56491**
314.94 (a)(7)(i) revised; eff. 7–15–09 2861
314.96 (a)(2) revised; (a)(3) removed...**39609**
  (a)(1) amended; eff. 7–15–09 2861
314.100 Revised **39609**
314.101 (f)(1)(ii) revised; (f)(2) amended **39609**
314.102 (b) amended; (d) revised **39609**
314.103 (c)(1) amended **39609**
314.105 (b) amended..........................**39609**
314.107 (b)(3)(v) amended **39609**
314.110 Revised **39609**

Federal Register—page where a regulation has been revised

Federal Register—page where a regulation has been withdrawn

B. *State Law*

Information on each state can be found on its web home page, which will contain links to the state constitution, code, courts, and administrative law and regulations. Many states use a basic web address based on their postal abbreviations; for example, www.nv.gov for Nevada or www.ca.gov for California. Others use their names spelled in full: www.oregon.gov or www.michigan.gov. Still others use addresses with the extension *us*; New York State's website address, for example, is www.state.ny.us and Colorado's is www.state.co.us. Any search engine will lead you to the site of any particular state you might be looking for.

Table 2.2, on page 56, lists websites for each state's statutory code. Table 2.3, on page 57, lists court websites for each state.

1. State Legislatures and State Statutes

Each state has its own legislature. Like the federal Congress, most state legislatures are broken into two separate houses. Similar to federal bills, state bills must pass each house (and receive the governor's signature) before they become law.[19]

State constitutions. Each states has its own constitution, which is subordinate to the U.S. Constitution but which may enumerate more rights for its own citizens. The District of Columbia does not have its own constitution. A state's constitution usually is found in the first volume of the state's code and can be accessed through the index accompanying the state statutes or on the Web.

State statutes are laws passed by a state's legislature. They are published in three separate forms:

1. The first form of publication is a **slip law,** which is published in a separate pamphlet or a single sheet containing the text of the law immediately after enactment.
2. The second form of publication is a **session law,** which is published in a volume that contains all the laws passed by a legislative body during each year or session. Session laws are arranged chronologically and are snapshots of the statutory law at the time.
3. The final form of publication is in either the official or annotated **codes or statutes** (see page 58), which are arranged by subject matter. They are the preferred citations and most often used by lawyers because they are easy to access by way of a topical or popular name index. The volumes contain collections of all statutes in that particular jurisdiction and are arranged in broad topics called titles. The code contains the current laws (whereas session laws are snapshots of the law in time). State codes vary in quality and quantity. Some states use commercial publishers for their official codes; other states publish

---

19. To see an example of how states enact law, see the following website on the process used in California: www.leginfo.ca.gov/bil2lawd.html.

their codes themselves, usually more slowly than commercial publishers do. Bluebook Table 1 (T.1) and ALWD Appendix 1 list each state's official code.

To access state constitutions and statutes for particular states, go to that state's website.

Table 2.2. Websites for Statutes in U.S. States and Territories

ALABAMA	http://alisondb.legislature.state.al.us/acas/
ALASKA	www.legis.state.ak.us/basis/folio.asp
AMERICAN SAMOA	www.asbar.org/Newcode/asca.htm
ARIZONA	www.azleg.state.az.us/ArizonaRevisedStatutes.asp
ARKANSAS	http://courts.state.ar.us
CALIFORNIA	www.leginfo.ca.gov/calaw.html
COLORADO	www.state.co.us/gov_dir/leg_dir/olls/colorado_revised_statutes
CONNECTICUT	www.cga.ct.gov/asp/menu/Statutes.asp
DELAWARE	http://legis.delaware.gov/?as_sitesearch=&q=statutes
DISTRICT OF COLUMBIA	www.dccouncil.washington.dc.us/dcofficialcode
FLORIDA	www.flsenate.gov/Laws/Statutes
GEORGIA	www1.legis.ga.gov/legis/2009_10/10sumdoc.pdf
GUAM	www.justice.gov.gu/compileroflaws/gca.html
HAWAII	www.capitol.hawaii.gov/session2011/
IDAHO	www.legislature.idaho.gov/idstat/TOC/IDStatutesTOC.htm
ILLINOIS	www.ilga.gov/legislation/ilcs/ilcs.asp
INDIANA	www.ai.org/legislative/ic/code/
IOWA	www.legis.state.ia.us/IowaLaw.html
KANSAS	www.kscourts.org
KENTUCKY	www.lrc.state.ky.us/statrev/frontpg.htm
LOUISIANA	www.legis.state.la.us/lss/tsrssearch.htm
MAINE	www.mainelegislature.org/legis/statutes/
MARYLAND	http://mlis.state.md.us/asp/web_statutes.asp
MASSACHUSETTS	http://www.malegislature.gov/Laws/GeneralLaws/
MICHIGAN	www.legislature.mi.gov/(S(j4e1uc55ax45k2451zqi3b45))/mileg.aspx?page=home
MINNESOTA	www.revisor.mn.gov/statutes/
MISSISSIPPI	www.mlc.lib.ms.us/servicestolibraries/StateDocuments/SDDPonline.html
MISSOURI	www.moga.mo.gov/statutesearch/
MONTANA	http://msl.mt.gov/About_MSL/commission/statutes.asp
NEBRASKA	http://nebraskalegislature.gov/laws/browse-statutes.php
NEVADA	www.leg.state.nv.us/nrsindex/index.html
NEW HAMPSHIRE	http://gencourt.state.nh.us/rsa/html/indexes/default.html
NEW JERSEY	http://lis.njleg.state.nj.us/cgi-bin/om_isapi.dll?clientID=263247&depth=2&expandheadings=off&headingswithhits=on&infobase=statutes.nfo&softpage=TOC_Frame_Pg42
NEW MEXICO	http://www.conwaygreene.com/nmsu/lpext.dll?f=templates&fn=main-h.htm&2.0
NEW YORK	http://public.leginfo.state.ny.us/menugetf.cgi?COMMONQUERY=LAWS
NORTH CAROLINA	www.ncga.state.nc.us/gascripts/Statutes/Statutes.asp
NORTH DAKOTA	www.legis.nd.gov/information/statutes/cent-code.html
OHIO	http://codes.ohio.gov/orc
OKLAHOMA	www.oklegislature.gov/osStatuesTitle.html
OREGON	www.leg.state.or.us/ors/
PENNSYLVANIA	www.legis.state.pa.us/cfdocs/legis/LI/Public/cons_index.cfm
RHODE ISLAND	www.courts.ri.gov
SOUTH CAROLINA	www.scstatehouse.gov/
SOUTH DAKOTA	http://legis.state.sd.us/statutes/index.aspx
TENNESSEE	www.tn.gov/sos/acts/
TEXAS	www.statutes.legis.state.tx.us/
UTAH	www.le.state.ut.us/~code/code.htm
VERMONT	www.leg.state.vt.us/statutesMain.cfm
VIRGINIA	http://leg1.state.va.us/000/src.htm
WASHINGTON	http://apps.leg.wa.gov/rcw/
WEST VIRGINIA	www.legis.state.wv.us/WVCODE/Code.cfm
WISCONSIN	http://legis.wisconsin.gov/rsb/stats.html
WYOMING	http://legisweb.state.wy.us/statutes/statutes.aspx?dir=new

Table 2.3. Websites for Courts in U.S. States and Territories

ALABAMA	http://judicial.alabama.gov
ALASKA	www.state.ak.us/courts
AMERICAN SAMOA	www.justice.gov/jmd/ls/americansamoa
ARIZONA	www.azcourts.gov
ARKANSAS	http://courts.state.ar.us
CALIFORNIA	www.courtinfo.ca.gov
COLORADO	www.courts.state.co.us
CONNECTICUT	www.jud.ct.gov
DELAWARE	http://courts.delaware.gov
DISTRICT OF COLUMBIA	www.dccourts.gov
FEDERATED STATES OF MICRONESIA	www.paclii.org/fm/courts.html
FLORIDA	www.flcourts.org
GEORGIA	www.georgiacourts.org
GUAM	www.guamsupremecourt.com
HAWAII	www.courts.state.hi.us
IDAHO	www.isc.idaho.gov
ILLINOIS	www.state.il.us/court
INDIANA	www.in.gov/judiciary
IOWA	www.iowacourts.state.ia.us
KANSAS	www.kscourts.org
KENTUCKY	http://courts.ky.gov
LOUISIANA	www.louisiana.gov/Government/Judicial_Branch/
MAINE	www.courts.state.me.us
MARSHALL ISLANDS	www.paclii.org
MARYLAND	www.courts.state.md.us
MASSACHUSETTS	www.mass.gov/courts
MICHIGAN	www.courts.michigan.gov
MINNESOTA	www.courts.state.mn.us
MISSISSIPPI	www.mssc.state.ms.us
MISSOURI	www.courts.mo.gov
MONTANA	http://courts.mt.gov
NEBRASKA	http://court.nol.org
NEVADA	www.nevadajudiciary.us
NEW HAMPSHIRE	www.courts.state.nh.us
NEW JERSEY	www.judiciary.state.nj.us
NEW MEXICO	www.nmcourts.com
NEW YORK	www.courts.state.ny.us
NORTH CAROLINA	www.nccourts.org
NORTH DAKOTA	www.ndcourts.com/court/courts.htm
NORTHERN MARIANA ISLANDS	www.cnmilaw.org
OHIO	www.sconet.state.oh.us
OKLAHOMA	www.oscn.net
OREGON	www.oregon.gov/OJD/courts
PENNSYLVANIA	www.courts.state.pa.us
PUERTO RICO	www.ramajudicial.pr
RHODE ISLAND	www.courts.ri.gov
SOUTH CAROLINA	www.judicial.state.sc.us
SOUTH DAKOTA	www.sdjudicial.com
TENNESSEE	www.tsc.state.tn.us
TEXAS	www.courts.state.tx.us
UTAH	www.utcourts.gov
VERMONT	www.vermontjudiciary.org
VIRGIN ISLANDS	www.visupremecourt.org
VIRGINIA	www.courts.state.va.us
WASHINGTON	www.courts.wa.gov
WEST VIRGINIA	www.state.wv.us/wvsca/wvsystem.htm
WISCONSIN	www.wicourts.gov
WYOMING	www.courts.state.wy.us

Annotated State Statute

Chapter number and name

Outline

Definition section

History of statute

Relevant articles

Cases discussing and interpreting the statute

Text of statute

CHAPTER 96. FALSE DISPARAGEMENT OF PERISHABLE FOOD PRODUCTS

Section
96.001. Definition.
96.002. Liability.
96.003. Proof.
96.004. Certain Marketing or Labeling Excluded.

Westlaw Electronic Research

See Westlaw Electronic Research Guide following the Preface.

§ 96.001. Definition

In this chapter, "perishable food product" means a food product of agriculture or aquaculture that is sold or distributed in a form that will perish or decay beyond marketability within a limited period of time.

Added by Acts 1995, 74th Leg., ch. 80, § 1, eff. Sept. 1, 1995.

Historical and Statutory Notes

Section 2 of Acts 1995, 74th Leg., ch. 80 provides:

"This Act takes effect September 1, 1995, and applies only to information disseminated on or after that date."

Law Review and Journal Commentaries

Let them eat beef: The constitutionality of the Texas False Disparagement of Perishable Food Products Act. 29 Tex.Tech.L.Rev. 851 (1998).

Notes of Decisions

Perishable food product   1

_____

1. Perishable food product

Live cattle are not "perishable food product" for purposes of Texas' False Disparagement Of Perishable Food Products Act. Texas Beef Group v. Winfrey, N.D.Tex.1998, 11 F.Supp.2d 858, affirmed 201 F.3d 680, rehearing and suggestion for rehearing en banc denied 212 F.3d 597. Libel And Slander ⬳ 130

§ 96.002. Liability

(a) A person is liable as provided by Subsection (b) if:

(1) the person disseminates in any manner information relating to a perishable food product to the public;

(2) the person knows the information is false; and

(3) the information states or implies that the perishable food product is not safe for consumption by the public.

2. State Courts and State Cases

a. *State Courts*

Each state has its own court system. Although state court systems differ from each other, in every jurisdiction a case starts in a trial court and has an opportunity for at least one appeal.

- **Trial courts:** Some jurisdictions have multiple trial courts, such as one for criminal cases and one for civil cases.
- **Appellate courts:** Many states have an intermediate appellate court so that a litigant has two opportunities for appeal: one to the intermediate appellate court and one to the highest state court. In these types of jurisdictions, there may be more than one intermediate appellate division.

To understand your particular state's court structure, consult Bluebook Table 1 (T1) or ALWD Appendix 1. Below is a diagram of the hierarchy of a typical state's court system:

Supreme Court
↑
Court of Appeals
↑
Trial Court

b. *State Cases*

- **What:** State cases are written by state judges. These judges decide on specific cases and thereby create common law and interpret state statutes and constitutions. Only the written opinion of the court is considered case precedent. However, when published, editors include other helpful information such as the following:
    - **Citation and Heading:** The citation includes the case name, reporter (sometimes there is an official and an unofficial reporter provided in a parallel citation), and the year of the decision. The heading contains a bit more detail by providing the name of the court as well as the actual date of the decision.
    - **Case synopsis:** The editors usually provide a summary of the opinion
    - **Headnotes:** These are short paragraphs that summarize key points of the opinion. Usually, editors will provide corresponding numbers to the text of the opinion, or, in online materials, headnotes may be hyperlinked to the text of the opinion. West also provides key numbers to these headnotes. (For more on using key numbers, see chapter 3, page 113.)
    - **Names:** Here, the editor will provide the names of the attorneys as well as the names of the judge who wrote the opinion. Per curium

means that no one particular judge is taking credit for the opinion. En banc means that the full appellate court has heard the argument and rendered a decision (as opposed to a three-judge panel).

- **Written Opinion:** The actual opinion appears next in the text and is the only part of the published decision you should cite.

These published opinions become binding precedent. However, only the cases chosen by the courts for publication are considered "published." As a result, only the published opinions will ultimately be placed in the reporters. Although many unpublished decisions are available through services such as Westlaw and Lexis, most jurisdictions do not rely on unpublished decisions as binding precedent, so lawyers are wary of citing them in court documents. Check your jurisdiction's local rules to determine whether unpublished decisions may be cited.

- **Where:** State cases are published in chronological and subject-matter forms:
  - The **chronological form** of publication is through state or regional reporters (see Anatomy of a Case, page 62). The regional reporters and their corresponding states are as follows:
    - **Atlantic Reporter** (A., A.2d): Connecticut, Delaware, District of Columbia, Maine, Maryland, New Hampshire, New Jersey, Pennsylvania, Rhode Island, Vermont
    - **North Eastern Reporter** (N.E., N.E.2d): Illinois, Indiana, Massachusetts, New York, Ohio
    - **North Western Reporter** (N.W., N.W.2d): Iowa, Michigan, Minnesota, Nebraska, North Dakota, South Dakota, Wisconsin
    - **Pacific Reporter** (P., P.2d): Alaska, Arizona, California, Colorado, Hawaii, Idaho, Kansas, Montana, Nevada, New Mexico, Oklahoma, Oregon, Utah, Washington, Wyoming
    - **South Eastern Reporter** (S.E., S.E.2d): Georgia, North Carolina, South Carolina, Virginia, West Virginia
    - **South Western Reporter** (S.W., S.W.2d): Arkansas, Kentucky, Missouri, Tennessee, Texas
    - **Southern Reporter** (So., So. 2d): Alabama, Florida, Louisiana, Mississippi
  - The **subject-matter** form of publication is in state or regional digests (see page 63). However, the cases in the digests are not printed in full; instead, they are summaries of cases grouped by subject matter and function as an index to the reporters. Each reporter has its own digest and an index to the digest. The digests are a form of access into the chronological reporters.
- **Why:** Your ultimate goal is to find a case within the chronological reporter. However, you would start with the chronological reporter only if you had a citation or the plaintiff's or defendant's name (to check the names tables). Most of the time, you will be searching for cases based on subject matter. Most researchers begin on Lexis or Westlaw with word searches based on specific terms to narrow the issue. For print research, the best place to begin your common law research is through the digests if avail-

able in your library. Each digest contains an index and then volumes, arranged alphabetically by subject matter. These subjects have been created and maintained by publishers who act as the researchers' first set of eyes to cull and sort case law. Once you find your subject matter, the digest will provide citations to the reporters as well as a short annotation summarizing the case. You should never cite directly to the digest.

- **How:** For more information on finding information on state cases, see chapter 3, page 137.[20] For information on citations for state cases, see chapter 4, pages 260 (Bluebook) and 208 (ALWD).

---

20. A tutorial on researching state cases can be found at www.ll.georgetown.edu/tutorials/cases/index.cfm.

Anatomy of a State Court Case

380   **831 NEW YORK SUPPLEMENT, 2d SERIES**

Attorneys

Citation — 37 A.D.3d 368

Name of case —
Juan O. GARCIA, Plaintiff–Respondent,

Ella Garcia, Plaintiff,

v.

Tom STICKEL, et al., Defendants–Appellants.

Judges —

Court — Supreme Court, Appellate Division, First Department.

Date case decided — Feb. 27, 2007.

Beginning of opinion —
Background: Malpractice action was brought against attorneys. The Supreme Court, Bronx County, Yvonne Gonzalez, J., denied attorney's motions to rejection plaintiff's errata sheets and for summary judgment. Attorneys appealed.

Editor's synopsis (not part of judge's opinion) —

Holdings: The Supreme Court, Appellate Division, held that:

Headnote number—refers to headnote one —
(1) plaintiff's errata sheets should have been rejected, and

(2) attorneys were entitled to summary judgment.

Reversed.

Headnote number—references part of case where this legal issue is discussed —
1. **Pretrial Procedure** ⬤➡139

Plaintiff's errata sheets should have been struck since plaintiff failed to timely submit a statement of the reasons for the numerous changes in his deposition testimony indicated thereon. McKinney's CPLR 3116(a).

Key number —
2. **Judgment** ⬤➡185.3(4)

Headnote—editor's summary of key parts of law —
Affidavits submitted by plaintiffs in opposition to summary judgment in their legal malpractice action were insufficient to raise an issue of fact as to notice of the alleged defective condition, a "missing" ladder rung, and whether, but for the alleged malpractice, plaintiffs would have prevailed in the underlying action in which they were represented by defendants.

Law Offices of Tom Stickel, Bronx (Ramon A. Pagan of counsel), for Stickel appellants.

Ohrenstein & Brown, LLP, New York (Serena W. Richardson of counsel), for Schneider, Kleinick, Weitz, Damashek & Shoot, appellant.

Alexander J. Wulwick, New York, for respondent.

ANDRIAS, J.P., FRIEDMAN, SULLIVAN, WILLIAMS, CATTERSON, JJ.

Order, Supreme Court, Bronx County (Yvonne Gonzalez, J.), entered August 9, 2005, which denied defendants' motions seeking rejection of plaintiff's errata sheets and summary judgment, unanimously reversed, on the law, without costs, and the motions granted. The Clerk is directed to enter judgment in favor of defendants dismissing the complaint.

[1] Plaintiff's errata sheets should have been struck since plaintiff failed to timely submit a statement of the reasons for the numerous changes in his deposition testimony indicated thereon (*see* CPLR 3116[a]; *Schachat v. Bell Atl. Corp.*, 282 A.D.2d 329, 723 N.Y.S.2d 465 [2001]; *Rodriguez v. Jones*, 227 A.D.2d 220, 642 N.Y.S.2d 267 [1996]).

[2] Defendants' motions for summary judgment in this action to recover for alleged legal malpractice should have been granted since plaintiff's unrevised testimony and the affidavits submitted in opposition to the motions were insufficient to raise an issue of fact as to notice of the alleged defective condition, a "missing" ladder rung, and whether, but for the alleged malpractice, plaintiffs would have prevailed in the underlying action in which they were represented by defendants.

WEST KEY NUMBER SYSTEM

The New York Digest

LABOR RELATIONS ⌐372.1 — Topic and key number

For references to other topics, see Descriptive-Word Index

conclude that community college's alleged retaliatory conduct in reducing number of hours of part-time teacher after she had voiced teachers' common concerns was not improper employer practice under Taylor Law on ground there was no indication in record that, at time complaints were voiced, teachers were seeking to form employee organization or to be represented by such organization. McKinney's CPLR 7801 et seq.; McKinney's Civil Service Law §§ 201 et seq., 201, subds. 5, 6(a), 7(a), 202, 209–a, subds. 1, 3.

> Rosen v. Public Employment Relations Bd., 510 N.Y.S.2d 180, 125 A.D.2d 657, appeal granted 519 N.Y.S.2d 1029, 70 N.Y.2d 605, 513 N.E.2d 1309, affirmed 530 N.Y.S.2d 534, 72 N.Y.2d 42, 526 N.E.2d 25.

N.Y.A.D. 4 Dept. 1997. Protection of statute prohibiting discrimination by employer based on individual's membership in union or any exercise of rights granted under National Labor Relations Act (NLRA) or under Taylor Law extends to members of any union, and is not limited to members of unions subject to NLRA or Taylor Law. National Labor Relations Act, § 1 et seq., as amended, 29 U.S.C.A. § 151 et seq.; McKinney's Labor Law § 201–d, subd. 2, par. d.

> Muhitch v. St. Gregory the Great Roman Catholic Church and School, 659 N.Y.S.2d 679, 239 A.D.2d 901.

N.Y.Sup. 1996. Discrimination against employee for union membership chills, if not kills, employee's federal and state law rights to engage in collective activity. McKinney's Civil Service Law §§ 202, 203.

> Devine v. New York Convention Center Operating Corp., 639 N.Y.S.2d 904, 167 Misc.2d 372.

⌐369–370.1. *For other cases see earlier editions of this digest, the Decennial Digests, and WESTLAW.*

Library references
> C.J.S. Labor Relations.

⌐370. **Employment.**

⌐371. —— **During strike.** •

E.D.N.Y. 1999. National Labor Relations Act (NLRA) preserves to employers the right to permanently replace economic strikers as an offset to the employees' right to strike. National Labor Relations Act, § 1 et seq., as amended, 29 U.S.C.A. § 151 et seq.

> Van-Go Transport Co., Inc. v. New York City Bd. of Educ., 53 F.Supp.2d 278.

"Market participant" exemption to National Labor Relations Act (NLRA) preemption did not apply to school board's policy of refusing to conditionally certify a replacement workforce for contractor's striking workers since policy was a regulatory policy which board incorporated into every contract it negotiated with its contractors. National Labor Relations Act, § 1 et seq., as amended, 29 U.S.C.A. § 151 et seq.

> Van-Go Transport Co., Inc. v. New York City Bd. of Educ., 53 F.Supp.2d 278.

"Peripheral concerns" exception to National Labor Relations Act (NLRA) preemption did not apply to school board's policy of refusing to conditionally certify a replacement workforce for contractor's striking workers since the state action could not realistically be said to involve matters that were peripheral to federal law; board's regulatory action directly curtailed an important right guaranteed to an employer under federal labor law. National Labor Relations Act, § 1 et seq., as amended, 29 U.S.C.A. § 151 et seq.

> Van-Go Transport Co., Inc. v. New York City Bd. of Educ., 53 F.Supp.2d 278.

N.Y. 2000. The *"Triborough* Doctrine," under which terms and conditions of an expired collective bargaining agreement may continue in effect until new agreement is negotiated between public employer and its employees, cannot supersede an employer's rights under federal law to replace temporarily or permanently a striking worker.

> In re Goodman, 709 N.Y.S.2d 884, 95 N.Y.2d 15, 731 N.E.2d 600.

N.Y.Sup. 1990. Hiring of workers to replace strikers is lawful under federal law.

> Amalgamated Transit Union, Local 1202 AFL-CIO, CLC v. Greyhound Lines, Inc., (GLI), 561 N.Y.S.2d 118, 148 Misc.2d 601.

Law Rev. 1993. Workplace Fairness Act. John P. Furfaro and Maury B. Josephson.
> 209 N.Y.L.J. 3 (April 2, 1993).

⌐372. **Discharge.**

Library references
> C.J.S. Labor Relations § 356 et seq.

⌐372.1. —— **In general.**

C.A.2 1967. J. P. Stevens & Co. v. N. L. R. B., 380 F.2d 292, certiorari denied 88 S.Ct. 564, 389 U.S. 1005, 19 L.Ed.2d 600, motion granted in part 464 F.2d 1326, decision supplemented 1972 WL 12082, certiorari denied 93 S.Ct. 1357, 410 U.S. 926, 35 L.Ed.2d 587. — Key number / Court name and date / Case summary

C.A.2 (N.Y.) 1985. Discharge of Conrail employee for disloyalty after he represented, as an attorney, Conrail employees in actions against Conrail was not precluded by provisions of Railway Labor Act, on theory that by barring the union from employing counsel of its choosing, employee's discharge interfered with union's right to organize as it saw fit, since his — Citation to case

Table 2.4. Websites for More Information on Courts in U.S. States and Territories

ALABAMA	http://judicial.alabama.gov
ALASKA	www.state.ak.us/courts
AMERICAN SAMOA	www.justice.gov/jmd/ls/americansamoa
ARIZONA	www.azcourts.gov
ARKANSAS	http://courts.state.ar.us
CALIFORNIA	www.courtinfo.ca.gov
COLORADO	www.courts.state.co.us
CONNECTICUT	www.jud.ct.gov
DELAWARE	http://courts.delaware.gov
DISTRICT OF COLUMBIA	www.dccourts.gov
FEDERATED STATES OF MICRONESIA	www.paclii.org/fm/courts.html
FLORIDA	www.flcourts.org
GEORGIA	www.georgiacourts.org
GUAM	www.guamsupremecourt.com
HAWAII	www.courts.state.hi.us
IDAHO	www.isc.idaho.gov
ILLINOIS	www.state.il.us/court
INDIANA	www.in.gov/judiciary
IOWA	www.iowacourts.state.ia.us
KANSAS	www.kscourts.org
KENTUCKY	http://courts.ky.gov
LOUISIANA	www.louisiana.gov/Government/Judicial_Branch/
MAINE	www.courts.state.me.us
MARSHALL ISLANDS	www.paclii.org
MARYLAND	www.courts.state.md.us
MASSACHUSETTS	www.mass.gov/courts
MICHIGAN	www.courts.michigan.gov
MINNESOTA	www.courts.state.mn.us
MISSISSIPPI	www.mssc.state.ms.us
MISSOURI	www.courts.mo.gov
MONTANA	http://courts.mt.gov
NEBRASKA	http://court.nol.org
NEVADA	www.nevadajudiciary.us
NEW HAMPSHIRE	www.courts.state.nh.us
NEW JERSEY	www.judiciary.state.nj.us
NEW MEXICO	www.nmcourts.com
NEW YORK	www.courts.state.ny.us
NORTH CAROLINA	www.nccourts.org
NORTH DAKOTA	www.ndcourts.com/court/courts.htm
NORTHERN MARIANA ISLANDS	www.cnmilaw.org
OHIO	www.sconet.state.oh.us
OKLAHOMA	www.oscn.net
OREGON	www.oregon.gov/OJD/courts
PENNSYLVANIA	www.courts.state.pa.us
PUERTO RICO	www.ramajudicial.pr
RHODE ISLAND	www.courts.ri.gov
SOUTH CAROLINA	www.judicial.state.sc.us
SOUTH DAKOTA	www.sdjudicial.com
TENNESSEE	www.tsc.state.tn.us
TEXAS	www.courts.state.tx.us
UTAH	www.utcourts.gov
VERMONT	www.vermontjudiciary.org
VIRGIN ISLANDS	www.visupremecourt.org
VIRGINIA	www.courts.state.va.us
WASHINGTON	www.courts.wa.gov
WEST VIRGINIA	www.state.wv.us/wvsca/wvsystem.htm
WISCONSIN	www.wicourts.gov
WYOMING	www.courts.state.wy.us

3. State Agencies and State Administrative Law

State agencies fall under the state's executive branch. Agencies on the state level create and enforce regulations on a variety of matters such as housing, utilities, and public health. Each state has its own agencies, which can be found by consulting the state's website.

- **What:** Each state agency creates administrative laws, which include rules and regulations, decisions, and a variety of other documents particular to that agency. These documents mirror the form and function of federal administrative law.
- **Where:** States publish their administrative laws in a wide variety of formats. Some states' publications are similar to federal administrative law in that they have subject sets similar to the subject-matter codification of the C.F.R. that are sometimes supplemented by chronological sets similar to the Federal Register. In other states, regulations are published only by the agency itself. Some states have sold the rights to publish their state administrative codes to private publishers.
- **Why:** You might be asked to find regulations promulgated by a particular state.
- **How:** To find the administrative law resources for a particular state, go to that state's website, then click on the administrative law link. You can also consult the following sources: BNA's Directory of State Administrative Codes and Registers and The Book of the States (Council of State Governments). Westlaw and Lexis also publish selected states' administrative laws.

For additional information on finding state administrative law, see chapter 3, page 151. For information on citing state administrative law, see chapter 4, page 265 (Bluebook) and page 211 (ALWD).

II. SECONDARY SOURCES

Secondary sources are materials that discuss and comment on primary law. They are written by scholars, judges, and others to provide commentary and background materials on the law. Although they are not the law itself, secondary sources can help a legal researcher understand a particular body of law as well as find primary law on a subject. They are especially helpful for first-year students, who tend to know very little about most legal subjects, as well as for experts in a particular field, who refer to these sources when developing law in their areas. Information on each of the following most widely used secondary sources listed below can be found at the page number indicated:

- Legal Encyclopedias (C.J.S. and Am. Jur.), below
- American Law Reports (A.L.R.), page 74
- Hornbooks and Treatises, page 80

A. *Legal Encyclopedias*

- **What:** Legal encyclopedias look and function like general encyclopedias in that they are alphabetically arranged into volumes that contain specific topics. Each encyclopedia contains an index, usually located at the end of the volumes, as well as an index to each volume and a table of contents to each topic.
- **Why:** Legal encyclopedias provide very basic introductions to a specific legal topic, but they do not analyze the law or explain its application. You would use an encyclopedia if you need an elementary context for a particular law or if you need a more detailed definition than found in Black's Law Dictionary. A state encyclopedia may be helpful if you are trying to find whether a state has a particular law (i.e., whether Maryland has the death penalty). While legal encyclopedias contain footnotes to legal citations, these citations are only a small sample.
- **Where and How:** Three sets of encyclopedias are most often used by lawyers:
  - **Corpus Juris Secundum (C.J.S.).** This West publication (see pages 68-69) is a set of dark blue volumes that uses the key number system. (For more on the key number system, see chapter 3, page 113.) The set contains pocket parts, which are located at the back of each volume and reference recent citations. C.J.S. contains lengthy footnotes since it has its origins in West's exhaustive publication philosophy.
    - **To access from Westlaw:** Type CJS in the box labeled Search These Databases.
    - **To access from WestlawNext:** Click on Secondary Sources on the All Content tab in the Browse section. Click Text and Treatises; then click Corpus Juris Secundum.
  - **American Jurisprudence 2d (Am. Jur. 2d).** This encyclopedia set (see pages 70-71) was originally published by Lawyers Cooperative Publishing, but is now a part of West Group. It contains pocket parts, which are located at the back of each volume and reference recent citations. Unlike C.J.S., Am. Jur. 2d has a New Topics binder, located at the end of the set, that introduces new topics. It also contains a "Deskbook," which serves as a handy reference tool that lists items such as the following: addresses and phone numbers of federal departments; historical documents; financial and annuity tables; arbitration rules.
    - **To access from Lexis:** Go to "Source—Legal—Secondary Sources—American Jurisprudence 2d" (see page 122).
    - **To access from Westlaw:** Type AMJUR in the box labeled Search These Databases (see page 119).

- **To access from WestlawNext:** Click on Secondary Sources on the All Content tab in the Browse section. Click Text and Treatises; then click American Jurisprudence 2d. Users can limit a search in American Jurisprudence 2d by using the Table of Contents.

- **State Encyclopedias.** Many states publish their own encyclopedias (see pages 72-73), which function similarly to the national sets referenced above. They have names such as Encyclopedia, Jurisprudence, or Practice. State encyclopedias can be very helpful because they might contain a history of the law in that state as well as citations to statutes and useful cases on point. Remember to look for pocket parts and be wary of citing to these encyclopedias in legal documents. Most state encyclopedias are only available in either Westlaw or Lexis—not both.

    - **To access from Westlaw:** View Westlaw Directory—U.S. State Materials—Forms, Treatises, CLEs and Other Practice Materials (see page 119).

    - **To access from WestlawNext:** Click on Secondary Sources on the All Content tab in the Browse section. Click Text and Treatises; then click on the state of interest.

    - **To access from Lexis:** Go to Source—Legal—Secondary Legal —Jurisprudence & A.L.R. (see page 122).

    - **To access from Lexis Advance:** Click on Content Type; then look within Analytical Materials.

For more information on an online tutorial on using state secondary sources, see www.ll.georgetown.edu/tutorials/second/index.cfm. Citation to a legal encyclopedia is rarely done in court documents.

C.J.S.

Title

Author

Outline

Scope

Other C.J.S. entries

References to Westlaw

FALSE PERSONATION
John A. Gebauer, J.D.

I. IN GENERAL

§ 1 What constitutes offense
§ 2 Definitions
§ 3 Statutory provisions
§ 4 —Under federal law

II. PROCEEDINGS AGAINST FALSE PERSONATORS

§ 5 Indictment or information
§ 6 Evidence
§ 7 Trial and review

Scope

This title discusses the crime of falsely personating another, by deceptively assuming and acting in the character of another person, or by assuming to be a public officer, or a person having any special authority or privilege, and acting in such assumed capacity. Also discussed is the nature and extent of criminal responsibility for false personation, and the prosecution and punishment of such acts.

Treated Elsewhere

False personation as an element of forgery, see C.J.S., Forgery §§ 1 et seq.

Fraud, generally, see C.J.S., Fraud §§ 1 et seq.

Larceny, generally, see C.J.S., Larceny §§ 1 et seq.

Offense of obtaining money or property false pretenses, see C.J.S., False Pretenses §§ 1 et seq.

Offenses involving fraudulent misuse of credit cards or charges by unauthorized users, see C.J.S., Interest and Usury; Consumer Credit §§ 523 to 529

Research References

Westlaw Databases

All Federal & State Cases (ALLCASES)
All Federal Cases (ALLFEDS)
American Law Reports (ALR)
West's A.L.R. Digest (ALRDIGEST)
Wharton's Criminal Law (CRIMLAW)
United States Code Annotated (USCA)

KeyCite®: Cases and other legal materials listed in KeyCite Scope can be researched through the KeyCite service on Westlaw®. Use KeyCite to check citations for form, parallel references, prior and later history, and comprehensive citator information, including citations to other decisions and secondary materials.

I. IN GENERAL   Research References

627

C.J.S. *(continued)*

§ 1   CORPUS JURIS SECUNDUM

West's Key Number Digest
False Personation ⊙1, 2

A.L.R. Library
A.L.R. Index, Impersonation
West's A.L.R. Digest, False Personation ⊙1, 2

§ 1   What constitutes offense

Research References

West's Key Number Digest, False Personation ⊙2

> **To constitute the offense of false personation, there must be an untrue or false personation of the officer or person designated in the statute, with, ordinarily, an intent to defraud.**

To constitute the offense of false personation there must be an untrue or false personation under circumstances covered by the statute.[1] The gravamen of the crime of false personation consists of falsely representing some other person or acting in a character unlawfully assumed in order to deceive others, and thereby gain some profit or advantage, or enjoy some right or privilege, appertaining to the party so personated.[2] The advantage to be gained, however, need not be monitary, or even material.[3] Moreover, under some authority, showing that the defendant sought to gain something of value through impersonation is not element of the offense of false personation.[4]

False personation can be accomplished by actions or conduct or by outward indicia such as signs or advertising.[5] It is a holding out whereby a person induces others to believe that he or she can lawfully engage in a particular activity or exercise certain authority.[6] Such holding out or false personation may involve verbal declarations as well as other manifestations of authority.[7]

Giving a false name is not impersonation unless the name given is that of a real person,[8] and a statute forbidding the impersonation of another does not apply to a defendant who provides false information.[9] Moreover, the ancient customs of masquerade and trick-or-treating antedate, and have survived, enactment of false personation statutes, which clearly

Analysis of topic

[Section 1]

[1]U.S.—Shepherd v. U.S., 177 F.2d 938 (10th Cir. 1949).

  Okla.—Raymer v. State, 27 Okla. Crim. 398, 228 P. 500 (1924).

[2]Colo.—Alvarado v. People, 132 P.3d 1205 (Colo. 2006).

  N.J.—State v. Thyfault, 121 N.J. Super. 487, 297 A.2d 873 (County Ct. 1972), aff'd, 126 N.J. Super. 459, 315 A.2d 424 (App. Div. 1974).

[3]D.C.—Gary v. U.S., 955 A.2d 152 (D.C. 2008).

  N.Y.—People v. Chive, 189 Misc. 2d 653, 734 N.Y.S.2d 830 (City Crim. Ct. 2001).

[4]Ill.—People v. Reyes, 328 Ill. App. 3d 918, 263 Ill. Dec. 614, 768 N.E.2d 374 (2d Dist. 2002).

[5]D.C.—Gary v. U.S., 955 A.2d 152 (D.C. 2008).

  Ga.—Self v. State, 245 Ga. App. 270, 537 S.E.2d 723 (2000).

  N.J.—State v. Thyfault, 121 N.J. Super. 487, 297 A.2d 873 (County Ct. 1972), aff'd, 126 N.J. Super. 459, 315 A.2d 424 (App. Div. 1974).

[6]N.J.—State v. Thyfault, 121 N.J. Super. 487, 297 A.2d 873 (County Ct. 1972), aff'd, 126 N.J. Super. 459, 315 A.2d 424 (App. Div. 1974).

[7]U.S.—Pierce v. U.S., 86 F.2d 949 (C.C.A. 6th Cir. 1936).

  N.J.—State v. Thyfault, 121 N.J. Super. 487, 297 A.2d 873 (County Ct. 1972), aff'd, 126 N.J. Super. 459, 315 A.2d 424 (App. Div. 1974).

[8]Cal.—Lee v. Superior Court, 22 Cal. 4th 41, 91 Cal. Rptr. 2d 509, 989 P.2d 1277 (2000).

  Conn.—State v. Bradley, 60 Conn. App. 534, 760 A.2d 520 (2000).

  Ind.—Brown v. State, 868 N.E.2d 464 (Ind. 2007).

  N.Y.—People v. Sadiq, 236 A.D.2d 638, 654 N.Y.S.2d 35 (2d Dep't 1997).

[9]Ga.—Brown v. State, 225 Ga. App. 750, 484 S.E.2d 795 (1997).

False date of birth

  Colo.—People v. Peay, 5 P.3d 398 (Colo. Ct. App. 2000).

  N.Y.—People v. Danisi, 113 Misc. 2d 753, 449 N.Y.S.2d 874 (Dist. Ct. 1982).

Inaccurate social security number

  Colo.—People v. Jones, 841 P.2d 372 (Colo. Ct. App. 1992).

Footnotes and references to cases supporting concepts

Title

Author

FALSE PERSONATION
Maria Del Rio, J.D.

Outline

I. IN GENERAL

§ 1   Generally
§ 2   Proscribed conduct, generally
§ 3   Misrepresenting personal information to police officer
§ 4   Intent, or possibility of doing injury, or of receiving or conferring benefit
§ 5   Federal statutes
§ 6   Participation; conspiracy

II. FALSE PERSONATION OF GOVERNMENT OFFICERS OR EMPLOYEES

§ 7   Generally
§ 8   Federal statutes
§ 9   Validity of statutes
§ 10   Affirmative defenses

III. PRACTICE AND PROCEDURE

§ 11   Accusatory pleadings
§ 12   Jury's role and instructions
§ 13   Evidence

Scope

Scope

This article discusses the crime of falsely personating another, with discussion of the offense generally, particular acts as constituting criminal violations, and procedural matters relating to such offense.

Federal Aspects

Federal Aspects

This article covers various federal statutes making it a crime to pretend to be or to act under the authority of the United States, including any department, agency, or officer thereof, or of a foreign government.

Treated Elsewhere

Other Am. Jur. entries

Aliens: false claims of citizenship or nationality, see Am. Jur. 2d, Aliens and Citizens §§ 2708 to 2711

Business or trade secrets, impersonation of person for purpose of obtaining, as invasion of person's right to privacy, see Am. Jur. 2d, Privacy § 76

Checks drawn payable to imposter or fictitious payee, see Am. Jur. 2d,

193

American Jurisprudence, 2d *(continued)*

§ 1

Trial Strategy
Scams and Cons, 74 Am. Jur. Proof of Facts 3d 63

§ 1 Generally

Research References
Other research references
West's Key Number Digest, False Personation 🖚1, 2
Scams and Cons, 74 Am. Jur. Proof of Facts 3d 63

False personation is the crime of pretending to be another person under proscribed circumstances.[1] Ancient customs of masquerade and trick-or-treating antedate, and have survived, enactment of false personation statutes, which clearly are not designed to eliminate these innocuous practices.[2] Statutes prohibiting impersonation have two purposes: to prevent harm to the person falsely represented, and to ensure the integrity of judicial and governmental processes.[3]

Analysis of topic

§ 2 Proscribed conduct, generally

Research References
West's Key Number Digest, False Personation 🖚1, 2

One does not commit false personation merely by happening to resemble another person; rather, one must intentionally engage in a deception that may fairly be described as noninnocent behavior, even if, in some instances, it might not stem from an evil motive.[1] Giving a false name does not constitute false personation unless the name

---

[Section 1]

[1]People v. Vaughn, 196 Cal. App. 2d 622, 16 Cal. Rptr. 711 (2d Dist. 1961); People v. Danisi, 113 Misc. 2d 753, 449 N.Y.S.2d 874 (Dist. Ct. 1982).

To prove false impersonation, state must show: (1) assumption by one person of another person's character; (2) intentional impersonation of that character; and (3) such person either (i) does any act whereby, if it were done by the person falsely personated, might make him liable to any suit or prosecution, or to pay any sum of money, or to incur any charge, forfeiture, or penalty; or (ii) accrues any benefit as a result of the personation. Barkus v. State, 1996 OK CR 45, 926 P.2d 312 (Okla. Crim. App. 1996).

[2]People v. Rathert, 24 Cal. 4th 200, 99 Cal. Rptr. 2d 779, 6 P.3d 700 (2000).

[3]Lee v. Superior Court, 22 Cal. 4th

41, 91 Cal. Rptr. 2d 509, 989 P.2d 1277 (2000).

Purpose of statute proscribing the giving of false information to a police officer is to require the defendant to give sufficient information to allow law enforcement to locate the person if he does not appear in court. In re Kelly W., 95 Cal. App. 4th 468, 115 Cal. Rptr. 2d 536 (2d Dist. 2002).

The objective of a false personation statute is to prevent the wasted time and effort spent searching for the real identity of persons who give false pedigree information to the police. In re Travis S., 96 N.Y.2d 818, 728 N.Y.S.2d 411, 752 N.E.2d 848 (2001).

[Section 2]

[1]People v. Rathert, 24 Cal. 4th 200, 99 Cal. Rptr. 2d 779, 6 P.3d 700 (2000).

Footnotes to cases
supporting content

196

Maryland State Encyclopedia

Topic name

Author

Scope

Cross-references to
other similar topics in
encyclopedia

Other research references

NAMES

Robert F. Koets, J.D.

Scope of Topic

This article discusses the naming of individuals as a means of
unique identification, the procedures involved in a change of
name, and the naming or change of name of minors by their
parents or on their own initiative.

Treated Elsewhere

Filing of agent's certificate placing on record names of true owners of business conducted by agents, see M.L.E., Agents and Factors § 131.

Use of personal or corporate name as unfair competition, see
M.L.E., Monopolies and Unfair Trade § 7.

Validity of deed as affected by fact that names of grantees in
deed were assumed names, see M.L.E., Conveyancing § 33.

Names of organizations are considered in specific M.L.E. titles,
as, for example, Corporations § 31 and Banks and Trust
Companies § 24. Change of name incident to adoption is
discussed in M.L.E., Adoption § 44.

Research References

Text References

57 Am Jur 2d, Name § 1 et seq.
65 C.J.S. Names § 1 et seq.

West's Digest References

West's Maryland Digest 2d, Names   1 et seq.

Annotation References

ALR Digest: Name § 1 et seq.
ALR Index: Assumed or Fictitious Names, Change of Name, Idem
Sonans, Maiden Name, Middle Name or Initial, Names.

Forms References

13B Am Jur Legal Forms 2d, Name.
18A Am Jur Pleading and Practice Forms, Annotated (Revised),
Name.

Statutory References

Md Rule 15-901

Page 327

Maryland State Encyclopedia *(continued)*

MARYLAND LAW ENCYCLOPEDIA

> **KeyCite®:** Cases and other legal materials listed in KeyCite Scope can be researched through West Group's KeyCite service on Westlaw®. Use KeyCite to check citations for form, parallel references, prior and later history, and comprehensive citator information, including citations to other decisions and secondary materials.

Table of Parallel References:

To convert General Index references to section references in this volume, or to ascertain the disposition (or current equivalent) of articles in the prior edition of this publication, see the Table of Parallel References at the beginning of this volume.

§ 1 Generally

§ 2 Change of name

§ 3 Minors

§ 1 Generally

West's Maryland Digest 2d, Names ⟐ 1 et seq.

A name is the designation or appellation which is used to distinguish one person from another, and, since the person's identity is the essential thing, if that is certain, a variance in the name is often immaterial.[1] Generally, the law recognizes only one given or Christian name, and the insertion or omission of a middle name or initial is therefore immaterial and may be disregarded.[2]

In the absence of a statute to the contrary, a person may adopt any name by which he or she may become known, and by which he or she may transact business and execute contracts and sue or be sued, and that may be done without regard to the person's true name.[3]

---

[1]Romans v. State, 178 Md. 588, 16 A.2d 642 (1940).

[2]White v. McClellan, 62 Md. 347 (1884).

[3]Hardy v. Hardy, 269 Md. 412, 306 A.2d 244 (1973); Romans v. State, 178 Md. 588, 16 A.2d 642 (1940); Klein v. Klein, 36 Md. App. 177, 373 A.2d 86 (1977) (at common law, a person could take any name he or she pleased, so long as it was not done for fraudulent purposes or to interfere with the rights of others).

Forms: Fictitious or assumed name. 18A Am Jur Pleading and Practice Forms, Annotated (Revised), Name §§ 47-62.

Fictitious or assumed name. 13B Am Jur Legal Forms 2d, Name §§ 182:11-182:28.

Page 328

Analysis

Footnotes to cases supporting content

B.   *American Law Reports (A.L.R.)*

- **What:** American Law Reports (A.L.R.), see pages 76-79, combines features of an encyclopedia with those of a case reporter. It is like an encyclopedia in that it contains annotations and footnotes to particular legal topics. However, a topic covered in A.L.R. is much more detailed than one covered in an encyclopedia, and it also discusses and analyzes national trends. The distinctive feature of A.L.R. that resembles a case reporter is that it contains the full text of selected cases to act as a reference point for the analytical discussion of the particular legal topic. Cases are selected for discussion if they contain novel or important issues. A.L.R. was originally published by Lawyers Cooperative, which published selective opinions. Therefore, one limitation of the series is that coverage is not comprehensive.

- **Why:** A.L.R. is a fantastic source if you are looking to learn all you can about a particular topic in a very short time. If your topic or case is the subject of an A.L.R. annotation, you will have found a gold mine. First, A.L.R. will print, in full, a representative case on that topic. Next, it will print a lengthy (sometimes 40-page) annotative section discussing that topic, including context, particular issue, a survey of states including distinctions among jurisdictions, and citations to other sources within each jurisdiction. As a result, A.L.R. annotations can be quite helpful in discussing, comparing, and citing law from various jurisdictions. If you find your case has been addressed or your particular point of law has been analyzed, then the annotation will be extremely helpful and well worth using. However, because the series is not comprehensive and is often confusing with its many series, it is not always efficient.

- **Where and How:** A.L.R. (now published by West Group) contains seven series: A.L.R., A.L.R.2d, A.L.R.3d, A.L.R.4th, A.L.R.5th, A.L.R.6th, and A.L.R. Federal (A.L.R. Fed., A.L.R. Fed. 2d). A researcher can use the index and digest to find relevant annotations. If an annotation has been superseded, the researcher need only read the later annotation. However, if it has been supplemented, the researcher should consult both annotations. The "Annotated History Table," located in the index, shows if an annotation has been supplemented or superseded. In addition, the researcher should consult pocket parts within each volume for updates. A.L.R. annotations usually contain the following:
  - A scope note, which describes coverage in the annotation
  - A summary of the case
  - An outline of the annotation
  - Extensive research references
  - An in-depth index
  - A table of cases
  - An annotation text
  - To access online:

- **Westlaw:** Type ALR in the box labeled Search These Databases.
- **WestlawNext:** Click on Secondary Sources on the All Content tab in the Browse section, then click American Law Reports under By Type.

For more information on an online tutorial on using secondary sources, see www.ll.georgetown.edu/tutorials/second/index.cfm. Citation to a legal encyclopedia is rarely done in court documents.

American Law Reports

Volume number and citation of annotation

125 ALR Fed 273

Title of annotation

WHO, OTHER THAN SPECIFICALLY EXCLUDED PERSONS, IS "EMPLOYEE" UNDER § 4(a)(1) OF AGE DISCRIMINATION IN EMPLOYMENT ACT OF 1967 (29 USCS § 623(a)(1))

by
Francis M. Dougherty, J.D.

Author

Scope of annotation

The Age Discrimination in Employment Act (ADEA) (29 USCS §§ 621 et seq.) prohibits discrimination in employment practices and decisions against workers between the ages of 40 and 70, on account of age, and also prohibits the placing of help wanted advertisements which indicate preferences based on age. The definition of the term "employee" for purposes of the ADEA is important in determining who is protected by the ADEA and who is an employer for ADEA purposes, since only employers who are engaged in an industry affecting commerce and have a certain number of employees are subject to the Act. Despite the importance of determining who is an employee, the term is defined simply as an individual employed by an employer, except that the term does not include certain enumerated individuals. In light of the vagueness of the definition and the importance attached thereto, it is not surprising that a considerable amount of litigation has been generated in which the courts were called upon to determine who, other than specifically excluded persons, is an employee for purposes of the ADEA. Thus, an independent sales representative was held by the court in Hayden v La-Z-Boy Chair Co. (1993, CA7 Ind) 9 F3d 617, 63 BNA FEP Cas 273, 63 CCH EPD ¶ 42664, 125 ALR Fed 717, to be an independent contractor and therefore not covered by the ADEA.

Location of full text of A.L.R.

Hayden v La-Z-Boy Chair Co., is fully reported at page 717, infra.

American Law Reports *(continued)*

ADEA "Employee" 125 ALR Fed
125 ALR Fed 273

TABLE OF CONTENTS

Table of Contents

---◇---

ARTICLE OUTLINE

Outline

American Law Reports *(continued)*

125 ALR Fed ADEA "Employee"
125 ALR Fed 273

       [a] Held not to be employees
       [b] Held to be employees
§ 11. Conjugal partnership
§ 12. Corporate entity
§ 13. Officer, director, or shareholder of corporation
       [a] Generally
       [b] Held not to be employees
       [c] Held to be employees
§ 14. —Professional corporations
       [a] Held not to be employees
       [b] Held to be employees

IV. STATUS OF OTHER INDIVIDUALS OR ENTITIES

§ 15. Salaried workers
§ 16. Hourly workers
§ 17. Part-time workers
§ 18. Former employees of defendant
§ 19. Individuals demoted from employee to nonemployee status
§ 20. Individual in position obtained by fraud
§ 21. Individuals employed in United States by foreign employer
§ 22. Prisoners
§ 23. Unpaid volunteers
§ 24. Physician with emergency room privileges

—◇—

RESEARCH REFERENCES

TOTAL CLIENT-SERVICE LIBRARY® REFERENCES

    The following references may be of related or collateral interest to a user of this annotation:

Annotations

See the related annotations listed in § 1[b].

Encyclopedias and Texts

45A Am Jur 2d, Job Discrimination §§ 111-114
21 Federal Procedure, L Ed, Job Discrimination §§ 50:306-50:347
Employment Coordinator EP-17,156 et seq.
Employment Discrimination Coordinator 24,101 et seq.

Practice Aids

12 Federal Procedural Forms, L Ed, Job Discrimination §§ 45:251 et seq.
5A Am Jur Pl & Pr Forms (Rev), Civil Rights, Forms 131, 132

275

References to other resources

American Law Reports Index

125 ALR Fed	ADEA "EMPLOYEE"

125 ALR Fed 273

INDEX

Each annotation has an index to locate relevant information within the annotation

C.   *Hornbooks and Treatises*

1.   Hornbooks

- **What:** Hornbooks are legal aids created for a student audience, namely the audience using the legal casebook method developed by Langdell. These textbooks, usually written by one or more law professors, contain excerpts from cases in a particular field of law, such as contracts. The cases are often explained, questioned, and placed in a context within the book.
- **Why:** Hornbooks are used by students in class and in studying for exams.
- **Where and How:** Consult your law library or bookstore to find an appropriate hornbook. Usually, they are arranged by subject matter or assigned by your professor.

2.   Treatises

- **What:** Treatises are legal aids that also cover one particular area of law, but they are more extensive than hornbooks (they are often published in multiple volumes). They are often written for the practitioner. They contain lengthy footnotes, critical analyses, and sometimes historical or social debates on issues particular to that topic. They are written by scholars, and different treatises are relied on more heavily than others. For example, Weinstein on Evidence or Prosser on Torts is often used by practitioners.
- **Why:** Many practitioners rely heavily on treatises in their particular legal areas. Because they are written by real experts who have spent their careers focusing on the law and explaining and discussing it, treatises play an integral role in the law firm. Consulting a treatise is like asking for help from the smartest student in the class.
- **Where and How:** To find relevant treatises, you should consult your law library's catalog or a book titled Law Books in Print. If you specialize in an area of practice, your office library will usually contain a relevant treatise. Most treatises are available only in print form. If you are working in a law firm, you will often find a treatise in the office of a partner who specializes in that particular subject.

For information on citing treatises or hornbooks, see chapter 4, page 266 (Bluebook) and page 212 (ALWD).

D.   *Law Reviews*

- **What:** Law reviews are student-run organizations that publish heavily footnoted articles, usually written by professors, and notes, written by students. Law reviews, such as the Georgetown Law Journal, publish on any topic chosen and are edited by its students. Other law reviews, such as the American Criminal Law Review, publish in the area of one particular topic.[21]

- **Why:** Law review articles are scholarly documents designed to stimulate thought, argue for a position, or criticize a case. Therefore, you would not use them to find objective explanations of the law. Instead, the value of a law review article is the work done by the author; in writing the critical piece, the author performs thorough research into that particular area of the law and provides prolific footnotes detailing that research. While the commentary often gives useful insight into a subject and its historical or political underpinnings, the footnotes almost always provide helpful references to cases, statutes, and other authorities on the subject matter. These footnotes provide a gold mine in terms of legal sources.

- **Where and How:** To find law review articles on a particular area of law, you can use a number of sources:

  - **Index to Legal Periodicals and Books (ILP)** contains law review articles dating back to 1908 and focuses on academic reviews. Users search the index by using author names, law review titles, or specific cases or statutes. The index is available in a print version, a CD version (WilsonDisc), or online via Lexis and Westlaw, where it is called Legal Periodicals and Books. You can also subscribe to the Web version.[22]

  - **Current Law Index (CLI)** dates back only to 1980, so its coverage is not as comprehensive. However, it covers a wider range of periodicals and newspapers than does the Index to Legal Periodicals and Books; it also includes practitioners' publications. It is published 12 times a year in single editions and is then republished in a cumulative volume. Its online version, **LegalTrac,** is available on Lexis and Westlaw. You can subscribe to LegalTrac directly online as well. Here, you can search by keyword and by author. Once you have a citation, you can search in other sources (such as Lexis, Westlaw, HeinOnline, and E-Journal Finder) to find the article.
    - **Lexis:** Go to Look for a Source—Legal—Secondary Legal—Annotations and Indexes.
    - **Westlaw:** Type LRI or ILP in the box labeled Search These Databases.

  - **HeinOnline** is a retrieval source for dozens of academic journals. It houses all but the most recent issue of journals in PDF format for easy access. Most law libraries subscribe to HeinOnline.[23] You can search HeinOnline by citation, title, author, or keyword, or by using a table of contents for individual publications (see above).

---

21. For more information on using law journals, see the tutorial for using secondary sources at http://www.ll.georgetown.edu/tutorials/second/index.cfm. For information on citations for law journal articles, see chapter 4, page 267 (Bluebook) and 212 (ALWD).

22. Visit the Index to legal Periodicals online at http://www.hwwilson.com/Databases/legal.htm.

23. http://www.heinonline.org/.

- **Westlaw and Lexis** both publish full-text articles from many law reviews, and they are easy to access. Searching here differs from using the journal indexes because you can search full text, not just the title and subject headings. In addition, you can search each section as well as footnotes for content that does not appear in the indexes. Lexis and Westlaw usually update their sites more frequently than the journal indexes. However, you are likely to find a great deal of "hits" in searching on Lexis and Westlaw since their databases are very large. In addition, coverage for the journals is very mixed, with some starting in the 1990s. On Westlaw, some law reviews publish only selected articles before 1994. To search these databases, do the following:
  - **Lexis:** Go to Look for a Source—Secondary Legal—Law Reviews and Journals.
  - **Lexis Advance:** Click on Content Type; then look within Analytical Materials.
  - **Westlaw:** Type JLR in the box labeled Search These Databases.
  - **WestlawNext:** Click on Secondary Sources on the All Content tab in the Browse section, then click Law Reviews and Journals under By Type.
- **E-Journal Finder.** This source leads you to journals that publish only electronic versions.[24]

HeinOnline

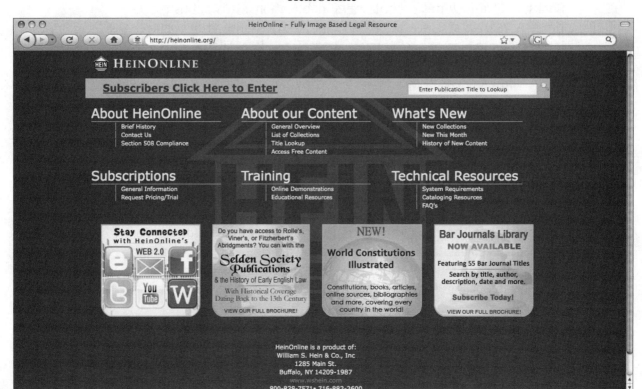

---

24. To access the E-Journal Finder, see http://www.ohiolink.edu/resources/ejournals.php.

Law Review Article

485

An Autobiography of a Digital Idea: From Waging War against Laptops to Engaging Students with Laptops

Diana R. Donahoe

Title and author

Introduction

What are *your* students doing on the other side of their laptops as they peer over their screens during class? Perhaps you are frustrated because you know what they are doing; they are checking e-mail, Twittering, and IM-ing their friends. If you feel as if you are losing your students' attention to the lure of the laptop,[1] you are not alone. Many law professors feel as if they are fighting a battle against the students' laptops in the classroom.[2] Some professors have turned off the wireless routers in their classrooms while others forbid the use of computers altogether.[3] Most professors continue to lecture using the Socratic Method[4] though many students no longer are paying attention.[5] As a

Beginning of article

Diana R. Donahoe has taught at Georgetown University Law Center since 1993. She is professor and former director and chair of Legal Research and Writing. In 2008, she was the recipient of Georgetown's Frank Flegal Award (best teacher award).

Footnote references

1. *See* Marilyn W. Walter, Retaking Control Over Teaching Research, 43 J. Legal Educ. 569, 569 (1993) (students "believe computers can do everything books can do only better and faster").

2. *Compare* David Cole, Laptops vs. Learning, Geo. L. Res Ipsa Loquitur 56 (2007) *with* Diana R. Donahoe, Laptops for Learning, Geo. L. Res Ipsa Loquitur 57 (2007). Previously, in 2001, Ian Ayers wrote an op-ed article in The New York Times arguing against the use of laptops in the classroom, claiming they were simply distractions in the classroom. Ian Ayers, Lectures vs. Laptops, N.Y. Times, Mar. 20, 2001.

3. *See* Paul L. Caron & Rafael Gely, Taking Back the Law School Classroom: Using Technology to Foster Active Student Learning, 54 J. Legal Educ. 551, 556 (2004) (describing professors at the University of Texas and Georgetown University Law Center who have forbidden laptop and wireless devices in the classroom). In some schools, the wireless router is off by default and professors must choose to turn it on to access the Internet in class.

4. *See id.* at 554 (describing the inadequacies of the Socratic Method). According to Caron and Gely, the theory behind the Socratic Method is that students who are not called on to speak still will follow the dialogue, answering the questions to themselves while the student in the hot seat is asked to answer out loud. *Id.* at 555.

5. Scott Carlson, The Net Generation in the Classroom, 52 Chronicle of Higher Educ. 7 (2005).

E. Restatements

- **What:** Restatements (see page 85) are similar to treatises in that they cover one particular area of the law. They are written by committees of scholars, judges, and lawyers and published by the American Law Institute,[25] which is a nonprofit organization for lawyers' continuing education. However, unlike treatises, Restatements do not contain a great amount of detail or practitioner's hints.[26]

  There are thirteen Restatements, each addressing a particular area of law, such as the most widely used, Restatement on Torts and Restatement on Contracts. Although they are not the law, they are so authoritative that courts often specifically adopt a particular Restatement as the law in that jurisdiction. The thirteen Restatements cover these areas of the law:
  - Agency
  - Conflict of Laws
  - Contracts
  - Foreign Relations
  - Judgments
  - Law Governing Lawyers
  - Property Restitution Security
  - Suretyship & Guaranty
  - Torts
  - Trusts
  - Unfair Competition

- **Why:** You would use a Restatement if you need a neutral, concise, black-letter statement of the law. A Restatement is also a useful tool for studying for law school exams. Beware, however: The Restatement might not be the law of your particular jurisdiction, and it does not provide you with analyses of, details or hints about, or answers to a specific legal question.

- **Where and How:** Each Restatement has its own index and is organized by subsection to that topic. The Restatements "state" the law as well as provide commentary, examples, and analysis about the law and its development. The Restatements 2ds also provide cross-references to the key number system and to American Law Reports (A.L.R.). Each Restatement is updated by an appendix, which may contain several volumes. To access online:
  - **Lexis:** Go to Source—Secondary Legal—Restatements.
  - **Lexis Advance:** Click on Content Type; then look within Analytical Materials.
  - **Westlaw:** View Westlaw Directory—Forms, Treatises, CLEs and Other Practice Material—Restatements of the Law & Uniform Laws.
  - **WestlawNext:** Click on Secondary Sources on the All Content tab in the Browse section, then click Restatements & Principles of the Law under By Type.

---

25. To access the American Law Institute's web site, see http://www.ali.org/ali_old/thisali. htm.

26. For more information on using Restatements, see the tutorial on secondary sources at http://www.ll.georgetown.edu/tutorials/second/index.cfm. For information on citations to Restatements, see chapter 4, page 264.

Restatement

TOPIC 3.   ACCIDENTAL ENTRIES ON LAND

§ 166. Non-liability for Accidental Intrusions

Except where the actor is engaged in an abnormally dangerous activity, an unintentional and non-negligent entry on land in the possession of another, or causing a thing or third person to enter the land, does not subject the actor to liability to the possessor, even though the entry causes harm to the possessor or to a thing or third person in whose security the possessor has a legally protected interest.

Beginning of entry

See Reporter's Notes.

Comment:

Comment

a. As to the carrying on of an abnormally dangerous activity, see § 165 and Comments *a* and *d* to that Section. As to intrusions under mistake, see § 164.

b. The early English common law seems to have imposed liability upon one whose act directly brought about an invasion of land in the possession of another, irrespective of whether the invasion was intended, was the result of reckless or negligent conduct, or occurred in the course of an abnormally dangerous activity, or was a pure accident, and irrespective of whether harm of any sort resulted to any interest of the possessor. All that seems to have been required was that the actor should have done an act which in fact caused the entry. At the present time, however, except in the case of one carrying on an abnormally dangerous activity, an unintentional and non-negligent entry or remaining on land in the possession of another or causing a third person or thing so to enter or remain is not a trespass on land and imposes no liability upon him. This is true although harm results to the land or to some other interest of the possessor.

Illustrations:

Illustrations

    1. A is walking along the sidewalk of a public highway close to the border of B's land. Without fault on his part, A slips on a piece of ice, and falls against and breaks a plate glass window in B's store adjoining the sidewalk. A is not liable to B.

    2. A, while driving his automobile along the street in the exercise of due care, is suddenly overcome by a paralytic

See Appendix for Reporter's Notes, Court Citations, and Cross References

III.　STUDY AIDS—RESEARCH SOURCES

A.　*Quick References and Checklists*

📝　1.　Statutes: Quick Reference

United States Constitution

The U.S. Constitution creates the broad governmental framework, describes governmental powers and restraints, defines political relationships, and enumerates individual rights and liberties. It is found in print version in the first volume of the federal code (U.S.C., U.S.C.A., U.S.C.S.).

The U.S.C.A. and U.S.C.S. are often more helpful than the U.S.C. because they are published more frequently and are annotated.

Federal Statutes

Federal statutes are laws passed by the U.S. Congress. They are found in chronological order in the session law, which is published in a volume that contains all the laws passed by a legislative body during each year or session. Session laws are published (very slowly) in the Statutes at Large (Stat.). Federal statutes are found in subject order in either the official or annotated codes. These are the preferred codes to cite to and are easier to use. They can be accessed by way of topical or popular name indexes, and the volumes contain collections of all statutes in that particular jurisdiction and are arranged in broad topics called titles.

The official code is the United States Code (U.S.C.), and the annotated codes are the United States Code Annotated (U.S.C.A.) and the United States Code Service (U.S.C.S.). The annotated codes have indexes, usually located at the end of the set of volumes, and can be accessed either with the books or on Lexis or Westlaw.

The commercial annotated codes (U.S.C.A. and U.S.C.S.) are usually the easiest source to use for a researcher. They are updated more frequently than the official code, and the subject-matter organization is easier to use than the Statutes at Large. The annotations are helpful tools for finding additional sources that interpret the code provision.

State Constitutions

Each state may have its own constitution, which is subordinate to the U.S. Constitution but which can provide additional rights to the citizens of that state. They are usually found in the first volume of the state code and are found in the index. State constitutions are also usually found on the state's website. If you are looking for a particular provision, however, or want to find other sources interpreting a provision, you may want to use the print source rather than the Web source because it provides an index and annotations.

State Statutes

State statutes or codes are laws passed by a state's legislature. They are found in chronological order in the session law, which is published in a volume that contains all the laws passed by a legislative body during each year or session. State statutes are also found in subject-matter order in either the official or annotated codes or statutes. They are the preferred citation and most often used by lawyers because they are easy to access by way of topical or popular name index.

The annotated codes are usually easier to use because of their subject-matter arrangement, indexing, and annotations. They are also frequently more current than the government-published official code or session laws.

 ## 2. Courts and Cases: Quick Reference

Federal Courts

The federal court system is hierarchical. At the lowest level, trials are held in the U.S. district courts. The first level of appeal is in the courts of appeals, or circuit courts. The district courts and the courts of appeal are broken down geographically into circuits. There are 11 numbered circuits as well as the D.C. Circuit and the Federal Circuit. Each circuit has its own district court and appellate court judges. The highest appeal is held in the U.S. Supreme Court.

Federal Cases

Federal cases are the written opinions of federal judges in particular cases; they make up the common law and interpret federal statutes and the constitution. They are published chronologically in the federal reporters. Supreme Court decisions are found in the United States Reports (U.S.), the official reporter, and in two commercial reporters, the Supreme Court Reporter (S. Ct.) and the United States Supreme Court Reports, Lawyers' Edition (L. Ed., L. Ed. 2d). The commercial reporters both contain annotations. Courts of appeals decisions are found in the Federal Reporter (F., F.2d, F.3d), which is published commercially and contains annotations. District court decisions are found in the Federal Supplement (F. Supp., F. Supp. 2d), which contains annotations. The Federal Rules Decisions (F.R.D.) also contains district court decisions, and the Federal Reporter (F.) contains cases decided between 1880 and 1932.

Federal cases are found in subject-matter order in the federal digests. These digests provide summaries of cases grouped by subject matter, and they function as an index to the reporters. Each reporter has its own corresponding digest.

Ultimately, you must find the case in and cite to the reporters, but you can find a case in a reporter only if you have the citation or the name of one of the parties to check the names table. Therefore, the best place to begin your common law research is through the digests. Once you find your subject matter, the digest will provide citations to the reporters as well as a short annotation summarizing the case. You should never cite directly to the digest.

State Courts

Every state has its own court system, and many differ in their structures. However, in all states, cases begin at the trial level and have the opportunity for at least one appeal. Many states have intermediate appellate courts, providing two opportunities for appeal along with the state supreme court. Table 1 in the Bluebook can help you understand the court system of a particular state.

State Cases

State cases are the opinions of state judges. They decide specific cases, creating common law and interpreting statutes and constitutions. Cases are published chronologically in state or regional reporters. Regional reporters include the Atlantic Reporter (A., A.2d), North Eastern Reporter (N.E., N.E.2d), North Western Reporter (N.W., N.W.2d), Pacific Reporter (P. P.2d), South Eastern Reporter (S.E., S.E.2d), South Western Reporter (S.W., S.W.2d), and Southern Reporter (So., So. 2d).

Cases are found in subject-matter order in the state or regional digests. These provide summaries of cases grouped by subject matter and function as an index to the reporters. Each reporter has its own digest and an index to the digest. The digests are a form of access into the chronological reporters.

Ultimately, you must find the case in and cite to the reporters, but you can find a case in a reporter only if you have the citation or the name of one of the parties to check the names table. Therefore, the best place to begin your common law research is through the digests. Once you find your subject matter, the digest will provide citations to the reporters as well as a short annotation summarizing the case. You should never cite directly to the digest.

3.   Secondary Sources: Quick Reference

Secondary Sources: What, Why, Where, and How

Source	What is it?	Why would you reach for it?	Where can you find it?	How do you use it?
Legal Encyclopedias	An encyclopedia covering legal topics, organized alphabetically by topic.	To provide a basic, elementary background on a legal issue or to determine if a certain state has a particular law.	C.J.S. is found in the books or on Westlaw or WestlawNext. Am. Jur. is found in the books and on Lexis, Lexis Advance, Westlaw, and WestlawNext. Many state encyclopedias are found in the books or on Lexis, Lexis Advance, Westlaw, or WestlawNext.	C.J.S., published by West, uses the key number system. Generally, these encyclopedias are indexed, with the index found at the end of volumes on the shelf, or can be searched online in Lexis, Lexis Advance, Westlaw, and WestlawNext.
American Law Reports (A.L.R.)	A more detailed encyclopedia, with extensive annotations on legal issues. A.L.R. also includes the full text of relevant or important cases and annotations, and discusses and analyzes national trends.	To learn a lot about a particular topic in a short amount of time or to get a national overview of a particular topic and get citations to continue your research in more detail.	A.L.R. contains seven series: A.L.R., A.L.R.2d, A.L.R.3d, A.L.R.4th, A.L.R.5th, A.L.R.6th, and A.L.R. Federal (A.L.R. Fed., A.L.R. Fed. 2d). It is found both in book form and on Lexis and Westlaw.	Use the index and digest to locate relevant topics. If an annotation has been superseded, read only the later one. If it has been supplemented, read both. Annotations usually contain a scope note, summary of the case, outline of the annotation, research references, in-depth index, table of cases, and annotation text.
Treatises and Hornbooks	Hornbooks are legal aids for the student audience on a particular area of law. Treatises are similar legal aids for the practitioner, but often with greater detail and analysis.	To study for a law school exam (hornbooks) or to get an explanation of an issue in your practice area from one of the leading scholars in the field (treatises).	These sources are typically found in book form and are located using either a library catalog or the book Law Books in Print. At firms, treatises are often found in the offices of partners who specialize in that practice area.	Treatises are updated annually and contain indexes and tables for easy reference.

Source	What is it?	Why would you reach for it?	Where can you find it?	How do you use it?
Law Reviews	Scholarly periodicals, published by student-run organizations at law schools, containing scholar-written articles and student-written notes. Articles are typically written from the author's individual perspective to stimulate thought, argue a position, or criticize a case.	To mine the footnotes for helpful sources, such as cases, statutes, and other authorities. Law review articles often provide insight into the issue, but should not be taken to be an objective explanation of the law.	Law reviews are published in print and online. HeinOnline houses back issues of legal periodicals in pdf format, and articles can be searched and retrieved in full text on Lexis, Lexis Advance, Westlaw, and WestlawNext although coverage for many journals is mixed. Older articles may be available only in the bound print editions of the journal.	The Index to Legal Periodicals and Books can be used, in print form, using a CD-ROM, or on Lexis and Westlaw (called "Legal Periodicals and Books") to access articles via author, title, or specific case/statute (dating back to 1908). The Current Law Index (CLI) is more comprehensive, but dates back to 1980 and is found in the books or on Lexis and Westlaw. Lexis and Westlaw also provide extensive search and retrieval options for law reviews.
Restatements	A restatement of the law in a particular area (e.g., torts) written by a committee of scholars, judges, and lawyers, and published by the American Law Institute. Although these are not the law, they are very authoritative and are adopted as the law in many jurisdictions.	To get a neutral, concise, black-letter statement of the law. The Restatement may not be the law in your particular jurisdiction, however, and it will not provide you with hints or explanation regarding how the law is to be applied.	The Restatement can be found in book form, on Lexis, Lexis Advance, Westlaw, or on WestlawNext. There are a total of 13 Restatements.	Each Restatement is indexed and organized by subsection within the overall topic. The Restatements state the law and provide commentary, examples, and analysis of the law and its development. The Restatement 2ds also provide cross-references to the key number system and A.L.R. Each Restatement is updated by an appendix.

📝 4. Administrative Law: Quick Reference

Federal Agencies

Federal agencies fall under the executive branch. They are created through congressional legislation that defines the specialized topic and mission of the agency. Once established, an agency may issue rules and regulations pertaining to its mission and hear and settle disputes arising from them. Law produced by agencies is called administrative law.

Federal Administrative Law

Administrative rules and regulations are published in the Federal Register and the Code of Federal Regulations (C.F.R.). The Federal Register is published daily (based on work days), and all issues within a year constitute a single volume. A table of contents page lists all executive agencies and documents produced by each agency.

The C.F.R. arranges administrative rules and regulations chronologically. It is arranged in a format similar, almost parallel, to the U.S. Code. The regulations are arranged in 50 titles, some of which match the titles of the U.S.C. The titles are then divided into chapters, which regulate a particular agency. The C.F.R. is updated quarterly, and each year's volumes are a different color.

The List of Sections Affected (L.S.A.) is published monthly and contains the finalized and proposed changes made since the latest publication of the C.F.R. The L.S.A. arranges final regulations by C.F.R. title and section and provides page references to the Federal Register. The L.S.A. arranges proposed changes by title and part and references pages in the Federal Register.

Federal Administrative Agency Decisions

Administrative agencies exercise a quasi-judicial power in that they make decisions involving issues arising under their regulations. Many agencies publish these opinions in their own reporters, such as the Federal Trade Commission Reports or Agriculture Decisions. In addition, these decisions may be found on an agency's website or sometimes on Lexis or Westlaw.

State Agencies and Administrative Law

State agencies fall under a state's executive branch. Agencies on the state level create and enforce regulations on a variety of matters such as housing, utilities, and public health.

Each state agency creates administrative law, which includes rules and regulations, decisions, and a variety of other documents particular to that agency. These documents mirror the form and function of federal administrative law.

States differ in the manner in which they publish administrative law. To determine the administrative law resources for a particular state, you can consult the following sources: BNA's Directory of State Administrative Codes and Registers and The Book of the States (Council of State Governments). Westlaw and Lexis also publish selected states' administrative laws.

5.   Legislative History: Quick Reference

Why: Legislative history provides an understanding of the context in which Congress or a state legislature wrote a particular bill. It is often used (to a greater or lesser degree) in the interpretation of a law, although it is only persuasive authority.

What: Legislative history encompasses several types of sources:

- Amendments and prior versions of bills, to compare what was added or removed during the legislative process;
- Subcommittee hearings, providing views of various groups who took an interest in the bill;
- Committee reports, including the purposes and recommendations of a committee; Congressional floor debates, indicating the intent of individual congresspersons.
- Congressional floor debates, indicating the intent of individual congresspersons.

Of these, committee reports are generally the most important and useful source.

Where: Legislative history is available in print and online sources.

- In print:
  - USCCAN
    - Full text of selected committee reports
    - Bill information and list of reports for all federal laws passed
  - Congressional Information Service (CIS) Provides comprehensive records, but only as abstracts (not full text)
  - Congressional Record
    - Includes floor debates from both houses, published daily
- Online:
  - Thomas, via the Library of Congress
  - Lexis databases (current session)
    - Bills—Legis; Bills
    - Hearings—Legis; Hearing
    - Committee reports—Legis; CMTRPT
    - Floor debates—Legis; Record
  - Westlaw databases (current session)
    - Bills—Cong-BillTXT
    - Hearings—USTestimony
    - Committee reports and floor debates—LH
  - WestlawNext databases (current session)
    - Bills—Proposed and Enacted Legislation
    - Hearings—USTestimony
    - Committee reports and floor debates—Proposed and Enacted Legislation—Capitol Watch

Prior congressional sessions are available in the print and online sources as well.

6. What Source Do I Look In?: Checklist

Where to Find ...

Information on a topic you know little about	**Treatise or hornbook:** read an expert's in-depth discussion of a legal topic targeted toward a practitioner or student audience, respectively.	
	Legal encyclopedia: read a basic overview of a particular legal topic with some annotations to cases on point.	
A general nationwide survey on a topic	**American Law Reports (A.L.R.):** read an in-depth survey of a specific topic, including annotations with references to legal sources from many jurisdictions.	
	Restatement: read a black-letter statement of the law in many jurisdictions.	
	West's 50 State Surveys: quickly find links to statutes from all 50 states addressing a specific legal topic.	
Information on a specific topic, for which you want to find ...	**Cases** that address that topic	**Case digest:** look up the topic in the index to find sections of the digest with annotations and citations to relevant cases.
		American Law Reports (A.L.R.): find citations and summaries of cases from many jurisdictions addressing your topic.
		Legal encyclopedia: examine the footnotes from a topical encyclopedia entry for links to some cases discussing the topic.
	Statutes that address that topic	**Annotated code:** look up the topic in the index volume of the code for your jurisdiction to find statutes addressing your topic.
	Administrative regulations that address that topic	**CIS Index to the Code of Federal Regulations:** look up the topic in the CIS Index to find C.F.R. sections addressing your topic.
	Other sources that address that topic	**Law reviews:** survey the footnotes for many citations to primary and secondary sources on a given legal topic.
The citation to a case	**Case reporter:** look up the citation in the reporter for the appropriate jurisdiction.	
The name of the parties to a case (but not its citation)	**Case reporter:** find the decision's citation by looking up the party names in the reporter's names table.	

The citation to a statute, for which you need ...	The **statute** itself	**Official or annotated code:** look up the citation in the code volumes for the appropriate jurisdiction.
	Cases discussing the statute	**Annotated code:** the annotations following the statute will include brief summaries and citations of cases discussing and interpreting the statute.
	Administrative regulations implementing the statute	**Annotated code:** the annotations will include citations to implementing regulations.
		C.F.R.: locate the given U.S.C. section in the C.F.R.'s table of authorities to find citations to implementing regulations.
The name of a legislative act (but not its citation)	**Official or annotated code:** look up the act's name in the popular names table for the code to find its citation.	
The citation to an administrative regulation	**C.F.R.:** find administrative regulations that were in force as of the publication date; each volume is updated annually. If you have a C.F.R. citation, check it in the L.S.A. and Federal Register for up-to-date changes.	
	Federal Register: find recently issued administrative regulations, updated daily.	
The proper citation form for a source	**Bluebook:** use the United States Jurisdictions Table (T.1) to find the proper citation format for your jurisdiction.	
	ALWD: use Appendix 1 to find the proper citation format for your jurisdiction.	

B.   Quizzes

⦿? 1.   Research Sources (in General): Quiz

1. The Restatements of the Law published by the American Law Institute

    A. are the same as statutes.
    B. have the same force and effect as law.
    C. can be adopted by a jurisdiction.
    D. codify the common law.
    E. A and B.

2. The print version of the United States Code Annotated can be a better resource than the print version of the United States Code because

    A. the U.S.C.A. contains an index and the U.S.C. does not.
    B. the U.S.C.A. contains annotations and the U.S.C. does not.
    C. the U.S.C.A. is updated more frequently than the U.S.C.
    D. A, B, and C.
    E. B and C.

3. What legal research resource combines the features of an encyclopedia with those of a case reporter, allowing users to learn the basic information within a legal topic with annotations and footnotes, while discussing, comparing, and citing law from various jurisdictions?

   A. Corpus Juris Secundum (C.J.S.)
   B. American Jurisprudence (Am. Jur.)
   C. American Law Reports (A.L.R.)
   D. United States Code
   E. Black's Law Dictionary

4. Sarah, a law student, is writing a scholarly article on a legal topic area with which she is not very familiar. She should begin researching this topic area by

   A. searching Lexis or Westlaw for statutes related to the legal topic area.
   B. reading a hornbook to gain background in the legal topic area.
   C. searching the Internet for key terms of art.
   D. searching Google for law review articles related to her topic.
   E. A and C.

5. Which of the following states is NOT a part of the Tenth Circuit?

   A. Nebraska
   B. Oklahoma
   C. Wyoming
   D. Colorado

6. Which source for federal administrative materials is published most frequently?

   A. The Code of Federal Regulations (C.F.R.)
   B. The e-CFR
   C. The Federal Register
   D. The List of Sections Affected (L.S.A.)

7. Which of the following would you NOT find in Corpus Juris Secundum?

   A. A short sample of relevant case annotations
   B. Topics organized by West's key number system
   C. Pocket parts with citations to more recent material
   D. A "New Topics" binder at the end of the set

8. Which of the following statements is true?

   A. Hornbooks and treatises are updated annually.
   B. Most law review articles are written from an objective point of view.
   C. Looseleaf binders are often used for academic research but are rarely used by practitioners.
   D. Restatements are not necessarily the law, but are often adopted by courts as the law in that jurisdiction.

9. Which of the following is NOT the abbreviation for a federal case reporter?

    A. F. Supp. 2d
    B. F. Ed. 3d
    C. L. Ed. 2d
    D. S. Ct.

10. Which of the following statements is true?

    A. Session laws are rarely used for statutory research.
    B. Every state has its own official, unannotated code.
    C. State constitutions may limit the rights granted its citizens by the U.S. Constitution.
    D. Official state codes are generally updated more frequently than their annotated counterparts.

Answer Key on page 309

🗔? 2.   Congress and Federal Statutes: Quiz

1. Which version of the federal code contains the text of the United States Constitution in its first volume?

    A. United States Code (U.S.C.)
    B. United States Code Annotated (U.S.C.A.)
    C. United States Code Service (U.S.C.S.)
    D. All of the above

2. Of the following, which is the LEAST useful source for finding a statute if you know its subject matter but not its date of enactment or citation?

    A. Statutes at Large
    B. United States Code (U.S.C.)
    C. United States Code Annotated (U.S.C.A.)
    D. United States Code Service (U.S.C.S.)

3. Which of the following is NOT true about the U.S.C.A. and U.S.C.S.?

    A. They are published more frequently than the U.S.C.
    B. They are the official compilations of the federal code.
    C. They are indexed by topic and by popular names.
    D. They are accessible in both book and online formats.

4. Of the following, which is the MOST useful for locating case decisions relating to constitutional issues?

    A. United States Constitution
    B. United States Code Annotated (U.S.C.A.)
    C. United States Code (U.S.C.)
    D. Session Laws from Statutes at Large

Answer Key on page 309

🔍 3. Federal Courts and Federal Cases: Quiz

1. You have just been convicted of a crime in the Idaho federal district court. To which court can you now appeal your conviction?

    A. The Court of Appeals for the Ninth Circuit
    B. The United States Supreme Court
    C. The Idaho Supreme Court
    D. The Court of Appeals for the Federal Circuit

2. The court from Question 1 has ruled on your appeal and the decision is now published. In what reporter are you most likely to find this published decision?

    A. U.S.
    B. F.3d
    C. F. Supp. 2d
    D. F.R.D.

3. What is the official reporter for the United States Supreme Court?

    A. The Supreme Court Reporter
    B. The United States Supreme Court Reports
    C. The Federal Reporter
    D. The United States Reports

4. Which of the following is true?

    A. Appeals from the D.C. federal district court go to the Court of Appeals for the Fourth Circuit.
    B. Federal digests publish summaries of federal cases organized chronologically.
    C. Federal reporters for district court decisions are published by the courts themselves.
    D. If you do not have a citation but do have a party's name in a case, you can start with the reporters by using the names tables.

Answer Key on page 309

🔍 4. Federal Administrative Law: Quiz

1. Federal administrative agencies are a part of what branch of government?

    A. Legislative
    B. Executive
    C. Judicial
    D. None of the above

2. How often is a single title of the Code of Federal Regulations updated?

    A. Daily
    B. Monthly

C. Quarterly

D. Yearly

3. Which of the following is true?

    A. Each of the 50 C.F.R. titles covers the same topic as its U.S.C. counterpart with the same title number.

    B. All Federal Register regulations published in a given day constitute a single volume.

    C. The L.S.A. arranges proposed changes by Federal Register publication and provides page references to the C.F.R.

    D. None of the above

4. Which of the following is NOT a source for locating decisions from administrative agency hearings?

    A. Some agency websites

    B. Reporters published by some agencies

    C. The Federal Reporter

    D. Lexis and Westlaw

Answer Key on page 309

😯 5. State Legislatures and State Statutes: Quiz

1. Which of the following is true?

    A. State constitutions are usually included in the first volume of the state's code.

    B. Every jurisdiction has created its own constitution.

    C. State constitutions may not enumerate more rights for their citizens than does the U.S. Constitution.

    D. State constitutions are not subordinate to the U.S. Constitution.

2. Yesterday, the Maryland state legislature passed a law regulating gambling. Where are you most likely to find the text of this law?

    A. The state constitution

    B. An official state code

    C. A slip law pamphlet

    D. A session law volume

3. Which of the following is always true about official state code compilations?

    A. They are organized chronologically.

    B. They can be accessed via a topical or popular names index.

    C. They include annotations to relevant case decisions.

    D. None of the above.

4. Which of the following is NOT a state's official statutory compilation? (Hint: Refer to Bluebook Table T.1.)

    A. Hawaii Revised Statutes
    B. West Virginia Code
    C. Connecticut General Statutes Annotated
    D. New Mexico Statutes 1978

Answer Key on page 309

6. State Courts and State Cases: Quiz

1. Which court has final say over the interpretation of New York state law?

    A. United States Supreme Court
    B. New York Supreme Court
    C. New York Court of Appeals
    D. New York Supreme Court, Appellate Division

2. If you are researching employment discrimination cases in Wyoming and have a citation to a case you are interested in, which of the following would be the most likely place to find your case?

    A. North Western Reporter
    B. Pacific Reporter
    C. North Western Digest
    D. Pacific Digest

3. If you do not have a citation to a Wyoming case you are interested in, but you know its subject matter, which of the following would be the best place to start your research?

    A. North Western Reporter
    B. Pacific Reporter
    C. North Western Digest
    D. Pacific Digest

4. Where in the Bluebook can you find details by state on which reporter should be cited for cases in that state?

    A. Table 1
    B. Table 7
    C. Rule 3
    D. Rule 10

5. Which of the following is NOT true?

    A. You should never cite to a state or regional digest.

    B. The state and regional digests contain the full text of case decisions.

    C. State and regional digests act as an index to the reporters and also have their own indexes.

    D. State and regional digests are organized alphabetically by subject matter.

Answer Key on page 309

8? 7. Legislative History: Quiz

1. Legislative history is considered binding authority when interpreting a statute. **True** or **False**?
2. State legislative history is not always available online. **True** or **False**?
3. History for laws included in the Sources of Compiled Legislative Histories is easy to research because the relevant legislative histories have already been compiled for you. **True** or **False**?
4. Congressional Information Service (CIS) includes the full text of legislative history for a given bill. **True** or **False**?
5. Subcommittee hearings are available on Thomas, Lexis, and Westlaw. **True** or **False**?
6. Legislative history includes which of the following?

    A. Working versions of bills prior to the final. **True** or **False**?

    B. Committee reports and subcommittee hearings. **True** or **False**?

    C. Transcripts of House and Senate floor debates. **True** or **False**?

Answer Key on page 310

8? 8. Looseleaf Services: Quiz

1. The two major looseleaf service publishers are Lexis and West. **True** or **False**?
2. Looseleaf services are used by practitioners but not by academic researchers. **True** or **False**?
3. Looseleaf services are constantly revised and kept very current. **True** or **False**?
4. A looseleaf service contains a compilation of statutes, regulations, and cases, but includes no commentary. **True** or **False**?
5. Most practitioners rely heavily on looseleaf services. **True** or **False**?
6. A looseleaf service includes a section describing how best to use the service. **True** or **False**?

Answer Key on page 310

📇? 9. Secondary Sources: Quiz

1. Hornbook is to student as _____ is to practitioner.

    A. legal encyclopedia
    B. American Law Reports
    C. treatise
    D. Restatement

2. Which of the following is an advantage of a Restatement over a treatise?

    A. A Restatement covers its area of law in extensive detail.
    B. A Restatement is often adopted by courts as an authoritative statement of the law in that jurisdiction.
    C. A Restatement includes excerpts from cases in its area of law.
    D. Both A and B.

3. Which of the following is a difference between American Law Reports (A.L.R.) and American Jurisprudence 2d (Am. Jur. 2d)?

    A. A.L.R. covers topics in much more detail than Am. Jur. 2d.
    B. Am. Jur. 2d contains annotations to relevant cases, but A.L.R. does not.
    C. An A.L.R. article discusses many different legal topics, but an entry in Am. Jur. 2d discusses only one.
    D. An A.L.R. article provides only a basic introduction to a legal topic, but an entry in Am. Jur. 2d covers it in depth.

4. Which of the following accurately describes law review articles?

    A. They are written from a neutral, objective point of view.
    B. They provide extensive footnotes referring to supporting cases, statutes, and other legal authorities.
    C. They are published by the American Law Institute.
    D. They provide a concise, authoritative statement of the law.

Answer Key on page 310

CHAPTER 3

Research Strategies

This chapter informs you of your many options as a legal researcher and helps you choose efficient and effective strategies. Here, you will learn how the American legal system guides your research, how to choose between book research and online research, how to determine your research strategies for particular sources, and how to update the law to ensure that it is timely and accurate.

3. Continuing Research: Checklist ☑
4. Binding vs. Persuasive Law: Quick Reference 🗒
5. West's Key Number System: Quick Reference 🗒
6. Collecting Information: Quick Reference (Note-Taking Chart) 🗒
7. Note-Taking Chart: Quick Reference (Note-Taking Chart: Example) 🗒
8. Updating the Law: Quick Reference 🗒

Statutes
9. Finding Statutes: Quick Reference 🗒
10. Strategies for Researching Statutes: Checklist ☑

Cases
11. Finding Cases: Quick Reference 🗒
12. Strategies for Researching Cases: Checklist ☑

Legislative History, Administrative Law, and Looseleafs
13. Finding Legislative History: Quick Reference 🗒
14. Strategies for Researching Legislative History: Checklist ☑
15. Finding Administrative Law: Quick Reference 🗒
16. Strategies for Researching Administrative Law: Checklist ☑
17. Using Looseleaf Services: Quick Reference 🗒

B. Quizzes
1. Research Strategy (in General): Quiz ⚲?
2. Binding v. Persuasive Law: Quiz ⚲?
3. Finding Statutes: Quiz ⚲?
4. Finding Cases: Quiz ⚲?
5. Updating: Quiz ⚲?

I.   THE AMERICAN LEGAL SYSTEM

A.   *Civics, Federalism, and Interaction*

1.   Civics Lesson

While most countries rely solely on their civil codes as laws, the United States, considered a "common law country," has three bodies of government that create laws:

1. Congress or the legislature creates constitutions and statutes:
   a. Found in state or federal codes
   b. First published in slip laws and session laws
2. Courts create cases or court opinions:
   a. Found in state, regional, or federal reporters
   b. First published in slip opinions
3. The executive branch, through its agencies, creates regulations:
   a. Found in the Code of Federal Regulations or the state's equivalent
   b. First published in the Federal Register or the state's equivalent

2.   Federalism

a.   *Federal and State Government*

To complicate matters, states and the federal government have their own legislatures, courts, and agencies. These are parallel systems, and the type of issue dictates which body of law and which branch of government applies. This seemingly confusing system arose as a result of the states trying to retain their rights when the federal Constitution was ratified.

b.   *Federal and State Court Systems*

The federal and state court systems have parallel structures and similar functions. Usually, federal courts will hear matters that relate to federal law. They therefore apply the relevant federal law. State courts will usually hear matters that relate to state law; they therefore apply the relevant state law. However, in some instances, federal law applies within a state court, while state law might apply in federal court. For example:

A federal court might hear a case based on "diversity of citizenship," a concept you will learn about in Civil Procedure. In this situation, the federal court will apply the particular state law, and it will be bound by the decisions of the state court applying state law.

A state court is bound by the U.S. Constitution. The state must uphold the same rights as those granted in the U.S. Constitution, although it may grant additional rights. Therefore, a state judge is bound by both the state and federal constitutions.

The U.S. Supreme Court is binding, in most situations, on all courts—both state and federal.

At times, the appropriate law is ambiguous and litigated. The balance of power between state law and federal law, federalism, is constantly shifting.

3. Legal Interaction

The starting point in legal analysis is usually statutes. Courts often define, apply, and analyze the terms of those statutes. Courts also determine whether a statute is constitutional. The courts, through their decisions, create legal precedent, which should be followed by other courts within that jurisdiction under the concept of *stare decisis*. When a court determines that a statute is unconstitutional, that statute is no longer good law. When a legislature determines that a court has misinterpreted a legal term of art within a statute, the legislature can rewrite the statute.

When no statute is applicable, often there is common law, or case law, that applies. In these instances, a judge's opinion or a series of court opinions create a body of law. At times, the legislature will codify a body of case law.

Congress has also empowered agencies to create their own law through regulations. These laws are specific to a particular area such as environment, food and drug, and housing. Courts can interpret regulations to ensure that they are constitutional and being applied correctly by agencies.

B. *Primary Law vs. Secondary Sources*

Primary law is the actual law such as statutes, rules, cases, and regulations.

Secondary sources are materials that discuss and comment on primary law such as law review articles, legal encyclopedias, and hornbooks. Secondary sources are persuasive law.

C. *Stare Decisis*

Stare decisis is a core concept of the American legal system. It means that current cases are treated consistently with past precedent. Stare decisis has a number of benefits to litigants. First, it permits them to predict the outcome of a legal issue or dispute. Oftentimes, clients ask lawyers for advice as to whether they are permitted to perform a certain action; lawyers look to past cases to determine whether the requested action is permitted under the law. Clients can then rely on the prior cases, through the doctrine of stare decisis, to determine whether to perform the particular action. Second, lawyers look to prior decisions to determine whether to bring lawsuits and to determine how best to defend lawsuits. Third, stare decisis provides parties with fair treatment under the law. Each party is treated similarly, based on case precedent.

Stare decisis, while a core concept of the American legal system, operates with some flexibility. Because no one case is exactly like a prior case, courts can still follow precedent but massage the law to fit the current facts. As such, case law develops over time, often by adding new elements to a rule or applying exceptions to existing rules. At times, however, courts do overtly overrule previous decisions. When they do so, the courts often justify these rulings based on changes in circumstances or societal values.

Stare decisis has both vertical and horizontal limitations. On a horizontal level, a court is bound only by decisions of other courts within its jurisdiction. For example, the state of New Jersey is not bound by cases from North Dakota. Likewise, except in certain situations, state courts are not bound by cases from federal courts nor are federal courts bound by state court opinions.

On a vertical level, courts are bound only by decisions from courts on a higher level. Thus, trial courts are bound by appellate court decisions within that jurisdiction, but appellate courts are not bound by decisions from their trial courts.

Cases that must be followed under stare decisis are referred to as binding or mandatory case law, while cases that are not binding are called persuasive.

D. *Binding Law vs. Persuasive Law*

An important distinction in primary law is mandatory or binding law versus law that is merely persuasive.

Mandatory or binding law is law that is binding in that jurisdiction; it must be followed under the principle of stare decisis. For example, a trial court in Maryland must follow Maryland state codes and decisions from higher Maryland courts because they are binding authorities.

Persuasive law is law from a lower court or a different jurisdiction that gives guidance but does not have to be followed. For example, a New York court does not have to follow a California court's decision. Likewise, a justice who sits on the Supreme Court of California, that state's highest court, is not required to follow a California trial judge's opinion.

The distinction between mandatory and persuasive law is important when deciding the best cases to rely on when writing a legal document. Usually, you want to show the judge that she is bound by certain law. However, at times, you will need to rely on persuasive authority. For example, although an opinion from the same level court is not binding on that court (one trial court judge is not bound by his colleague's opinion) because it is technically only persuasive authority, an opinion from the same-level court would be extremely relevant to the judge making the decision. In addition, when no binding authority exists on an issue, you will need to use persuasive authority to make your argument.

II.   STRATEGIES FOR THE RESEARCH PROCESS

For an overview of the legal research process, see page 7 in chapter 1. In addition, you will find a start-to-finish example of a legal research plan on page 12 of chapter 1. To view students' testimonials about conducting legal research, go to http://www.aspenlawschool.com/books/donahoe.

A.   *Asking the Right Questions* ─────────────▷

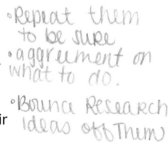

person assigning Topic
•Don't assume you have everything

Most assignments are <u>given orally by busy supervising attorneys</u>. Therefore, when a supervisor presents you with an assignment, you should assume he has not provided you with all the details necessary to answer the legal question. It is imperative that you ask the right questions before you leave his office. While there is no set list of exact questions that must be asked in each situation, there are a number of categories that will help your research:

1. **Asking fact questions:** Ask the supervisor for details about the factual situation of the client. Often, the attorney has met with the client, but you have not. Filling in the facts will help you understand the issue.
2. **Framing the issue:** Often the supervisor has not fully thought out the legal issue he wants you to address. Therefore, repeating the issue to the partner to ensure that you understand it often helps the partner think it through as well. Before you leave the office, you and the partner should be very clear on the issue that is to be addressed.

•Repeat them to be sure
•agreement on what to do.

3. **Brainstorming research strategies:** Because supervising attorneys have had years of research experience and are often specialists in their fields, it is a good idea to ask your supervisor for any research strategies she might have to begin the project. Often, the supervisor will be a gold mine for resources, save you time, and be thankful that you thought to solicit her advice.

•Bounce Research ideas off Them

4. **Taking notes:** It is imperative to take copious notes throughout these assignment meetings for a number of reasons: (a) you cannot remember all the details; (b) you want to refer back to the issue you and the partner have framed; (c) you want your notes to memorialize the facts as they exist at the time as they might change or expand as discovery proceeds (a change in facts could change your analysis).

•Must!
•Recall
•Prove Billing

The items on the above list should be addressed in the supervisor's office. Once you leave the office, you need to immediately take notes on your notes. If you focus your attention on another matter or attend another meeting, you will waste time later trying to recreate your conversation with the supervisor. Therefore, when you return to your office, take five to ten minutes to reconstruct the assignment to stay focused.

B. *Staying Focused*

When you return to your office with a new assignment from a supervising attorney, be sure to focus on the assignment while the information is fresh:

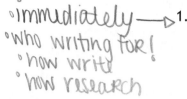

1. **Write down the issue statement:** You and the supervisor have framed the issue; now, write it down in a lucid manner. A question presented, a one-sentence issue, or a brief paragraph will work. This issue statement will serve as a crutch as you find tangential arguments and issues throughout your research. Carry it with you to the library or tape it onto your computer as you do your online research.

2. **Ask yourself about the assignment:**
    a. Who is your audience? Are you writing for a judge, a client, the supervising attorney, the other side? Your answer will dictate the way in which you draft your document. What is the purpose? Are you writing to inform or to win or both? Are you writing with the idea of settlement or to litigate? What is your strategy?
    b. What is the scope of your document? How long should it be? How much time, and
    c. How much money can you spend on it?
    d. Time management is an important part of being a lawyer. Consult your calendar for every assignment and make sure you have time to meet your deadline.

3. **Create a list of key words:** Whether you are using the books or computer sources, you will be more efficient if you create search terms or key words before you begin to research.

4. **Devise a research sources strategy:** You should not dive into research without deciding on a strategy. What sources would be the best starting points? If you list research sources in the order you think will be most helpful, you will be more efficient when you begin your research. The least efficient researcher is the one who roams the library or cyberspace without a game plan.

C. *Taking Notes*

Once you begin your research, taking notes is imperative for a number of reasons:

1. **Take Notes to Keep a Record of Where You Have Researched.** As you gather information, you will find sources that are both useful and not useful. Keep track of both. Invariably, you will need to go back and find more law. If you have kept notes on the sources that were not helpful, you will not waste time repeating research. In addition, if your notes indicate which sources were most helpful, you can focus your energy on those sources when you continue researching.

2. **Take Notes to Keep a Record of What You Have Found.** As you are researching, you will need to keep track of the law that you think is relevant. Be sure to note the citation as well as the name of the case or statute or source. Locating the source later will be just as important as finding its full name. Note: Just because a source has cited the law, do not assume it is the official cite. You will still need to check the Bluebook or ALWD before filing a document with citations.

3. **Take Notes on the Law You Have Read.** As you read the law, take notes—either by hand or on the computer. Note the facts as well as the law. Try to categorize each piece of law you read; sometimes a case might fall into more than one category. Some people use charts, graphs, or separate computer files to take notes as they read the law to easily find information later in a useful, organized fashion. For help in taking notes, see the Note-Taking Chart on page 166.

D. *Deciding When to Stop*

In practice, stopping your research is often dictated by time constraints (e.g., an hour lunch break in the courtroom), client's financial restraints (e.g., a small budget), or a deadline. In an ideal world, you would stop researching when you know you have found the law. However, oftentimes it is difficult to tell whether you have found all or enough of the relevant law. Some cues will tell you that your research has been thorough:

1. You start finding the same cases cited over and over.
2. You Shepardize or KeyCite the law and no new citations appear.
3. You read a secondary source about your issue and it all makes sense.
4. You have followed your research strategy list and checked every source.
5. You have researched online and in the books and the research is redundant.
6. You are able to write a logical document without any holes in legal reasoning.
7. Your opponent's document cites the same law (or less).

III. BOOK RESEARCH VS. ONLINE RESEARCH

Caution
free - vary in
quality, quantity

Legal research can be accomplished through traditional law books as well as through modern computer resources. Historically, the law has developed through an organizational scheme modeled around legal books. However, computer resources are changing some research methods and ways of thinking about legal organization. This section first provides historical background for context about legal thinking and the development of computer researching. Next, it provides strategies for researching using legal books, specifically using West's key number system, as well as strategies for using computer research, mainly through Lexis and Westlaw and free Internet sources.

A. *The Historical Debate*

U.S. law, modeled on the British legal system, started as a common law system where cases were reported by individual members of the bar who sat in courtrooms, kept notes, and compiled reporters that were neither systematic nor structured. In the early nineteenth century, "official reporters" developed but remained similar to the unofficial reporters in that they had no organizational scheme and published only selected cases. As a result, lawyers used their memories to find law as opposed to any external system.

In the mid-nineteenth century, industrialization caused a dramatic increase in legal activity. Some publishers wanted to continue publishing selected decisions only; others, including John West, who was a salesman, not a lawyer, decided to publish most cases instead of selected ones. As a result, lawyers were unable to use memory to recall the huge number of cases now being reported.

To meet demand for a system to access the plethora of cases, West developed the American digest system, an organizational system of classification of law. The digest classified all areas of law into seven major categories: persons, property, contracts, torts, crimes, remedies, and government. These areas mirror the current traditional first-year law school curricula, which was simultaneously developed at Harvard Law School by Dean Langdell. Each of the seven categories was further subdivided into 430 key numbers: "the key number system." These key numbers were further subdivided. West editors became the primary classifiers. As they read cases, they decided which categories of law and key numbers to assign to the cases.

The digest with its key number system became the primary method for lawyers to locate case law. As a result, lawyers began to organize the law into the scheme developed by West and followed by law schools adopting Harvard's Langdellian curriculum. The West system became a national system with reporters spanning the country. As a result, the national legal structure has developed around the categories of the digest, and American lawyers now rely on the organizational paradigm developed by West to find law using the books.

The computer age has thrown a wrench into the digest system. While the digest is based on organization, computer searching, by nature, has no organizational scheme at all. Instead, it is based on text searching. Words and facts are the basis for computer searching, not ideas and legal concepts. Lexis and Westlaw have become the primary services for legal online searching. These services cost a fee for practicing attorneys, but are often paid for by law schools so that they students can use them for free. Some free sites are located on the Web, such as findlaw.com and Google Scholar. In addition, many courts have websites where local decisions and dockets are searchable. One of the widely recognized advantages to online searching is that the law is updated frequently. Some legal researchers are liberated by the computer system as they can find cases based on judge, opposing counsel, or date. Others are still uncomfortable with the computer system because the nationally developed organizational scheme is not readily apparent, context is missing, and endless screens are hard to bring to internal order. The best researchers are those who can combine the organizational scheme of the book world with the text-based searches online. Strategies for both types of research are provided below.

To read an article by this author discussing more of the differences between online and book research, see http://www.law.georgetown.edu/faculty/donahoe.

B. *Key Number System*

The key number system was developed by West as a method to organize the growing number of published cases. The system breaks all possible legal categories into seven major categories:

- Persons
- Property
- Contracts
- Torts
- Crimes
- Remedies
- Government

These large categories are then subdivided into over 430 topics. Each topic is further subdivided into a more detailed outline, using specific numbers. The result is a **key number,** which includes a topic and a number.

The editors at West (and Westlaw) use the key number system to categorize cases. Thus, a case may fit into a number of key numbers and is cataloged accordingly in multiple key number locations. The key numbers appear in case digests as well as on the Westlaw site (see below and page 115) and are arranged in both places alphabetically.

In addition, each case published by West (or Westlaw) contains headnotes located at the beginning of the opinion. A headnote provides a key number (see page 116) along with an annotation explaining the key number. Any one case may have multiple headnotes for multiple key numbers. In addition, the headnote provides a paragraph number where that legal issue is discussed in the case. The headnote number can make reading a case more efficient as you can turn (or link) directly to the paragraph in the text listed in the headnotes.

Westlaw Key Numbers

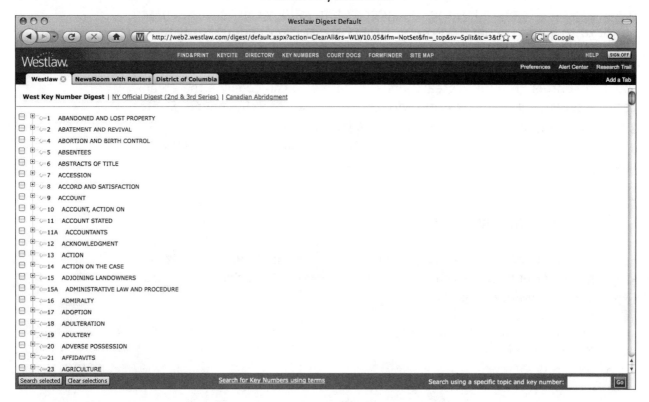

Key Numbers in Digests

81E F P D 4th—491   **PRODUCTS LIABILITY**   ☞**417**

For references to other topics, see Descriptive-Word Index

scription drug to her physicians constituted negligence on patient's part was question of comparative negligence to be determined by jury.

> Nichols v. McNeilab, Inc., 850 F.Supp. 562.

D.N.H. 2005. Under New Hampshire law, whether a plaintiff's injuries are indivisible, for purposes of contribution and apportionment between joint tortfeasors, is a question of law for the trial judge in a crashworthiness case.

> McNeil v. Nissan Motor Co., Ltd., 365 F.Supp.2d 206.

D.N.M. 2005. City's negligence was not so extraordinary as to be independent intervening cause of accident involving asphalt emulsion distributor used in road resurfacing work, but evidence of city's negligence was sufficient to go to jury on issue of comparative fault in operator's products liability action.

> Morales v. E.D. Etnyre & Co., 382 F.Supp.2d 1278.

E.D.N.Y. 1989. Evidence that plaintiff in asbestos-related personal injury action continued smoking despite knowing of health hazards and that smoking aggravates effects of asbestosis was sufficient to create jury issue as to whether plaintiff was contributorily negligent. Fed.Rules Civ.Proc.Rule 50(b), 28 U.S.C.A.

> In re Joint Eastern and Southern Districts Asbestos Litigation, 124 F.R.D. 538, affirmed Johnson v. Celotex Corp., 899 F.2d 1281, certiorari denied 111 S.Ct. 297, 498 U.S. 920, 112 L.Ed.2d 250.

M.D.Pa. 1992. Even if apportionment of liability was appropriate in asbestos case, issue should have been raised before case was submitted to jury.

> Sealover v. Carey Canada, 791 F.Supp. 1059, reversed 996 F.2d 42.

E.D.Tenn. 2000. Under Tennessee law, the comparative fault of a plaintiff in a products liability action is a matter ordinarily left to the jury.

> Martin v. Michelin North America, Inc., 92 F.Supp.2d 745.

☞**416. —— Misuse of product.**

C.A.7 (Ind.) 1987. Evidence that heart catheter was designed for general and variable therapeutic purposes, but not specifically for kind of use to which operating surgeon put catheter in open-heart surgery, and evidence that operating surgeon sutured catheter in manner not intended by manufacturers, raised jury question on defense of misuse in strict products liability suit against manufacturers to recover damages sustained when catheter broke and portion remained inside patient's heart. IC 33–1–1.5–4 (1982 Ed.).

> Phelps v. Sherwood Medical Industries, 836 F.2d 296.

C.A.10 (Okla.) 2004. Under Oklahoma law, issue of whether injuries sustained by passenger involved in motor vehicle accident resulted from passenger's misuse of vehicle's front seat by riding in a reclined position was for jury in personal injury suit brought by passenger against automobile manufacturer alleging that passenger's injuries resulted from a flawed seat belt system and seat design.

> Cummings v. General Motors Corp., 365 F.3d 944, as modified on denial of rehearing.

M.D.Ala. 1995. In action brought under Alabama Extended Manufacturer's Liability Doctrine (AEMLD), ordinarily, whether someone misused allegedly defective product is factual issue for jury.

> Dickerson v. Cushman, Inc., 909 F.Supp. 1467.

D.Colo. 1988. Injured worker's failure to follow warning supplied with machine causing injury did not as matter of Colorado law, bar his products liability claim alleging design defect; question of misuse of product was properly submitted to jury, presence or absence of warning is merely one factor of several to consider in determining whether product is defective or unreasonably dangerous, and warnings and instructions, even when they are adequate, are not substitute for safe design.

> McHargue v. Stokes Div. of Pennwalt, 686 F.Supp. 1428.

S.D.Fla. 1990. Plaintiff did not misuse motorcycle as a matter of law by riding it at high speed along dirt trails.

> Mendez v. Honda Motor Co., 738 F.Supp. 481.

☞**417. —— Assumption of risk.**   *— Key number*

C.A.11 (Ala.) 1992.   *— Court and date* Contributory negligence questions in actions under Alabama Extended Manufacturer's Liability Doctrine are normally for jury, and trial court must be careful not to construe the phrase "intended use" so   *— Case summary* strictly as to actually resolve questions of contributory negligence or assumption of risk without submitting those issues to jury.

> Goree v. Winnebago Industries, Inc., 958   *— Case citation* F.2d 1537.

C.A.11 (Ala.) 1986. Whether wood cutter appreciated danger of using chain saw without a chain brake due to illiteracy and a low level of intelligence, thereby rendering defense of assumption of risk unavailable to chain saw manufacturer under Alabama Extended Manufacturer's Liability Doctrine, was for jury in products

† This Case was not selected for publication in the National Reporter System
For cited U.S.C.A. sections and legislative history, see United States Code Annotated

Key Numbers in Cases

676 **11 FEDERAL SUPPLEMENT, 2d SERIES**

their May 8, 1998 "Order on Rule to Show Cause" against the plaintiffs.

It is so ORDERED

Key number ─────

Headnote number ─────

Case summary on this issue ─────

Willie BARRON, Jr., Plaintiff,

v.

Marvin T. RUNYON, Defendant.

No. CIV. A. 98–100–A.

Name of case ─────

Court ─────

United States District Court, E.D. Virginia, Alexandria Division.

Date case decoded ─────

July 7, 1998.

Employee brought action against employer, alleging that he was unlawfully terminated for absences protected by the Family Medical Leave Act (FMLA). Employer moved for summary judgment. The District Court, Ellis, J., held that: (1) as applied to employee, effective date of FMLA was one year after the date of enactment; (2) employee, who sought intermittent leave under the FMLA to care for his wife, was only required to establish his eligibility for the first absence related to that leave; and (3) triable issues existed regarding whether employee was terminated for taking leave protected by the FMLA.

Summary of case (written by publisher) ─────

Motion denied.

1. Civil Rights ⚷102.1

For purposes of employee's action under the Family Medical Leave Act (FMLA) where a collective bargaining agreement (CBA) covering the employee was in effect on the date of enactment of the Act, effective date of FMLA was one year after the date of enactment, though both employer and employee's union voluntarily adopted terms of FMLA and explicitly made them effective with respect to their employees on an earlier

date. Family and Medical Leave Act of 1993, § 2 et seq., 29 U.S.C.A. § 2601 et seq.

2. Statutes ⚷250

Private parties have no power to change or vary, by fiat or agreement, the effective date of a legislative enactment; only Congress can set a law's effective date.

3. Civil Rights ⚷173.1

Employee who sought intermittent leave under the Family Medical Leave Act (FMLA) to care for his wife was only required to establish his eligibility for the first absence related to that leave, and was not required to reestablish eligibility for each subsequent absence taken for the same reason during the following 12 months. Family and Medical Leave Act of 1993, §§ 101(2)(A), 102(a)(1), (b)(1), 29 U.S.C.A. §§ 2611(2)(A), 2612(a)(1), (b)(1); 29 C.F.R. §§ 825.100(a), 825.110(a)(2), 825.203(a), (c)(1).

4. Civil Rights ⚷173.1

An employee who is eligible for intermittent leave under the Family Medical Leave Act (FMLA) need only establish his eligibility on the occasion of the first absence, and not on the occasion of each subsequent absence. Family and Medical Leave Act of 1993, §§ 101(2)(A), 102(a)(1), 29 U.S.C.A. §§ 2611(2)(A), 2612(a)(1); 29 C.F.R. §§ 825.100(a), 825.110(a)(2), 825.203(a), (c)(1).

5. Civil Rights ⚷173.1

For purposes of the Family Medical Leave Act (FMLA), a series of absences, separated by days during which the employee is at work, but all of which are taken for the same medical reason, subject to the same notice, and taken during the same 12–month period, comprises one period of intermittent leave. Family and Medical Leave Act of 1993, §§ 101(2)(A), 102(a)(1), (b)(1), 29 U.S.C.A. §§ 2611(2)(A), 2612(a)(1), (b)(1); 29 C.F.R. §§ 825.100(a), 825.110(a)(2), 825.203(a), (c)(1).

6. Federal Civil Procedure ⚷2497.1

Genuine issues of material fact regarding whether employee was terminated for taking leave that was covered by the Family Medical Leave Act (FMLA) or for taking leave that was not protected under such Act

C. *Strategies for Book Research*

1. **Think Like a Legal Editor:** Because the books are organized around legal subjects organized over 100 years ago, it is helpful for the legal researcher to think like a legal editor. A legal editor reads recent law and tries to classify it into preexisting categories. Therefore, a legal researcher can find law more easily if she tries to determine how her issue would be classified under these categories, starting from a broad topic, such as contracts, and then narrowing the subject, such as offer or acceptance.

2. **Use Legal Terms of Art:** When using book sources to search for law, use legal terms of art. Therefore, while the word "Walmart" is not a useful research term, the word "employer" might be very useful to find cases on point. "Labor" could also prove to be a helpful term of art when looking for cases involving Walmart. It is often useful for the novice researcher to scan the indexes of legal sources to determine legal terms of art that might be helpful.

3. **Use the Indexes and Digests:** Book sources are organized extremely well with thorough indexes. The cases are organized through the digest system, which also has an index. Using the indexes and digests saves time and money when using the books.

4. **Look at Pocket Parts and Supplements:** Because the books are not updated daily, it is important to check for supplements and pocket parts for recent law. Each set of legal resources should either have a supplement, usually located at the end of the volumes, or a pocket part, which is a paperback pamphlet located at the back of each book. These updates contain recent law. Therefore, if you check a source but do not look in its pocket part, you might miss an important part of the law.

5. **Determine a Research Path:** Heading to the library without a game plan is going to be frustrating and time consuming. Therefore, before you begin your research, determine which sources you think would be most helpful, list a number of legal terms of art that might prove to be productive, and devise a method for note-taking so that you do not repeat research.

    a. **If You Know Nothing About your Legal Topic,** consider researching first in a background and context. (For more on secondary sources, see page 65 in chapter 2.) Often, the secondary source will provide you with a crash course in the subject area and help you narrow your focus.

    b. **If You Know Your Jurisdiction,** go right to that section of your library and focus on the books from your jurisdiction. Do not waste your time with persuasive authority, especially in the initial stages of your research.

    c. **If You Have One Known Source** and have read it carefully, look for other cites referenced in that source and then shepardize or key cite that source to find other sources.

For a comprehensive example of a research strategy example, see page 12 in chapter 1.

For strategies on researching particular sources, see the section "Strategies for Particular Sources," starting on page 129.

D.　*Strategies for Online Research*

Online legal research is offered for free and by commercial services. While there are a number of commercial services,[1] this section primarily focuses on the two major commercial services, Westlaw and Lexis, as well as free Internet sites that are useful for legal research.

Lexis and Westlaw compile primary and secondary legal sources, organize them by type, and publish them on their online databases. Because the full text of thousands of publications is online, users can search the text for key terms to find the documents they need. In addition, these online services are updated frequently so that a user can access recent law.

Online research can be done on websites other than Lexis and Westlaw. Legal websites such as findlaw.com and Google Scholar provide legal search engines on the Web. In addition, government web sites such as THOMAS and regulations.gov are useful for specific legal sources. The trick is to spend time as a student learning how to use all these services efficiently and effectively so that when you start practice, you can be cost-effective in your research.

1.　Commercial Online Legal Research Services

Lexis and Westlaw are the most commonly used legal research services. While your law school will most likely provide you access to both services, your employer will be willing to pay for only one, if any. Therefore, as a student, you should try to learn both to be prepared for your first job.

To further complicate matters, both Lexis and Westlaw have recently introduced new platforms to provide more intuitive search techniques and tools for organizing your research. As a result, each service now has two separate platforms and only some employers have begun to make the switch to the newer web sites. This section will discuss both versions of Westlaw and both versions of Lexis.

a.　*Westlaw*

Westlaw now has two platforms: Westlaw and WestlawNext. They exist on separate web sites and can both be accessed through lawschool.westlaw.com. This book often refers to both generally as "Westlaw."

---

1. Loislaw and BloombergLaw are also available for a fee.

i.   Westlaw (Traditional Westlaw)

Traditional Westlaw is organized around thousands of databases (such as "Federal Materials") and files within those databases (such as "federal statutes"). The main databases are listed in the directory. By using a Boolean word search or a natural language search, the user can focus on specific materials located within each database and file. In addition, a researcher can find a source by citation, by party name, by key number, or by using the table of contents. In order to update the law or find its history, users can click on "KeyCite" or the flags located on each document. Payment for Westlaw is usually determined by a flat rate or by each search.

Traditional Westlaw

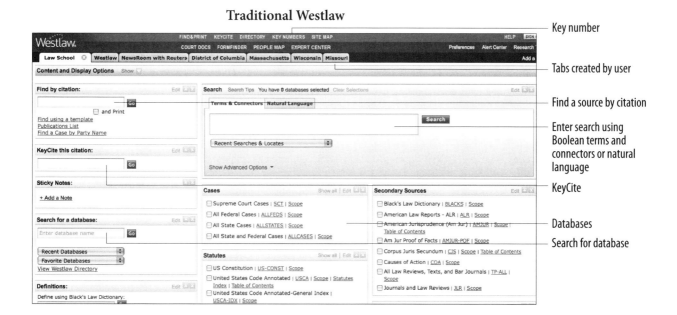

ii.   WestlawNext

WestlawNext is West's new platform, designed to be more user-friendly for the "Google generation" and to provide organizational tools for the legal researcher. While a user can still start with a database (by clicking on the tabs instead of a directory), a user can alternatively begin with a search in the search box found at the top of the screen. Here, the user can type a citation, a specific name of a case or other source, or a word search. These word searches need not be in Boolean or natural language format. WestlawNext uses data it has collected from experienced legal researchers conducting similar searches to find the best documents for that particular search. The results are collected from all core content (unless you select a specific database or file) and are ranked by relevance. The content type (such as cases, statutes, regulations) can be found on the left side of the screen if the user wants to narrow the type of search to a particular source. In addition, the user can further narrow the results by other filters such as date or key number. The user can also access Key Cite to update the law and look for history.

WestlawNext

History

Search box (by citation, name, or Google-type search)

Narrow by jurisdiction

Tabs

Items frequently used by user

Content types

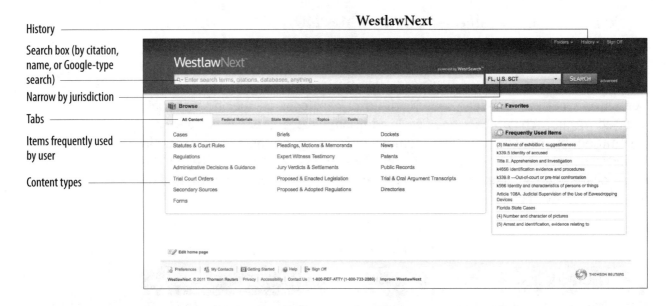

WestlawNext

Narrow by jurisdiction

Search box

Folders

KeyCite flag

Click to view case in full

Content types

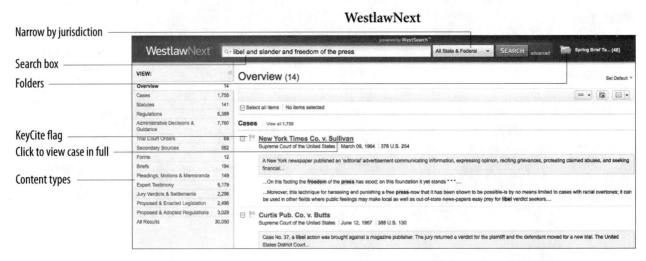

In addition, WestlawNext provides workflow and organizational tools for the legal researcher. First, a user can highlight and take notes on research found. Second, the researcher can save full documents as well as highlighted material and notes to specific folders created and organized by the user directly in WestlawNext. These folders can be further organized, shared, and accessed in the future without incurring any additional hourly charge. WestlawNext has been optimized for mobile devices such as iPads and iPhones, and a user can send results to her Kindle instead of printing. Payment for WestlawNext is usually determined by each document accessed by the user as opposed to each search performed.

Viewing Documents in Westlaw: There are different ways to display your search results.

Westlaw offers the following displays:

- **Result screen:** Appearing on left, lists documents retrieved by date. Each entry includes excerpts from document showing where search terms appear. (Click Hide Terms to make these disappear.)
- **Full Text:** By clicking on the name in the result screen, you will retrieve the full text of the document on the right screen. Your terms will be highlighted.
- **Doc button:** Takes you to the next document retrieved.
- **Term button:** Takes you to the next search term in that document.

WestlawNext offers the following displays:

- **Result screen:** Three columns are displayed on the result screen. The center column lists excerpts of documents retrieved in order of relevancy with terms highlighted in yellow. The left column features the core content categories and available filters. The terms used to narrow your results will display in purple. The right column lists some of the most relevant secondary sources in your search result.
- **Full Text:** By clicking on the name in the result screen, you will retrieve the full text of the document on the right screen. Your terms will be highlighted. Arrows at the top of the screen will allow you to toggle to the next result, next search term, or the full list.

b. Lexis

Lexis now has two platforms, Lexis and Lexis Advance. They exist on separate web sites and can both be accessed through lexisnexis.com/lawschool. This book often refers to both generally as "Lexis."

i. Lexis (Traditional Lexis)

Traditional Lexis is organized around databases. Legal researchers usually focus their research in the "legal" source and then choose from the sources listed within that tab (such as U.S. Supreme Court Briefs). By using a Boolean word search or a natural language search, the user can focus on specific materials located within each source. In addition, a researcher can get a document by citation, by party name, or by docket number. In order to update the law or find its history, users can click on "Shepards" or the colored symbols located

Traditional Lexis

Shepard's

Get a document

Various sources or
databases

Get a document

Search by topic or
headnote

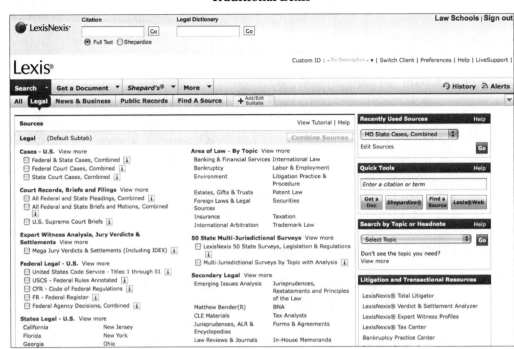

on each document. Payment for Lexis is usually determined by a flat rate or by
each search.

ii. *Lexis Advance*

Lexis Advance is Lexis's new platform, designed to transform the way
legal research is conducted and to provide organizational tools for the legal
researcher. The homepage features a "workspace carousel" that allows a user
to focus on quick tips, work folders, history, or support. In addition, a red
search box appears on the top of the screen so that users can type in a search
without first selecting a specific database. The word search need not be a specific type of search; instead, the user enters a Google-type search and Lexis's
search technology intuitively picks up the search and decides whether to use
natural language or Boolean searching for the most effective results. On Lexis
Advance, an "or" is presumed between words, whereas Google presumes an
"and." Thus, Lexis Advance returns a broader scope of results. Tab filters allow
a user to filter the search by content types, jurisdiction, or practice area if
desired. Once results are displayed, the user can further narrow the results by
other filters such as date, timeline, or headnote number. In addition, the "legal
issue trail feature" can lead the user to similar concepts in other documents.
The user can also Shepardize each document found.

Lexis Advance

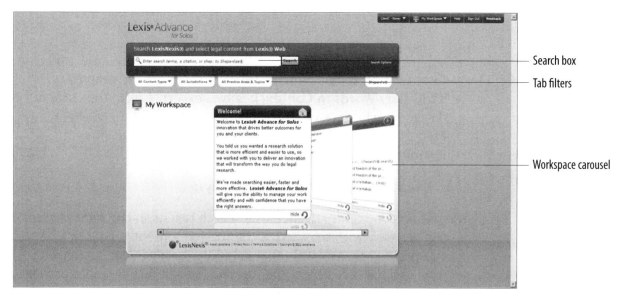

Search box

Tab filters

Workspace carousel

Lexis Advance

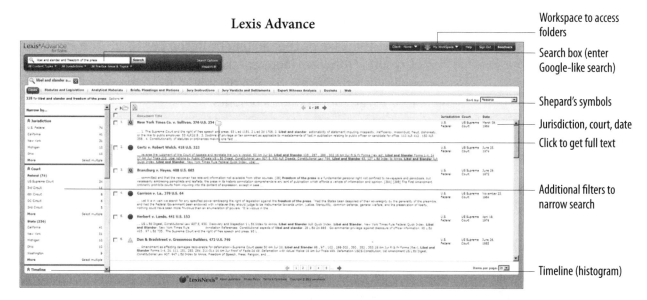

Workspace to access folders

Search box (enter Google-like search)

Shepard's symbols

Jurisdiction, court, date

Click to get full text

Additional filters to narrow search

Timeline (histogram)

In addition, Lexis Advance provides note-taking and organizational tools for the legal researcher. First, a user can highlight and take notes on research found. Second, the researcher can save full documents and searches, as well as highlighted material and notes to specific folders created and organized by the user directly in Lexis. Payment for Lexis Advance is usually determined by a monthly flat rate subscription price.

Viewing Documents in Lexis: There are different ways to display your search results.

Traditional Lexis offers the following displays:

- **Cite:** Lists all the documents retrieved through the search.
- **KWIC (Key Words in Context):** Shows excerpts from the current document where search terms appear.
- **Full:** Displays the full text of the document.
- **Custom:** Permits selection of certain segments.

Lexis Advance offers the following displays:

- **Result screen:** Lexis Advance lists search results in the right pane of the browser, with tabs across the top for content type. Click on the tabs to see results within that category. Narrow your search with filters on the left side of the screen. You can filter by date or view the historical activity related to your search with the histogram in the left column.
- **Full Text:** By clicking on the name in the result screen, you will retrieve the full text of the document in the center of the screen. Tabs of results from previous searches are located across the top of the panel, with the latest results displayed in a new window, allowing you to toggle between documents.

c. Search Strategies

As in book research, it is important to develop a strategy before logging on to Westlaw or Lexis, and those strategies differ on each of their platforms. Unlike traditional web surfing, surfing for legal research can be a costly time waster. Getting to know your way around the legal databases and other online legal sources will help save time. Both services are constantly updated so it makes sense for you to familiarize yourself with the most recent versions of each by accessing the relevant tutorials.

- For Westlaw and WestlawNext Tutorials, consults West's eLearning Center.[2]
- For Lexis Tutorials, see LexisNexis online.[3]
- For Lexis Advance tutorials, click on the support folder within the carousel on the homepage.

Use the tips below to help plan your online time.

a. **Narrowing the Database:** It is often efficient to narrow your database. For example, if you want only cases from Missouri state court, use the

---

2. For the West Learning Center, see http://www.westelearning.com/rc2/login.asp.

3. For Lexis tutorials, see http://www.lexisnexis.com/lawschool/content/aspx?articleid=436 &topicd=30.

Missouri State Cases database. Databases can be narrowed by topic, jurisdiction, and practice area. For example, suppose you want to research tax amnesty. There is a specific tax-related Law Reviews database on Westlaw. If you simply used the All Law Reviews database to search for "amnesty," you would find a lot of irrelevant articles.

b. **Brainstorm Search Terms:** When crafting your search, think of narrow search terms that would be found in a useful document. This process is like looking in an index in the library. Start with the general topic and write down some of the key legal terms. Then try to narrow the topic into subtopics with key words for each subtopic. Try to include synonyms in your list. If you do not know enough about a topic to make a list of search terms, you may need to go back to the library and look up your topic in a secondary source. (For more on using secondary sources, see page 65 in chapter 2.)

Once you have the correct database and relevant search terms, your objective is to find a manageable number of documents that discuss the topic that interests you. In WestlawNext and Lexis Advance, you can just type in your search terms. However, for traditional Lexis and Westlaw, you will need to create a specific Boolean or natural language search.

Natural language searching provides documents that include the language you specify most often. Natural language searching is useful when your search terms are broad; it is similar to surfing on the Web. It often leads to more search terms, which can then be used in terms and connectors searching.

Terms and connectors searching provides all of the documents in the database that meet the specifications of the search. Terms are the words the computer searches for, and connectors are the symbols that show the relationships between the terms. Terms and connectors work together to link search terms using the Boolean language. For example, you can specify that one term be in the same sentence as another. You can limit by date. You can search only within specified fields, such as title or author for an article, or judge or party name for a case.

Some basic terms and connectors:

- And
- Or
- /p = within same paragraph
- /s = within same sentence
- /3 = within that number of words (you can specify any number)
- ! = different forms of same word (e.g., host! will search for host, hostess, hosts, hosted)
- * = to substitute for a single letter (e.g., wom*n will search for woman and women)

c. **Segment and field searches or filters:** All the platforms provide a way to narrow the results of a search. Each document is divided or narrowed into different sections, such as title, author, date, judge, etc. Lexis refers to these sections as segments and Westlaw refers to them as fields. Lexis Advance calls them filters and WestlawNext labels them as "narrow"—both appear in those new platforms on the left side of the results screen. You can use these filters to narrow your search and focus on just that one part of the document.

d. Use Online Databases to Update the Law

It is always necessary to update the law, that is, to determine whether a source you would like to cite represents current law. Lexis and Lexis Advance use the Shepard's system for their updating databases, and they have purchased the Shepard's trademark. Westlaw and WestlawNext use a similar system called KeyCite, which uses multicolored flags to indicate whether a source has been overruled, amended, or has some negative history. For specifics on updating, see page 156.

2.   Evaluate the Credibility of Internet Sources

A source found on Lexis or Westlaw is reliable because it is a primary source or editor-reviewed secondary source. However, other websites can be less reliable. It is important to determine whether a source is credible before citing to it. Look to see who has published the site; .gov or .edu sites are usually much more reliable than .coms.

3.   Free Internet Sources—Save Time and Money

Lexis and Westlaw are free to most law students. This is an excellent time to learn how to navigate these sites effectively. However, use this time to practice cost-effective research as well by becoming familiar with the databases and platforms available within Lexis and Westlaw.

In addition, before logging on to Lexis or Westlaw, consider whether there are any free sources that you can use instead. Often, an Internet site is the easiest way to find information, and many of them are referenced throughout this book. The next two pages gather those sites in one place.

a. Cases

Finding cases online is still probably best on Lexis and Westlaw. However, more and more courts are posting opinions on their Web sites and providing access to their dockets. Google scholar is also now posting cases online. For more about finding Supreme Court cases, see chapter 2, page 32. Some courts are beginning to post cases on their web sites. To look in particular jurisdictions, try the websites in the tables provided in chapter 2 (see pages 36 and 57).

b. *Statutes, Legislative Information, and Administrative Law*

Finding statutes online is easier than finding cases. Most codes are now available online. To look in particular jurisdictions, try the websites in the table provided in chapter 2 (see page 56). For legislative history of federal statutes, the government website, THOMAS, provides in-depth information. Table 3.1, below, provides a number of easily accessible government resources.

Table 3.1. Online Resources for U.S. Statutes and Legislative and Other Government Material

U.S. Government Resources	
United States Code	http://www.gpoaccess.gov/uscode/index.html
U.S. House of Representatives	http://www.house.gov/
U.S. Senate	http://www.senate.gov/
Administrative Law, Administrative Agencies, and Executive Materials	
Code of Federal Regulations (C.F.R.)	http://www.gpoaccess.gov/cfr/index.html
Proposed Regulations	http://www.regulations.gov
Federal Register	http://www.gpoaccess.gov/fr/index.html
Index of Federal Agencies	http://www.washlaw.edu/doclaw/executive5m.html
A-Z Index of U.S. Government Departments and Agencies	http://www.usa.gov/Agencies/Federal/All_Agencies/index.shtml
U.S. Government Printing Office Access	http://www.gpo.gov/
Environmental Protection Agency	http://www.epa.gov/
Federal Trade Commission	http://www.ftc.gov/
The White House	http://www.whitehouse.gov/
Legislative History	
Library of Congress	http://www.thomas.gov/
Other Government Material	
U.S. Constitution (through archives)	http://www.archives.gov/exhibits/charters/constitution.html
U.S. Constitution (through Findlaw)	http://www.findlaw.com/casecode/constitution/
Bill of Rights	http://www.archives.gov/exhibits/charters/bill_of_rights.html
Declaration of Independence	http://www.archives.gov/exhibits/charters/declaration.html

c. *Law School Sites*

Many law schools also compile legal materials. These are extremely useful because these Web sites are usually developed by law librarians—the experts at legal research.

Table 3.2. Law School Resources for Online Research

Cornell Law School	http://www.lawschool.cornell.edu/
Georgetown Law Library	http://www.ll.georgetown.edu/
Washburn University School of Law	http://www.washlaw.edu/

d. *Search Engines*

Using traditional search engines and legal search engines can also yield results. However, consider using sites such as Google for fact investigations and broad legal issues instead of for specific law in a particular jurisdiction.

Table 3.3. Useful Search Engines for Legal Research

American Bar Association	http://www.abanet.org/
Bloomberg Law (fee based)	https://www.bloomberglaw.com/
Findlaw	http://www.findlaw.com/
Google	http://www.google.com/
Google Scholar	http://scholar.google.com/
LawCrawler	http://lawcrawler.findlaw.com/
Law Guru	http://www.lawguru.com/
LLRX	http://www.llrx.com/
Loislaw (fee based)	http://www.loislaw.com/
Martindale-Hubbel	http://www.martindale.com/
VersusLaw (fee based)	http://www.versuslaw.com/

IV.   STRATEGIES FOR PARTICULAR SOURCES

The following section provides various strategies for finding particular sources. Try to learn all the strategies and then determine which strategy is most efficient and effective for you.

A.   *Finding Constitutions and Statutes*

Constitutions are usually found in the first volume of the federal code (U.S.C.) or state code. Each set of volumes for the code has an index; therefore, you may access parts of the Constitution using the code's index. The U.S.C.A. and U.S.C.S., as well as state annotated codes, provide annotations to cases and other sources that interpret particular parts of the Constitution. In addition, you can search the full text of the Constitution online.[4] For more information on constitutions and statutes, see page 27 in chapter 2.

As noted above, statutes are usually easier to find in the books than online. To find them using book sources, you need to find the particular set of volumes for your statute's code. Each state has its own statutory code. The federal code is found in the following resources:

1. United States Code (U.S.C.), the official version printed by the government
2. United States Code Annotated (U.S.C.A.)
3. United States Code Service (U.S.C.S.).

Each statutory code has its own index, usually located at the end of the set. State statutes are arranged in a similar fashion. There are a number of ways to search statutes:

1. By number
2. By name
3. By subject

1. **By number:**
   a. **Books:** If you have a specific cite to a statute, e.g., 12 U.S.C. § 323, you would go to the volume that contains title 12 and find section 323 in numerical order.
   b. **Online:**
      i. *Westlaw:* Type the citation under Find.
      ii. *WestlawNext:* Type the citation into the main search box.
      iii. *Lexis:* Type the citation under Get A Document.
      iv. *Lexis Advance:* Type the citation into the main search box.
2. **By name:**
   a. **Books:** Some codes have popular names (such as the Civil Rights Act). The U.S.C., U.S.C.A., U.S.C.S, and many state codes have

---

4. http://www.findlaw.com/casecode/constitution.

alphabetically arranged popular names tables, usually located at the end of the set. Here, you can look up the statute's name to retrieve its citation.

b. **Online:** Westlaw and Lexis both have popular names table links.

   i. *Westlaw:* Look in the directory under USCA-POP.

   ii. *WestlawNext:* Click on Tools & Resources on the right side of the screen.

   iii. *Lexis:* Under Find a Source, type "popular names."

3. **By subject:**

a. **Books:** If you do not know the citation or the name of the statute, but have only a general idea of the subject matter, you will need to brainstorm descriptive words to search the index to the code, usually located at the end of each volume set. For example, to find a particular New York statute on retaliatory action by an employer using descriptive words, you would do the following:

   i. Look through New York's Code index (see page 132) for key words that would relate to the relevant law. Here, you need to think like a legal editor (see page 117). A term such as "Labor and Employment" might be useful. For example, under "Labor and Employment," you will find "Retaliatory action" and a reference to Labor § 740 (see page 133).

   ii. Next, find the Labor volume of the New York Code (which is arranged alphabetically) (see pages 132-135). Within that volume, find Labor § 740. This will lead you to the relevant statute (see page 133).

   iii. If you are using an annotated code, you will also find other sources that reference that particular provision. These annotations are important in your research since they provide legislative histories, cases, and other sources that analyze your statute. You should look up these other sources to thoroughly analyze the statute (see page 129).

   iv. For all above book methods, be sure to check the pocket parts or supplements in the books to determine if the statutes have been recently updated, amended, or discussed.

   v. Be sure to update your statute to make sure it is still good law. (For more on updating, see page 156.)

b. **Online:** Although searching for statutes is usually easier in the books, there are times when online searching is more efficient. For example, if asked to find similar laws in multiple jurisdictions, online searching is easier. Both Lexis and Westlaw have the full text of the U.S. Code, all the state codes, and a single database of all 50 states.

   i. *Westlaw:* To search the U.S. Code, go to "Directory—U.S. Federal Materials—Statutes—United States Code Annotated" (see page 29). Click on the search box and use descriptive word searching. To search the N.Y. Code (see page 133), go to "Directory—U.S. State Materials—Statutes—Statutes Annotated—Individual States—N.Y." (or other options such as "All States"). Click on the search box and use descriptive word searching. See what words lead you to Labor § 740.

ii. *WestlawNext:* To search the U.S. Code, enter "U.S. Code" in the main text box and click Search. You can also click the All Content tab under the Browse section, then click Statutes and Court Rules. Click United States Code Annotated (U.S.C.A.) to view the table of contents of the USCA. A third way to access the U.S. Code is to click the Federal Materials tab, then click United States Code Annotated (USCA). To search the N.Y. Code, enter "N.Y. Code" in the main text box and click Search. You can also click the State Materials tab and select a state from the list; then click the link to that state's statutes under Statutes and Court Rules. To search using the table of contents, scroll down the alphabetized list of the code and click on "Labor Law;" then click on "Article 20-C-Retaliatory Action by Employers."

iii. *Lexis:* To search the U.S. Code (see page 29), go to "Federal Legal—U.S.—United States Code Service 1-50." Here, you can either browse the table of contents or create a search using descriptive words. To search the N.Y. Code (see page 133), go to "State Legal—N.Y." See what words lead you to Labor § 740. To search using the table of contents, scroll down the alphabetized list of code until you reach "Labor Law." Check the box to the left of "Labor Law" and type "Section 740" in the Search box.

iv. *Lexis Advance:* To search the U.S. Code, enter "U.S. Code" in the main text box and click Search. You can also click the All Content Types tab; select Statutes & Legislation; then click on United States Code Annotated (U.S.C.A.). A third way to access the U.S. Code is to click the All Jurisdictions tab, then select U.S. Federal. To search the N.Y. Code, enter "N.Y. Code" in the main text box and click Search. You can also click the All Jurisdictions tab, then select "New York."

For more on Finding Statutes on Westlaw and Lexis, see http://www.ll.georgetown.edu/tutorials/lexiswestlaw/index.cfm.

New York Code Index

Topic heading ──────

LABOR AND EMPLOYMENT—Cont'd
Restrooms and toilets—Cont'd
  Stations—Cont'd
    Employees, **LAB 381**
  Street, surface and electric railroads, **LAB 378**
  Telecommunications, **LAB 378, 381**
  Tenant factory building, duties of owners and occupiers, **LAB 316**
  Terminals, **LAB 378**
    Employees, **LAB 381**
  Tunnels, **LAB 404**
  Video tapes, **LAB 203–c**
Retail mercantile establishment, questioning of persons detained, defense of employee, **GEN B 218**

Specific topic ──────

Retaliatory actions,
  Arbitration, dismissal or other disciplinary action, **CIV S 75–b**
  Attorneys fees, court costs, **LAB 740**
  Blood and transfusion services, work hours, **LAB 202–j**
  Collectively negotiated agreement, arbitration, **CIV S 75–b**
  Commence action in suit of competent jurisdiction, **CIV S 75–b**
  Compensation for lost wages, **LAB 740**
  Complaints of violations, **LAB 215**
  Defenses, **LAB 740**
  Definitions, **LAB 740**
    Public employer, **CIV S 75–b**
  Disclosure,
    Disciplinary action, **CIV S 75–b**
    Substantial and specific damages to public health or safety, **LAB 740**

Subtopic and key number ──────

Employer, definitions, **LAB 740**
    Public employer, **CIV S 75–b**
  Existing rights shall not be diminished, **LAB 740**
  Good faith effort of appointing authority, provide with information, **CIV S 75–b**
  Governmental body, definitions, public employer, **CIV S 75–b**
  Health care fraud, definitions, **LAB 740**
  Improper governmental action, definitions,
    Dismissal or discipline by public authority because of disclosure, prohibition, **CIV S 75–b**
    Public employers, **CIV S 75–b**
  Injunction, **LAB 740**
  Jurisdiction, **LAB 740**
  Law, rule or regulation, definitions, **LAB 740**
  Medical and surgical care and assistance, officers and employees, **LAB 741**
    Actions and proceedings, **LAB 740**
  Military forces, spouses, leaves of absence, **LAB 202–i**
  Personnel action, definitions, public employer, **CIV S 75–b**
  Prohibitions, retaliatory action against, **LAB 740**
  Public body, definitions, **LAB 740**
  Public employer, definitions, **CIV S 75–b**
  Reasonable costs, disbursements, attorney fees, **LAB 740**
  Reinstatement, **LAB 740**

LABOR AND EMPLOYMENT—Cont'd
Retaliatory actions—Cont'd
  Retaliatory personnel action, definitions, **LAB 740**
  Rights of personnel action not impaired, **CIV S 75–b**
  School officers and employees, **EDUC 3028–d**
  Supervisor, definitions, **LAB 740**
  Testifies before public body, **LAB 740**
  Violation, civil action may be instituted, **LAB 740**
  Waiver of rights and remedies, **LAB 740**
Retirement and Pensions, generally, this index
Review. Appeal and review, generally, ante
Sabbath, generally, this index
Safety, **LAB 200**
  Areas of construction, excavation and demolition work, **LAB 241**
  Devices, cleaning exterior building surfaces, protection of persons engaged in, **LAB 202**
  Employees, duty to protect, **LAB 200**
  Glazing materials, liability, **GEN B 389–p**
  High voltage lines, prevention of accidents, **LAB 202–h**
  Occupational Health and Safety, generally, this index
  Standards and procedures applicable, persons handling energized high voltage lines, **LAB 207–a**
Scaffolds, generally, this index
School buildings and sites, cost of labor index, monthly establishment, **LAB 21**
Schools and school districts,
  As excluding day student, **LAB 511**
  Certificates and certification, generally, ante
  Child of school age, **EDUC 3216**
  Definitions, camps and camping, **LAB 511**
  Obtaining vocational experience in participation in school to employment program not deemed to be employee, **EDUC 4606**
  Visiting lecturers, **EDUC 3006**
Sealed records, conviction for noncriminal offense, discrimination, **EXEC 296**
Seats, female employees, **LAB 203–b**
Second hand watches, offenses, **GEN B 392**
Second offense of violation of labor law, punishment, **LAB 213**
Self employed persons,
  Employees, definitions, Workers Compensation Law, **WORK C 2**
  Group or blanket accident and health insurance, demonstration programs, **INS 1123**
  Retirement trusts,
    Savings and loan associations as trustee, **BANK 382–a**
    Savings banks as trustee, **BANK 237**
  Taxation, exemption, persons 65 years of age or over, **RPTL 467**
  Trusts and trustees,
    Conveyance, **EPTL 7–2.1**
    Perpetuities, **EPTL 9–1.7**
Seniority, restoration of, complaints of employer violations, employer who penalizes because of, **LAB 215**

New York Annotated Code

ARTICLE 20–C—RETALIATORY ACTION BY EMPLOYERS

Article number and name

Section

740. Retaliatory personnel action by employers; prohibition.
741. Prohibition; health care employer who penalizes employees because of complaints of employer violations.

Section of this statute

Cross References

Retaliatory action by public employers, see Civil Service Law § 75–b.

Other references

Law Review and Journal Commentaries

1985 survey of New York law: labor relations law. Christensen. 37 Syracuse L.Rev. 579 (1986).

United States Code Annotated

Prohibited personnel practices, see 5 USCA § 2302.

§ 740. Retaliatory personnel action by employers; prohibition

1. Definitions. For purposes of this section, unless the context specifically indicates otherwise:

Definition section

(a) "Employee" means an individual who performs services for and under the control and direction of an employer for wages or other remuneration.

(b) "Employer" means any person, firm, partnership, institution, corporation, or association that employs one or more employees.

(c) "Law, rule or regulation" includes any duly enacted statute or ordinance or any rule or regulation promulgated pursuant to any federal, state or local statute or ordinance.

(d) "Public body" includes the following:

(i) the United States Congress, any state legislature, or any popularly-elected local governmental body, or any member or employee thereof;

(ii) any federal, state, or local judiciary, or any member or employee thereof, or any grand or petit jury;

(iii) any federal, state, or local regulatory, administrative, or public agency or authority, or instrumentality thereof; or

(iv) any federal, state, or local law enforcement agency, prosecutorial office, or police or peace officer.

(e) "Retaliatory personnel action" means the discharge, suspension or demotion of an employee, or other adverse employment

108

New York Annotated Code *(continued)*

RETALIATORY ACTION BY EMPLOYERS   **§ 740**
Art. 20–C

Historical and Statutory Notes

History of the statute

L.2002, c. 24 legislation
  Subd. 4, par. (d). L.2002, c. 24, § 2, added par. (d).

L.1984, c. 660 legislation
  Section 3 of L.1984, c. 660, provided:

"This act [adding this article and Civil Service Law § 75–b] shall take effect September first, nineteen hundred eighty-four and shall apply to any retaliatory personnel action taken on or after such date."

Legislative Histories

Legislative history

L.1984, c. 660: For memorandum of the State Executive Department, see McKinney's 1984 Session Laws of New York, p. 3389.

Cross References

Cross references

Costs, disbursements and attorney's fees, see CPLR § 8303.

Injunctions, see generally, CPLR § 6301 et seq.

Prevention of unfair labor practices, see Labor Law § 706.

Unfair labor practices, see Labor Law § 704.

West's McKinney's Forms

Other references

Complaint in action by employee against employer for illegal suspension and termination in violation of "whistle blower" statute, defamation, reinstatement and damages, see SCL, LABOR § 740, Form 1.

American Law Reports

Liability for retaliation against at-will employee for public complaints or efforts relating to health or safety. 75 ALR4th 13.

Law Review and Journal Commentaries

1998–99 survey of New York law, business associations. William D. Harrington, 50 Syracuse L.Rev. 341 (2000).

Employees face danger under New York's whistleblower statute. Jack A. Raisner, 216 N.Y.L.J. 1 (Oct. 17, 1996).

Is there Whistleblower protection for private employees in New York? Sandra J. Mulllings, 69 N.Y.St.B.J. 36 (Feb. 1997).

1990 Survey of New York law: Employment law. Minda. 42 Syracuse L.Rev. 491 (1991).

1996–97 survey of New York law, business associations. William D. Harrington, 48 Syracuse L.Rev. 387 (1998).

Truth-in-hiring claims and the at-will rule. Sandra J. Mullings, 1997 Colum.Bus.L.Rev. 105.

Utilization of the disclaimer as an effective means to define the employment relationship. Michael A. Chagares. 17 Hofstra L.Rev. 365 (1989).

Wieder v. Skala: A chink in the armor of the at-will doctrine or a lance for law firm associates? Sandra J. Mullings, 45 Syracuse L.Rev. 963 (1995).

New York Annotated Code *(continued)*

§ 740 RETALIATORY ACTION BY EMPLOYERS
Art. 20–C
Library References

American Digest System
Master and Servant ☜30(6.5).

Encyclopedias
53 NY Jur 2d, Employment Relations § 478.
C.J.S. Employer–Employee Relationship §§ 68, 70, 72, 79.

Texts and Treatises
5 Carmody-Wait 2d (Rev ed), Complaints Answer Counterclaim with Forms § 29:454.
5A Carmody-Wait 2d (Rev ed), Complaints in Particular Actions Answer Counterclaim with Forms § 31:14.
Employment in New York §§ 13:203.2, 13:405.1, 13:405.5.

West's New York Practice Series
Pleadings, state and city law complaint forms, see Taber, 13 New York Practice Series § 3.10.

Westlaw Research
In a caselaw database, run TO(255) or 255k[add key number] to retrieve cases related to Master and Servant.

United States Supreme Court

Civil rights conspiracy statute, prohibition on intimidation or retaliation against witnesses in federal court proceedings, at-will employees, injury to person or property, see Haddle v. Garrison, 1998, 119 S.Ct. 489.

> Reference to U.S. S.Ct. case

Notes of Decisions

Attorney fees 18
Commencement of action 6
Construction with federal laws 2
Construction with other laws 1
Damages 17
Danger to public health or safety 13
Defenses 16
Disclosures 9
Discovery 10
Employees 4
Employers 5
Limitations 7
Pleadings 8
Proof of actual violation 14
Purpose 3
Remedies 15
Res judicata or collateral estoppel 19
Retaliatory personnel action 11
Violations of law 12

> Summaries of cases that interpret or reference this statute

1. Construction with other laws

Employee's claim that private employer violated New York whistleblower law, New York Election Law, and New York and Federal Constitutions when employer fired executive employee for accepting elective position as mayor would be dismissed; whistleblower law was limited to matters involving health or safety hazards, Election Law provided no private right of action, and Constitutions contained no pertinent self-executing provisions. Ribando v. Silhouette Optical, Ltd., 1994, 871 F.Supp. 675.

New Jersey law applied to employee's wrongful discharge action because New Jersey had greatest interest in protecting employees in its state and thus had the paramount interest in the lawsuit; employee's former office was in New Jersey, employee was informed of his discharge in New Jersey, and employee would not be able to maintain his claim under either New York or Ohio law, the other two states with contacts to the litigation. Littman v. Firestone Tire & Rubber Co., 1989, 709 F.Supp. 461.

2. Construction with federal laws

Although former employee was barred from pursuing qui tam claims under False Claims Act due to failure to comply with Act's filing and service require-

B. *Finding Cases*

This section explores research strategies for finding cases. For more information on finding cases, refer to chapter 2. Information on finding federal cases appears on page 38; state case information is on page 59.

1. Getting Started

There are a number of factors to consider before you start researching case law.

1. It is important to focus on a particular **jurisdiction** whenever possible. Are you looking for cases in a particular federal circuit or a particular state? Knowing your jurisdiction will substantially limit the number of cases found.
2. It is important to understand the **hierarchy** of cases and the difference between mandatory and persuasive law (see page 108). (Bluebook Table 1 and ALWD Appendix 1 list the hierarchy for each jurisdiction.) A case from a higher court in your jurisdiction carries greater weight than a lower case in your jurisdiction or one from a different jurisdiction.
3. The **date** of a decision is important. Recent decisions carry great weight. Older decisions that have been followed over long periods of time also carry great weight. On the other hand, be wary of relatively old decisions that are rarely followed or new decisions that contradict overwhelming precedent.
4. Cases do get overturned. Therefore, it is imperative that you update your cases before you rely on them as good law. (For more on updating cases, see page 156.)

Cases are found in a number of different locations.

a. *Federal Case Law*

Supreme Court Cases
United States Reports (U.S.)
Supreme Court Reporter (S. Ct.)
United States Supreme Court Reports, Lawyers' Edition (L. Ed., L. Ed. 2d)

Circuit Court Cases
Federal Reporter (F., F.2d, F.3d)
Federal Cases (F. Cas.)

District Court Cases
Federal Supplement (F. Supp., F. Supp. 2d)
Federal Cases (F. Cas.)
Federal Rules Decisions (F.R.D.)

b.   State Case Law

Regional Reporters
1. **Atlantic Reporter** (A., A.2d): Connecticut, Delaware, District of Columbia, Maine, Maryland, New Hampshire, New Jersey, Pennsylvania, Rhode Island, Vermont
2. **North Eastern Reporter** (N.E., N.E.2d): Illinois, Indiana, Massachusetts, New York, Ohio
3. **North Western Reporter** (N.W., N.W.2d): Iowa, Michigan, Minnesota, Nebraska, North Dakota, South Dakota, Wisconsin
4. **Pacific Reporter** (P., P.2d): Alaska, Arizona, California, Colorado, Hawaii, Idaho, Kansas, Montana, Nevada, New Mexico, Oklahoma, Oregon, Utah, Washington, Wyoming
5. **South Eastern Reporter** (S.E., S.E.2d): Georgia, North Carolina, South Carolina, Virginia, West Virginia
6. **South Western Reporter** (S.W., S.W.2d): Arkansas, Kentucky, Missouri, Tennessee, Texas
7. **Southern Reporter** (So., So. 2d): Alabama, Florida, Louisiana, Mississippi

State Reporters

Most states also have their own reporters. See Bluebook Table 1 (T1) or ALWD Appendix 1.

2.   Strategies

There are a number of strategies for finding federal and state case law. The strategy that works best for you will be determined not only by your preferences, but also by the resources available and the starting point for your research. Your starting point might be any one of the following:

1. **Case citation**
2. **Case name**
3. **Subject matter**

a.   Case Citation

To find a case using its citation is relatively easy.

a. **Books:** First, you need to find the correct set of reporters (see locations of law above). Second, find the correct volume and page number in the reporter to locate the case itself. For example, 212 S. Ct. 301 is found in the 212th volume of the Supreme Court Reporter on page 301.
b. **Online:**
   i. *Westlaw:* Go to Find and type the citation.
   ii. *WestlawNext:* Type the citation in the main text box and click Search.

iii. *Lexis:* Go to Get A Document and type the citation.
iv. Lexis Advance: Type the citation in the main text box and click Search.

b.   Case Name

a. **Books:** To find a case using its name, go to the end of the reporter set where you will find a digest. Each digest has a volume labeled "Table of Case Names" that lists cases and their citations in alphabetical order by first party name. Some tables also have a "Defendant-Plaintiff Table" that lists cases and their citations in alphabetical order by defendants' names. Remember to check pocket parts.

b. **Online:**
   i. *Westlaw:* Go to Find and search by case name.
   ii. *WestlawNext:* Type the name(s) of one or more of the parties in the main text box and click Search.
   iii. *Lexis:* Go to Get A Document and choose Get By Party Name.
   iv. Lexis Advance: Type the name(s) of one or more of the parties in the main text box and click Search.

c.   Subject Matter: Using the Books

Finding cases by subject matter is a bit trickier and requires multiple strategies, depending on the circumstances. A thorough researcher uses a variety of strategies and multiple sources. Below, you will read strategies for finding cases by subject matter using both book sources and online sources. But before you begin, you need to be familiar with the key number system developed by West. (For more on the key number system, see page 113.)

a. **One Good Case:** Often times, a supervising attorney will provide you with one case on point. This case can be a gold mine if used properly. First, it will cite to other helpful sources, such as cases, statutes, rules, or secondary sources. Second, if it is a case published by West, it will provide key numbers, the system designed by West to arrange the law into topics. If, for example, your supervisor gives you the case, Remba v. Federation Employment & Guidance Serv., 545 N.Y.S.2d 140 (App. Div. 1989), as a starting point or for background information, you could use this case to
   i. find other law on the point; or
   ii. find key numbers that would lead you back to the digests for more cases on the point.

b. **Statutes Annotated:** If there is a statute on point, often cases have cited to the statute. To find these cases, you should research annotated statutes in your particular jurisdiction. For example, if you were looking for cases on retaliatory action taken by employers in New York State, you could:

    i. Search the index for the N.Y. State Annotated Code (McKinney's Consolidated Laws of N.Y.) (see page 132) or Consolidated Laws Service. Under "Labor and Employment" you will find "retaliatory action" and a definition section for "employers" and a citation to Labor § 740 (see prior page 132).

    ii. Within the volumes of the annotated code (see page 133), you would find Labor § 740. Here, you find (1) the statute, (2) its history and research references, and (3) case notes, which provide annotations to cases that have cited the statute (see prior pages 134-135).

    iii. Remember to check the pocket parts of the book to look for more recent annotations.

  c. **Case Digests:** A case digest arranges case annotations by topics. To use the digest to find New York cases on unfair labor practices, you could do one of the following:

    i. Search the index to the New York digests, usually located at the end of the digest volumes. Under "Labor Relations—Discrimination," you will find "Unfair labor practices, employer practices" and a reference to "Labor Key Number 368" (see page 140). This reference is a key number under the West key number system. It refers to the topic "Labor," and its subsection 368 (see page 141).

    ii. Next, you find the Labor digest and look up number 368 (see page 141). Here, you will find a number of case annotations on your topic. Read through them to find relevant cases and note the citations. Be sure to read the key numbers surrounding your key number because they are often on the same topic or related ones.

    iii. In addition, each digest topic will have a table of contents at the beginning of the section. So, if you turn to the beginning of the "Labor" section of the digest, you will find a table of contents for the key numbers of that topic. These will help you further refine your research.

    iv. Remember to check the pocket part of the digest for recent annotations.

    v. Once you have noted relevant cases, you can go to the reporters and look up those cases.

    vi. Be sure to update (see page 156) all the cases you cite to make sure they are good law.

Index to New York Digest

LABOR

References are to Digest Topics and Key Numbers

LABOR RELATIONS—Cont'd

CONTRACTS. See heading **LABOR ORGANIZATIONS**, CONTRACTS.

COSTS,
Actions against employers or employers' organizations,
Generally, **Labor** ☞ 776
Breach of contract, **Labor** ☞ 778
Injunction,
Permanent injunction, **Labor** ☞ 997
Proceedings for violation or enforcement, **Labor** ☞ 1020

CREATION of relationship,
Unfair labor practices, **Labor** ☞ 369

CRIMES. See subheading OFFENSES under this heading.

DAMAGES,
Actions against employers or employers' organizations,
Generally, **Labor** ☞ 776
Breach of contract, **Labor** ☞ 778
Permanent injunction, **Labor** ☞ 996

DECLARATORY judgment. See heading **DECLARATORY JUDGMENT**, generally.

DEMOTION,
Unfair labor practices,
Generally, **Labor** ☞ 387
Evidence,
Sufficiency and weight, **Labor** ☞ 573

DEPARTMENTS. See heading **LABOR RELATIONS BOARDS**, generally.

DISCHARGE,
Black lists. See subheading BLACK list under this heading.
Labor disputes. See heading **LABOR DISPUTES AND CONCERTED ACTIVITIES**, DISCHARGE.
Labor relations board proceedings. See heading **LABOR RELATIONS BOARDS**, DISCHARGE.
Service letters. See subheading SERVICE letters under this heading.
Unfair labor practices. See subheading UNFAIR labor practices under this heading.

DISCRIMINATION,
Closed or union shop agreements. See heading **CLOSED OR UNION SHOPS**, CONTRACTS.
Contracts,
Validity or propriety of terms, **Labor** ☞ 250

LABOR RELATIONS—Cont'd
DISCRIMINATION—Cont'd

Exercise of rights, discrimination due to, **Labor** ☞ 26.5
Unfair labor practices,
Employer practices,
Generally, **Labor** ☞ 368
Evidence, sufficiency and weight of evidence, **Labor** ☞ 558
Labor organizations or employees,
Acts causing employer discrimination, **Labor** ☞ 395.2
Seniority, **Labor** ☞ 391

DISMISSAL,
Injunction proceedings,
Dismissal before hearing, **Labor** ☞ 947

DISOBEDIENCE, discharge for,
Unfair labor practice, **Labor** ☞ 373

DISPUTES and concerted activities. See heading **LABOR DISPUTES AND CONCERTED ACTIVITIES**, generally.

DOMINATION of union by employer. See heading **LABOR ORGANIZATIONS**, EMPLOYER-DOMINATED or favored organizations.

DUE process,
Generally, **Const Law** ☞ 275(5)
Injunction, **Const Law** ☞ 275(4)
Railway labor, **Const Law** ☞ 275(6)

DUES. See heading **LABOR ORGANIZATIONS**, DUES.

EDUCATION,
Inclusion of educational employment within acts, **Labor** ☞ 51, 52

EMPLOYEES included within labor acts,
Generally, **Labor** ☞ 63
Agricultural laborers, **Labor** ☞ 65
Guards, **Labor** ☞ 66
Managers, **Labor** ☞ 67
Strikers, **Labor** ☞ 68
Supervisors, **Labor** ☞ 67
Terminated employees, **Labor** ☞ 68

EMPLOYER-DOMINATED organizations. See heading **LABOR ORGANIZATIONS**, EMPLOYER-DOMINATED or favored organizations.

EMPLOYERS' liability. See heading **EMPLOYERS' LIABILITY**, generally.

EMPLOYERS' organizations. See heading **EMPLOYERS' ORGANIZATIONS**, generally.

Key number

New York Digest

☞367 LABOR RELATIONS

30 N Y D 4th—846

For later cases, see same Topic and Key Number in Pocket Part

Act (NLRA) are not limited to those explicitly set forth in section of NLRA setting forth rights of employees as protected against private interference. National Labor Relations Act, § 7, as amended, 29 U.S.C.A. § 157.

    Delta-Sonic Carwash Systems, Inc. v. Building Trades Council, AFL-CIO, 640 N.Y.S.2d 368, 168 Misc.2d 672.

Machinists preemption doctrine concerns activity that was neither arguably protected against employer interference by sections of National Labor Relations Act (NLRA) setting forth employees' rights and prohibiting interference with, restraint, or coercion of employees in exercise of such rights, nor arguably prohibited as unfair labor practice by NLRA. National Labor Relations Act, §§ 7, 8(a)(1), (b), as amended, 29 U.S.C.A. §§ 157, 158(a)(1), (b).

    Delta-Sonic Carwash Systems, Inc. v. Building Trades Council, AFL-CIO, 640 N.Y.S.2d 368, 168 Misc.2d 672.

N.Y.Sup. 1985. College violated provisions of the Taylor Law [McKinney's Civil Service Law § 209–a, subd. 1], which prohibit an employer from interfering with an employee organization, when it retaliated against employee by reducing her working hours in response to that employee's complaints, on behalf of other employees, about terms and conditions of employment, notwithstanding that at time complaints were voiced employees were not seeking to form an employee organization or to be represented by one. McKinney's Civil Service Law § 202.

    Rosen v. Public Employment Relations Bd., 490 N.Y.S.2d 705, 128 Misc.2d 628, reversed 510 N.Y.S.2d 180, 125 A.D.2d 657, appeal granted 519 N.Y.S.2d 1029, 70 N.Y.2d 605, 513 N.E.2d 1309, affirmed 530 N.Y.S.2d 534, 72 N.Y.2d 42, 526 N.E.2d 25.

☞368. Discrimination in general.

Library references

    C.J.S. Labor Relations §§ 349, 350, 351.

C.A.2 (N.Y.) 1980. It is not sufficient merely to demonstrate discriminatory conduct and resulting encouragement or discouragement of union membership in order to establish unfair labor practice in violation of section of National Labor Relations Act, but, rather, added element of unlawful intent is also required. National Labor Relations Act, § 8(a)(3) as amended 29 U.S.C.A. § 158(a)(3).

    B. G. Costich & Sons, Inc. v. N. L. R. B., 613 F.2d 450.

Where employers made contributions to union pension fund on behalf of casual employees who were union members but not on behalf of nonunion casual employees but where bargaining agreement also contained union security clause requiring that all employees in bargaining unit join union after 30 days of employment and, pursuant to terms of pension plan, participating employees became eligible for normal pension benefits after the age of 60 if they accumulated at least 15 years of credited service, employers' conduct did not constitute unfair labor practice under National Labor Relations Act section prohibiting employer from encouraging or discouraging union membership. National Labor Relations Act, § 8(a)(3) as amended 29 U.S.C.A. § 158(a)(3).

    B. G. Costich & Sons, Inc. v. N. L. R. B., 613 F.2d 450.

N.D.N.Y. 1998. Violation of National Labor Relations Act (NLRA) section making it an unfair labor practice to discriminate in regard to hire or tenure of employment or any term or condition of employment to encourage or discourage membership in any labor organization is comprised of two elements: (1) discrimination, (2) resulting in a discouragement of union membership. National Labor Relations Act, § 8(a)(3), as amended, 29 U.S.C.A. § 158(a)(3).

    Dunbar v. Colony Liquor and Wine Distributors, L.L.C., 15 F.Supp.2d 223.

For purpose of the National Labor Relations Act (NLRA) section making it an unfair labor practice to discriminate in regard to hire or tenure of employment or any term or condition of employment to encourage or discourage membership in any labor organization, issue if whether there has been discouragement of union membership normally turns on whether the discriminatory conduct was motivated by an antiunion purpose, though proof of anti-union motivation may be unnecessary where the discriminatory conduct is inherently destructive of employee interests. National Labor Relations Act, § 8(a)(3), as amended, 29 U.S.C.A. § 158(a)(3).

    Dunbar v. Colony Liquor and Wine Distributors, L.L.C., 15 F.Supp.2d 223.

N.D.N.Y. 1998. Unfair labor practice occurs where employer enforces facially neutral policies in discriminatory manner against pro-union employees. National Labor Relations Act, § 8, as amended, 29 U.S.C.A. § 158.

    Dunbar v. Landis Plastics, Inc., 996 F.Supp. 174, remanded 152 F.3d 917.

S.D.N.Y. 1992. NLRA prohibits discrimination based on nonmembership in union. National Labor Relations Act, § 8(b)(2), 29 U.S.C.A. § 158(b)(2).

    U.S. v. International Broth. of Teamsters, Chauffeurs, Warehousemen and Helpers of America, AFL-CIO, 808 F.Supp. 276, order clarified 828 F.Supp. 258.

N.Y.A.D. 2 Dept. 1986. It was not irrational for Public Employment Relations Board to

Annotations in right margin: Key number · Court and date · Summary of case · Citation

For legislative history of cited statutes, see McKinney's Consolidated Laws of New York

d. Subject Matter: Online

Many of the same strategies for finding cases using books also work with online sources.

a. **One Good Case:** If you have a good case on Westlaw or Lexis, you can link to other cases cited within that case. Also, you can click on the key numbers on Westlaw, located in the beginning of the case before the judicial opinion, to link directly to the key number system to find other cases listed under that key number. This method is very effective for finding cases that West editors have categorized under that key number. Be careful to take notes as you research using this strategy as you can become looped within a key number as you find case after case; keep track of the cases you have read.

b. **Key Numbers:** In Westlaw, you can access the key number system directly by clicking on the More menu, located at the top of the Westlaw screen. Click on the arrow to scroll down to Key Numbers and Digests; here the key numbers will be listed in alphabetical order so that you can find a relevant key number for your cases. (See above.) In WestlawNext, click the Tools tab in the Browse section; then click West Key Number System. You can also click "Cases that cite this headnote" to find a list of citing references that discuss the legal issues summarized in the headnote.

c. **Searches:** Within a specified directory, you can use key terms to search for cases. The tricks here are to search in a specific directory and to create your search terms and connectors carefully. (For more on formulating a search strategy, see page 124.)

C. Finding Legislative History

Legislative history refers to the documents that are made as Congress transforms a bill into a law. These documents can be important in determining congressional intent of a particular law. However, there is an ongoing debate about the relevance of legislative history as political motivations come into play when laws are made. Legislative documents are only persuasive authority.

Legislative history is made by the federal Congress as well as by state legislatures. Below are strategies for finding federal legislative history. Finding state legislative history is not as easy. Often, you must visit the state itself to access the legislative history from that particular branch of government. Some states have placed their legislative histories on their state homepages, but not all states have done so.

If you are asked to find the legislative history of a particular federal law, there are many sources available.

First, you should have a basic understanding as to how laws are made. (See page 144 for an overview.)

Compiled legislative histories—histories that someone else has taken the time to put together, often on major legislation—are excellent sources if they include your bill. Check the Sources of Compiled Legislative Histories, a book that lists all available published legislative histories by public law number. If your law does not have an already compiled legislative history, you will need to create your own. You can use book sources and online services. The following is a list of book sources and online sources, as well as a list of most useful legislative history documents.

1. Book Sources

There are three print sources that are most useful for finding federal legislative history: USCCAN, CIS, and the Congressional Record.

a. USCCAN

This source (see pages 145-146) publishes selected committee reports for legislation enacted since 1949. Committee reports are often the most useful documents for determining congressional intent. Although USCCAN provides the full text for only select reports, it provides the bill number, date of enactment, and list of all committee reports for every law passed. It also provides the full text of public laws, presidential messages, and cites to the Congressional Record. To use USCCAN, you should find the public law number and year your bill was enacted into law. (You can find this information through the U.S. Code.) Then, you can find the full text of your public law through the relevant volume of federal legislative histories. This source references page numbers for the selected legislative history documents, which can be found in the legislative history volumes of USCCAN. Thus, you will need to use two different volumes of USCCAN to find your bill and legislative history.

b. CIS (Congressional Information Service)

Instead of providing full text of selected documents like USCCAN, CIS (see pages 147-148) provides comprehensive legislative histories. However, finding each source is not as easy as in USCCAN. You can search CIS by subject, name, committee, public law number, bill number, or document number, but you are usually provided only an abstract of that piece of history. To find the full text, you will need to go to another source, such as CIS microfiche or Congressional Universe on the Web.

c. Congressional Record

This hefty set of books contains the text of the congressional debates of both houses. The daily edition is published every day Congress is in session. Page numbers begin with S for Senate, H for House, E for Extension of Remarks, and D for Daily Digest. A permanent bound edition is also published, but the volumes are published very slowly and have a different numbering system from the daily edition. Therefore, you will need to use the Index or Daily Digest to find relevant pages to the bound edition.

How a Bill Becomes Law

1. **IDEA:** A bill starts as an idea, either from a constituent, a congressperson, or the president.

2. **INTRODUCTION:** A bill is then introduced to one house (or both). Usually, it is introduced by a congressperson. At this point, the bill receives a number: an H.R. number if it is introduced in the House of Representatives, or an S. number if it is introduced in the Senate.

3. **COMMITTEE:** The bill is then sent to a relevant committee(s) or subcommittee(s), which might hold hearings. During markup sessions, the bill becomes amended or it might be "tabled" and die. If the committee decides to present the bill to the house, it will write a report.

4. **CHAMBER FLOOR:** The bill is then sent to the floor of that chamber, where it is debated, amended, and voted on. If passed, the bill becomes an act of that house, called an engrossed bill, and is sent to the other chamber. If the bill is not passed, it dies.

5. **OTHER CHAMBER:** An engrossed bill then goes to the other chamber of Congress, either the House or Senate, and goes through the same process, where it might die in committee or on the chamber floor. If it is passed by the second chamber in the same form as the first chamber, it goes to the president. If it is passed in a different form, it can go back to the first chamber to see if that chamber concurs in its new form. Otherwise, it goes to a conference committee.

6. **CONFERENCE COMMITTEE:** The conference committee is staffed from members of both the House and the Senate. This committee discusses only those parts of the bill on which the chambers disagree. It may file a report. If it cannot agree, the bill can die or continue to be debated in conference committee. If the conference committee does agree to certain amendments, the bill goes back to a vote in each chamber. If the bill or certain amendments do not pass, the bill or the amendments die or may return to the conference committee. If it does pass, the bill goes to the president.

7. **PRESIDENT:** If the president signs the bill, it becomes a law. If the president vetoes the bill, Congress can override the veto by two-thirds vote by both chambers. If the president takes no action for ten days and Congress is in session, the bill becomes law. If the president takes no action for ten days and Congress is not in session, the bill is considered to have been vetoed by "pocket veto."

IDEA

INTRODUCTION
Receives Bill #H.R. 601 S. 601

COMMITTEE
Subcommittee
- Hearings
- Bill might die in committee
- Bill might be amended in markup session

Full Committee
- Amend
- Committee report

CHAMBER FLOOR
- Debate
- Vote
- Bill might die
- If passed, bill moves on as an engrossed bill

OTHER CHAMBER
Goes through same process:
- Hearings
- Committee report
- Debate
- Vote

CONFERENCE COMMITTEE
Conference report

PRESIDENT
- Sign = Law
- Veto = Dies or goes back to both chambers of Congress for two-thirds vote
- No action = Law (if Congress is in session)
- No action = Pocket veto (if Congress is not in session)

USCCAN Index

INDEX
References are to Pages

JOHN W. MCCARTER
Regent, Smithsonian Institution, joint resolution, **122 Stat. 655**

JOHN W. WARNER RAPIDS
Rappahannock River, designation,
122 Stat. 4772

JOINT RESOLUTIONS
Army, reserves, centennial, **122 Stat. 701**
Burma, exports and imports, **122 Stat. 2649**
Fish and game, Arctic Ocean, management,
122 Stat. 1569
Great Lakes and tributary waters, interstate
compacts, **122 Stat. 3739**
John W. McCarter, regent, Smithsonian Institution, **122 Stat. 655**
Native American Heritage Day,
122 Stat. 4035, Leg. Hist. 1667
One hundred eleventh Congress, first session,
time, **122 Stat. 4846**
Presidential electors, counting, time,
122 Stat. 4846
Secretary of State, compensation and salaries,
122 Stat. 5036
Very Energetic Radiation Imaging Telescope
Array System (VERITAS) project,
122 Stat. 3738, Leg. Hist. 1500

JUANITA MILLENDER-MCDONALD HIGHWAY
Generally, **122 Stat. 5005, Leg. Hist. 2193**

**JUDGE RICHARD B. ALLSBROOK POST
OFFICE**
Generally, **122 Stat. 732**

JUDGES
Appointments,
Administrative patent judges,
122 Stat. 3014
Administrative trademark judges,
122 Stat. 3014
District of Columbia, superior court,
122 Stat. 696, Leg. Hist. 40

**JUDICIAL ADMINISTRATION AND TECHNICAL
AMENDMENTS ACT OF 2008**
Generally, **122 Stat. 4291**

JULIA M. CARSON POST OFFICE BUILDING
Generally, **122 Stat. 738**

JUSTICE DEPARTMENT
Succession, executive order, **B108**

JUVENILE DELINQUENTS AND DEPENDENTS
Reentry, demonstration projects or programs,
122 Stat. 657, Leg. Hist. 24

K.T. SAFETY ACT OF 2007
Generally, **122 Stat. 639**

**KEEPING THE INTERNET DEVOID OF SEXUAL
PREDATORS ACT OF 2008**
Generally, **122 Stat. 4224**

**KENDALL FREDERICK CITIZENSHIP
ASSISTANCE ACT**
Generally, **122 Stat. 2319**

**KENNETH JAMES GRAY POST OFFICE
BUILDING**
Generally, **122 Stat. 3009**

**KENNETH PETER ZEBROWSKI POST OFFICE
BUILDING**
Generally, **122 Stat. 4210**

KIDS ACT OF 2008
Generally, **122 Stat. 4224**

KOOCHICHING COUNTY
Minnesota, deeds and conveyances,
122 Stat. 4837, Leg. Hist. 2137

KOREA
Associations. **Korean War Veterans Associa-
tion, Incorporated**, generally, this index
Exports and imports,
North Korea,
Blocking property, executive order, **B42**
Termination, proclamation, **A107**
Weapons, **122 Stat. 4842**
North Korea,
Exports and imports,
Blocking property, executive order, **B42**
Termination, proclamation, **A107**
Human rights, **122 Stat. 3939,
Leg. Hist. 1607**

**KOREAN WAR VETERANS ASSOCIATION,
INCORPORATED**
Charters, **122 Stat. 2419**

LABOR AND EMPLOYMENT
Defense department, **122 Stat. 3, S3**
Federal labor-management relations program,
exemptions, executive order, **B106**
Genetic testing, discrimination, ——————— Reference to statute
122 Stat. 881, Leg. Hist. 66, S14
Human trafficking, **122 Stat. 5044**
National disability employment Awareness
Month, 2008, proclamation, **A152**
National Employer Support of the Guard and
Reserve Week, 2008, proclamation, **A130**
Unemployment compensation,
122 Stat. 5014
Veterans, **122 Stat. 4145, Leg. Hist. 1722**

USCCAN

PUBLIC LAW 110–233 [H.R. 493]; May 21, 2008

GENETIC INFORMATION NONDISCRIMINATION ACT OF 2008

For Legislative History of Act, see Report for P.L. 110–233 in U.S.C.C. & A.N.
Legislative History Section

For Signing Statement of Act, see Statement for P.L. 110–233 in U.S.C.C. & A.N.
Signing Statement Section

An Act To prohibit discrimination on the basis of genetic information with respect to health insurance and employment.

Be it enacted by the Senate and House of Representatives of the United States of America in Congress assembled,

SECTION 1.   SHORT TITLE; TABLE OF CONTENTS.

Genetic
Information
Non-
discrimination
Act of 2008.
42 USC 2000ff
note.

(a) SHORT TITLE.—This Act may be cited as the "Genetic Information Nondiscrimination Act of 2008".

(b) TABLE OF CONTENTS.—The table of contents of this Act is as follows:

SEC. 2.   FINDINGS.

42 USC 2000ff
note.

Congress makes the following findings:

(1) Deciphering the sequence of the human genome and other advances in genetics open major new opportunities for medical progress. New knowledge about the genetic basis of illness will allow for earlier detection of illnesses, often before symptoms have begun. Genetic testing can allow individuals to take steps to reduce the likelihood that they will contract

122 STAT. 881

CIS Index

General aviation

"Navy Aviation: V-22 Cost and Capability To Meet Requirements Are Yet To Be Determined", H701-38

"Navy Aviation: V-22 Development—Schedule Extended, Performance Reduced, and Costs Increased", H701-38

"Report to the Secretary of the Army: Improved Planning Needed by the Corps of Engineers To Resolve Environmental, Technical, and Financial Issues on the Lake Pontchartrain Hurricane Protection Project", S321-12.1

see also Government Accountability Office

General aviation

DOT programs, FY2009 approp, H181-23

FAA programs extension and revision, H751-2

Flight service station program transition to contractor ops, status review, H751-21

General Dynamics Corp.

Navy nuclear submarine program review, H201-75.2

Shipbuilding industrial base status and future needs, H181-40.2

Shipbuilding industrial base status and Navy shipbuilding costs reduction and process modernization efforts, H201-49.2

General Dynamics Land Systems

DOD mine resistant ambush protected vehicles program status, H201-72.2

General Electric Co.

Clean coal power technological innovations and global climate change mitigation review, H361-11.2

Freight rail infrastructure capacity expansion investment incentives estab, H751-38.3

Renewable energy resources technologies dev, intl efforts review, S361-22.2

General Mills, Inc.

Employment discrimination based on sexual orientation, prohibition, H341-26.2

General Motors Corp.

Automobile fuel efficiency technology dev and use, transportation sector efforts, H181-67.1

Energy storage R&D programs review, H701-34.2

Social science research role in energy policy, H701-9.1

General Physics Corp.

Terrorism involving radiological weapons, US preparedness, S481-19.2

General Services Administration

Administrator alleged misconduct, issues review, H601-12, H601-13

Approp, FY2009, H181-35, H181-45.4, H183-6, S183-8

Budget proposal, FY2009, H180-2

Capitol visitor center construction and mgmt ops, status review, H751-3.3

DC Old Post Office Bldg redev measures estab, H753-21, S323-32, PL110-359

Energy conservation by Fed Govt, H751-17, H751-17.2

Energy efficiency in transportation systems and Fed bldgs, promotion measures estab, H753-40

Fed agency property repair and maintenance backlogs review, GAO rpt, J942-602

Fed bldgs capital improvement programs, FY2008 budget proposal, H751-31

Fed bldgs energy efficiency measures, GSA implementation, GAO letter, J942-582

Fed contractor oversight, GSA database and Fed agency debarment procedures requirement estab, H603-5

Fed property mgmt, GSA program estab, H603-10

Fed property mgmt reform issues, S481-34.2

Fed Protective Service ops and funding challenges, GAO rpt, J942-293

Fed services procurement process, issues and improvement measures, S481-38.1

Global climate change mitigation, Fed, State, and private sector energy efficiency promotion and greenhouse gas emissions reduction efforts, H751-38.1

Hurricane Katrina disaster response, Fed recovery efforts, S321-3.1

Hurricane Katrina disaster response, Fed small business contracting review, H721-22.1, H721-41.1

Natl Park Service payments to Pacific Gen, Inc subcontractors, authority estab, S311-12, S313-37

Navy boat barrier procurement review, H201-78

Ohio and Minn public lands conveyance, H753-34, PL110-427

Small business access to Fed contracting opportunities, H721-78.1

Small businesses owned by minorities and women, Fed contracting opportunities, S721-7.1

Sr Exec Service and Postal Career Exec Service gender, racial, and ethnic diversity, Fed agencies promotion efforts, H601-22.2

State, local, and tribal purchase of GSA security and safety equipment, authorization, S483-6

State, local, and tribal purchase of security and safety equipment, use of GSA Fed supply schedules authority estab, PL110-248

"State of the Portfolio FY2007", S481-34.2

Telecommunications system contract transition efforts, GAO rpt, J942-353

Telecommunications use for work at home or remote locations by Fed agencies, promotion, H601-44.1, S481-31.1

Telecommunications use for work at home or remote locations by Fed agencies, promotion measures estab, H603-11

see also Office of the Inspector General, GSA

see also Public Buildings Service

Generalized System of Preferences

Trade preferences for developing countries, GAO rpt, J942-150

Trade preferences programs, extension and revision, PL110-436

Generations Invigorating Volunteering and Education Act

House consideration of legislation, committee rule, H683-13

Index of Subjects and Names

Generic Drug Enforcement Act

Prescription drugs generic versions approval activities, FDA debarment authority for criminal activity, staff rpt, H362-3

Generic Pharmaceutical Association

Pharmaceutical sales on Internet and prescription drug imports into US, safety and regulatory issues, S521-48.3

Genetic Alliance

Genetic info basis for insurance or employment discrimination, prohibition, H361-2.2

Genetic diseases

see Hereditary diseases

Genetic engineering

see Biotechnology

Genetic Information Nondiscrimination Act ⟶ Reference to statute

Genetic info basis for insurance or employment discrimination, prohibition, H361-2, PL110-233

Genetic info basis for insurance or employment discrimination, prohibition, Democratic policy rpt, S962-170

Genetic info basis for insurance or employment discrimination, prohibition, Republican policy paper, S962-176

House consideration of legislation, committee rule, H683-27

Medicare and Medicaid programs, revision, PL110-275

Genetic Information Nondiscrimination in Employment Coalition

Genetic info basis for insurance or employment discrimination, prohibition, H361-2.2

Genetic Nondiscrimination Study Commission

Estab, PL110-233

Genetics

CDC programs, FY2009 approp, H181-75

Genes and genomic invention, patent issues, H521-16

Genetic and human modification technologies, intl regulations review, H381-83

Genetic info basis for insurance or employment discrimination, prohibition, H361-2, PL110-233

Genetic info basis for insurance or employment discrimination, prohibition, Democratic policy rpt, S962-170

Genetic info basis for insurance or employment discrimination, prohibition, Republican policy paper, S962-176

"Human Gene Transfer Research: An Overview of the State of the Science and U.S. Efforts To Address Related Ethical and Social Issues", H381-83

Natl Human Genome Research Inst programs, FY2008 approp, S181-22.7

Natl Human Genome Research Inst programs, FY2009 approp, H181-74

Natl Inst of Gen Medical Sciences programs, FY2009 approp, H181-74

NSF programs, FY2009 approp, H181-7

Plant genetic resources intl access system treaty, Pres message, S385-9

Stem cell research status and Fed funding issues, S431-2 *(S181-1)*

see also Biotechnology

CIS

| **Public Law 110-233** | **122 Stat. 881** |

Genetic Information Nondiscrimination Act of 2008

May 21, 2008

Public Law

1.1   Public Law 110-233, approved May 21, 2008. (H.R. 493)

(CIS08:PL110-233   42 p.)

"To prohibit discrimination on the basis of genetic information with respect to health insurance and employment."

Amends the Internal Revenue Code of 1986, the Employee Retirement Income Security Act of 1974, the Public Health Service Act, and other acts to prohibit employment and health insurance discrimination against groups or individuals based on genetic information.

Authorizes health insurance issuers to request, but not require, genetic information for research purposes, and provides that issuers that obtain genetic information incidental to requesting, requiring or purchasing other information are not in violation of the prohibition on collection of genetic information.

Directs HHS to revise Health Insurance Portability and Accountability Act of 1996 regulations to treat genetic information as health information.

Provides for establishment of the Genetic Nondiscrimination Study Commission six years after enactment of this act.

Amends the Fair Labor Standards Act of 1938 to increase civil penalties for child labor violations.

P.L. 110-233 Reports

106th Congress

2.1   S. Rpt. 106-82 on S. 326, "Patients' Bill of Rights Act of 1999," June 17, 1999.

(CIS99:S433-1   173 p.)
(Y1.1/5:106-82.)

Recommends passage, with an amendment in the nature of a substitute, of S. 326, the Patients' Bill of Rights Act of 1999, to improve the quality of health care services provided to patients.

Title II, the Genetic Information Nondiscrimination in Health Insurance Act of 1999, to amend ERISA, the Public Health Service Act, and the Internal Revenue Act of 1986 to prohibit group health plans and health insurance issuers offering group or individual coverage from denying or canceling coverage, or changing premiums or conditions for coverage on the basis of predictive genetic information or a request for genetic services.

 Includes additional, minority, and supplemental views (p. 96-109).
 S. 326 is similar to S. 300 and related to four other bills.

108th Congress

2.2   S. Rpt. 108-122 on S. 1053, "Genetic Information Nondiscrimination Act of 2003," July 31, 2003.

(CIS03:S433-12   61 p.)
(Y1.1/5:108-122.)

Recommends passage, with an amendment in the nature of a substitute, of S. 1053, the Genetic Information Nondiscrimination Act of 2003, to amend the Internal Revenue Code of 1986 and three other acts to prohibit employment and health insurance discrimination against individuals on the basis of predictive genetic information or information regarding requests for or receipt of genetic services.
 S. 1053 is related to S. 16 and numerous other bills.

110th Congress

2.3   H. Rpt. 110-28, pt. 1 on H.R. 493, "Genetic Information Nondiscrimination Act of 2007," Mar. 5, 2007.

(CIS07:H343-3   73 p.)
(Y1.1/8:110-28/PT.1.)

Recommends passage, with an amendment in the nature of a substitute, of H.R. 493, the Genetic Information Nondiscrimination Act of 2007, to amend the Employee Retirement Income Security Act of 1974, the Public Health Service Act, and the Social Security Act to prohibit health insurance discrimination against individuals on the basis of information regarding requests for or receipt of genetic services or for requirement of genetic testing, and to prohibit employment discrimination on the basis of genetic information.
 Includes minority views (p. 65-73).
 H.R. 493 is related to 109th Congress H.R. 1227 and five other bills.

2.4   H. Rpt. 110-28, pt. 2 on H.R. 493, "Genetic Information Nondiscrimination Act of 2007," Mar. 26, 2007.

(CIS07:H783-3   51 p.)
(Y1.1/8:110-28/PT.2.)

Recommends passage, with an amendment in the nature of a substitute, of H.R. 493, the Genetic Information Nondiscrimination Act of 2007, to amend the Internal Revenue Code of 1986 and three other acts to prohibit health insurance discrimination against individuals on the basis of information regarding requests for or receipt of genetic services or for requirement of genetic testing, and to prohibit employment discrimination on the basis of genetic information.
 Includes additional views (p. 51).

2.5   H. Rpt. 110-28, pt. 3 on H.R. 493, "Genetic Information Nondiscrimination Act of 2007," Mar. 29, 2007.

(CIS07:H363-7   73 p.)
(Y1.1/8:110-28/PT.3.)

Recommends passage, with an amendment in the nature of a substitute, of H.R. 493, the Genetic Information Nondiscrimination Act of 2007, to amend the Employee Retirement Income Security Act of 1974, the Public Health Service Act, and the Social Security Act to prohibit health insurance discrimination against individuals on the basis of information regarding requests for or receipt of genetic services or for requirement of genetic testing, and to prohibit employment discrimination on the basis of genetic information.
 Includes additional views (p. 64-73).
 H.R. 493 is related to 109th Congress S. 306.

---

2. Online Sources

The most useful online sources for legislative history are THOMAS (see below),[5] Lexis, and Westlaw.[6] The following are the most significant pieces of legislative history and how to find them online:

THOMAS

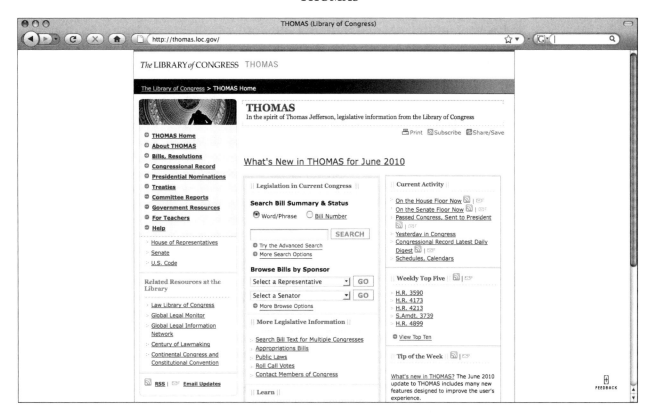

a. Bills

Bills are often amended during the legislative process; thus, comparing the different versions of a bill may help determine its intended meaning. The bill number is often the best way to trace legislative history. To find bills online, follow any of these links:

- *THOMAS:* Allows access to bills from 1989 to present.
- *Westlaw:*
  - For current Congress: Cong-BillTXT database
  - For previous Congresses starting in 1985: Cong-BillTxt104-Cong-BillTxt109 databases
- *WestlawNext:* Click on Proposed & Enacted Legislation under the All Content tab.

---

5. http://thomas.loc.gov.

6. For a tutorial on researching secondary sources on Lexis and Westlaw, see http://www.ll.georgetown.edu/tutorials/lexiswestlaw/index.cfm.

- *Lexis:*
  - For current Congress, Short Name—Legis; Bills
  - For previous Congresses starting in 1989, Short Name—Legis; BTX101-BTX109

b. *Hearings*

Subcommittee hearings (either House or Senate) provide the views of various groups, individuals, or organizations interested in the bill and thus are not as relevant to legislative intent. To find hearings online, follow any of these links:

- *Westlaw:* USTestimony database (January 1993 – date)
- *WestlawNext:* Click on Proposed & Enacted Legislation under the All Content tab; then click Capitol Watch under the Tools & Resources tab on the right side of the screen.
- *Lexis:* Short Name—Legis: Hearing (July 1993 – date)

c. *Committee Reports*

These reports may be created by the House, Senate, or Conference Committees and are the most important source of legislative history. They usually reprint the bill, explain its purpose, and provide reasons for the recommendation of the committee. To find committee reports online, follow any of these links:

- *THOMAS:* 1995 – date
- *Westlaw:* LH database (1990 to present comprehensive) (reprinted USCCAN reports from 1948-1989)
- *Lexis:* Short Name—Legis; CMTRPT (1990 to date)
- *WestlawNext:* Click on Proposed & Enacted Legislation under the All Content tab; then click Capitol Watch under the Tools & Resources tab on the right side of the screen.

d. *Congressional Debates*

Congressional debates are published in the Congressional Record and are the proceedings of the debates on the Senate and House floors. These are not as helpful for legislative history as they might show the intent of one congressperson but not necessarily the intent of the legislative body. To find the Congressional Record online, follow any of these links:

- *THOMAS:* For the daily edition
- *Westlaw:* LH database for the daily edition
- *WestlawNext:* Click on Proposed & Enacted Legislation under the All Content tab; then click Capitol Watch under the Tools & Resources tab on the right side of the screen.
- *Lexis:* Short Name—Legis; Record—for the daily edition.

D. *Finding Administrative Law*

Administrative law consists of rules, regulations, and decisions created by federal or state agencies. While this section focuses mainly on finding federal administrative law, parallel methods of research apply within each state. For more information on administrative law, see chapter 1, page 4.

1. Finding Regulations

There are many ways to research administrative law, depending on your starting point. If you are working with a particular statute and want to find regulations that implement that statute, you would start with the code provision itself. For finding regulations by topic, you usually will begin with the Code of Federal Regulations (C.F.R.)[7] rather than the Federal Register,[8] because the C.F.R. is a topical compilation of all the regulations and is updated each year. If you were looking for a recent regulation, the Federal Register would be the best place to start. A specific agency's website is also a good starting point.

Starting with a **code section** to find regulations that implement it:

a. Start with the annotated code, either U.S.C.A. or U.S.C.S., for federal law or your state's annotated code. In the annotations, you will find references to regulations and their citations. You can either use the books for these sources or log on to Lexis or Westlaw.

b. You can also use the C.F.R. table of authorities (see page 152),[9] which contains a numerical list of the regulations arising out of each U.S.C. section. This source is also available in book form (usually located next to the C.F.R.) and online for free at the C.F.R. website.[10]

c. Once you find your regulation cite, simply look it up in the official C.F.R., the C.F.R. online (see page 152), Lexis or Westlaw, or in the Federal Register.[11]

Starting with a topic to find regulations about the topic:

a. *Books:* You can start your topic search in the C.F.R. index, which is not very effective because it contains only broad terms. A better source is the CIS Index to the Code of Federal Regulations, which is more comprehensive than the C.F.R. index; it is usually located near the C.F.R. itself.

b. *Free Online Site:* You can directly search the C.F.R. online.[12]

c. **Lexis and Westlaw** both allow you to access and search the Federal Register (issues since 1980) and the C.F.R.

---

7. http://www.gpoaccess.gov/cfr/index.html.
8. http://www.gpoaccess.gov/fr/index.html.
9. http://www.gpoaccess.gov/cfr/index.html.
10. http://www.gpoaccess.gov/cfr/index.html.
11. http://www.gpoaccess.gov/fr/index.html.
12. http://www.gpoaccess.gov/cfr/index.html.

C.F.R. Table of Authorities

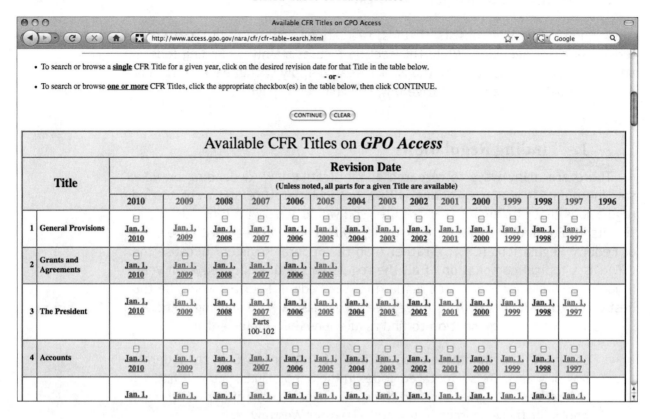

C.F.R. Online

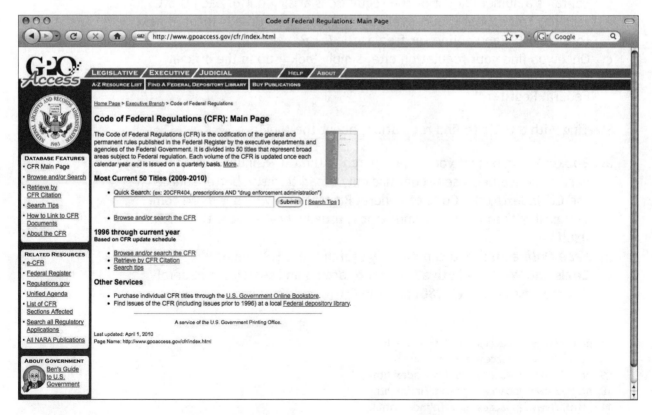

- Westlaw: Federal Register: FR database
    - Current C.F.R.: C.F.R. database
    - Previous year C.F.R.: e.g., CFR03
    - Combined files in six major areas: FSEC-CODREG
  - WestlawNext: Federal Register: FR database
    - Current C.F.R.: C.F.R. database
    - Previous year C.F.R.
  - Lexis: Federal Register: Genfed Library; Fedreg file
    - Current C.F.R.: C.F.R. file
    - Previous year C.F.R.: e.g., CFR03
    - Both Federal Register and C.F.R: ALL REG

Starting with the **Federal Register** if you are looking for a recent rule, regulation, proposed rule, or commentary:

a. *Federal Register Index:* This index is issued monthly and is arranged alphabetically by agency. Each issue is cumulative, so the December issue covers the year.
b. *CIS Federal Register Index:* This index is issued weekly with cumulative volumes issued periodically and permanent bound volumes issued twice a year. It indexes each issue of the Federal Register either by subject, name, C.F.R. section numbers affected, federal docket numbers, and Calendar of Effective Dates and Comment Deadlines.
c. *Federal Register[13] online:* Log on and follow the instructions for searching on this free website.

Starting with a **particular agency** and looking for regulations and administrative decisions created by that agency:

a. Click on Administrative Agencies.[14] Here, you can locate particular agencies websites.
b. Each agency has its own method of searching for regulations and administrative decisions. Therefore, it is important to spend some time browsing your particular agency's website.

2. Updating Regulations

Because the C.F.R. is reissued in quarterly installments each year, there are always volumes of the C.F.R. that are not up to date. It is important to update administrative law because regulations can change often, and new rules may be proposed that affect your regulation.

Before you update a regulation to ensure that it is still being enforced, you need to know the date of the regulation. If you are using an online version, look for the "currency date," usually located near the top of the document. If you are using the book form of the C.F.R., check the date on the cover of the volume.

---

13. http://www.gpoaccess.gov/fr/index.html.
14. www.usa.gov/Agencies/Federal/All_Agencies/Index.html.

List of Sections Affected (L.S.A.)

26 **LSA—LIST OF CFR SECTIONS AFFECTED**

CHANGES APRIL 1, 2008 THROUGH JANUARY 30, 2009

TITLE 21 Chapter I—Con.

17.1 (c) through (g) redesignated as (e) through (i); new (c) and (d) added.................**66752**
17.2 Revised................................**66752**
56.102 (b)(12) amended; eff. 7–14–09....................................2368
56.106 Added; eff, 7–14–09.................2368
73.100 (d) revised; eff. 1–5–11.............216
73.2087 (c) revised; eff. 1–5–11...........216
101 Technical correction..................**66754**
Uniform compliance date **74349**
101.22 (k)(2) revised; eff. 1–5–11..........216
101.72 Revised; eff. 1–1–10..............**56486**
101.80 Regulation at 72 FR 52789 confirmed............................**30301**
101.81 (c)(2)(iii)(C) revised; (c)(2)(iii)(D) added................**23953**
Regulation at 73 FR 9947 confirmed **47829**
111.75 (c)(3) correctly revised.........**27727**
179.26 (b) table amended................**49603**
189.5 (a)(1) revised; (e) added; interim....................................**20793**
201.66 Regulation at 73 FR 403 confirmed............................**63897**
203.3 (q) revised....................**59500**
203.22 (h) and (i) added..............**59500**
205.3 (h) revised....................**59501**
208.20 Regulation at 73 FR 404 confirmed............................**63897**
209 Regulation at 73 FR 404 confirmed **63897**
210 Technical correction..............**63361**
210.2 (c) added....................**40462**
210.3 Regulation at 72 FR 68068 withdrawn..........................**18440**
(b)(6) revised....................**51931**
211 Technical correction..............**63361**
211.48 Regulation at 72 FR 68068 withdrawn..........................**18440**
211.67 Regulation at 72 FR 68068 withdrawn..........................**18440**
(a) revised......................**51931**
211.68 Regulation at 72 FR 68068 withdrawn..........................**18440**
(c) added........................**51932**
211.72 Regulation at 72 FR 68068 withdrawn..........................**18440**
Revised..........................**51932**
211.82 Regulation at 72 FR 68069 withdrawn..........................**18440**
(b) revised......................**51932**
211.84 Regulation at 72 FR 68069 withdrawn..........................**18440**
(c)(1), (d)(3) and (6) revised...........**51932**

211.94 Regulation at 72 FR 68069 withdrawn..........................**18440**
(c) revised......................**51932**
211.101 Regulation at 72 FR 68069 withdrawn..........................**18440**
(c) and (d) revised................**51932**
211.103 Regulation at 72 FR 68069 withdrawn..........................**18440**
Revised..........................**51932**
211.110 Regulation at 72 FR 68069 withdrawn..........................**18440**
(a) introductory text revised; (a)(6) added....................**51932**
211.113 Regulation at 72 FR 68069 withdrawn..........................**18440**
(b) revised......................**51932**
211.160 Regulation at 72 FR 68069 withdrawn..........................**18440**
(b)(1) revised....................**51932**
211.182 Regulation at 72 FR 68069 withdrawn..........................**18440**
Revised..........................**51933**
211.188 Regulation at 72 FR 68070 withdrawn..........................**18440**
(b)(11) revised....................**51933**
312.3 (b) amended..................**22815**
312.84 (c) amended.................**39607**
312.120 Revised....................**22815**
314.3 (b) amended.......**39607, 49609, 56491**
314.50 (d)(5)(vi)(b) amended.............**39608**
314.60 (b) and (c) redesignated as new (c) and (d); new (b) added; heading, (a), new (c)(1)(iii) and (iv) revised; new (c)(2) amended..................**39608**
314.65 Amended **39609**
314.70 (c)(6)(iii) introductory text and (A) revised **49609**
314.71 (c) amended................**39609**
314.81 (b)(2)(ii) redesignated as (b)(2)(ii)(a); (b)(2)(ii)(b) added **56491**
314.94 (a)(7)(i) revised; eff. 7–15–09 2861
314.96 (a)(2) revised; (a)(3) removed............................**39609**
(a)(1) amended; eff. 7–15–09...........2861
314.100 Revised **39609**
314.101 (f)(1)(ii) revised; (f)(2) amended..........................**39609**
314.102 (b) amended; (d) revised **39609**
314.103 (c)(1) amended **39609**
314.105 (b) amended................**39609**
314.107 (b)(3)(v) amended **39609**
314.110 Revised **39609**

The next thing you need to do is check to see if there have been any changes to your rule or regulation published in the Federal Register since the currency date you found above. If you are using an online version (C.F.R., Lexis, or West-law), simply search in the Federal Register for your particular C.F.R. citation or log onto List of Sections Affected (L.S.A.) (see previous page).[15] If you are using the books, you will need to find the book version of the L.S.A., usually located at the end of the C.F.R. set and in the last Federal Register issue of each month. Once you have found the correct date of the L.S.A., you will need to look at each subsequent L.S.A. to ensure that nothing has changed since your currency date. The L.S.A. does not bring a search completely up to date, however. For a thorough search, you must consult a similar list found in the last Federal Register issue of each month.

3.   Administrative Decisions

Regulations may have been challenged in court. First, the case would be litigated before an administrative judge. This administrative decision may be appealed to the federal courts. To research the judicial treatment of regulations, you should check in Shepard's C.F.R. Citations, which is found in book form as well as on Lexis. In addition, an agency's website often posts administrative judicial opinions.

E.   Using Looseleaf Services

- **What:** Looseleaf services are research sources arranged by topic and issued in looseleaf binders. The benefit to the binders is that information can be easily added, omitted, or exchanged as the law changes. Thus, the publication is in a constant process of revision and is very current. The advantage of the topical arrangement is that practicing lawyers can subscribe to a looseleaf service in a specialized practice area and closely follow the developments in that field.

    Looseleaf services vary in content and organization, depending on the publisher and the subject area. However, most of them contain up-to-date coverage and information regarding court decisions, statutes, administrative regulations, practice tips, forms, and developing legal trends. In addition, they contain user guides and various indexes and finding tools.

- **Why:** Most practitioners, especially those in the regulatory field, rely heavily on looseleaf services. Often times, a practitioner will rely on a looseleaf service as a total library for his practice since it contains the code, regulations, cases, and commentary in a particular area of law in an up-to-date, organized fashion. Looseleaf services are often expensive because their publishers spend enormous amounts of time bringing together primary sources from disparate places into one organized unit.

---

15. http://www.gpoaccess.gov/lsa/about.html.

- **Where and How:** Commerce Clearinghouse (CCH) and the Bureau of National Affairs (BNA) are two of the major looseleaf publishers. To use a looseleaf service, you should (1) be sure you have found the most useful looseleaf service, and (2) be sure to read the directions.

  1. **Finding your looseleaf service:** Looseleaf services are used mainly by practicing lawyers, and certain looseleafs have become the bibles of their fields. Therefore, it is always a good idea to check with a supervising attorney for the most relevant service; at times, you may see the set sitting on the attorney's shelf. As a student, you should check with your local librarian to find the looseleaf preferred in your field. Typical subjects for looseleaf reports are criminal law, tax, evidence, and bankruptcy. Another source is a book called Legal Looseleafs in Print. Every law library should subscribe either to the print or the online version.

  2. **Using your looseleaf service:** Read the directions. All looseleaf services have a section on how to use the service. You will save time by reading this section. It explains the information included in the set, the indexing tools, the finding aids, and the format of the service. The more in-depth a service, the more necessary it is that you read the "how to" section.

V. UPDATING THE LAW

Before you rely on any law by citing to it in a legal document, you must determine whether it is still good law through "updating." Updating is essential because the law is fluid: statutes are amended, cases are reversed, and laws are massaged through time. A fatal mistake is to rely on a case that is no longer good law. For a case illustrating the importance of updating the law, see Glassalum Eng'g Corp. vs. 392208 Ontario Ltd., 487 So.2d 87 (1986) where an attorney was chastised by the court for relying on a case that was no longer good law.

Historically, updating was performed through a set of books called Shepard's Citations, which was started in 1873 by a man named Frank Shepard. *Shepardizing* became the term lawyers used to refer to updating the law. If you went to law school ten years ago or more, you would have been taught to use the bulky, maroon volumes of Shepard's, which was a tedious and intimidating process. However, Shepard's is now available online through Lexis. In 1997, Westlaw introduced its own online citator, KeyCite.

Shepard's and KeyCite are now the main citator tools for lawyers. They are used for a number of purposes: (1) to update the law; (2) to indicate the law's frequency of citation and treatment by other sources; and (3) to find other sources that have referred to your law. When used to research law, Shepard's and KeyCite can prove very useful since they not only provide links to all sources that have cited your law, but they also break down those sources by headnote, date, jurisdiction, and depth of discussion.

Currently, most lawyers use the online version of the citators, either Key-Cite or Shepard's.

KeyCite: Westlaw

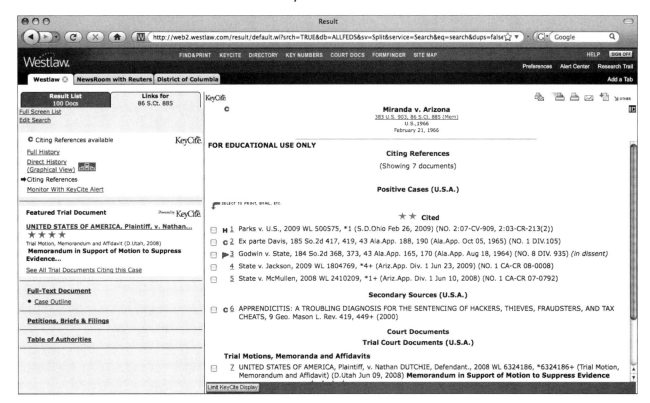

A. *KeyCite*

KeyCite was developed by West to compete with Shepard's. It is found only online on Westlaw, and it provides up-to-date information on cases, statutes, and administrative materials.

To access KeyCite in Westlaw, you can click on the KeyCite tab and enter a citation or simply click on the colored flag that appears next to the law you are reading. The colored flag system in KeyCite signals the type of treatment of your law. For example, if you are reading a case and you see a red flag next to that case, you should be wary of its precedential value as it might have been reversed or overturned.

Once you have accessed KeyCite, you will be given a full citation and history of your law. After the direct history, any negative history will be listed. Be sure to read the cases listed for negative treatment; at times, only part of the case might be overturned. By clicking on Citing References, you will be provided a list of sources that have cited your law and the symbols for the treatment by these sources. You may search these references through the popup menu at the bottom of the page by the following "segments":

- *Jurisdiction:* You can locate all sources in Hawaii, for example, that have cited your law.
- *Headnote:* You can search for sources related to specific headnotes in your law.
- *Date:* You can search by date.

KeyCite Flags and Symbols for Westlaw and WestlawNext

Westlaw	WestlawNext	Description of WestlawNext Interface, Feature, or Functionality
Checking Citations (continued)		
KeyCite status flags	KeyCite status flags and descriptions	KeyCite flags still warn you of negative treatment; new flag descriptions tell you why. The description displayed next to the KeyCite flag at the top of the document indicates the most negative treatment affecting a document (e.g., *Reversed by Hat v. Depositors Ins. Co. 9th Cir. (Cal.), July 30, 2009*).
▶	⚑	A red flag indicates a case is no longer good law for at least one point of law it contains or that a statute has been amended, repealed, superseded, held unconstitutional, or preempted.
▷	⚐	A yellow flag indicates a case has some negative history or that a statute has been renumbered, proposed legislation affecting it is available, or its validity has been called into doubt by a court.
H	No equivalent status flag	If a document has some history, the number of history documents is displayed on the History tab. Click the **History** tab to view the history of the document.
C	No equivalent status flag	If a document has citing references, the number of references is displayed on the Citing References tab. Click the **Citing References** tab to view all citing references.
Depth of treatment stars	Depth of treatment bar	The depth of treatment bar indicates the extent to which the citing case, administrative decision, or brief discusses the cited case . The bar has four sections to indicate the extent to which the cited case is discussed.
KeyCite quotation marks	KeyCite quotation marks ❞	Quotation marks in a KeyCite result indicate that the citing case, administrative decision, or brief directly quotes the cited case.
Direct History (Graphical View)	Appellate History diagram	Click the **History** tab. Direct appellate history for the case is displayed in a diagram. The cases included in the direct history and related references are listed in the left column.
Limit KeyCite History Display	History views	On the History tab, choose a view (e.g., **Negative Direct History**) from the drop-down list on the toolbar.
Citing References: Limit KeyCite Display	Citing References filters	On the Citing References tab, click a content type in the left column under *View* to limit the citing references by content type (e.g., *Cases* or *Secondary Sources*). Depending on the content type you have chosen, you can further narrow your citing references by selecting a filter under *Narrow* in the left column (e.g., *Jurisdiction, Date, Depth of Treatment, Headnote Topics, Treatment Status,* and *Reported Status* for cases).
		To search for specific terms within the citing references, type a Terms and Connectors query in the *Search within results* text box in the left column and click **Continue**. Then click **Apply Filters**.
Table of authorities	Under development	

- *Document type:* You can search, for example, for cases, administrative law, or secondary sources.
- *Depth of treatment:* Westlaw uses star symbols for depth of treatment, and WestlawNext uses a bar. The more stars or bars, the more treatment from that citing source. (See the KeyCite Flags and Symbols link above for more about star and bar symbols.)
- *Locate:* You can enter search terms to further narrow your search.

Furthermore, you can search by key number by clicking on the link at the bottom of the page. For more tips on using KeyCite, see the guide on the Westlaw website.[16]

B.   *Shepard's Online*

Using Shepard's on Lexis and Lexis Advance is also convenient. Shepard's provides up-to-date citations to statutes, cases, and administrative materials.

---

16. http://www2.westlaw.com/CustomerSupport/KnowledgeBase/Technical/WestlawCreditCard/WebHelp/Checking_a_Document_in_KeyCite.htm.

To access Shepard's on Lexis and Lexis Advance, you can click on the Shepard's link or click on the Shepard's signal for the treatment of the law you are reading. For example, if a case you are reading has a red stop sign, you should be wary of its precedential value. A tutorial on using Shepard's is available at the Georgetown Law Library website.[17]

Shepard's: Lexis

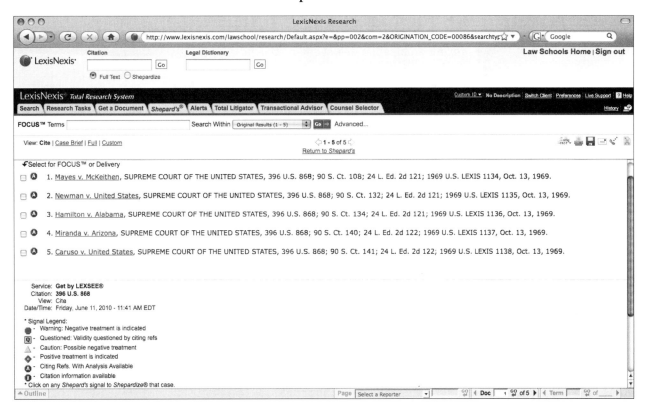

Once you have accessed Shepard's, you will be given the law's direct history and citations to later sources. Be sure to read the cases listed for negative treatment; at times, only part of the case might be overturned. These citations in Shepard's will include an editor's assessment of this source's treatment of the case. So, for example, if a source distinguishes or criticizes your law but does not reverse it, you will see a yellow triangle located next to that source. (See page 160 for **Shepard's Symbols**.) You may organize these sources by their treatment, their kind of law (e.g., statutes, secondary sources), and by headnote number.

_____

17. http://www.ll.georgetown.edu/tutorials/lexiswestlaw/index.cfm.

Shepard's Symbols

Warning: Negative treatment indicated
The red Shepard's signal indicates that citing references in the Shepard's Citations Service contain strong negative history or treatment of your case (for example, overruled or reversed by).

 Caution: Possible negative treatment indicated
The yellow Shepard's signal indicates that citing references in the Shepard's Citations Service contain history or treatment that may have a significant negative impact on your case (for example, limited or criticized by).

 Case has been questioned
The yellow Q symbol indicates a more specific form of negative treatment, that the case has been questioned by other cases.

 Positive treatment indicated
The green Shepard's signal indicates that citing references in the Shepard's Citations Service contain history or treatment that has a positive impact on your case (for example, affirmed or followed by).

 Cited and neutral analysis indicated
The blue "A" Shepard's signal indicates that citing references in the Shepard's Citations Service contain treatment of your case that is neither positive nor negative.

 Citation information available
The blue "I" Shepard's signal indicates that citing references are available in the Shepard's Citations Service for your case, but the references do not have history or treatment analysis (for example, the references are law review citations).

Note: Not every case will have a signal indicator.

VI. STUDY AIDS—RESEARCH STRATEGIES

A. Quick References and Checklists

Research Strategies in General

 1. Before Beginning Research: Checklist

✓ **Get the facts.**
- Who are the parties involved?
- Where is the relevant jurisdiction?
- What happened and when?
- Why did the events occur?
- Ask any other relevant factual questions.

✓ **Consider the assignment.**
- Purpose:
  - Objective or persuasive?
  - Writing to inform, to settle, to litigate ...?
- Audience: a judge, your client, your supervising attorney, the other side ...?
- Scope: how long and comprehensive should the end product be?
- View: formality, tone, theory of the case?
- Deadline: when is the assignment due?

✓ **Spot the legal issues.**
- What potential civil claims might exist?
- What potential criminal charges might exist?
- Discuss with supervising attorney.

✓ Create issue statements.
- Summarize the legal issue in context.
- One approach: question presented format
  - "Under": what jurisdiction and applicable law?
  - "Did/Can/Will": what is the legal issue?
  - "When": what are the key significant facts?
- Create an issue statement for each primary legal issue.

✓ **Brainstorm initial search terms.**
- Use key words from issue statement.
- Begin with broad, categorical terms.
- Use legal terms of art.

✓ **Plan a research strategy.**
- Does your supervising attorney have any suggestions for starting points?
- Time management: How much time will you spend on research? How much on writing? How much will it cost?
- Take thorough notes both before and during research.

☑ 2.   Initial Research: Checklist

✓ **Decide on a starting point.**
  - Create a separate file for each claim.
  - Attack each claim individually.
  - If you know little or nothing about the topic, consult a secondary source:
      - Legal encyclopedia: for basic information on a legal issue.
      - Restatement, treatise, hornbook: for concise overview of the law (though not necessarily applicable to your jurisdiction).
      - A.L.R.: for a lot of information and citations on a particular topic.
      - Law review: for many citations on a particular topic (though not written from an objective point of view).
  - If your supervising attorney gives you a case or statute:
      - Read the initial source carefully.
      - Shepardize or KeyCite it to find other sources.

✓ **Conduct print research.**
  - Think like a legal editor: organize in standard categories (such as first-year courses).
  - Browse table of contents and index for search terms.
  - If you find something possibly relevant, browse nearby sections. If you do not find anything, broaden search terms.

✓ **Conduct online research.**
  - Use narrow and appropriate databases.
  - Examine key number references (on Westlaw and WestlawNext).
  - Create appropriate natural language/terms and connectors searches.

✓ **Identify elements of legal issue.**
  - Look for a statute on point.
  - Find cases that identify the legal elements.
  - Consider whether administrative regulations would be applicable.

✓ **Take thorough notes.**
  - Track the legal elements you have investigated.
  - Track the sources you have used.
      - Which sources provided the legal elements?
      - Which sources were helpful for further analysis?
      - Which sources were not helpful?
  - Take notes on the application of the legal elements to the factual situation.

---

3.   Continuing Research: Checklist

✓ **Narrow search terms and connectors.**
  - Use specific terms of art found in earlier research.
  - Narrow from topics to subtopics.

- Use connectors to ensure terms in searches are close to one another (/s).
- Use narrower databases.

✓ **Expand research to other sources.**
- Look up materials referenced from secondary sources.
- Look up related statutory provisions referenced in annotated codes.
- Look up cases referenced in annotated codes.
- Look up cases cited in case decisions you have already found.
- Shepardize or use KeyCite to find cases that cite to case decisions you have already found.

✓ **Update to verify good law.**
- Shepard's (Lexis and Lexis Advance)
  - Look for red stop sign or yellow warning sign for possible reversal, overturning, or negative treatment.
  - Review decisions that indicate negative treatment of your case and determine whether they affect your use of the case.
  - Organize by treatment, type of law, or headnote.
- KeyCite (Westlaw and WestlawNext)
  - Look for red or yellow flag for possible reversal, overturning, or negative treatment.
  - Review decisions that indicate negative treatment of your case and determine whether they affect your use of the case.
  - Restrict by jurisdiction, headnote, date, particular terms.

✓ **Know when to stop.**
- Is your research repeatedly leading you to the same cases?
- Have you Shepardized or KeyCited your sources without finding new citations? Do you understand the nuances of each legal element?

📝 4. Binding vs. Persuasive Law: Quick Reference

Binding law is law that must be followed in that jurisdiction.

Persuasive law is law that a jurisdiction may look to for guidance but is not obligated to follow. Ordinarily, if there is sufficient binding law to support your position, persuasive authority is not necessary. However, if you are attempting to convince a court to adopt a new approach that is supported in persuasive authority from other jurisdictions, using that authority may be helpful.

State Courts

On matters of state law in state trial court, precedents from higher state courts are binding. For example, a California trial court must follow precedent from the California Supreme Court. Precedent from other courts at the same level (e.g., another trial court) is usually only persuasive, not binding.

Federal Courts

Federal district courts must follow the precedents from that particular circuit's court of appeals. For example, a federal district court in North Carolina must follow precedent from the Fourth Circuit Court of Appeals and the U.S. Supreme Court. However, a federal district court is bound only by the court of appeals for the circuit in which it is located. For example, precedent from the D.C. Circuit is only persuasive in a federal district court in Wyoming. Precedent from the U.S. Supreme Court is binding in all courts. As in the state courts, precedent from other courts at the same level (e.g., another circuit court) is usually only persuasive, not binding.

Secondary Sources

Secondary sources, such as law review articles, are only persuasive authority.

Statutes

A statute is considered to be binding law within the jurisdiction in which it was enacted. For example, a state statute in California is binding in California, but only persuasive in other states.

📝 5. West's Key Number System: Quick Reference

West Publishing and Westlaw use their key number system to categorize every case they publish. Cases often fit into a number of different key numbers and are catalogued accordingly in multiple key number locations. All legal topics are divided into the following categories:

- Persons
- Property
- Contracts
- Torts
- Crimes
- Remedies
- Government

These larger categories are then subdivided into over 430 topics. Each topic is divided into a more detailed outline, using specific numbers. This results in the creation of a key number—including both a topic and a specific number.

If you can identify one or more key numbers relevant to your research topic, they can be a helpful tool for finding related cases.

---

6. **Collecting Information: Quick Reference**

Note-Taking Chart

WHO	WHERE	WHAT

PARTIES	JURISDICTION	OBJECTS	CLAIMS/CHARGES & DEFENSES

Research Strategies—Study Aid Material

7.   Note-Taking Chart: Quick Reference

Note-Taking Chart: Example

Name	Facts	Holding	Reasoning
Jones v. U.S. 779 A.2d 277 2001	A. After observing Jones drop two baggies on the ground, three officers approached Jones and picked up the bags, which contained a substance that later proved to be crack cocaine. B. The officers asked Jones "for his ID, if he had ID at that time, or if he didn't have his ID what is his name, address, where he lives, things like that." C. After these questions were posed to him, Jones stated that "he was holding for those two guys." D. At the time that he made these comments, Jones had not been advised of his rights under Miranda.	Not an interrogation; appellate court didn't address issue of custody.	A. "Interrogation" is not only express questioning but also words or actions on the part of police that the police should know are reasonably likely to elicit an incriminating response from the suspect. B. Given the lack of the slightest logical nexus between the officer's question and the defendant's statement, it is difficult to understand how the judge could reasonably have found anything other than the statements were voluntary and spontaneous.
Dancy v. U.S. 745 A.2d 259 2000	A. Officer came to defendant's hospital room, where he saw him alone. B. Officer told D that he had an arrest warrant for him, about the police investigation (including what the police had found of defendant's role), and the penalty in the event of conviction. C. D responded by asking if "the girl" (person who drove Ds to the murder scene) was being charged and whether "Mike" (another D) was "finished. D. Officer asked D if he would be willing to talk about his involvement. E. D said that he wanted to speak to his lawyer, at which point officer read him his Miranda rights.	D was "interrogated" for Miranda purposes.	A. Officer should have known that his words were reasonably likely to elicit incriminating evidence. B. There were no other circumstances to indicate that the officer's words had any purpose other than getting the D to incriminate himself. C. Officer in this case also admitted that he made statements in an effort to get D to talk about his involvement.

 ## 8.   Updating the Law: Quick Reference

Before relying on any piece of law by citing to it in a legal document, you must update it to make sure it is still good law. The process of updating a piece of law through Shepard's or KeyCite can also aid you in your research by identifying other sources that have cited that particular piece of law. For example, by using either Shepard's or KeyCite on a statute, you can identify all other cases and secondary sources that have cited that statute. They also break down those sources by headnote, date, jurisdiction, and depth of discussion.

Updating the law was traditionally a lengthy process using the book form of Shepard's. Most lawyers today, however, use the online version of Shepard's, found on Lexis and Lexis Advance, or a similar resource, KeyCite, found on Westlaw and WestlawNext.

Shepard's

To access Shepard's on Lexis or Lexis Advance, click on the Shepard's link or the Shepard's signal for the treatment of the law you are reading. Make sure to read through any sources with negative treatment; sometimes only one part of a case is overturned. Also note the court issuing any case with negative treatment; your case can be directly overturned only by courts with jurisdiction over it, so negative treatment from another state may not be significant. The citations provided by Shepard's will include an editor's assessment of this source's treatment of the case. So, for example, if a source distinguishes or criticizes your law but does not reverse it, you will see a yellow triangle located next to that source. You may organize these sources by their treatment, their kind of law (e.g., statutes, secondary sources), and by headnote number.

Shepard's also has a system of symbols to indicate the type of treatment a source has received. For example, be wary of a case displaying a red stop sign; this symbol indicates negative treatment.

KeyCite

To access KeyCite, click on the KeyCite tab and enter your citation. If you have already pulled up a piece of law and wish to update it, simply click on the colored flag next to the case. Clicking on Citing References will provide a list of sources that have cited your law and the symbols for the treatment by these sources. You can also search these references through the pop-up menu at the bottom of the page. As discussed above, be sure to read through sources with negative treatment to determine their impact on the validity of your law.

The colored flags in Westlaw and WestlawNext indicate the type of treatment a source has received. Make sure you understand this system so you can recognize quickly when a source is likely to be good law. Westlaw uses star symbols for depth of treatment, and WestlawNext uses a bar. The more stars or bars, the more treatment from that citing source.

Statutes

📝 9. Finding Statutes: Quick Reference

Finding statutes is usually easier in the books than online. Each state has its own statutory code; the federal code is found in the United States Code (U.S.C., the official government-published version), the United States Code Annotated (U.S.C.A.), or the United States Code Service (U.S.C.S.). Statutes are also found on Westlaw and Lexis.

Constitutions are typically found in the first volume of the code. The index is usually located at the end of the set. The full text of the U.S. Constitution can also be searched at http://www.findlaw.com/casecode/constitution. Statutes can be searched in three ways:

1. **By number**
   - *Online:* Westlaw: Type the citation under Find. WestlawNext: Type the citation in the main text box. Lexis: Type the citation under Get A Document. Lexis Advance: Type the citation in the main text box.
   - *Books:* If you have a specific cite to a statute, e.g., 12 U.S.C. § 323, you would go to the volume that contains title 12 and find section 323 in numerical order.

2. **By name**
   - *Online:* Lexis and Westlaw both have links to popular names tables. In Westlaw, look in the directory under USCA-POP. In WestlawNext, click on Tools and Resources on the right side of the screen. In Lexis, under Find A Source, type "popular names."
   - *Books:* Some codes have popular names (such as the Civil Rights Act). The U.S.C., U.S.C.A., U.S.C.S, and many state codes have popular names tables, usually located at the end of the set. Here, you can look up the name alphabetically to retrieve the citation to the statute itself.

3. **By subject**
   - *Online:* Although searching for statutes is usually easier in the books, there are times when online searching is more efficient. For example, if asked to find similar laws in multiple jurisdictions, online searching is easier. Both Lexis and Westlaw have the full text of the U.S. Code, all the state codes, and a single database of all fifty states. In Lexis, to search the U.S. Code, go to "**Federal Legal—U.S.—United States Code Service 1-50.**" Here, you can either browse the table of contents or create a search using descriptive words. In Lexis Advance, enter "**U.S. Code**" in the main text box and click Search. You can also click the **All Content Types** tab; select **Statutes & Legislation**; then click on **United States Code Annotated (U.S.C.A.)**. A third way to access the U.S. Code is to click the **All Jurisdictions** tab, then select **U.S. Federal**. In Westlaw, to search the U.S. Code, go to "**Directory—U.S. Federal Materials—Statutes—United States Code Annotated (or other options).**" Click on the Search box and use descriptive word searching. In WestlawNext, enter "**U.S. Code**" in the main text box and click Search. You can also click the **All Content** tab under the Browse section; click **Statutes and Court Rules**; then click **United States Code Annotated (U.S.C.A.**") to view the table of contents of the U.S.C.A. A third way to access the U.S. Code is to click the **Federal Materials** tab, then click **United States Code Annotated (U.S.C.A.)**.

- *Books:* If you do not know the citation or the name of your statute, but only have a general idea of the subject matter, you will need to brainstorm descriptive words to search the index to the code, usually located at the end of each volume set.

✅ 10. Strategies for Researching Statutes: Checklist

✓ **Determine the appropriate jurisdiction.**
  - Federal
  - State

✓ **Conduct print research.**
  - Locate the annotated code for your jurisdiction. If you have a citation to a statute:
    - Find the volume corresponding to the first number in the citation.
    - Turn to the section corresponding to the second number in the citation.

✓ If you have the name of a legislative act:
  - Use the code's popular names table to find its citation.

✓ If you know only the general subject matter:
  - Brainstorm descriptive search words and legal terms of art.
  - Browse the code's table of contents for more terms.
  - Browse the index for relevant key words.
  - Read statutes referenced from the index.
  - Check pocket parts or supplements for updates or amendments.

✓ **Conduct online research.**
  - If you have a citation to a statute:
    - Lexis: Go to "Get a Document," then "by Citation," and type in cite.
    - Lexis Advance: Type the citation in the main text box and click Search.
    - Westlaw: Go to "Find " then type in cite.
    - WestlawNext: Type the name of the legislative act in the main text box and click Search.
  - If you have the name of a legislative act:
    - Lexis: For federal, go to "Search," then "Find a Source," and type "popular names."
    - Lexis Advance: Type the name of the legislative act in the main text box and click Search.
    - Westlaw: For federal, search in the database USCA-POP.
    - WestlawNext: Type the name of the legislative act in the main text box and click Search.
  - If you know only the general subject matter:
    - Brainstorm descriptive search words and legal terms of art.
    - Find the appropriate state code database:
      - Browse the code's table of contents.

- Formulate a natural language or terms and connectors search.

✓ **Check for other provisions or statutes on point.**
  - Look for statutory definitions of terms.
  - Look up statutes referred to in the statute you found.
  - Examine surrounding statutes for relevance.

✓ **Update to verify that the statute is still good law.**
  - Shepard's (Lexis and Lexis Advance)
    - Look for red stop sign or yellow warning sign for possible negative treatment.
    - Review decisions that indicate negative treatment of the statute.
  - KeyCite (Westlaw and WestlawNext)
    - Look for red or yellow flag for possible negative treatment.
    - Review decisions that indicate negative treatment of the statute.

Cases

 ## 11. Finding Cases: Quick Reference

Getting Started

There are a number of factors to consider before you start researching case law.

1. First, it is important to focus on a particular jurisdiction whenever possible. Are you looking for cases in a particular federal circuit or a particular state? Knowing your jurisdiction will substantially limit the number of cases found.

2. Second, it is important to understand the hierarchy of cases and the difference between mandatory and persuasive law. (Table 1 in the Bluebook lists the hierarchy for each jurisdiction.) A case from a higher court in your jurisdiction carries greater weight than a lower case or one from a different jurisdiction.

3. Third, the date of a decision is important. Recent decisions carry great weight. Older decisions that have been followed over a long period of time also carry great weight. On the other hand, be wary of relatively old decisions that are rarely followed or new decisions that contradict overwhelming precedent.

4. Cases do get overturned. Therefore, it is imperative that you update your cases before you rely on them as good law.

Strategies

Your starting point could be any of the following:

- **A case citation**
  - *Books:* First, you would need to find the correct set of reporters (see locations of law above). Second, find the correct volume and page number in the reporter to locate the case itself. For example, 212 S. Ct. 301 would be found in the 212th volume of the Supreme Court Reporter on page 301.
  - *Online:* In Westlaw, enter the citation in the Find field. In Lexis, type the citation under Find A Document. For Lexis Advance and WestlawNext, enter the citation in the main search box.
- **A case name**
  - *Books:* To find a case using its name, go to the end of the reporter set where you will find a digest. Each digest has a volume labeled "Table of Case Names," which lists cases and their citations in alphabetical order by first party name. Some tables also have a "Defendant-Plaintiff Table," which lists cases and their citations in alphabetical order by defendant's names. Remember to check pocket parts.
  - *Online:* In Westlaw, go to Find, by title. In Lexis, under Get A Document, choose By Party Name. For Lexis Advance and WestlawNext, type the name(s) of one or more of the parties in the main text box and click Search.
- **Subject Matter**
  - *One Good Case:* Often, a supervising attorney will provide you with one case on point. This case can be a gold mine if used properly. First, it will cite to other sources, either other cases or statutes, rules, or secondary sources that might also provide other relevant law. Second, if it is a case published by West, it will provide key numbers, the system designed by West to arrange the law into topics.
  - *Statutes Annotated:* If there is a statute on point, often cases have cited to the statute. To find these cases, you should research annotated statutes in your particular jurisdiction. Remember to check pocket parts of the books for more recent annotations.
  - *Case Digests:* A case digest arranges case annotations by topics. The index is usually located at the end of the volumes. Each digest topic also has its own table of contents at the beginning of the section. Remember to check pocket parts for more recent annotations. Once you have found relevant cases, look them up in the reporter. Remember to update all cases to make sure they are still good law.
- **Subject Matter: Online**
  - *One Good Case:* If you have a good case on Westlaw or Lexis, you can link to other cases cited within that case. Also, you can click on the key numbers on Westlaw and WestlawNext, located in the beginning of the case before the judicial opinion, to link directly

to the key number system to find other cases listed under that key number. This method is very effective for finding cases that West editors have categorized under that key number. Be careful to take notes as you research using this strategy as you can become looped within a key number as you find case after case; keep track of the cases you have read.

- *Key Numbers:* In Westlaw and WestlawNext, you can access the key number system directly by clicking on the More menu, located at the top of the Westlaw screen. Click on the arrow to scroll down to Key Numbers And Digests; here the key numbers are listed in alphabetical order so that you can find the relevant key numbers for your cases.

- *Searches:* Within a specified directory, you can use key terms to search for cases. The tricks here are to search in a specific directory and to create your search terms and connectors carefully.

📝 12. Strategies for Researching Cases: Checklist

✓ **Determine the appropriate jurisdiction.**
- Federal or state?
- Which district or circuit?

✓ **Focus on cases that are**
- In your particular state or federal circuit.
- Binding rather than persuasive.
- More recent.

✓ **Conduct print research.**
- Locate the case reporters and digests for your jurisdiction. If you have a citation to a case:
  - Find the volume corresponding to the first number in the citation.
  - Turn to page corresponding to the second number in the citation.
  - Read that case to find other cases, statutes, secondary sources.
  - If published by West, examine that case's key numbers to identify topics for further research.
- If you have the name of the parties in a case:
  - Use the digest's table of case names volume to find the case citation.
  - Look up the case citation in the reporter for the decision's full text.
- If you have a relevant statute:
  - Look up the statute in the annotated code.
  - Read the annotations to locate cases that have cited the statute.
  - Look up case citations in the reporter for the decision's full text.

- If you know only the general subject matter:
  - Brainstorm descriptive search words and legal terms of art.
  - Browse the digest's index for relevant key words.
  - Locate topics in the digest referenced from the index.
  - Browse the digest topic's table of contents for specific subtopics.
  - Read the case annotations and locate interesting cases in the reporters.
- Check pocket parts or supplements for more recent decisions and annotations.

✓ **Conduct online research.**
  - If you have a citation to a case:
    - Lexis:
      - Go to "Get a Document," then "by Citation," and type in cite.
      - Read the case and investigate other cases it cites.
    - Lexis Advance:
      - Enter the citation in the main text box and click Search.
      - Read the case and investigate other cases it cites.
    - Westlaw:
      - Type in cite in the Retrieve a Document or "Find by Citation box.
      - Read the case and investigate other cases it cites.
      - Follow the links for any relevant headnotes and key numbers.
    - WestlawNext:
      - Enter the citation in the main text box and click Search.
      - Read the case and investigate other cases it cites.
      - Follow the links for any relevant headnotes and key numbers.
  - If you have the name of the parties in a case:
    - Lexis:
      - Go to "Get a Document," then "by Party Name."
      - Enter at least one of the party's names.
      - Select the appropriate jurisdiction.
      - Restrict by date (optionally) and click "Search."
    - Lexis Advance:
      - Select the appropriate jurisdiction.
      - Enter at least one of the party's names in the main text box and click Search.
    - Westlaw:
      - Under "Finding Tools," select "Find a Case by Party Name."
      - Enter at least one of the party's names.
      - Select the appropriate jurisdiction and click "Go."

- WestlawNext:
  - Select the appropriate jurisdiction.
  - Enter at least one of the party's names in the main text box and click Search.
- If you have a relevant statute:
  - Enter the citation for the statute.
  - Read the annotations to locate cases that have cited the statute.
  - Click on cases in the annotations to read the decisions' full text.
- If you know only the general subject matter:
  - Brainstorm descriptive search words and legal terms of art.
  - Find the appropriate federal or state case database.
  - Formulate a natural language or terms and connectors search.
  - Browse the key number directory for topic and subtopic terms (Westlaw only).
✓ **Update to verify that the case is still good law.**
  - Shepard's (Lexis or Lexis Advance)
    - Look for red stop sign or yellow warning sign for possible negative treatment.
    - Review decisions that indicate negative treatment of the case.
  - KeyCite (Westlaw or WestlawNext)
    - Look for red or yellow flag for possible negative treatment.
    - Review decisions that indicate negative treatment of the case.

Legislative History, Administrative Law, and Looseleafs

13.   Finding Legislative History: Quick Reference

What Is Legislative History?

Legislative history is the collective term for all the documents produced as a bill becomes a law in Congress. It can include the text of the bill itself and any versions and amendments, the text of congressional debates, the text of committee hearings, and committee reports. These documents can be important in determining the legislative intent behind a particular law, but there is an ongoing debate as to the usefulness of legislative history. Legislative history is only persuasive authority.

How Do You Research Federal Legislative History?

When researching the legislative history of a bill or law, first check to see if there is already a **compiled legislative history** on that particular piece of legislation. Check the Sources of Compiled Legislative Histories, a book that lists all available published legislative histories by public law number. If there is not already a compiled legislative history available, you will have to create your own. There are a number of sources for legislative history.

- Book Sources
  - **USCCAN:**
    - *What it provides:* USCCAN provides the full text for selected committee reports; it also provides the bill number, date of enactment, and list of all committee reports for every law passed. Additionally you can find the full text of public laws, presidential messages, and cites to the Congressional Record.
    - *How to use it:* First, find the public law number for your bill and the year it was enacted into law; you can find this information using the U.S. Code. Then, you can find the full text of your public law in the relevant volume of federal legislative histories. This source references page numbers for the selected legislative history documents, which are found in the legislative history volumes of USCCAN. You will need to use two different volumes of USCCAN to find your bill and legislative history.
  - **CIS (Congressional Information Service):**
    - *What it provides:* Unlike USCCAN, CIS does not provide the full text of pieces of legislative history. Instead, it gives a comprehensive legislative history for a particular piece of law, but it provides only a brief abstract of each piece of history.
    - *How to use it:* You many search CIS by subject, name, committee, public law number, bill number, or document number. To find the full text of a given piece of history, however, you will have to go to another source, such as CIS microfiche or Congressional Universe on the Web.
  - **Congressional Record**
    - *What it provides:* This hefty set of books contains the text of the congressional debates of both houses.
    - *How to use it:* The daily edition is published every day Congress is in session. Page numbers begin with S for Senate, H for House, E for Extension of Remarks, and D for Daily Digest. A permanent bound edition is also published, but the volumes are published very slowly and have a different numbering system from the daily edition. Therefore, you will need to use the Index or Daily Digest to find relevant pages to the bound edition.
- **Online Sources**
  - **THOMAS:**
    - *What it provides:* For free, THOMAS provides the text of bills from 1989 to the present, committee reports from 1995 to the present, and congressional debates from the daily edition.
    - *How to use it:* Go to http://thomas.loc.gov and enter the bill number for your piece of legislation.

- **Lexis**
  - *What it provides:* Bills (1989 to the present), hearings (July 1993 to the present), congressional debates, and committee reports (1990 to the present).
  - *How to use it:* To find bills for the current congress, go to "Short Name—Legis; Bills." To find bills for previous congresses starting in 1989, go to "Short Name—Legis; BTX101-BTX106." To find hearings, go to "Short name—Legis; Hearing." To find committee reports, go to "Short Name—Legis; CMTRPT." To find congressional debates, go to "Short Name—Legis; Record."
- **Westlaw**
  - *What it provides:* Bills (1985 to the present), hearings (Jan. 1993 to the present), congressional debates, and committee reports (1990 to the present).
  - *How to use it:* To find bills for the current Congress, go to the Cong-BillTXT database. To find bills for previous Congresses starting in 1985, go to the Cong-BillTxt104-Cong-BillTxt106 databases. To find hearings, go to the USTestimony database. To find committee reports, go to the LH database. To find congressional debates, go to the LH database for the daily edition.
- **WestlawNext**
  - *What it provides:* Bills (1985 to the present), hearings (Jan. 1993 to present), congressional debates, and committee reports (1990 to the present).
  - *How to use it:* Click on Proposed & Enacted Legislation under the All Content tab.

---

 14. **Strategies for Researching Legislative History: Checklist**

✓ **THOMAS:**
- Free source for text of:
  - Bills (1989 – present)
  - Committee reports (1995 – present)
  - Congressional debates (from daily edition)
- Go to http://thomas.loc.gov and enter legislation's bill number.

✓ **Print Compilations:**
- USCCAN
  - Check U.S. Code to find public law number and year of enactment.
  - Use that information to look up full text of public laws in USCCAN federal legislative histories.
  - From there, look up the referenced USCCAN legislative history volumes for full text of selected committee reports and other legislative history materials.

- Congressional Information Service (CIS)
  - Search by subject, name, committee, public law number, etc.
  - Provides a comprehensive legislative history for laws, but only a brief abstract of each piece of legislative history.
- Congressional Record
  - Use Index or Daily Digest to find relevant pages in bound edition.
  - Page numbers are based on source:
    - S – Senate
    - H – House
    - E – Extension of Remarks
    - D – Daily Digest
  - Contains text of congressional debates (House and Senate).

✓ **Westlaw:**
- From a U.S.C.A. provision:
  - In the sidebar, choose "Legislative History," then "Text Amendments."
  - Click on the public laws indicated.
- Search the appropriate database:
  - Bills:
    - CONG-BILLTXT (current session)
    - US-BILLTRK (summaries and status for currently introduced legislation)
      - CONG-BILLTXT104 [105, ...] (for the 104th, ... session)
  - Hearings: USTESTIMONY
  - Committee reports: LH
  - Congressional debates: LH (for daily edition)

✓ **WestlawNext:**
- From a U.S.C.A. provision:
  - Click on the History tab and/or the Context & Analysis tab.
- Search the appropriate database:
  - Bills:
    - Click on Proposed & Enacted Legislation; select Federal; then select Congressional Bills.
    - Click on Bill Tracking under the Tools & Resources tab on the right side of the screen.
  - Hearings: Type "Congressional Testimony" in main text box and click Search, or click on Proposed & Enacted Legislation under the All Content tab; then click Capitol Watch under the Tools & Resources tab.
  - Committee Reports and Congressional Debates: Click on Proposed & Enacted Legislation under the All Content tab; then click Capitol Watch under the Tools & Resources tab.

✓ **Lexis:**
- From a U.S.C.S. provision:
  - In the Practitioner's Toolbox, choose "History."
  - Click on the public laws indicated.

- Search the appropriate database:
  - Bills:
    - Legis; Bills (current session)
    - Legis; BTX101 [102, ...] (for the 101st, ... session)
  - Hearings: Legis; Hearing
  - Committee reports: Legis; CMTRPT
  - Congressional debates: Legis; Record (for daily edition)

 ## 15. Finding Administrative Law: Quick Reference

Getting Started

Administrative law consists of rules, regulations, and decisions created by federal or state agencies. When searching for administrative law, your research process will differ, depending on your starting point. You can start with any of the following:

Start with a code section to find regulations that implement it.

- Start with the annotated code, either U.S.C.A. or U.S.C.S. for federal law or your state's annotated code. In the annotations, you will find references to regulations and their citations. You can either use the books for these sources or log on to Lexis or Westlaw.
- You can also use the C.F.R. table of authorities, which contains a numerical list of the regulations arising out of each U.S.C. section. This source is also available in book form (usually located next to the C.F.R.) and online for free at http://www.gpoaccess.gov/cfr/index.html.
- Once you find your regulation cite, simple look it up in the C.F.R. or in the Federal Register.

Start with a topic to find regulations about that topic.

- **Books:** You can start your topic search in the C.F.R. index, which is not very effective because it only contains broad terms. A better source would be CIS Index to the Code of Federal Regulations, which is more comprehensive than the C.F.R. index; it is usually located near the C.F.R. itself.
- **Free Online Site:** You can directly search the C.F.R. online at http://www.gpoaccess.gov/cfr/index.html.
- **Lexis and Westlaw:** Both online services allow you to access and search the Federal Register (issues since 1980) and the C.F.R. Start with the Federal Register if you are looking for a recent rule, regulation, proposed rule, or commentary.
- **Federal Register Index:** This index is issued monthly and is arranged alphabetically by agency. Each issue is cumulative so that the December issue covers the year.
- **CIS Federal Register Index:** This index is issued weekly with cumulative volumes issued periodically and permanent bound volumes issued twice

a year. It indexes each issue of the Federal Register either by subject, name, C.F.R. section numbers affected, federal docket numbers, and Calendar of Effective Dates and Comment Deadlines.
- **Free Online Site:** Go to http://www.gpoaccess.gov/fr/index.html and follow the instructions for searching on this free website.

Start with **a particular agency** to look for regulations and administrative decisions created by that agency.

- Locate your particular agency's website using a search engine or linking from another site. The following sites provide links to agency sites:
  - *Washburn University School of Law Agency Index:* http://www. washlaw.edu/doclaw/executive5m.html
  - *Federal Web Locator* (The Villanova Center for Information Law and Policy): http://www.lib.auburn.edu/madd/docs/fedloc.html
  - *FirstGov:* http://firstgov.gov/Agencies/Federal/All_Agencies/ index.shtml
- Each agency has its own method of searching for regulations and administrative decisions, so spend some time browsing your particular agency's website.

Updating Regulations

Remember that it is essential to update administrative law because it changes frequently. First, find the date of the regulation you have found. In online sources, this will be the "currency date" near the top of the document; in print sources, this will be the date on the cover of the volume. Next, check to see if any changes to your regulation have been published in the Federal Register since the date you found. In online versions, simply search using your regulation's citation or look in the List of Sections Affected (L.S.A.). If you are using the books, find the book version of the L.S.A., usually located at the end of the C.F.R. set and in the last Federal Register issue of each month. Once you have found the correct date of the L.S.A., you will need to look at each subsequent L.S.A. to ensure that nothing has changed since your currency date. The L.S.A. does not bring a search completely up to date, however. For a thorough search, you must consult a similar list found in the last Federal Register issue of each month.

Administrative Decisions

To research the judicial treatment of regulations, check in Shepard's C.F.R. Citations, which is found in book form as well as in Lexis. In addition, agency websites often post administrative judicial opinions.

16. Strategies for Researching Administrative Law: Checklist

✓ **Choose an appropriate starting point.**
- If you have a relevant statute:
  - Option 1: Look up statute in U.S.C.A. or U.S.C.S., and follow annotations to find citations to regulations.
  - Option 2: Use the C.F.R. Table of Authorities (in print or online) to find a list of regulations associated with each U.S.C. section.
  - After finding the regulation cite, look it up in C.F.R. or the Federal Register.
- If you have only a general topic:
  - Books: Use CIS Index to the Code of Federal Regulations.
  - Online: Search C.F.R. at GPOAccess, or on Lexis or Westlaw.
- If you are looking for a recent regulation:
  - Books: Search the Federal Register Index or the CIS Federal Register Index.
  - Online: Search the Federal Register at GPOAccess.
- If you are looking for regulations associated with a particular agency, start with that agency's website.

✓ **Update any regulations you find.**
- Check the date of the regulation you find.
  - Books: date on cover of volume
  - Online: "currency date"
- Check for any changes to regulation since that date.
  - Books: Look in the List of Sections Affected (L.S.A.) volume for each month following the date you found.
  - Online: Search using the regulation's citation or use the L.S.A.
  - To be thorough, consult the list of affected sections from the last Federal Register issue of each month.

___

 17. Using Looseleaf Services: Quick Reference

Looseleaf services are research sources arranged by topic and issued in looseleaf binders. They vary in content and organization, depending on publisher and subject area. However, most of them contain up-to-date coverage and information regarding court decisions, statutes, administrative regulations, practice tips, forms, and developing trends in the law. In addition, they contain user guides and various indexes and finding tools. Looseleaf services tend to be most useful in heavily regulated, highly technical areas of law, such as tax law. Commerce Clearinghouse (CCH) and the Bureau of National Affairs (BNA) are two of the major looseleaf publishers.

When presented with a topic of research that you believe may be covered in a looseleaf service, the first task is to identify the appropriate one. The easiest way to do this is to ask your supervising attorney; the relevant looseleaf service is likely on the bookshelves in his or her office. As a student, you should ask a reference librarian which looseleaf service is appropriate for your field. A source called *Legal Looseleafs in Print* is also helpful; most libraries have this either in book form or online.

When you have found the appropriate looseleaf service, read the directions section to learn how to use it. All looseleaf services have this section, which explains the information included in the set, the indexing tools, the finding aids, and the format of the service.

B. Quizzes

⚇? 1. Research Strategy (in General): Quiz

Questions 1-2 are based on the following hypothetical:

Our client is a fifty-five-year-old computer programmer who was recently terminated from his job at Techno Inc., a locally owned technology services company based in Cincinnati, Ohio. He believes he was improperly terminated based on his age. He offers the fact that all of the new programmers have been twenty-five years old or younger and that several of the older programmers have been terminated for "other" reasons. The client would like to sue Techno Inc. for wrongful termination under the Ohio state law. Your supervising attorney recalls that Ohio has passed legislation called Protecting Workplace Age Diversity. This act protects employees over the age of fifty from being wrongfully terminated within two years before reaching retirement age.

1. Which of the following statements describes the most effective way to begin your research?

   A. Having been provided with a known authority, the Ohio Protecting Workplace Age Diversity Act, I would begin my research by looking up the Ohio Protecting Workplace Age Diversity Act in the index or popular name table of the United States Code because the United States Code is the official federal code.

   B. Having been provided with a known authority, the Ohio Protecting Workplace Age Diversity Act, I would begin my research by looking up the Ohio Protecting Workplace Age Diversity Act in the index or popular name table of Page's Ohio Revised Code Annotated because Page's Ohio Revised Code Annotated is the official Ohio code and is the only source of primary law.

   C. Having been provided with a known authority, the Ohio Protecting Workplace Age Diversity Act, I would begin my research by looking up the Ohio Protecting Workplace Age Diversity Act in the index or popular name table of Page's Ohio Revised Code Annotated or Baldwin's Ohio Revised Code Annotated because either of these annotated codes would provide me with both the text of the statute and the annotations to cases interpreting the statute.

D. Having been provided with descriptive words "age diversity," I would begin my research by using Lexis or Westlaw to search these descriptive words on the ALL STATES database because this search will yield both relevant statutory provisions and cases.

E. Having been provided with descriptive words "age diversity," I would begin my research by looking up these descriptive words in the index of the official Ohio code and the Midwestern digest.

F. Having been provided these descriptive words "age diversity," I would begin my research by entering these terms in the main text box of Lexis Advance or WestlawNext; select Ohio from the jurisdiction list; then click Search.

G. C and F.

2. After finding the Protecting Workplace Age Diversity Act, you begin to analyze the statute to determine its applicability to our client's situation. In interpreting the statute, which of the following statements accurately reflects the techniques that you should employ?

A. You should look only to the plain meaning of the statutory language because that is the most important tool of statutory interpretation.

B. You should not waste time looking up the legislative history of the Ohio Protecting Workplace Age Diversity Act because the intent of the legislature is not a reliable tool of statutory interpretation given compromises in lawmaking.

C. You should use statutory definitions, if available, before relying on dictionary definitions.

D. You should consider policy as a tool of statutory interpretation only if your case is pending before an appellate court.

E. You should rely exclusively on case law from the Ohio Supreme Court interpreting the statute because that is the only binding authority.

3. When researching using Westlaw and updating the law using the KeyCite feature, a blue "H" next to a relevant case indicates

A. positive treatment by subsequent courts of law.

B. that the case or administrative decision has some history, but it is not known to be negative history.

C. that the case or administrative decision has citing references but no direct or negative indirect history.

D. that the case or administrative decision most closely matches your search terms.

E. none of the above.

4. When researching using WestlawNext and viewing Citing References, a bar with all four bars full indicates

A. positive treatment by subsequent courts of law.

B. negative treatment by subsequent courts of law.

C. that the case has been discussed by four other cases, administrative decisions, or briefs.

D. that the citing case, administrative decision, or brief discusses the cited case in great depth.

E. none of the above.

5. When researching using Lexis and updating the law using the Shepardize feature, a yellow triangle appearing next to a case name indicates

A. that not many cases have subsequently cited that principal case.

B. that citing references are available in the Shepard's Citations Service for your case.

C. that citing references in the Shepard's Citations Service contain history or treatment that may have a significant negative impact on your case.

D. that citing references in the Shepard's Citations Service contain treatment of your case that is neither positive nor negative.

E. that the case is good law.

Questions 6-7 are based on the following hypothetical:

You work for a Montana state congressperson who wants to pass legislation to help reduce the number of pedestrian injuries. She asks you to find out whether Montana already has a statute that criminalizes jaywalking.

6. How could you begin your research most efficiently?

A. Use Lexis or Westlaw to search the ALL STATES database for the term "jaywalking."

B. Make a list of possible search terms and go to the index of the Montana statutes.

C. Use Lexis or Westlaw to find law review articles about traffic fatalities and the response of law enforcement officials.

D. Use the Montana Digest to find Montana cases that discuss hit-and-run accidents.

E. A and B.

7. You find a jaywalking statute in Montana. Now you want to find cases in which the Montana courts have discussed the jaywalking statute. What is the most effective way to find these cases?

A. Look at the annotations located below the text of the statute.

B. Use Lexis or Westlaw to search the ALL STATES database for the term "safety."

C. Go to the index to the Montana Digest and look for an entry for "jaywalking."

D. Type the citation for the statute into Shepard's on Westlaw.

E. A and D.

8. You clerk for a federal judge. He has a number of attorneys in his chambers for a status conference. They are discussing the case France v. United States, 460 F.2d 478 (9th Cir. 1966). The judge asks you to bring him a copy of the

case right away. You walk across the hall into your office. What is the most efficient method for you to find the case?

    A. Use Black's Law Dictionary.

    B. Use Lexis or Westlaw and type in the citation.

    C. Look in the digest using West's national key number system.

    D. Call the librarian in the courthouse and ask him to bring you a copy.

    E. B and C.

9.   Your supervising attorney asks you to find law review articles on intentional infliction of emotional distress. What is the most effective way to find these articles using Lexis Advance or WestlawNext?

    A. On Lexis Advance or WestlawNext, type "intentional infliction of emotional distress" in the main text box and click Search.

    B. On WestlawNext, type "law reviews" in the main text box and select Law Reviews & Journals from the drop down list; then type "intentional infliction of emotional distress" in the main text box and click Search.

    C. On Lexis Advance, click on Content Type: select Analytical Materials; then type "intentional infliction of emotional distress" in the main text box and click Search.

    D. A and C.

    E. B and C.

Questions 10-12 are based on the following hypothetical:

Your firm has been retained to represent Tasha Harrison. Harrison recently received a popular hair treatment at a Beverly Hills salon in California. Apparently, during the treatment Harrison suffered chemical burns to her scalp and neck. You attended a meeting with the senior partner and Harrison to learn more about the facts of the case and her injuries.

10. The senior partner believes that there is a statute in California that regulates cosmetologists, beauticians, and hairstylists. He asks you to research this potential statutory claim. Which of the following is the most effective and efficient way to begin your research?

    A. Find West's California Reporter because you may find factually similar cases in order to predict the result of possible litigation for your client.

    B. Find West's Annotated California Codes because it will provide both the governing statutory language and case annotations that interpret the statutory provisions.

    C. Search the Internet for Deering's California Codes, Annotated, because it is free for all attorneys and a more efficient method to find both statutory language and case annotations.

    D. A and C, but not B.

    E. A, B, and C.

11. The senior partner has asked you to draft a memo that will explain a potential cause of action against the hairstylist. Why might you plan to begin your research by checking secondary sources?

   A. Secondary sources, written by scholars in their fields of specialization, often address interesting and developing areas of the law, and citing them might be helpful to courts in your jurisdiction—especially if this is a new issue in the jurisdiction.
   B. The Restatement (Second) of Torts is a secondary source that sets forth the elements of tort claims, such as negligence, and its enumeration of such elements would be binding authority in any jurisdiction should the client pursue a negligence claim against the hairstylist.
   C. Secondary sources often collect citations to statutes and cases from several jurisdictions, providing you with binding secondary authority.
   D. Reading secondary sources could provide background and context that would allow for more critical reading of primary sources and could provide citations to statutes and cases that will aid your research of primary authority in your jurisdiction.
   E. A and D.

12. As you consider beginning your research online for primary authority, which of the following statements is true?

   A. A Natural Language search using Lexis or Westlaw is a good method to begin the research because it is easy to craft using a few keywords that describe the topic and will yield a few key documents at the beginning of my research.
   B. A Natural Language search using Lexis or Westlaw is a precise and thorough search method that will retrieve every relevant document.
   C. A Terms and Connectors search using Lexis or Westlaw may be more effective after I have found a few cases that help me understand the terms and relationships between those terms within the legal issue I am researching.
   D. A and B.
   E. A and C.

Answer Key on page 310

⚇? 2.   Binding vs. Persuasive Law: Quiz

1. You are clerking for a judge in the United States District Court for the Eastern District of Virginia. He asks you to research cases interpreting a particular provision of the federal Endangered Species Act. Your research uncovers a prior decision authored by a judge on the same court. That decision is:

   A. Binding, because it is a federal court decision interpreting a federal statute.
   B. Binding, because it was decided by the same United States District Court.

    C. Persuasive, because federal judges are not bound by precedent when interpreting federal statutes.

    D. Persuasive, because it was decided by the same United States District Court.

    E. None of the above.

2. Your law firm has been retained to represent a manufacturer for injuries caused by a defective soda bottle; the case is before the California Court of Appeal. A senior partner has asked you to find cases construing California product liability law. Which of the following authorities is the most binding?

    A. Johnson v. Kwik-Dry, Inc., 143 F.2d 548 (C.D. Ca. 2001)

    B. Hatfield v. McCoy International, 264 P.3d 703 (Cal. 2000)

    C. Potter v. Diagon Alley Broom Co., 188 F.2d 341 (9 th Cir. 2004)

    D. Matthews v. Orange Fizz Co., 280 P.3d 557 (Cal. Supr. 2005)

    E. McNee v. Calif. Mopeds, Inc., 242 P.3d 819 (Cal. App. 2003)

3. You sue for breach of contract in Texas state court. A decision by the United States District Court for the Southern District of Texas applying Texas contract law is:

    A. Binding, because federal court decisions always bind state courts.

    B. Binding, because it is a federal court decision construing state law.

    C. Persuasive, because it is a federal court decision construing state law.

    D. Persuasive, because federal courts have the final say on questions of state law.

    E. None of the above.

4-5: A sues B in for an alleged violation of the federal Americans with Disabilities Act (ADA) in the United States District Court for the District of Colorado.

4. A 12-year-old decision by the United States Court of Appeals for the Seventh Circuit interpreting the ADA is:

    A. Persuasive, because the United States Court of Appeals for the Seventh Circuit is not a higher court with direct appellate jurisdiction.

    B. Persuasive, because only Supreme Court decisions on matters of federal law have the power to bind other federal courts.

    C. Binding, because the United States Court of Appeals for the Seventh Circuit is a higher level federal court with direct appellate jurisdiction.

    D. Binding, because the Seventh Circuit decision has stood for 12 years without being overturned.

    E. None of the above.

5. A two-week old decision by the United States Court of Appeals for the Tenth Circuit interpreting the ADA is:

    A. Persuasive, because the United States Court of Appeals for the Tenth Circuit is not a higher court with direct appellate jurisdiction.

B. Persuasive, because only Supreme Court decisions on matters of federal law have the power to bind other federal courts.
C. Persuasive, because it is only two weeks old and has not withstood the test of time.
D. Binding, because the decisions by a United States Court of Appeals bind all federal courts.
E. Binding, because the United States Court of Appeals for the Tenth Circuit is a higher court with direct appellate jurisdiction.

Answer Key on page 310

⚇? 3.   Finding Statutes: Quiz

Your client, Mr. Fairbanks, was arrested for drunk driving in Virginia on his way home to Maryland. He has come to you asking for advice about the charges he is facing. You have not worked on any drunk driving cases previously and are unfamiliar with the relevant law.

1. How could you efficiently locate the Virginia statute criminalizing drunk driving?

    A. Search the "All State Statutes" database on Lexis or Westlaw for the term "drunk driving."
    B. Check the print index of the annotated code of Virginia for the term "drunk driving" or "driving while intoxicated."
    C. Consult a criminal law treatise or hornbook.
    D. All of the above.

2. What would be an advantage of locating the statute in the print volumes rather than using Lexis or Westlaw?

    A. You could easily flip through and browse nearby sections, which are likely related to the drunk driving statute.
    B. The print version of the official, unannotated code is guaranteed to have the most up-to-date version of the statute.
    C. Statutes in the print version of annotated codes are organized by key number, making it easier to locate statutes related to drunk driving.
    D. All of the above.

3. Your supervisor mentions that Virginia recently passed the Stop Drunk Driving in Virginia Act of 2007. How would you efficiently find the statutes corresponding to this act?

    A. Search the table of contents of the code of Virginia in the books.
    B. Type the name of the act into the Find by Citation box on Lexis or Westlaw.
    C. Search the popular names table from the code of Virginia for the name of the act.
    D. B and C.

4. If you want to compare the sentencing statutes from many different states to see what penalties they impose on drunk drivers, which of the following would be a useful source?

  A. An A.L.R. article on point.
  B. A treatise on tort law.
  C. A "50 State Surveys" annotation from West on point.
  D. All of the above.
  E. A and B.

Answer Key on page 310

👤? 4. Finding Cases: Quiz

Your supervising attorney is preparing a case addressing capital punishment in Connecticut, which she will be arguing before the Connecticut Appellate Court. She asks you to write a memo on the issue and gives you a citation to the state statute on capital punishment.

1. Which of the following would NOT be an effective way to find cases interpreting the statute?

  A. Look up the statute in the official Connecticut code.
  B. Look up the statute in the annotated Connecticut code.
  C. Look up the topic "Capital Punishment" in the index for the Atlantic regional case digest.
  D. Search the Connecticut cases database on Lexis or Westlaw for the term "capital punishment."

2. Which of the following secondary sources would be most effective for finding Connecticut cases interpreting the statute?

  A. A criminal law hornbook.
  B. A civil law treatise.
  C. A Restatement.
  D. A law review article on capital punishment.
  E. An A.L.R. article on capital punishment.

3. You have found a case on topic. However, you see on Westlaw or Westlaw-Next that a red flag appears at the top of the page. Should you use this case in your memo?

  A. Yes, because you may use any published case.
  B. Possibly, but you should Shepardize or KeyCite the case to see what portion of the case is no longer good law.
  C. Possibly, but you should look up the case in the supplement to the print reporter to see what portion of it is no longer good law.
  D. No, because a case with a red flag has been overruled and may not be used at all.
  E. Red flags appear in Lexis, not Westlaw.

4. You have found several more cases on topic, none of which has been overruled or challenged. Which case is binding on the court that your supervisor will be addressing? (Note that the citations given below are for fictional cases.)

    A. 304 Conn. Supp. 190 (Super. Ct. 2002)
    B. 293 A.2d 405 (Conn. 1995)
    C. 67 F.3d 107 (2d Cir. 2006)
    D. 310 A.2d 211 (Conn. App. Ct. 1999)
    E. 324 P.2d 657 (1983)

5. You have found another case, 230 F. 109 (2d Cir. 1826), which discusses capital punishment in Connecticut. The Westlaw page for this case does not show a red or yellow flag or any symbol at all. Why might you still not want to use this case?

    A. It has no citing references and therefore has not been followed by any published decisions (according to Westlaw).
    B. It is a case from a federal court of appeals and its interpretation of Connecticut state law is not binding.
    C. It is a very old case, and the court likely will not consider it to be very influential on its decision.
    D. All of the above.

Answer Key on page 310

⚇? 5. Updating: Quiz

1. You have found a case that is directly on point and want to use it in a memo for a partner. Must you update it?

    A. No, if it's not being submitted to the court, you don't have to update every case.
    B. Yes, you must update every case you rely on in any document to make sure it is still good law.
    C. Yes, because updating the case may help you find additional helpful sources.
    D. Answers B and C are both correct.

2. You have found a case in Westlaw or WestlawNext with a red flag. Can you use it in your brief?

    A. Yes, a red flag means there has been some negative treatment, but you can use it anyway.
    B. You must update the case to find out how much negative treatment the case has received. If the KeyCite report indicates that the case has been overruled by another case, however, you cannot use it.

  C. You must update the case to find and read the cases giving it negative treatment. It is possible that a case may have overruled one part of your case, but not the rest of it.

  D. No, a red flag means the case has been overruled, so you should not use it.

3. Why might you want to update a statute?

  A. To make sure it is still good law

  B. To find cases that interpret that statute

  C. No reason, because cases cannot overrule statutes.

  D. Answers A and B are both correct.

4. You have found a case in Lexis or Lexis Advance with a yellow triangle. Can you use it in your brief?

  A. No, a yellow triangle means that the case has been questioned, so to be safe, you should not use it.

  B. Yes, there would be a red stop sign if it had been overruled, so it is probably fine to use.

  C. You should update the case and see what negative treatment it has received before using it.

  D. You should use a case only if it has a green symbol associated with it.

Answer Key on page 311

CHAPTER 4

Citation

CITATION

This chapter covers the essentials of citation, addressing the two most used authorities: the ALWD citation manual and the Bluebook.

I. ALWD and the Bluebook
   A. ALWD
   B. The Bluebook
II. Strategies for Using ALWD
   A. The Purpose of Citation
   B. Design, Layout, and Basic Citation Rules of ALWD Citation
      1. ALWD Design
      2. ALWD Layout
      3. ALWD Basic Citation Rules
         a. Cases
         b. Constitutions
         c. Statutes
         d. Federal Administrative, and Executive Materials
         e. Books, Treatises, and Other Nonperiodic Materials
         f. Legal and Other Periodicals
   C. Often-Used ALWD Rules
      • Typefaces
      • Spelling and Capitalization
      • Basic Structure and Signals
      • Subdivisions and Pinpoint Cites
      • Short Citations
      • Abbreviations
      • Numbers
      • Quotations
      • Cases
      • Constitutions
      • Statutes
      • Administrative and Executive Materials
      • Books, Reports, and Other Nonperiodic Materials
      • Periodicals
      • Electronic Media
III. Study Aids—ALWD Citation
   A. ALWD Quick References and Checklists
      1. ALWD in General: Quick Reference 📋
      2. Typefaces: Checklist ☑

- Cases
- Constitutions
- Statutes
- Administrative and Executive Materials
- Books, Reports, and Other Nonperiodic Materials
- Periodical Materials
- Electronic Media

V. Study Aids—Bluebook Citation

   A. Bluebook Quick References and Checklists
      1. The Bluebook in General: Quick Reference 🗒
      2. Typefaces: Checklist ☑
      3. Basic Structure and Signals: Checklist ☑
      4. Signals: Checklist ☑
      5. Subdivisions and Pinpoint Cites: Checklist ☑
      6. Short Form Citations: Checklist ☑
      7. Abbreviations: Checklist ☑
      8. Cases: Checklist ☑
      9. Constitutions: Checklist ☑
      10. Statutes: Checklist ☑
      11. Administrative and Executive Materials: Checklist ☑
      12. Books, Reports and Other Nonperiodic Materials
      13. Periodicals: Checklist ☑
      14. Electronic Media: Checklist ☑

   B. Bluebook Quizzes
      1. Typefaces: Quiz ⚲?
      2. Basic Structures and Signals: Quiz ⚲?
      3. Citation Signals: Quiz ⚲?
      4. Order and Punctuation of Signals and Citations: Quiz ⚲?
      5. Subdivisions and Pinpoint Cites: Quiz ⚲?
      6. Short Form Citations: Quiz ⚲?
      7. Abbreviations: Quiz ⚲?
      8. Cases: Quiz ⚲?
      9. Constitutions: Quiz ⚲?
      10. Statutes: Quiz ⚲?
      11. Administrative and Executive Materials: Quiz ⚲?
      12. Books, Reports and Other Nonperiodic Materials: Quiz ⚲?
      13. Periodicals: Quiz ⚲?
      14. Electronic Media: Quiz ⚲?

   C. Bluebook Self-Assessment
      1. Bluebook Citation Self-Assessment ⚲?

I. ALWD AND THE BLUEBOOK

What follows is not intended to substitute for The Bluebook or ALWD Citation Manual but is only a guide to their use.

Finding the authority referenced in a legal document is so important to the legal reader that rules have developed to standardize citation. Although most law students and practicing attorneys dislike citation rules, they are necessary to allow the reader to access the materials referenced. If a legal authority is improperly cited, the reader will have a difficult time finding the law. In addition, the legal reader might not trust the substance of the document; if the writer's citation is inadequate, then perhaps the research and writing are similarly inadequate or improper. Thus, citations for the legal reader are not only helpful for finding law, but they also have become a tool to measure the writer's credibility. Currently, there are two widely accepted citation reference manuals: the more recent ALWD (Association of Legal Writing Directors) and the more traditional Bluebook.

This book covers citation using both ALWD (starting on page 195) and the Bluebook (Starting on page 249), although you will probably learn only one of these citation reference manuals in your class.

A. ALWD

In 1997, the board of directors of the Association of Legal Writing Directors decided to create a citation manual to fulfill three primary goals: to simplify legal citation rules, to create one set of rules for all forms of legal writing, and to present these rules in a format that judges, lawyers, instructors, and students would find easy to use. The result was the *ALWD Citation Manual: A Professional System of Citation*, written primarily by Dean Darby Dickerson of Stetson University College of Law. Known as ALWD, this manual is now in its fourth edition, published in 2010 by Wolters Kluwer Law & Business.

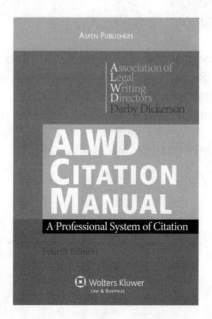

B.   The Bluebook

The first and most widely recognized citation standardization manual, titled *The Bluebook: A Uniform System of Citation,* was developed in the 1920s by a Harvard law student and is still published by the Harvard Law Review. The Bluebook is the traditional citation manual used by courts, lawyers, and law schools, despite complaints by some that the book is difficult to use and inconsistent in places. The Bluebook is currently in its nineteenth edition (2010), and it is now available online.[1]

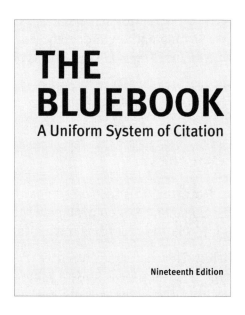

II.   STRATEGIES FOR USING ALWD

The trick for using ALWD is to learn these three things:

1. The purpose of citation
2. The design, layout, and basic citation rules of ALWD
3. Some of the often-used rules

A.   The Purpose of Citation

Lawyers use citation to provide authority in legal documents and to find the law referenced in legal documents. The *ALWD Citation Manual: A Professional System of Citation* (or ALWD for short) is designed to provide a uniform system of citation rules so that lawyers can easily find and reference legal sources. Eventually, when electronic filings are required with links to each cited source, citation might become obsolete. But until that time, lawyers are required to use citation that permits other lawyers easy access to their references. ALWD

---

1. http://www.legalbluebook.com/.

and the Bluebook are the most commonly used citation systems. Using correct citation adds credibility to your writing; if a judge can trust your citations, she can also trust your analysis.

B. Design, Layout, and Basic Citation Rules of the ALWD Citation Manual

1. ALWD Design

Unlike the Bluebook, the ALWD Citation Manual does not have separate citation formats for scholarly writing and legal documents. Thus, a citation based on ALWD style appears the same, regardless of the type of document you are writing.

2. ALWD Layout

ALWD is divided into seven parts:

Part 1: Introductory Material. This section summarizes the organization of the manual, discusses common citation problems that word processors may cause, and provides information regarding local citation formats.

Part 2: Citation Basics. This section contains the basic rules for citing a source, including typeface, abbreviations, spelling, capitalization, numbers, page numbers, citing particular sections or divisions of a source, internal cross-references, and short citation formats. A careful review of these fundamental rules is necessary before using ALWD to cite a source.

Part 3: Citing Specific Print Sources. This section focuses on print sources, both primary and secondary, and is divided into subsections by source type. At the beginning of each subsection, a "Fast Formats" table provides quick examples of correct citations for several commonly used sources.

Part 4: Electronic Sources. This section discusses the proper citation for electronic resources from LexisNexis, Westlaw, e-mail, and the Internet. It also provides information regarding the citation of sources available both in print and electronic formats.

Part 5: Incorporating Citations into Documents. This section explains how to place and use citations, how to use signals, how to order cited authorities, and when and how to include explanatory parentheticals.

Part 6: Quotations. This section discusses use of quotations, alteration of quoted material, and omission within quoted material.

Part 7: Appendices. The appendices contain more information about primary sources by jurisdiction, local court citation rules, abbreviations, federal taxation materials, federal administrative publications, and a sample legal memorandum showing proper citation placement.

ALWD also has a detailed table of contents and an index.

Throughout the manual, green triangles (▲) are used to designate spaces in citation formats, and green circles (●) are used to separate components of citations. On the inside front cover is a "Fast Format Locator" that gives the page numbers for the Fast Formats tables throughout the manual. On the inside back cover is a "Short-Citation Locator for Commonly Used Sources" that lists rule numbers for many short citation formats.

3.   ALWD Basic Citation Rules

a.   Cases (Rule 12)

Citation of a U.S. Supreme Court Case:

Lakeside v. Oregon, 435 U.S. 333, 345 (1978).

> Lakeside = plaintiff
> Oregon = defendant
> 435 = reporter volume #
> U.S. = reporter abbreviation
> 333 = first page
> 345 = specific page
> (1978) = date case decided

NOTE: Be sure to include both the first page of the cited case and a specific page if one is referenced.

Citation of a case decided by the U.S. Court of Appeals for the Eleventh Circuit:

Campbell v. Sikes, 169 F.3d 1353, 1366-67 (11th Cir. 1999).

> Campbell = plaintiff
> Sikes = defendant
> 169 = reporter volume #
> F.3d = reporter abbreviation
> 1353 = first page
> 1366-67 = specific pages
> 11th Cir. = court—this is necessary if it's not clear from reporter abbreviation
> 1999 = date case decided

Short form for cases:

Campbell, 169 F.3d at 1369.

> Campbell = plaintiff; use defendant's name in short cite if plaintiff's name is a
>   common litigant (i.e., United States)
> 169 = reporter volume #
> F.3d = reporter abbreviation
> 1369 = specific pages

b. Constitutions (Rule 13)

Citation of Section 2 of the Eighteenth Amendment to the U.S. Constitution:

U.S. Const. amend. XVIII, § 2.

> U.S. Const. = abbreviation of Constitution
> amend. = abbreviation of amendment
> XVIII = # of amendment
> § 2 = # of section if applicable

Citation of a state constitution:

N.C. Const. art. III, § 1.

> N.C. Const. = abbreviation of Constitution
> art. = abbreviation of article
> III = # of article
> §1 = # of section if applicable

c. Statutes (Rule 14)

Citation of an entire statue, as codified in the United States Code:

Federal Trademark Dilution Act, 15 U.S.C. § 1125 (2000).

> Federal Trademark Dilution Act = official name
> 15 = title #
> U.S.C. = abbreviation of code
> § 1125 = section #
> 2000 = date of code edition

Citation of an individual provision of the United States Code:

15 U.S.C. § 1125 (2000).

> 15 = title #
> U.S.C. = abbreviation of code
> § 1125 = section #
> 2000 = date of code edition

Short citation of provision of the United States Code:

Id. at § 1125 (where appropriate) or 15 U.S.C. § 1125.

> Id. at § 1125—use when referring to the immediately preceding authority

d. *Federal Administrative and Executive Materials (Rule 19)*

Citation of a particular provision of a regulation in the Code of Federal Regulations:

49 C.F.R. § 172.101 (2005).

---

49 = title #
C.F.R. = abbreviation of regulations
§ 172.101 = section #
2005 = date of C.F.R. edition

NOTE: Cite all final federal administrative rules and regulations to the C.F.R.

Short citation of particular provision of a regulation in the C.F.R.:

<u>Id.</u> at § 172.101 (where appropriate) or 49 C.F.R. at § 172.101.

<u>Id.</u> at § 172.101 (where appropriate)—use when referring to the immediately
   preceding authority
49 = title #
C.F.R. = abbreviation of regulations
at § 172.101 = section #

---

e. *Books, Treatises, and Other Nonperiodic Materials (Rule 22)*

Citation of a treatise:

William L. Prosser & W. Page Keeton, <u>Prosser and Keeton on the Law of Torts</u> § 3.65
(5th ed., West 1984).

William L. Prosser & W. Page Keeton = full name of 1st and 2nd authors
Prosser and Keeton on the Law of Torts = title of treatise
§ 3.65 = section #
5th ed. West, 1984—edition—if there is more than one—publisher, and date of
   edition

Short citation of a treatise:

Prosser & Keeton, <u>Prosser and Keeton on the Law of Torts</u> at § 3.65.

Prosser & Keeton = last name of 1st and 2nd authors
Prosser and Keeton on the Law of Torts = title of treatise
at § 3.65 = section #

NOTE: If using footnotes, use the following form.

Prosser & Keeton, <u>supra</u> n. 7, at § 3.65.

> Prosser & Keeton = last name of 1st and 2nd authors
> supra n. 7 = word supra & note number where full cite appears
> at § 3.65 = section #

Citation of a particular page in a novel:

J. K. Rowling, <u>Harry Potter and the Sorcerer's Stone</u> 125 (Scholastic 1997).

> J.K. Rowling—use full name of author unless author uses initials only
> Harry Potter and the Sorcerer's Stone = title of book
> 125 = section or page #
> Scholastic = publisher's name
> 1997 = year published

f. Legal and Other Periodicals (Rule 23)

Citation of particular pages within a law review article:

Mustave Hurt, <u>Unimaginable Pain</u>, 742 Geo L.J. 801, 831-32 (2003).

> Mustave Hurt = full name of author
> Unimaginable Pain = title of article
> 742 = journal volume #
> Geo. L.J. = abbreviation of journal
> 801 = first page of article
> 831-32 = specific pages
> 2003 = year published

Citation of a magazine article:

J. Madeleine Nash, <u>Fertile Minds</u>, Time 18 (Feb. 3, 1997).

> J. Madeline Nash = author's full name
> Fertile Minds = title of article
> Time = name of magazine
> 18 = first page
> Feb. 3, 1997 = cover date

Citation of a newspaper article:

Adam Gourna, <u>Celiac Disease: A Killer</u>, N.Y. Times F3 (Dec. 12, 1994).

> Adam Gourna = author's full name
> Celiac Disease: A Killer = headline
> N.Y. Times = abbreviation of newspaper
> F3 = page #
> Dec. 12, 1994 = date

C.   Often-Used ALWD Rules

The following are some of the most often-used rules in citation from the ALWD Citation Manual.

ALWD Typefaces (Rule 1)

ALWD RULE	KEY POINTS
Rule 1.1: Typeface Choices	- Most material should be presented in ordinary type. - Italics may be presented either with *slanted type* or <u>underlining</u>. - Periods are typically part of the citation component that they follow and should be underlined. - Commas are not typically part of the citation component and so should not be underlined. - Note that citations in law journals and book publishers that do not use the ALWD Citation Manual have different typeface conventions.
Rule 1.3: When to Use Italics in Citations	Italicize only the following: - Introductory signals - Internal cross-references - Case names, both in full and short citation formats - Phrases indicating subsequent or prior history - Titles of most documents - Topics or titles in legal encyclopedia entries - Names of Internet sites - The short forms <u>id.</u> and <u>supra</u>.
Rule 1.8: Italicizing Foreign Words	Generally italicize foreign words that have not been incorporated into normal English. Do not italicize words, such as ad hoc, amicus curiae, and habeus corpus, that have been incorporated into normal English. Consult Rule 1.8 or <u>Black's Law Dictionary</u> if you are unsure about a particular word.

ALWD Spelling and Capitalization (Rule 3)

ALWD RULE	KEY POINTS
Rule 3.1: Words in Titles	• Retain the spelling of the title of a source, such as a book or law review article, from the original source. • Change capitalization to conform to the following rules: • Capitalize the first word in the title. • Capitalize the first word in any subtitle. • Capitalize the first word after a colon or dash. • Capitalize all other words except articles, prepositions, the word "to" when used as part of an infinitive, and coordinating conjunctions. • Rule 3.1(c) contains special rules for capitalizing hyphenated words.
Rule 3.2: General Rules	Generally capitalize the following: • Professional titles and titles of honor or respect • Organization names • Proper nouns • Adjectives formed from proper nouns • Holidays, events, and epochs • Defined terms in a document
Rule 3.3: Capitalizing Specific Words	Certain words, such as "Act," "Board," and "Circuit," have special capitalization rules. Consult Rule 3.3 for the full list and accompanying rules.

ALWD Basic Structure and Signals (Rules 10, 43, and 44)

ALWD RULE	KEY POINTS
Rule 10: Internal Cross-References	• Internal cross-references may be used to reference text, footnotes, appendices, or any other internal material to avoid repeating text or to help readers. They may not be used to reference outside sources that have been cited elsewhere in the document. For those, use the appropriate short citation forms (see Rule 11). • To refer to material that appears earlier in the document, use supra. • To refer to material that will appear later in the document, use infra.
Rule 43: Citation Placement and Use Rule 43.1: Placement Options	• When a source relates to the whole sentence in the text, include the citation to that source in a separate citation sentence, beginning with a capital letter and ending with a period. • When a source relates to only part of a sentence in the text, include the citation as a clause within the sentence, immediately after the text it concerns, and set the clause off with commas. • Rule 43.1(e) discusses the use of footnotes in legal documents.

Rule 43.2: Frequency of Citation	Include a citation immediately after any sentence or portion thereof that contains a legal principle, legal authority, or thoughts borrowed from other sources.
Rule 44: Signals	• Signals are words or terms that inform readers about the type and degree of support (or contradiction) that the cited authority provides. • Use no signal if the cited authority directly supports the statement, identifies the source of a quotation, or merely identifies authority referred to in the text. • Signals that indicate support include: • See • Accord • See also • Cf. • Signals that indicate contradiction include: • Contra • But See • But cf. • Other signals indicate background material, See generally, indicate an example, See e.g., or draw a comparison, Compare … with …. • Signals should be capitalized if they begin a citation sentence, but not otherwise. Signals should be separated from the rest of the citation with one space, but no punctuation. Italicize or underline each introductory signal, unless it is used as a verb within the citation sentence. • Consult Rules 44.7 through 44.8 for specifics regarding the use of multiple signals or the same signal for multiple citations.
Rule 44.8: Order of Signals	• Signals of the same basic type are strung together within one citation sentence and are separated from each other by semicolons. • Signals of different types must be grouped in separate citation sentences. • Consult Rule 44.3 (Support, Comparison, Contradiction, and Background).
Rule 45.4: Order of Authorities Within Each Signal	• Constitutions; statutes; rules of evidence and procedure; treaties and international agreements; cases; case-related material; administrative and executive material; materials from intergovernmental organizations • Consult Rule 45 for more specifics.
Rule 46: Explanatory Parentheticals and Related Authority	• Parenthetical information explains the relevance of a particular authority to proposition given in the text. • If explanatory parenthetical information includes one or more full sentences, it should start with a capital letter and end with correct punctuation. • If the parenthetical information includes one or more full sentences, it should start with a capital letter and end with the correct punctuation. • Explanatory parenthetical phrases come before any citations concerning subsequent history or other related authority.

ALWD Subdivisions and Pinpoint Cites (Rules 5, 6, and 7)

ALWD RULE	KEY POINTS
Rule 5.1: Initial Pages	When citing a source with page numbers that is contained within a larger source (for example, a law review article), always include the initial page number of the source being cited.
Rule 5.2: Pinpoint Pages	• When citing specific material from a source, include a pinpoint page reference that provides the exact page on which the cited material is located. This rule applies both to material that is directly quoted and to specific information, such as a case holding, from a source. • Consult Rules 5.3 and 5.4 for details on how to cite consecutive pages or multiple pages within a source. • Consult Rule 5.5 for the format for star pagination. • Give page numbers or numbers before the date parenthetical, without any introductory abbreviation. • Use ", at" if a pinpoint page might be confused with the title. • If you are referring specifically to material on the first page of a source, repeat the page number. • When citing material within a concurring or dissenting opinion, give only the initial page of the case and the page on which the specific material appears. See Rule 12.5(d). • When citing material that spans more than one page, give the inclusive page numbers separated by the en dash (–) or the word "to." See Rule 5.3. • Cite nonconsecutive pages by giving the individual page numbers separated by a comma and a space (Rule 5.4).
Rule 6: Citing Sections and Paragraphs	If a source is divided into sections or paragraphs, cite the relevant subdivision using the section (§) and paragraph (¶) symbols, with a space between the symbol and the following number.
Rule 6.4: Subsections and Subparagraphs	Cite to the smallest subdivision possible when citing a section or paragraph. Use the original source punctuation to denote subsections. If the original source does not use punctuation to denote subsections, place subdivisions in parentheses, without inserting a space between the main and section and subdivision. Example: Fed. R. Civ. P. 26(a)(1)(D). Rules 6.6 through 6.10 address citation of multiple sections, subsections, paragraphs, and subparagraphs.
Rule 7: Citing Footnotes and Endnotes	• When citing a footnote or endnote, include the page on which the note begins and give the note number. • One note is abbreviated as "n."; multiple notes are abbreviated as "nn." Place one space between the abbreviation and the note number(s).

ALWD Short Citations (Rule 11)

ALWD RULE	KEY POINTS
Rule 11.2: Short Citation Format	• Only use short citation format after an authority has been cited once in full citation format and when the reader will not be confused as to which source is being referenced. • Rules for each specific type of source should be consulted to find the short citation format for that source. • For short form citations to cases, refer to Rule 12.20. • For short form citations for federal and state statutes, refer to Rule 14.6.
Rule 11.3: <u>Id.</u> as a Short Citation	• <u>Id.</u> generally replaces whatever portion of the immediately preceding citation is identical with the current citation. For example, if a full citation is provided for a law review article with pinpoint citation after one textual sentence, the citation for the next textual sentence may substitute "<u>id.</u>" for all the details regarding the article name, source name, and so on, and include only the new pinpoint page number: • Example: "And so it goes in Bankruptcy Court these days." Susan Dinero, <u>The Three Bs: Bankruptcy and Baby Boomers</u>, 105 Harv. L. Rev. 233, 245 (2002). Dinero adds, "And so it should." <u>Id.</u> at 246. • <u>Id.</u> may be used only to refer to the immediately preceding authority. In a paper with footnotes, if the preceding footnote has more than one citation, <u>id.</u> may not be used to refer because it would be unclear to the reader which citation is being referred to. • Italicize <u>id.</u> (if you use underlining to represent italics, underline the period in <u>id.</u> also). • Capitalize <u>id.</u> only if it begins a sentence.
Rule 11.4: <u>Supra</u> as a Short Citation	• <u>Supra</u> can be used to cross-reference a full citation provided previously in the document. • <u>Supra</u> is typically used for sources that are cited by author name, such as books and law review articles. Do not use <u>supra</u> as a short citation for cases, statutes, session laws, ordinances, legislative materials (other than hearings), constitutions, and administrative regulations. • Example: Baker, <u>supra</u> n. 3, at 55. *This citation provides the author name, the location of the original citation in the document, and a pinpoint citation to the page number in the original source.* • Rule 11.4(b)(2) states that legal writers should not use the <u>supra</u> format in documents that do not have footnotes or endnotes. • Rule 11.4(d) discusses the use of "hereinafter" to shorten <u>supra</u> citations or other short citations where a source has a particularly long title.

ALWD Abbreviations (Rule 2)

ALWD RULE	KEY POINTS
Rule 2: Abbreviations	• Abbreviations are often used in legal citation for common sources, such as legal periodicals and case names, and also for other less common words and phrases. • Consult Appendices 3, 4, and 5 for tables of standard abbreviations. Note that certain contractions may now be used as abbreviations. For example, Appendix 3 permits both "Govt." or "Gov't" as abbreviations for government. Once you choose the abbreviation, be consistent within your document. • Appendix 3 lists words, such as "commonwealth" or "insurance," that should be abbreviated in citations. Appendix 4 lists court abbreviations for both state and federal courts. • Appendix 5 lists abbreviations for legal periodicals, such as law reviews, including well-known law journals in some other English-language jurisdictions. • Appendix 5 also clarifies that commas should not be included in periodical abbreviations.

ALWD Numbers (Rule 4)

ALWD RULE	KEY POINTS
Rule 4: Numbers	• Numbers within citations should be presented as numerals unless the number appears in a title. If a number does appear in a title, present it as it is presented in the original. • Numbers within textual material may be presented as either numerals or words, but whichever you use, remain consistent. The convention in law is to present numbers zero to ninety-nine as words, and numbers above 100 as numerals. • Rule 4.3 addresses special rules for ordinal numbers (such as "first").

ALWD Quotations (Rules 47, 48, and 49)

ALWD RULE	KEY POINTS
Rule 47.4: Short Quotations	• If a quotation is fewer than fifty words, or runs fewer than four lines of typed text, simply enclose it in double quotation marks (" "). • Place the citation for the quoted material after the sentence containing the quoted material. In a footnoted document, place the note reference number immediately after the closing quotation mark, even if it is in the middle of the sentence. However, if a single textual sentence includes multiple quoted phrases from the same source and pinpoint reference, place the note reference number at the end of the sentence to reference all the quoted phrases.

Rule 47.4(d): Punctuation	Periods and commas should generally be placed inside quotations marks, regardless of whether they are part of the original quotation. Other punctuation, such as semicolons and question marks, should generally be placed outside the quotation marks unless they are part of the original quoted material.
Rule 47.5: Longer Quotations	If a quotation is fifty words or more, or exceeds four lines of typed text, present it as a block of type by single-spacing it and indenting it by one tab on both the right and left. Do not use quotation marks at the beginning or end of the block quotation. Separate the block quotation from the surrounding text by one blank line above and below.
Rule 47.7: Quotations within Quotations	• Within a short quotation, set off quotations with single quotation marks (' '). • Within a block quotation, set off quotations with double quotation marks (" ").
Rule 48: Altering Quoted Material Rule 48.1: Altering the Case of a Letter	When changing a letter from uppercase to lowercase, or vice versa, within a quotation, enclose the altered letter in brackets (for example, "[B]asketball" or "[f]ootball").
Rule 48.2: Adding, Changing, or Deleting One or More Letters	When adding, changing, or deleting letters from a quoted word, enclose the added, changed, or deleted material in brackets (indicate omitted or deleted material with empty brackets—[ ]).
Rule 48.4: Substituting or Adding Words	When substituting or adding words to a quotation, such as to clarify a detail for the reader, enclose those words in brackets.
Rule 48.5: Altering Typeface	When altering the typeface of quoted material, such as by adding or deleting italics for emphasis, describe the alteration in a parenthetical following the citation.
Rule 48.6: Mistakes within Original Quoted Material	When quoting material that contains mistakes, either correct the mistake and enclose changes in brackets as discussed above, or denote the mistake with "[sic]." Do not italicize or underline "[sic]."
Rule 49: Omissions within Quoted Material	• Use ellipsis to indicate omission of one or more words. An ellipsis consists of three periods with one space between each (. . .). Insert one space before and after the ellipsis as well. • Rule 49 contains many additional, more specific rules regarding the use of ellipses, particularly specifying spacing and punctuation.

ALWD Cases (Rule 12)

ALWD RULE	KEY POINTS
Rule 12.1: Full Citation Format	The general citation form for cases includes: Case Name, reporter volume number + reporter abbreviations + first page of case, page number (deciding court + date of decision). • Example: <u>N.Y. Times Co. v. Sullivan</u>, 144 So. 2d 25, 40-41 (Ala. 1962), <u>rev'd</u>, 376 U.S. 254 (1964).
Rule 12.2: Case Name	• Italicize or underline the case name, but not the comma following it. • If a caption on a case lists more than one case, cite only the first case listed. If a single case has two different names, use the one listed first. • Cite only the first-listed party on each side of the case, and do not use "et al." or other terms to denote any omitted parties. • If the party is an individual, use only the last name. If the party is an organization, include the organization's full name, but omit abbreviations such as "d/b/a" and any material following. Usually omit "The" when it appears as the first word in a party's name. • Generally, omit given names or initials of individuals, but not in names or businesses of firms. See Rule 12.2(e)(2). • Use the abbreviations listed in Appendix 3 to abbreviate listed words in case names pursuant to Rule 12.2(e)(3), unless doing so would create confusion for the reader. • Omit business firm designations such as "Inc." if the name of the firm also contains a word that clearly indicates the status of a business firm, such as "Ass'n." See Rule 12.2(e)(8). • Rule 12(g) now permits the use of "U.S." or "United States" when referring to the United States as a party in a case citation. • Omit "State of," "Commonwealth of," and "People of" unless citing decisions of the courts of that state, in which case only "State," "Commonwealth," or "People" should be retained. See Rule 12.2(h)(1). • Bankruptcy cases with two names follow Rule 12.2(p)(2). • If a case is unreported but available on electronic media, cite according to Rules 12.12, 12.13, 12.2. • Other more specific rules regarding the presentation of a case name in a citation sentence are provided in Rule 12.2.
Rule 12.4: Reporter Abbreviation	• After the volume number, include the abbreviation for the reporter in which the case appears. Abbreviations for reporters are found in Appendix 1. • When submitting a document to a state court, check the local rules for that court (see Appendix 2) to determine which reporter to cite to. Remember that some states require parallel citation (citation of both official and unofficial reporters). • When submitting a document to federal court, check the local rules for that court (see Appendix 2). • For U.S. Supreme Court cases, typically cite to only one reporter, preferably the United States Reports (abbreviated "U.S."), or to other reporters listed in Rule 12.4(c) if a "U.S." cite is not yet available.

Rule 12.6: Court Abbreviation	• Include the appropriate abbreviation for the court that decided the case in the parentheses following the page number, just before the year the case was decided. Check Appendices 1 and 4 for abbreviations of courts. • No court abbreviation is required for U.S. Supreme Court cases because the name of the reporter indicates that the case is a U.S. Supreme Court case. Simply include the year the case was decided in the parentheses.
Rule 12.8: Subsequent History	• Subsequent history should be included in a citation if the action is listed in Rule 12.8(a). Also indicate when a judgment in a cited case has been overruled. • Consult the rules in Rule 12.8 directly for formatting and other details.
Rule 12.9: Prior History	• Prior history may be included, but is never mandatory and should be used sparingly. • Prior history should be presented in the same manner as subsequent history.

Rule 12.20: Short Citation Format	• If id. is appropriate, use it as the preferred short citation for cases.
	• If all or part of a case name is not included in the textual sentence, include some portion of the case name in the short citation to identify it for the reader.
	   • Example: The judge thought otherwise and ruled against the defendant. Seel, 971 P.2d at 924.
	• If the case name, or part of it, is included in the textual sentence, simply include in the short citation the volume number, reporter abbreviation, the word "at," and then the pinpoint reference.
	   • Example: The judge in Seel thought otherwise and ruled against the defendant. 971 P.2d at 924.

ALWD Constitutions (Rule 13)

ALWD RULE	KEY POINTS
Rule 13.2: Full Citation Format for Constitutions Currently in Force	• A citation to a constitution currently in force should include the name of the constitution and a pinpoint reference. • Example: U.S. Const. amend. XIV, § 2. • Check Appendix 3C for appropriate abbreviations of article (art.), amendment (amend.), section (§), and clause (cl.). • Abbreviate United States (U.S.) if referring to the federal Constitution, or refer to Appendix 3A for the appropriate abbreviation if citing a state constitution (Rule 13.2 (a)). • Be as specific as possible with pinpoint references.
Rule 13.3: Full Citation Format for Constitutions No Longer in Force	For constitutions no longer in force, use the same citation format given in Rule 13.2, but use a parenthetical to explain why it is no longer in force and include the year in which it lost effect. • Example: U.S. Const. amend. XVIII (repealed 1933 by U.S. Const. amend. XXI).
Rule 13.4: Short Citation Format	If appropriate, use id. as the short-form citation for constitutional provisions.

ALWD Statutes (Rule 14)

ALWD RULE	KEY POINTS
Rule 14.2: Full Citation, Print Format for Federal Statutes Currently in Force	• Example: 18 U.S.C. § 1965 (2000). The official code for federal statutes is the United States Code, abbreviated "U.S.C." Do not include a publisher for U.S.C. • Make sure that the abbreviations of code names are properly formatted. There should be periods and no spaces between the letters of "U.S.C." See Appendix 1 to determine the proper abbreviation formats for state codes. • Use "§" to denote the section number of the code that you are citing. Leave a space between "§" and the section number, and use "§§" if you are citing multiple sections (Rule 14.2(c)). • Include the date of the code edition cited in a parenthetical following the section number (Rules 14.2(f)(1) and 14.2(f)(2)). • If citing to a code that is published, edited, or compiled by someone other than state officials, give the name of the publisher, editor, or compiler in the parenthetical phrase (14.2(e)). For example: (West 2006). • If the statute is commonly cited using a different name or is known by a popular name, give that name and the original section number preceding the normal citation format (14.2(g)).
Rule 14.3: Full Citation, Print Format for Federal Statutes No Longer in Force	Cite as described in Rule 14.2, but include a statement that the statute was repealed or superseded, with the year in which the statute ceased to be in force. • Example: 26 U.S.C. § 1071(a) (repealed 1995).

Rule 14.4: Full Citation, Print Format for State Statutes	Abbreviations and formats for state codes are included in Appendix 1.
Rule 14.6: Short Citation, Print Format for Federal and State Statutes	Use <u>id.,</u> if appropriate. Otherwise, use all required components of the full citation, but omit the date. • Example: The full citation "42 U.S.C. § 12101 (2000)" may be cited in short form as "42 U.S.C. § 12101."

ALWD Administrative and Executive Materials (Rule 19, Appendix 7(C))

ALWD RULE	KEY POINTS
Rule 19.1: Full Citation Format for Code of Federal Regulations	Whenever possible, cite all federal rules and regulations to the Code of Federal Regulations (C.F.R.) by title, section or part, and year. • Example: 28 C.F.R. § 540.71 (2003). • Example: 31 C.F.R. pt. 730 (2005). • Be sure to cite the most recent edition of C.F.R., according to Rule 19.1(d). • Do not leave spaces between the letters of "C.F.R." • Cite to arbitrations and administrative adjudications using Rule 19.5. • Advisory opinions from the United States Attorney general or Office of Legal Counsel are cited according to Rule 19.7 (full citation format) and Rule 19.8 (short citation format). • Presidential executive orders are found in title 3 of C.F.R. and should be cited to C.F.R. according to Rule 19.9, with a parallel citation to the United States Code if therein. However, if an executive order is not found in C.F.R., cite according to the federal Register. Examples of each citation format can be found in Rule 19.9.
Rule 19.2: Short Citation Format for Code of Federal Regulations	If <u>id.</u> is appropriate, use it as the preferred short citation for rules and regulations cited in the C.F.R. If <u>id.</u> is not appropriate, repeat all elements in the full citation except the date. • Example: 28 C.F.R. at § 540.90.
Rule 19.3: Full Citation Format for Federal Register	Cite final rules and regulations not yet entered in the C.F.R., proposed federal rules and regulations, and notices to the Federal Register. Include a pinpoint cite if appropriate, and use a full date. • Example: 70 Fed. Reg. 10868, 10870 (Mar. 5, 2005).
Rule 19.4: Short Citation Format for Federal Register	If <u>id.</u> is appropriate, use it as the preferred short citation for rules and regulations cited in the Federal Register. If <u>id.</u> is not appropriate, repeat all elements in the full citation except the date. • Example: 70 Fed. Reg. at 10875.
Appendix 7(C): Administrative Materials	See Appendix 7(C) for help in citing Treasury regulations and other federal taxation materials.

ALWD Books, Reports, and Other Nonperiodic Materials (Rule 22)

ALWD RULE	KEY POINTS
Rule 22.1: Full Citation Format	Cite books, treatises, reports, or other nonperiodic materials by author, title (italicized or underlined), pinpoint reference (if appropriate), edition (if any), publisher, and year. • Example: Joshua Dressler, <u>Understanding Criminal Law</u> §10.04 (3d ed., Lexis 2001). • When citing a publication for the first time, give the author's full name as it appears on the publication. However, do not include designations indicating academic degrees such as "Dr." • For works with two authors, give their names in the order in which they are listed on the title page, separated by "&" (Rule 22.1(a)(2(a) and Rule 22.1(a)(2)(b)). • Give the full name of the editor in a parenthetical as it appears in the publication. In the same parenthetical, after the full name of the editor, indicate the editor's title with "ed.," the name of the publisher (if other than the original publisher), and the year of publication (Rule 22.1(d)). • For specifics on works with translators, refer to Rule 22.1(e). • For works that have been published in only one edition, give the year of publication in parentheses (Rule 22.1(j)). • For works that have been published in multiple editions, cite the latest edition (Rule 22.1(f)(3)).
Rule 22.2: Short Citation Format for Works Other Than Those in a Collection	If <u>id.</u> is appropriate, use it as the preferred short citation for books. If <u>id.</u> is not appropriate, the format of the short citation varies. • Example (document without footnotes): Dressler, <u>Understanding Criminal Law</u>, at § 12.08. • Example (document with footnotes): Dressler, <u>supra</u> n. [note number], at § 12.08.

ALWD Periodicals (Rule 23)

ALWD RULE	KEY POINTS
Rule 23.1: Full Citation Format	• Cite to articles in law reviews, journals, newspapers, magazines, and other periodicals by author, title (italicized or underlined), volume number (if any), periodical abbreviation, first page, pinpoint reference (if appropriate), and date. Use Appendix 5 to abbreviate periodical names and to determine whether the journal you are citing is consecutively or nonconsecutively paginated. • Example (consecutively paginated periodical): Howard F. Chang, <u>Risk Regulation, Endogenous Public Concerns, and the Hormones Dispute: Nothing to Fear but Fear Itself?</u> 77 S. Cal. L. Rev. 743, 751 (2004). • Example (nonconsecutively paginated periodical): Linda Buckley, <u>A Hole in the Safety Net</u>, Newsweek 40 (May 13, 2002).

Rule 23.2: Short Citation Format	If <u>id.</u> is appropriate, use it as the preferred short citation for periodicals. If <u>id.</u> is not appropriate, the format of the short citation varies.
	• Example (document without footnotes): Chang, 77 S. Cal. L. Rev. at 752.
	• Example (document with footnotes): Chang, <u>supra</u> n. [note number], at 752.

ALWD Electronic Media (Rules 12, 14, and Part 4)

Rule 12.12: Cases Published Only on LexisNexis or Westlaw	Include the case name (italicized or underlined), the database identifier, the name of the database (either LEXIS or WL) plus a unique document number, and a parenthetical containing the court abbreviation and a full date.
	• Example: <u>Goodyear Tire & Rubber Co. v. Moore</u>, 2005 WL 1611323 (Va. App. July 12, 2005).
	Rule 12.12(d) explains how to format a docket number and when and how to include a docket number in a case citation.
	See below under "Rule 4" for information on citing Westlaw and Lexis formats, web sites, emails, CD-ROMs, and E-Readers.
Rule 14.5: Statutes Available on Electronic Databases	Cite statutes according to Rules 14.2 and 14.4. In addition, include in the date parenthetical the name of the database provider and information about the currency of the database.
	• Example: Ga. Code Ann. § 7-1-841 (Westlaw current through 2004 1st Spec. Sess.).
Part 4: Electronic Sources Rule 38: General Information About Online and Electronic Citation Formats	Cite only to print sources unless the material would be difficult for most readers to find or the source is more widely available in electronic form. In that case, include the electronic source information in a parenthetical. If a source is available in print, you may add a parenthetical with the electronic cite if it will help the reader access the source more easily.
	• Example: U.S. Census Bureau, <u>Statistical Abstract of the United States</u> 119 (121st ed. 2001) (available at http://www.census.gov/prod/2002pubs/01statab/stat-ab01.html).
Rule 39: Addresses Citation formats for documents found on commercial electronic databases such as LexisNexis or Westlaw.	• Unreported cases that are available on widely used electronic database such as LexisNexis or Westlaw can be cited to that database according to Rule 12.3. • If citing to a specific page of an opinion, place "at" after the database identifier and indicate the page number preceded by an asterisk. See Rule 12.12(b). • Cite statutes according to Rules 14.2 and 14.4. In addition, include in the date parenthetical the name of the database provider and information about the currency of the database (Rule 14.5).
Rules 38-42	For more about citing electronic sources, see Rules 38 through 42, which cover Westlaw and Lexis formats, web sites, email, CD-ROMs, and E-Readers.

III.   STUDY AIDS—ALWD CITATION

A.   *ALWD Quick References and Checklists*

📋 1.   ALWD in General: Quick Reference

To use ALWD effectively, you should understand the following:

- The purpose of citation
- The design, layout, and basic citation rules of ALWD
- Some often-used rules of ALWD

Purpose of Citation

The purpose of citation is to allow lawyers to easily find and reference legal sources.

Design, Layout, and Basic ALWD Citation Rules

- ALWD citation formats are the same for scholarly writing and legal documents.
- ALWD layout:
  - Part 1—Introductory Material
  - Part 2—Citation Basics
  - Part 3—Citing Specific Print Sources
  - "Fast Formats"—examples of citations for commonly used sources
  - Part 4—Electronic Sources
  - Part 5—Incorporating Citations into Documents
  - Part 6—Quotations
  - Part 7—Appendices
  - Detailed table of contents and an index
  - Green triangles (▲) designate spaces in citation formats.
  - Green circles (●) separate components of citations.
  - "Fast Format Locator" on inside front cover gives page numbers for Fast Format tables.
  - "Short Citation Locator for Commonly Used Sources" on inside back cover lists rule numbers for short citation formats.
- Basic ALWD Citation Rules
  - Legal and Other Periodicals: Rule 23

Often-Used Citation Rules in ALWD

- Typefaces: Rule 1
- Spelling and Capitalization: Rule 3
- Basic Structure and Signals: Rules 10, 43, and 44
- Subdivisions and Pinpoint Cites: Rules 5, 6, 7
- Short Citations: Rule 11
- Abbreviations: Rule 2

- Statutes: Rule 14
- Administrative and Executive Materials: Rule 19, Appendix 7C
- Books, Treaties, and Other Nonperiodic Materials: Rule 22
- Legal and Other Periodicals: Rule 23
- Electronic Media: Rules 12, 14, and Part 4

 ## 2.   ALWD Typeface Conventions: Checklist

✓ Rule 1 addresses typeface conventions for court documents. In court documents, underline (or italicize) the following:
- Introductory signals
- Internal cross-references
- Case names, in both full and short citation formats
- Phrases indicating subsequent or prior history
- Titles of most documents
- Topics or titles in legal encyclopedia entries
- Names of Internet sites
- The short forms <u>id.</u> and <u>supra</u>

✓ Note that citations in law journals and book publishers that do not use the ALWD Citation Manual have different typeface conventions.

 ## 3.   Basic Structure and Signals for ALWD Citations: Checklist

✓ Internal Cross-References: See Rule 10. Internal cross-references may be used to reference text, footnotes, appendices, or any other internal material to avoid repeating text or to help readers. They may not be used to reference outside sources that have been cited elsewhere in the document. For those, use the appropriate short citation forms (see Rule 11). Use <u>supra.</u> to refer to material that appears earlier in the document and <u>infra.</u> to refer to material that appears later in the document.

✓ Citation Placement and Use and Placement Options: See Rule 43. When a source relates to the whole sentence in the text, include the citation to that source in a separate citation sentence, beginning with a capital letter and ending with a period. When a source relates to only part of a sentence in the text, include the citation as a clause within the sentence, immediately after the text it concerns, and set the clause off with commas.

✓ Frequency of Citation: See Rule 43.2. Include a citation immediately after any sentence or portion thereof that contains a legal principle, legal authority, or thoughts borrowed from other sources.

✓ Categories of Signals: See Rule 44.3
- Signals that show support: <u>See</u>, <u>Accord</u>, <u>See also</u>, <u>Cf.</u>
- Signal that draws a comparison: <u>Compare</u> ... <u>with</u> ...
- Signals that indicate contradiction: <u>Contra</u>, <u>But see</u>, <u>But cf.</u>

- Signal that indicates background material: <u>See generally</u>
- Signal that indicates an example: <u>E.g.</u>

✓ Order of Signals: See Rule 44.8. Signals of the same basic type are strung together within one citation sentence and are separated from each other by semicolons. If there are signals of different types then they must be grouped in separate citation sentences. Follow order in Rule 44.3 (Support, Comparison, Contradiction, and Background).

✓ Order of Authorities Within Each Signal: See Rule 45 generally for more details within each category. Constitutions; statutes; rules of evidence and procedure; treaties and international agreements; cases; case-related material; administrative and executive material; materials from intergovernmental organizations.

✓ Parenthetical Information explains the relevance of a particular authority to proposition given in the text. See Rule 46.

- Explanatory parenthetical phrases that do not directly quote the authority usually begin with a present participle and usually do not begin with a capital letter.
- If the parenthetical information includes one or more full sentences, it should start with a capital letter and end with the correct punctuation.
- Explanatory parenthetical phrases come before any citations concerning subsequent history or other related authority.

4.   ALWD Citation Signals: Checklist

Signals in Text	Proposition	Cited Authority and Meaning
SUPPORT		
[No signal]		Directly states, identifies, or supports the proposition.
See; see also		Clearly supports; contains dicta that supports the proposition.
Cf.		Analogous proposition.
E.g.; see, e.g.,		Multiple authorities clearly state the proposition.
CONTRADICTION		
Contra		Directly states contrary proposition.
BACKGROUND		
See generally		Helpful, related background material.
COMPARISON		
Compare … with …		Comparison of cited authorities supports proposition.

5. ALWD Rules for Citing Subdivisions and Pinpoint Cites: Checklist

✓ Rule 5.2 addresses the proper format for citations to specific page numbers:

   a. Give page number or numbers before the date parenthetical, without any introductory abbreviation.
   b. Use ", at" if a pinpoint page might be confused with the title.
   c. If you are referring specifically to material on the first page of a source, repeat the page number.
   d. When citing material within a concurring or dissenting opinion, give only the initial page of the case and the page on which the specific material appears. See Rule 12.5(d).
   e. When citing material that spans more than one page, give the inclusive page numbers separated by the en dash (–) or the word "to." See Rule 5.3.
   f. Cite nonconsecutive pages by giving the individual page numbers separated by a comma and a space (Rule 5.4).

---

6. ALWD Rules for Short Form Citations: Checklist

✓ According to Rule 11.2(a), once you have provided one full citation to an authority, you are free to use a "short form" in later citations to the same authority. Use a short citation when:

   • it will be clear to the reader from the short form what is being referenced,
   • the earlier full citation falls in the same general discussion, and
   • the reader will have little more trouble quickly locating the full citation. General rule: Avoid confusion.

✓ For short form citations to cases, refer to Rule 12.20. Use first party's name, the volume number, reporter designation, and page number.

   • Example: <u>Youngstown</u>, 343 U.S. at 585.
   • Party Name: When using only one party name in a short form citation, use the name of the first party, unless that party is a geographical or governmental unit or other common litigant.

✓ Rule 14.6 gives the short form citation rules for federal and state statutes.

✓ <u>Id.</u>: Use to refer to the immediately preceding authority (Rule 11.3).

   • The "i" in "<u>id.</u>" is capitalized only when it begins a citation sentence.
   • To refer to a different page within the immediately preceding authority, add "at" and the new pinpoint cite.
   • <u>Id.</u> may be used only when the preceding citation cites to only one source.

✓ <u>Supra</u>: See Rule 11.4. Once a work in a periodical, book, legislative hearing, report, unpublished work, or nonprint resource has been fully cited, use "<u>id.</u>" to refer to material cited in the immediately preceding citation. Otherwise, use <u>supra</u> for legislative hearings, reports, unpublished materials, nonprint resources, periodicals, regulations, etc. that have previously been cited fully. <u>Supra</u> form generally consists of the last name of the author of the work (or the title if the author is not available), followed by a comma and the word "<u>supra</u> n.", the note number, "at" and the page number. (Rule 11.4(c)).

- Example: Reich, <u>supra</u> n. 18, at 6.

 ## 7.   ALWD Abbreviations: Checklist

✓ Rule 2.1 is the general rule on abbreviations. Appendices at the end of ALWD contain lists of specific abbreviations:
- General Abbreviations: Appendix 3
- Court Abbreviations: Appendix 4
- Abbreviations for Legal Periodicals: Appendix 5

✓ Spacing: Generally, close up adjacent single capitals (e.g., N.W.), but do not close up single capitals with longer abbreviations (e.g., D. Mass.). See Rule 2.2.

 ## 8.   ALWD Rules for Citing Cases: Checklist

✓ According to Rule 12.1, the general citation form for cases includes: Case Name, reporter volume number + reporter abbreviations + first page of case, page # (deciding court + date of decision).

✓ Case Names: Rule 12.2
    a. For case names that appear in textual sentences, refer to Rule 12.2:
- Italicize or underline the case name (Rule 12.2(a)), but not the comma following it.
- If a caption on a case lists more than one case, cite only the first case listed. If a single case has two different names, use the one listed first (Rule 12.2(b)). Bankruptcy cases with two names follow Rule 12.2(p)(2).
- Cite only the first-listed party on each side of the case, and do not use "et al." or other terms to denote any omitted parties (Rule 12.2(c)). If the party is an individual, use only the last name (Rule 12.2(d)). If the party is an organization, include the organization's full name, but omit abbreviations such as "d/b/a" and any material following (Rule 12.2(e)). Usually omit "The" when it appears as the first word in a party's name (Rule 12.2(e) and Rule 12.2(q)).
- Use the abbreviations listed in Appendix 3 to abbreviate listed words in case names pursuant to Rule 12.2(e)(3), unless doing so would create confusion for the reader.
- Omit "State of," "Commonwealth of," and "People of" unless citing decisions of the courts of that state, in which case only

"State," "Commonwealth," or "People" should be retained. See Rule 12.2(h)(1).

- Generally, omit given names or initials of individuals, but not in names or businesses of firms. See Rule 12.2(e)(2).
- Omit business firm designations such as "Inc." if the name of the firm also contains a word that clearly indicates its status as a business firm, such as "Ass'n." See Rule 12.2(e)(8).

b. For case names that appear in citations, refer to Rule 12. Note that case names in citations generally follow the rules in Rule 12.2, with the following modification:

- You may abbreviate any word in a party's name and any state, country, and geographic unit that appear in Appendix 3.

✓ Reporters: See Rule 12.3, 12.4, Chart 12.1, Appendix 1 and Appendix 2. Include the volume number of the reporter, followed by the abbreviated name of the reporter as found in Chart 12.1 and Appendix 1.

✓ Appropriate short form citations for cases are listed in Rule 12.20.

 ## 9. ALWD Rules for Citing Constitutions: Checklist

✓ Abbreviate United States (U.S.) if referring to the federal Constitution, or refer to Appendix 3A for the appropriate abbreviation if citing a state constitution (Rule 13.2(a)).

✓ Abbreviate "Constitution" as "Const." (Rule 13.2(a)).

✓ Refer to Appendix 3C for the appropriate abbreviations of article (art.), amendment (amend.), section (§), and clause (cl.).

✓ If the constitutional provision has been repealed, amended, or superseded, refer to Rule 13.3 for the appropriate citation format.

✓ Id. is the only acceptable format for short citations to constitutions (Rule 13.4).

 ## 10. ALWD Rules for Citing Statutes: Checklist

✓ Cite to the official federal and state codes whenever possible. The official federal code is the United States Code, "U.S.C." To determine the official code for a particular state, see Appendix 1 (Rule 14.1).

✓ Make sure that the abbreviations of code names are properly formatted. There should be periods and no spaces between the letters "U.S.C." See Appendix 1 to determine the proper abbreviation formats for state codes.

✓ Use "§" to denote the section number of the code that you are citing. Leave a space between "§" and the section number, and use "§§" if you are citing multiple sections (Rule 14.2(c)).

✓ Include the date of the code edition cited in a parenthetical following the section number (Rules 14.2(f)(1) and 14.2(f)(2)). If citing to a code that is published, edited, or compiled by someone other than state officials, give the name of the publisher, editor, or compiler in the parenthetical phrase (Rule 14.2(e)). For example: (West 2006).

✓ According to Rule 14.2(g), if the statute is commonly cited using a different name or is known by a popular name, give that name and the original section number preceding the normal citation format.

✓ If a statute appears in a supplement or pocket part, cite the statute according to Rule 8.1.

✓ If a statute has been invalidated, repealed, or amended, cite it in accordance with Rule 14.3. When citing a current version of a statute that has prior history, you may give the prior history in an explanatory parenthetical phrase according to Rule 14.2(h) and Rule 14.7(i).

✓ If a statute is previously cited, you may use a short form of the statute according to Rule 14.6. Use <u>id.</u>, if appropriate.

 ## 11. ALWD Citations for Administrative and Executive Materials: Checklist

✓ Whenever possible, cite all federal rules and regulations to the Code of Federal Regulations (C.F.R.) by title, section or part, and year using the format specified in Rule 19.

   a. Be sure to cite the most recent edition of C.F.R., according to Rule 19.1(d).

   b. Do not leave spaces between the letters of "C.F.R."

✓ According to Rule 19.3, if a rule or regulation has not yet been published in C.F.R., cite to the Federal Register. Administrative notices should also be cited to the Federal Register.

✓ To use a short citation to identify a rule or regulation, use one of the formats listed in Rule 19.2 for C.F.R. or Rule 19.4 for Federal Register.

✓ Cite to arbitrations and administrative adjudications using Rule 19.5.

✓ Advisory opinions from the United States Attorney General or Office of Legal Counsel are cited according to Rule 19.7 (full citation format) and Rule 19.8 (short citation format).

✓ See Appendix 7(C) for help in citing Treasury regulations and other federal taxation materials.

✓ Presidential executive orders are found in title 3 of C.F.R. and should be cited to C.F.R. according to Rule 19.9, with a parallel citation to the United States Code if therein. However, if an executive order is not found in C.F.R., cite according to the Federal Register. Examples of each citation format can be found in Rule 19.9.

✓ Patents should be cited according to the patent number and the date the patent was filed, using the format specified in Rule 19.13.

---

12. ALWD Citations for Books, Reports, and Other Nonperiodic Materials: Checklist

✓ According to Rule 22.1(a), when citing a publication for the first time, give the author's full name as it appears on the publication. However, do not include designations indicating academic degrees such as "Dr." For works with two authors, give their names in the order in which they are listed on the title page, separated by "&" (Rule 22.1(a)(2)(a) and Rule 22.1(a)(2)(b)).

✓ Rule 22.1(d) specifies the format for works with editors and Rule 22.1(e) specifies the format for works with translators. Give the full name of the editor in a parenthetical as it appears in the publication. In the same parenthetical, after the full name of the editor, indicate the editor's title with "ed.," the name of the publisher (if other than the original publisher), and the year of publication.

✓ For works that have been published in only one edition, give the year of publication in parentheses (Rule 22.1(j)). For works that have been published in multiple editions, cite the latest edition according to Rule 22.1(f)(3)).

 ## 13. ALWD Rules for Citing Periodical Materials: Checklist

✓ For consecutively paginated articles in law reviews, journals, newspapers, magazines, and other periodicals (Rule 23.1):

   a. Cite the author's full name as it appears in the publication according to Rule 22.1(a).

   b. Cite the full title of the article according to Rule 23.1(b).

   c. Cite the volume number, followed by the abbreviation for the periodical according to Appendix 5, and the page number on which the cited material begins.

   d. Indicate the date of publication in a parenthetical.

   e. If the piece you are citing is student-written, follow Rule 23.1(a)(2) and consult Sidebar 23.1.

   f. For book reviews reference Rule 23.1(b)(2).

 ## 14. ALWD Rules for Citing Electronic Media: Checklist

✓ Rule 39 addresses citation formats for documents found on commercial electronic databases such as LexisNexis or Westlaw.

   a. Unreported cases that are available on a widely used electronic database such as LexisNexis or Westlaw can be cited to that database according to Rule 12.13.

b. If citing to a specific page of an opinion, place "at" after the database identifier and indicate the page number preceded by an asterisk. See Rule 12.12(b).

c. Cite statutes according to Rules 14.2 and 14.4. In addition, include in the date parenthetical the name of the database provider and information about the currency of the database (Rule 14.5).

✓ Cite only to print sources unless the material would be difficult for most readers to find or the source is more widely available in electronic form. In that case, include the electronic source information in a parenthetical (Rule 38).

a. See Rule 40.1(d) for URL citation formats.

b. Personal e-mail correspondence may be cited according to Rule 32, but insert the designation "Email from" (Rule 41.1(a)). The e-mail addresses of the sender and recipient of the e-mail are not required. Include information that will assist the reader in finding a copy of the message (Rule 41.1(d)).

B. ALWD Quizzes

⚇? 1. ALWD Typeface Conventions: Quiz

Assume the following citations appear in court documents.

1. Choose the correct citation for Missouri v. Holland.

   A. <u>Missouri v. Holland, 252 U.S. 416</u> (1922).
   B. <u>Missouri v. Holland</u>, 252 U.S. 416 (1922).
   C. <u>Missouri v. Holland,</u> 252 U.S. 416 (1922).
   D. Missouri v. Holland, 252 U.S. 416 (1922).

2. Which citation does NOT have an error?

   A. See <u>Brown v. Board of Education</u>, 347 U.S. 438 (1954).
   B. <u>Brown</u>, 347 U.S. at 440.
   C. <u>Clark v. Davis,</u> 533 U.S. 678, 719 (2001) (citing <u>Evanson v. United States,</u> 345 U.S. 206 (1953)).
   D. Matt Corney, Red House (Oxford ed., Penguin Books 1979) (1899).

3. Which citation does NOT have an error?

   A. See <u>id.</u> at 348.
   B. <u>Id. at 348.</u>
   C. See <u>id.</u> at 348.
   D. See <u>id.</u> at 348.

4. Which citation does NOT have an error?

   A. Gretel C. Kovach, Use of False Hiring Data Found in Dallas Schools, N.Y. Times, Nov. 15, 2 A10.
   B. Greg Gelpi, Attorney Still Loves Fighting for Little Guys, <u>Augusta Chron.</u>, Dec. 8, 2008, at B.
   C. David Rudovsky, Police Abuse: Can the Violence Be Contained?, 27 Harv. C.R.-C.L. L. Rev 500 (1992).
   D. Andrew Rosenthal, <u>Medicine and the Law</u>, N.Y. Times A1 (June 15, 1990).

5. Which citation does NOT have an error?
   A. <u>Sciolino v. City of Newport News</u>, 480 F.3d 642, 647 (4th Cir. 2007) (Wilkinson, J., dissenting.
   B. Id. at 735.
   C. <u>Codd v. Velger</u>, 429 U.S. 624, 627 (1977).
   D. <u>U.S. Const.</u> amend XIV, § 1.

Answer Key on page 311

⚙? 2. Basic Structure and Signals for ALWD Citations: Quiz

Assume the following citations appear in court documents.

1. Choose the string citation without an error.
   A. <u>See</u> <u>Edwards v. Arizona</u>, 451 U.S. 477 (1981). <u>But see</u> <u>Berkemer v. MacCarty</u>, 468 U.S. 420 <u>Compare</u> <u>Orozco v. Texas</u>, 394 U.S. 324 (1969).
   B. <u>See</u> <u>Edwards v. Arizona</u>, 451 U.S. 477 (1981); <u>but see</u> <u>Berkemer v. McCarty</u>, 468 U.S. 420 (1984).
   C. <u>Edwards v. Arizona</u>, 451 U.S. 466 (1981). <u>See</u> <u>Berkemer v. McCarty</u>, 468 U.S. 420 (1984).
   D. <u>See</u> <u>Edwards v. Arizona</u>, 451 U.S. 477 (1981); <u>But see</u> <u>Berkemer v. MacCarty</u>, 468 U.S. 420 (1984).

2. Choose the string citation without an error.

   A. <u>See</u> <u>Edwards v. Arizona</u>, 451 U.S. 477 (1981); <u>State v. Bradshaw</u>, 457 S.E.2d 456 (W. Va. 2 <u>Orozco v. Texas</u>, 394 U.S. 324 (1969).
   B. <u>See</u> <u>Edwards v. Arizona</u>, 451 U.S. 477 (1981); <u>Orozco v. Texas</u>, 394 U.S. 324 (1969).
   C. <u>See</u> <u>State v. Bradshaw</u>, 457 S.E.2d 456 (W. Va. 1995); <u>State v. Singleton</u>, 624 S.E.2d 527 (2005).
   D. <u>See</u> <u>Edwards v. Arizona</u>, 451 U.S. 477 (1981); U.S. Const. amend V.

3. Choose the string citation without an error.
   A. <u>See</u> Greg Gelpi, <u>Attorney Still Loves Fighting for Little Guys</u>, Augusta Chron., Dec. 8, 2008, a <u>Swilley v. Alexander</u>, 629 F.2d 1018, 1020 (5th Cir. 1980).

B. <u>See</u> 42 U.S.C.A. § 1983 (2009); <u>Swilley v. Alexander</u>, 629 F.2d 1018, 1020 (5th Cir. 1980).

  C. <u>See</u> 42 U.S.C.A. § 1983 (2009); U.S. Const. amend XIV, § 1.

  D. <u>See</u> <u>Cox v. Roskelley</u>, 359 F.3d 1105, 1110 (9th Cir. 2002); <u>Codd v. Velger</u>, 429 U.S. 624, 62 (1977).

4. Choose the citation without an error.

  A. <u>Cox v. Roskelley</u>, 359 F.3d 1105, 1110 (9th Cir. 2002) (holding once stigmatizing information placed into Cox's personnel file, it became public record under Washington law).

  B. ("Nor shall any State deprive person of life, liberty, or property, without due process of the law Const. amend XIV, §1.

  C. Gretel C. Kovach, <u>Use of False Hiring Data Found in Dallas Schools</u> (newspaper ran article after obtaining report, marked highly confidential, through a records request), N.Y. Times, Nov. 15, A10.

  D. U.S. Const. ("Nor shall any State deprive person of life, liberty, or property, without due process law") amend XIV, § 1.

5. Choose the string citation without an error.

  A. <u>See also</u> <u>Miranda v. Arizona</u>, 384 U.S. 436 (1966); <u>see</u> <u>Edwards v. Arizona</u>, 451 U.S. 477 (1981).

  B. <u>See</u> S.C. Const. art. I, § 12; U.S. Const. art. IV, § 1.

  C. <u>See</u> <u>Miranda v. Arizona</u>, 384 U.S. 436 (1966); <u>see</u> <u>Edwards v. Arizona</u>, 451 U.S. 477 (1981)

  D. <u>See</u> <u>State v. Jameson</u>, 461 S.E.2d 67 (W. Va. 1995); <u>but see</u> <u>State v. Green</u>, 260 S.E.2d 257 (W. Va. 1979).

Answer Key on page 311

3. ALWD Citation Signals: Quiz

You are researching a state water quality issue for a partner at your firm, and you have uncovered a number of authorities that support, contradict, or supplement the following excerpt from a Maryland statute: Factories may not dispose of hazardous materials in the Chesapeake Bay. What signal would you use to best cite each authority described below?

1. A case decided by the Maryland Court of Appeals (the highest court in Maryland) that holds that factories cannot dispose of hazardous materials in Maryland rivers.

  A. No signal

  B. <u>But see</u>

  C. <u>See e.g.</u>

  D. <u>Cf.</u>

  E. <u>Contra</u>

2. A law review article that discusses hazardous waste disposal laws in several states on the eastern seaboard, including Maryland.

    A. No signal
    B. See generally
    C. See
    D. Cf.
    E. Contra

3. A Delaware statute that prohibits dumping of hazardous materials in the Chesapeake Bay.

    A. No signal
    B. See generally
    C. Accord
    D. Cf.
    E. See

4. One of several Maryland cases holding that factories may not dispose of hazardous waste in Maryland waters.

    A. No signal
    B. See e.g.
    C. See
    D. See generally
    E. Compare … with …

5. A Maryland Court of Appeals case holding that factories may not dispose of hazardous materials in the Chesapeake Bay.

    A. No signal
    B. See
    C. But see
    D. Contra
    E. Cf.

6. A Maryland Court of Appeals case holding that no individual or organization may dispose of polluting materials in the bays or other marshland areas of the state of Maryland.

    A. No signal
    B. Cf.
    C. See
    D. But see
    E. See e.g.

Answer Key on page 311

4. **ALWD Order and Punctuation of Signals and Citations: Quiz**

1. Select the correct citation sentence.
    A. <u>See</u> <u>Matthews v. Potter</u>, 19 P.2d 368 (Cal. 1999). <u>See also</u> <u>Morrison v. Perkins</u>, 56 P.2d 247 (Cal. 2000). <u>But see</u> <u>Smith v. Jennings</u>, 85 P.2d 465 (Cal. 2001).
    B. <u>See</u> <u>Matthews v. Potter</u>, 19 P.2d 368 (Cal. 1999); <u>see also</u> <u>Morrison v. Perkins</u>, 56 P.2d 247 (Cal. 2000); <u>but see</u> <u>Smith v. Jennings</u>, 85 P.2d 465 (Cal. 2001).
    C. <u>See also</u> <u>Morrison v. Perkins</u>, 56 P.2d 247 (Cal. 2000); <u>see</u> <u>Matthews v. Potter</u>, 19 P.2d 368 (Cal. 1999). <u>But see</u> <u>Smith v. Jennings</u>, 85 P.2d 465 (Cal. 2001).
    D. <u>See</u> <u>Matthews v. Potter</u>, 19 P.2d 368 (Cal. 1999); <u>see also</u> <u>Morrison v. Perkins</u>, 56 P.2d 247 (Cal. 2000). <u>But see</u> <u>Smith v. Jennings</u>, 85 P.2d 465 (Cal. 2001).

2. Which of the following is the correct order and punctuation of signals when more than one signal is used?

    A. <u>See</u>; <u>cf.</u>; <u>but see</u>; <u>see generally</u>.
    B. <u>See</u>; <u>cf.</u> <u>But see</u>. <u>See generally</u>.
    C. <u>See</u>. <u>But see</u>. <u>Cf.</u> <u>See generally</u>.
    D. <u>See</u>; <u>cf.</u> <u>But see</u>; <u>see generally</u>.
    E. <u>See</u>. <u>Cf.</u> <u>But see</u>. <u>See generally</u>.

3. A partner at your firm has asked you to revise a draft office memorandum containing the following sentence: <u>See e.g.</u> 18 U.S.C. § 588 (1998); 13 U.S.C. § 12 (1994); <u>Lineman v. Fawcett</u>, 689 U.S. 214 (1991); <u>Hingel v. Brown</u>, 855 U.S. 114 (1987); <u>Smith v. Tenorman</u>, 255 F.2d 2087 (2d Cir. 1997), <u>aff'd</u>, 225 U.S. 3 (1999); <u>Dohr v. Abrams</u>, 255 F. Supp. 2d 651 (D.D.C. 1989); <u>Masters v. Perlman</u>, 23 F.3d 785 (7th Cir. 1986). How would you revise this citation sentence?

    A. The ordering of citations is correct; no changes are necessary.
    B. The citations should be in the following order: <u>See e.g.</u> 18 U.S.C. § 588 (1998); 13 U.S.C. § 12 (1994); <u>Lineman</u>; <u>Smith</u>; <u>Hingel</u>; <u>Masters</u>; Dohr.
    C. The citations should be in the following order: <u>See e.g.</u>13 U.S.C. § 12 (1994); 18 U.S.C. § 588 (1998); <u>Lineman</u>; <u>Hingel</u>; <u>Smith</u>; <u>Masters</u>; <u>Dohr</u>.
    D. The citations should be in the following order: <u>See e.g.</u> 18 U.S.C. § 588 (1998); 13 U.S.C. § 12 (1994); <u>Lineman</u>; <u>Hingel</u>; <u>Dohr</u>; <u>Masters</u>; <u>Smith</u>.
    E. The citations should be in the following order: <u>See e.g.</u> 18 U.S.C. § 588 (1998); 13 U.S.C. § 12 (1994); <u>Lineman</u>; <u>Hingel</u>; <u>Masters</u>; <u>Smith</u>; <u>Dohr</u>.

Answer Key on page 312

♀? 5. ALWD Rules for Citing Subdivisions and Pinpoint Cites: Quiz

Assume the following citations appear in court documents.

1. Choose the correct citation for information on page 347 of <u>Beckwith v. United States</u>.

   A. <u>Beckwith v. United States</u>, 425 U.S. 341, 347 (1976).
   B. <u>Beckwith v. United States</u>, 425 U.S. 341, at 347 (1976).
   C. <u>Beckwith v. United States</u>, 425 U.S. 341, p. 347 (1976).
   D. <u>Beckwith v. United States</u>, 425 U.S. 341-47 (1976).

2. Choose the citation without an error.

   A. Christina M. Fernandez, <u>A Case-by-Case Approach to Pleading Scienter Under the Private Securities Litigation Reform Act of 1995</u>, 97 Mich. L. Rev. 2265, p. 2271 (1978).
   B. <u>Sciolino v. City of Newport News</u>, 480 F.3d 642 (4th Cir. 2007) (Wilkinson, J., dissenting, 654).
   C. <u>State v. Bradshaw</u>, 457 S.E.2d 456, 457, 459 (W. Va. 1995).
   D. <u>Codd v. Velger</u>, 429 U.S. 624 to 626 (1977).

3. Choose the citation without an error.

   A. 459 <u>State v. Bradshaw</u>, 457 S.E.2d 456 (W. Va. 1995).
   B. <u>Miranda v. Arizona</u>, 384 U.S. 436, 440 (1966).
   C. <u>Bishop v. Wood</u>, 426 U.S. 341 (1976) ("Fourteenth Amendment is not a guarantee against incorrect or ill-advised personnel decisions") 349.
   D. <u>State v. Mullens</u>, 172, 650 S.E.2d 169 (W. Va. 2007).

4. Choose the correct citation for information on page 2082 of the Michigan Law Review.

   A. Kim Scheppele, <u>Foreword: Telling Stories</u>, 87 Mich. L. Rev. 2073 (1989), 2082.
   B. Kim Scheppele, <u>Foreword: Telling Stories</u>, 2082, 87 Mich. L. Rev. 2073 (1989).
   C. Kim Scheppele, <u>Foreword: Telling Stories</u>, 87 Mich. L. Rev. 2073, 2082 (1989).
   D. Kim Scheppele, <u>Foreword: Telling Stories</u>, 87 Mich. L. Rev. 2073 at 2082 (1989).

5. Choose the correct citation for information on pages 479, 481, 485 in <u>Edwards v. Arizona</u>.

   A. <u>Edwards v. Arizona</u>, 451 U.S. 477, 479, 481, and 485 (1981).
   B. <u>Edwards v. Arizona</u>, 451 U.S. 477-85 (1981).
   C. <u>Edwards v. Arizona</u>, 451 U.S. 477 (1981) 479, 481, 485.
   D. <u>Edwards v. Arizona</u>, 451 U.S. 477, 479, 481, 485 (1981).

Answer Key on page 312

6. ALWD Rules for Short Form Citations: Quiz

Assume the following citations appear in court documents.

1. Choose the correct short citation for <u>Orozco v. Texas</u>, 394 U.S. 324, 327 (1969), if it is the only source in immediately preceding citation and cited page 327.

    A. <u>Id.</u>
    B. <u>Orozco v. Texas</u>, at 327.
    C. <u>Id.</u> at 327.
    D. <u>Orozco</u>, at 327.

2. Choose the correct short citation for <u>Orozco v. Texas</u>, 394 U.S. 324, 327 (1969), if the same cite was used three citations earlier.

    A. <u>Orozco v. Texas</u>, 394 U.S. at 327
    B. <u>Orozco</u>, 394 U.S. 324, 327.
    C. <u>Id.</u> at 327.
    D. <u>Orozco</u>, 394 U.S. at 327.

3. Choose the correct short citation for <u>Sciolino v. City of Newport News</u>, 480 F.3d 642, 654 (4th Cir. 2007), Judge Wilkinson's dissenting opinion, if the previous citation is from the same case but cites the majority.

    A. <u>Id.</u> at 654 (Wilkinson, J., dissenting).
    B. <u>Sciolino v. City of Newport News</u>, 480 F.3d 642, 654 (4th Cir. 2007) (Wilkinson, J., dissenting).
    C. Sciolino, 480 F.3d 642 at 654 (Wilkinson, J., dissenting).
    D. <u>Id.</u> (Wilkinson, J., dissenting) at 654.

4. Choose the correct short citation for 30 U.S.C. § 1330(a)(1) (2000) if the previous citation is 30 U.S.C. § 1331 (2000).

    A. 30 U.S.C. § 1330(a)(1) (2000).
    B. <u>Id.</u> (a)(1).
    C. <u>Id.</u> § 1330(a)(1).
    D. <u>Id.</u> at § 1330(a)(1).

5. Choose the correct short citation for Katherine Crytzer, You're Fired! Bishop v. Wood: When Does a Letter in Former Public Employee's Personnel File Deny a Due Process Liberty Right?, 16 Geo. Mason L. Rev. 447, 450 (2009), if it was used three citations earlier.

    A. Crytzer, <u>You're Fired!</u>, at 450.
    B. Crytzer, <u>supra</u>, at 450.
    C. Crytzer, 16 Geo. Mason L. Rev at 450.
    D. <u>Id.</u> at 450.

6. Choose the correct short citation for Deborah L. Rhode, <u>Justice and Gender</u> 56, 70-71 (Harv. U. Press 1989), if the immediately preceding cite is for the same source on page 60.

    A. <u>Id.</u> at 70-71.
    B. Rhode, <u>id.</u> at 70-71.
    C. Rhode, <u>Justice and Gender</u>, at 70-71.
    D. Rhode, <u>supra</u>, at 70-71.

7. Choose the correct short citation for <u>Orozco v. Texas</u>, 394 U.S. 324, 327 (1969), if it is one of three sources in the immediately preceding citation and cited on page 329.

    A. <u>Id.</u> at 327.
    B. <u>Orozco v. Texas</u>, at 327.
    C. <u>Id.</u> 394 U.S. 324, 327.
    D. <u>Orozco</u>, 394 U.S. at 327.

Answer Key on page 312

8? 7. ALWD Abbreviations: Quiz

Assume the following citations appear in court documents.

1. The following case appears in a textual sentence. Choose the answer that abbreviates the case name correctly.

    A. <u>NLRB v. General Hospital, Inc.</u>, 61 U.S. 3 (1951).
    B. <u>NLRB v. General Hosp., Inc.</u>, 61 U.S. 3 (1951).
    C. <u>N.L.R.B. v. General Hospital, Inc.</u>, 61 U.S. 3 (1951).
    D. <u>NLRB v. General Hospital, Incorporated</u>, 61 U.S. 3 (1951).

2. The following Ninth Circuit Court case appears in a citation sentence. Choose the answer that abbreviates the case name correctly.

    A. <u>Sunnyside Memorial School v. County Housing Department</u>, 537 F.2d 361, 366 (9th Cir. 1976).
    B. <u>Sunnyside Mem'l. Sch. v. County Hous. Dep't.</u>, 537 F.2d 361, 366 (9th Cir. 1976).
    C. <u>Sunnyside Meml Sch. v. County Hous. Dept</u>, 537 F.2d 361, 366 (9th Cir. 1976).
    D. <u>Sunnyside v. Mem'l Sch. v. County Hous. Dep't</u>, 537 F.2d 361, 366 (9th Circuit 1976).
    E. Both b and c are correct.

3. Choose the correct citation for the Federal Register.

    A. Importation of Dairy Products, 60 Federal Register 50379 (Sept. 29, 1995).
    B. Importation of Dairy Products, 60 F.R. 50379 (September 29, 1995).
    C. Importation of Dairy Products, 60 Fed. Reg. 50379 (Sept. 29, 1995).

D. Importation of Dairy Products, 60 Fed.Reg 50,379 (September 29, 1995).

4. Choose the correct citation for Rule 12(b)(2) of the Federal Rules of Civil Procedure.

    A. Fed. Rule Civ. P. 12(b)(2).
    B. Fed. R. Civ. P. 12(b)(2).
    C. Fed R Civ P 12(b)(2).
    D. Federal Rule of Civil Procedure 12(b)(2).

5. Choose the correct citation for an article in the George Mason Law Review.
    A. Kathy Crytzer, <u>Meeting of the Minds</u>, 16 Geo. Mason L. Rev. 447, 450 (2000).
    B. Kathy Crytzer, <u>Meeting of the Minds</u>, 15 G.M. L. Rev. 447, 450 (2000).
    C. Kathy Crytzer, <u>Meeting of the Minds</u>, 15 Geo. Mason L.R. 447, 450 (2000).
    D. Kathy Crytzer, <u>Meeting of the Minds</u>, 16 Geo Mason L Rev 447, 450 (2000).

Answer Key on page 313

? 8. ALWD Rules for Citing Cases: Quiz

Assume the following citations appear in court documents.

1. Choose the correct citation for <u>United States v. MacDonald</u>, decided in the Fourth Circuit Court of Appeals in 1976.

    A. 531 F.2d 196, 199, <u>United States v. MacDonald</u>, (4th Cir. 1976).
    B. <u>United States v. MacDonald</u>, 531 F.2d 196, 199 (4th Cir. 1976).
    C. <u>United States v. MacDonald</u>. 531 F.2d 196. 199 (4th Cir. 1976)
    D. <u>U.S. v. MacDonald</u>, 531 F.2d 196, 199 (4th Cir. 1976).

2. Choose the correct citation for Commonwealth of Pennsylvania v. Ferrone, decided in the Pennsylvania Superior Court in 1982. (Assume this citation appears in a court document submitted to a Pennsylvania court.)

    A. <u>Commonwealth v. Ferrone</u>, 448 A.2d 637 (Pa. Super. 1982).
    B. <u>Commonwealth of Pennsylvania v. Ferrone</u>, 448 A.2d 637 (Pa. Super. Ct. 1982).
    C. <u>Commonwealth of Penn. v. Ferrone</u>, 448 A.2d 637 (Pa. Super. 1982).
    D. <u>Penn. v. Ferrone</u>, 448 A.2d 637 (Pa. Super. Ct. 1982).

3. Choose the correct citation for <u>Miranda v. Arizona</u> in the United States Reports.

    A. <u>Miranda v. Arizona</u>, 384 S. Ct. 436 (1966).
    B. <u>Miranda v. Arizona</u>, 384 U.S. 436 (S. Ct. 1966).
    C. <u>Miranda v. Arizona</u>, 384 U.S. 436 (1966).
    D. <u>Miranda v. Arizona</u>, 384 U.S. 436 (U.S. 1966).

4. Choose the correct citation for <u>Johnson v. Seiler</u> decided by the Fourth Circuit Court of Appeals and reported in the Second Edition Federal Reporter.

 A. <u>Johnson v. Seiler</u>, 225 F.2d 308 (4th Cir. 1998).
 B. <u>Johnson v. Seiler</u>, 225 F.2d 308 (4th Cir. 1998).
 C. <u>Johnson v. Seiler</u>, 225 F.2d 308 (4th Circuit 1998).
 D. <u>Johnson v. Seiler</u>, 225 S.E.2d 308 (4th Cir. 1998).

5. Choose the correct citation for Justice Scalia's dissenting opinion in Jamison v. Blueline Railroad.

 A. <u>Jamison v. Blueline R.R.</u>, 338 U.S. 25, 47 (2004) (Scalia, J., dissenting) (rejecting Court's conception of the exclusionary rule).
 B. <u>Jamison v. Blueline R.R.</u>, 338 U.S. 25, 47 (2004). (Scalia, J., dissenting) (rejecting Court's conception of the exclusionary rule).
 C. <u>Jamison v. Blueline R.R.</u>, 338 U.S. 25, 47 (2004) (rejecting Court's conception of the exclusionary rule) (Scalia, J., dissenting).
 D. Jamison v. Blueline R.R., 338 U.S. 25, 47 (2004 Scalia J., dissenting) (rejecting Court's conception of the exclusionary rule).

6. Choose the correct citation for the unreported case of <u>Chavez v. Norton</u>, available on Lexis.

 A. <u>Chavez v. Norton</u>, No. 02-3924, 2004 U.S. App. LEXIS 2598713, 220 (3d Cir. Oct. 14, 2004).
 B. <u>Chavez v. Norton</u>, No. 02-3924, No. 02-3924, 2004 U.S. App. LEXIS 2598713 at *220 (3d Cir. Oct. 14, 2004).
 C. <u>Chavez v. Norton</u>, No. 02-3924, 2004 U.S. App. LEXIS 2598713, *220 (3d Cir. Oct. 14, 2004).
 D. <u>Chavez v. Norton</u>, No. 02-3924, 2004 U.S. App. LEXIS 2598713, at *220 (3d Cir. Oct. 14, 2004).

Answer Key on page 313

🔘? 9. ALWD Rules for Citing Constitutions: Quiz

Assume that the following citations appear in court documents.

1. Choose the correct citation format for the Fifth Amendment to the U.S. Constitution.

 A. U.S. Const. Amend. V.
 B. United States Constitution, amendment V.
 C. U.S. Const. amend. V.
 D. U.S. Const. amend V.

2. Which one of these citations to Article I, Section 1, of the Kansas Constitution is correct?

 A. Kan. Const. art. I, § 1.
 B. Kan. Const. art. I, sec. 1.

    C. Ka. Const. art. I, § 1,

    D. Kansas Constitution, art. 1, § 1.

3. What is the correct short citation format for Article II of the U.S. Constitution if it was cited in the immediately preceding section?

    A. Art. II.

    B. U.S. Const. II.

    C. II.

    D. <u>Id.</u>

4. Choose the correct format for citing the Eighteenth Amendment to the U.S. Constitution (repealed in 1933).

    A. U.S. Const. Amend. XVIII (repealed 1933).

    B. U.S. Const. amend. XVIII (repealed 1933).

    C. U.S. Const. amend. XVIII.

    D. U.S. Const. amend. XVIII, repealed 1933.

5. What is the correct citation format for Article II, Section 3, of the Pennsylvania Constitution?

    A. Pa. Const. art. II, § 3.

    B. Pen. Const. art. II, § 3.

    C. Pa. Const. Art. II, § 3.

    D. Pen. Const. art 2, § 3.

Answer Key on page 314

🯄? 10. ALWD Rules for Citing Statutes: Quiz

Assume that the following citations appear in court documents.

1. In the citation 28 U.S.C. § 585 (2000), what does the "28" signify?

    A. The section number of the statute

    B. The title number of the statute in the United States Code

    C. The session of Congress that enacted the statute

    D. The number of provisions in the cited statute

2. Choose the correct full citation for Title 42, Section 1975, of the United States Code.

    A. 42 USC § 1975 (2000).

    B. 42 U.S.C. § 1975.

    C. 42 U.S.C. § 1975 (2000).

    D. 42 U.S.C. §1975 (2000).

3. If using a short citation to refer to the statute from question 2, which one of the following options is an acceptable format?

    A. § 1975.
    B. 42 U.S.C.
    C. U.S.C. § 1975.
    D. 42.

4. Which of the following citations to the Internal Revenue Code is NOT correctly formatted?

    A. 26 U.S.C. § 153 (2000).
    B. I.R.C. § 153 (2000).
    C. 26 U.S.C. § 291 (2000).
    D. Int. Rev. Code § 291 (2000).

5. Choose the preferred citation format for the Indiana Code.

    A. Ind. Code § 3-5-1-1 (2008).
    B. Ind. Code Ann. § 3-5-1-1 (West 2006).
    C. Ind. Code Ann. § 3-5-1-1 (LexisNexis 2006).
    D. In. Code § 3-5-1-1 (2008).

6. Choose the correct citation for Federal Rule of Civil Procedure 11(a)(5).

    A. F.R.C.P. 11(a)(5).
    B. Fed R Civ P 11(a)(5).
    C. Fed. R. Civ. P. 11(a)(5).
    D. F.R.C.P. § 11(a)(5).

Answer Key on page 314

🔘? 11. ALWD Citations for Administrative and Executive Materials: Quiz

Assume that the following citations appear in court documents.

1. Which of the following citations to title 40, section 49.9861, of the Code of Federal Regulations is correct?

    A. 40 Code Fed. Reg. § 49.9861 (1999).
    B. 40 Code Fed. Reg. §49.9861 (1999).
    C. 40 C.F.R. § 49.9861 (1999).
    D. 40 C. F. R. § 49.9861 (1999).

2. Choose the correct short form citation to title 40, section 49.9861, of the Code of Federal Regulations.

    A. 40 C.F.R. § 49.9861 (1999)
    B. 40 C.F.R. at § 49.9861
    C. 40 C.F.R.
    D. 49.9861.

3. A rule is published on page 25684 of volume 74 of the Federal Register, but it has not yet been entered into the Code of Federal Regulations. Choose the correct citation for that rule.

    A. Airworthiness Directives, 74 Fed. Reg. 25684 (May 30, 2009) (to be codified at 14 C.F.R. pt. 39).
    B. Airworthiness Directives, 74 F.R. 25,684 (May 30, 2009) (to be codified at 14 C.F.R. pt. 39).
    C. Airworthiness Directives, 74 Fed. Reg. 25,684 (to be codified at 14 C.F.R. pt. 39).
    D. Airworthiness Directives, 74 Fed.Reg. 25684 (May 30, 2009) (to be codified at 14 C.F.R. pt. 39).

4. Which of the following citations to volume 24, page 2,834, of the Virginia Register of Regulations (dated June 9, 2008) is correct?

    A. 24 Va. Register 2,834 (June 9, 2008).
    B. 24 V.R.R. 2834 (June 9, 2008).
    C. 24 Va. Reg. Regs. 2834.
    D. 24 Va. Reg. Regs. 2,834 (June 9, 2008).

5. Choose the correct citation for a 1982 advisory opinion from the United States Attorney General, volume 43, page 369.

    A. 43 Op. Attorney General 369 (1982).
    B. 43 Op. Att'y Gen. 369 (1982).
    C. 43 Op. Att'y. Gen. 369 (1982).
    D. 43 Op. Atty. Gen. 369 (1982).

6. Presidential Executive Order 12001 is not in the Code of Federal Regulations, but it is found in volume 4, page 33709 of the Federal Register. Which of the following citations is correct?

    A. Exec. Order No. 12,001, 42 Fed. Reg. 33,709 (June 29, 1977).
    B. E.O. No. 12,001, 42 Fed. Reg. 33,709 (June 29, 1977).
    C. E.O. No. 12,001, 42 F.R. 33,709 (June 29, 1977).
    D. Exec. Or. No. 12001, 42 Fed. Reg. 33709 (June 29, 1977).

Answer Key on page 314

---

12. ALWD Citations for Books, Reports, and Other Nonperiodic Materials: Quiz

Assume that the following citations appear in court documents.

1. Choose the correct citation to page 171 of <u>The Nine: Inside the Secret World of the Supreme Court</u>, by Jeffrey Toobin.

    A. <u>The Nine: Inside the Secret World of the Supreme Court</u> 171 (Anchor Books, 2007) (2007) J Toobin.

   B. Toobin, J., <u>The Nine: Inside the Secret World of the Supreme Court</u> 171 (2007).

   C. Jeffrey Toobin, <u>The Nine: Inside the Secret World of the Supreme Court</u>, 171 (2007).

   D. Jeffrey Toobin, <u>The Nine: Inside the Secret World of the Supreme Court</u> 171 (Anchor Books 2007).

2. Which of the following citations to the tenth edition of <u>A History of the Modern World</u> to 1815, by R.R. Palmer, Joel Colton, and Lloyd Kramer (listed in this order on the title page), is correct?

   A. R.R. Palmer et al., <u>A History of the Modern World to 1815</u> (10th ed. McGraw-Hill, 2006).

   B. R.R. Palmer et al <u>A History of the Modern World to 1815</u> (10th ed. 2006).

   C. R.R. Palmer, Joel Colton and Lloyd Kramer, <u>A History of the Modern World to 1815</u> (10th ed.).

   D. Joel Colton, Lloyd Kramer & R.R. Palmer, <u>A History of the Modern World to 1815</u> (10th ed.).

3. Choose the correct citation to volume 2 of Michael Burlingame's <u>Abraham Lincoln: A Life</u>, published in 2008.

   A. Michael Burlingame, <u>Abraham Lincoln: A Life</u> vol. 2 (Johns Hopkins U. Press 2008).

   B. Michael Burlingame, <u>Abraham Lincoln: A Life</u> 2 (2008).

   C. 2 Michael Burlingame, <u>Abraham Lincoln: A Life</u> (Johns Hopkins U. Press 2008).

   D. Vol. 2 Michael Burlingame, <u>Abraham Lincoln: A Life</u> (2008).

4. Choose the correct citation for an originally unpublished letter from Alexander Hamilton to John Jay dated November 26, 1775, published on page 43 of <u>Alexander Hamilton: Writings</u>.

   A. Ltr. from Alexander Hamilton to John Jay (Nov. 26, 1775), in <u>Alexander Hamilton: Writings</u> 43 (2001).

   B. Letter to John Jay (Nov. 26, 1775), in <u>Alexander Hamilton: Writings</u> 43 (2001).

   C. Letter from Alexander Hamilton to John Jay (November 26, 1775), in <u>Alexander Hamilton: Writings</u> 43 (2001).

   D. Ltr. from Alexander Hamilton to John Jay (Nov. 26, 1775), in <u>Alexander Hamilton: Writings</u> 43 (Library of America 2001).

5. Which citation to the ninth edition of <u>Black's Law Dictionary</u>, published in 2009, is correct?

   A. <u>Black's Law Dictionary</u> (9th ed., West 2009).

   B. <u>Black's Law Dictionary</u> (9th ed. 2009).

   C. <u>Black's Law Dictionary</u> (9th edition 2009).

   D. <u>Black's Law Dictionary</u> (9th ed., West 2009).

Answer Key on page 315

? 13. ALWD Rules for Citing Periodical Materials: Quiz

Assume that the following citations appear in court documents.

1. Which of the following citations to a June 1, 2009, article on page E2 of the *San Francisco Chronicle* is correct?

    A. Peter Hartlaub, SFJazz Show Gets to the Roots, S.F. Chron., June 1, 2009, at E2.

    B. Peter Hartlaub, <u>SFJazz Show Gets to the Roots</u>, S.F. Chron. E2 (June 1, 2009).

    C. Hartlaub, Peter, <u>SFJazz Show Gets to the Roots</u>, S.F. Chron., June 1, 2009, at E2.

    D. Peter Hartlaub, <u>SFJazz Show Gets to the Roots</u>, <u>S.F. Chron.</u>, June 1, 2009, at E2.

2. Choose the correct citation to an April 2009 article by Eugene Volokh that appeared in volume 97 of the Georgetown Law Journal.

    A. Eugene Volokh, <u>Symbolic Expression and the Original Meaning of the First Amendment</u>, 97 Georgetown Law Journal 1057 (2009).

    B. Eugene Volokh, <u>Symbolic Expression and the Original Meaning of the First Amendment</u>, 97 Law J. 1057 (2009).

    C. Eugene Volokh, <u>Symbolic Expression and the Original Meaning of the First Amendment</u>, 97 Geo. L.J. 1057 (2009).

    D. Eugene Volokh, <u>Symbolic Expression and the Original Meaning of the First Amendment</u>, 97 J. 1057 (2009).

3. Which citation to a March 2007 student-written note, signed by Adrian Barnes and published in volume 1 the Columbia Law Review, is correct?

    A. Note, <u>Do They Have to Buy from Burma? A Preemption Analysis of Local Antisweatshop Procurement Laws</u>, 107 Colum. L. Rev. 426 (2007).

    B. Adrian Barnes, Note, <u>Do They Have to Buy from Burma? A Preemption Analysis of Local Antisweatshop Procurement Laws</u>, 107 Col. L.R. 426 (2007).

    C. Adrian Barnes, note, <u>Do They Have to Buy from Burma? A Preemption Analysis of Local Antisweatshop Procurement Laws</u>, 107 Colum. L. Rev. 426 (2007).

    D. Adrian Barnes, Student Author, <u>Do They Have to Buy from Burma? A Preemption Analysis of Local Antisweatshop Procurement Laws</u>, 107 Colum. L. Rev. 426 (2007).

4. Choose the correct citation to a nonstudent-written book review by Derrick A. Bell, Jr., reviewing <u>Just Schools: The Idea of Racial Equality in American Education</u> by David L. Kirp. The review appeared in the Texas Law Review in August 1983.

    A. Derrick A. Bell, Jr., <u>School Desegregation Postmortem</u>, 62 Tex. L. Rev. 175 (1983) (reviewing <u>Just Schools: The Idea of Racial Equality in American Education</u>).

B. Derrick A. Bell, <u>School Desegregation Postmortem</u>, 62 Tex. L. Rev. 175 (1983) (reviewing David L. Kirp, <u>Just Schools: The Idea of Racial Equality in American Education</u> (1982)).

C. Derrick A. Bell, Jr., <u>School Desegregation Postmortem</u>, 62 Tex. L. Rev. 175 (1983) (reviewing David L. Kirp, <u>Just Schools: The Idea of Racial Equality in American Education</u> (1982)).

D. Derrick A. Bell, Jr., <u>School Desegregation Postmortem</u>, 62 Texas L.R. 175 (1983) (reviewing David L. Kirp, <u>Just Schools: The Idea of Racial Equality in American Education</u> (1982)).

Answer Key on page 315

⚇? 14.   ALWD Rules for Citing Electronic Media: Quiz

Assume that the following citations appear in court documents.

1. Choose the correct citation format for a case that is unreported but is available on Westlaw and has been assigned a unique database identifier. There are no page numbers assigned to this case, but cite to screen two of the case.

   A. <u>Fenstermacher v. Telelect, Inc.</u>, No. 90-2159-O, 1992 WL 175114, at *2 (D. Kan. July 17, 1992).

   B. <u>Fenstermacher v. Telelect, Inc.</u>, 1992 WL 175114 at *2 (D. Kan. July 17, 1992).

   C. <u>Fenstermacher v. Telelect, Inc.</u>, No. 90-2159-O, 1992 WL 175114 at *2 (D. Kan. July 17, 1992).

   D. <u>Fenstermacher v. Telelect, Inc.</u>, No. 90-2159-O, 1992 WL 175114, at *2 (D. Kan. 1992).

   E. Both B and C are correct.

2. Which of the following citations to Baldwin's Kentucky Revised Statutes Annotated, as found on Westlaw is correct? Note that the Kentucky Statutes are current on Westlaw through the end of the 2008 legislation.

   A. Ky. Rev. Stat. Ann. § 38.100 (West, 2008).

   B. Ken. Stat. Ann. § 38.100 (West, Westlaw through 2008 legislation).

   C. Ky. Rev. Stat. Ann. § 38.100 (WL current through 2008 legislation).

   D. Ky. Rev. Stat. Ann. 38.100 (West, Westlaw through 2008 legislation).

3. The following New York Times article is available only on the Internet and is not available in traditional print format. Choose the correct citation format.

   A. Matthew Saltmarsh, Interest Rates Held Steady in Europe, N.Y. Times, June 4, 2009, http://www.nytimes.com/2009/06/05/business/%20 global/05euro.html?hpw.

   B. Matthew Saltmarsh, <u>Interest Rates Held Steady in Europe</u>, N.Y. Times (June 4, 2009), http://www.nytimes.com/2009/06/05/business/ global/05euro.html?hpw (accessed Oct. 12, 2010).

C. Matthew Saltmarsh, <u>Interest Rates Held Steady in Europe</u>, N.Y. Times, June 4, 2009, available http://www.nytimes.com/2009/06/05/business/ global/05euro.html?hpw.

    D. Matthew Saltmarsh, <u>Interest Rates Held Steady in Europe</u>, New York Times, June 4, 2009, http://www.nytimes.com/2009/06/05/business/ global/05euro.html?hpw.

4. The following article is available both in the print version of the New York Times and online. Choose the correct parallel citation.

    A. David Jolly, <u>Despite Devaluation Fear, Latvia Stands by Currency</u>, N.Y. Times, June 4, 2009, at B4, http://www.nytimes.com/2009/ 06/05/ business/global/05latvia.html?hpw.

    B. David Jolly, <u>Despite Devaluation Fear, Latvia Stands by Currency</u>, N.Y. Times, at B4, available http://www.nytimes.com/2009/ 06/05/business/global/05latvia.html?hpw (June 4, 2009).

    C. David Jolly, <u>Despite Devaluation Fear, Latvia Stands by Currency</u>, N.Y. Times, June 4, 2009, at http://www.nytimes.com/2009/ 06/05/business/global/05latvia.html?hpw.

    D. David Jolly, <u>Despite Devaluation Fear, Latvia Stands by Currency</u>, N.Y. Times B4 (June 4, 2009), http://www.nytimes.com/2009/06/05/business/global/05latvia.html?hpw (accessed Oct. 12, 2010).

5. Choose the correct citation to a fictional e-mail from George Ferman, Assistant Dean at Georgetown Law, to Alex Aleinikoff, Dean of Georgetown Law.

    A. E-mail from George Ferman, Asst. Dean, Georgetown L., to Alex Aleinikoff, Dean, Georgetown L. (Oct. 1, 2009, 08:15:01 EST) (on file with author).

    B. E-mail from George Ferman, Georgetown Law, Assistant Dean, to Alex Aleinikoff, Georgetown Law, Dean (Oct. 1, 2009, 08:15:01 EST) (on file with author).

    C. George Ferman, Asst. Dean, Georgetown L., to Alex Aleinikoff, Dean, Georgetown L. (Oct. 1, 2009, 08:15:01 EST) (on file with author).

    D. E-mail from George Ferman to Alex Aleinikoff (Oct. 1, 2009, 08:15:01 EST) (on file with author).

6. Which of the following citations to a commercial audio recording is correct?

    A. U2, <u>The Joshua Tree</u> (1987).

    B. U2, <u>The Joshua Tree</u> (Island Records).

    c. U2, CD, <u>The Joshua Tree</u> (Is. Recs., Inc. 1987).

    D. U2, <u>The Joshua Tree</u> (1987) (Island Records).

Answer Key on page 315

C. ALWD Citation Self-Assessment

INSTRUCTIONS: This self-assessment is designed to test your knowledge of the basic citation rules of ALWD covered in chapter 4. Read through the document, taking note of the numbered and highlighted passages. Each number and highlighted passage represents a question about which you should decide whether the citation is correct as is or whether a change is needed. If a change is needed, please make the correct change in citation format. When you are finished, check your work against the answer key on pages 316-320. The answer key also indicates for each item the applicable citation rule or form. This review will help you to assess your understanding of the ALWD citation forms and to more quickly and accurately provide citations for your own documents.

Civil Action No. 02-2332

UNITED STATES COURT OF APPEALS
FOR THE ELEVENTH CIRCUIT

DR. CHARLES OSSINING, Appellant,

v.

HARRISON BRUBAKER, ET AL., APPELLEES

ON APPEAL FROM UNITED STATES DISTRICT COURT
FOR THE SOUTHERN DISTRICT OF ALABAMA

BRIEF OF RESPONDENT

STATEMENT OF ISSUES PRESENTED FOR REVIEW

   I.   Whether an inmate, exhibiting no medical condition warranting special treatment, and having received adequate care for all documented symptoms, has an Eighth Amendment claim when, following self-diagnosis of a rare condition, the prison declined his request for a special diet and further unnecessary testing.
   II. Whether the trial court correctly found an inmate's First Amendment rights were not violated when the Warden reviewed and denied individual publications according to prison regulations in response to the unreasonable burden placed upon the prison's resources.

<u>STATEMENT OF THE CASE</u>

<u>Nature of the Case</u>

This is an appeal of summary judgment in a prisoner's rights case. Respondents request that summary judgment be affirmed as there are no genuine issues of fact in dispute, and that appellant's 42 U.S.C. § 1983 complaint be dismissed as treatment did not violate prisoner's constitutional rights. Appellant brings his claims under the First and Eighth Amendments #1 U.S. Const. Amend. I; #2 U.S. Const. amend. VIII.

#1 Keep as is/Change

#2 Keep as is/Change

Procedural History

Ossining alleges violations of his First and Eighth Amendment rights by the prison. The United States District Court for the Southern District of Alabama granted the defendant's motion for summary judgment. The District Court concluded that plaintiff's receiving of publications caused unreasonable burdens on the resources of the prison and that the prison was not deliberately indifferent to any serious medical needs of the plaintiff. #3 Ossining v. Brubaker, No. CIV.A.02-2332, 2003 U.S. Dist. LEXIS 5130 at *1 (S.D. Ala. Jan. 6, 2003).

#3 Keep as is/Change

STATEMENT OF FACTS

The prisoner, Dr. Charles Ossining, was convicted of Medicare fraud, mail fraud, and making false claims to the government. At the time of Ossining's incarceration in January 2002, a routine medical examination revealed he was in good health, without any notations of medical problems. (Brubaker Aff. 7.) After his arrival, Ossining received a considerable number of medical journals and newsletters pertaining to allergies. (Brubaker Aff. 8.) Ossining specifically ordered informational brochures concerning various types of allergies and treatments for the purpose of disseminating this information to other prisoners. (Ossining Aff. 4.) By the end of March, the infirmary reported a significant increase in prisoner visits: 15% higher than the same quarter a year before, and requests for allergy testing increased 100%. More than half of these requests were declined as these prisoners showed no symptoms warranting testing. Many inmates requesting allergy testing indicated Ossining had suggested they be tested for various allergies. (Brubaker Aff. 9.) Proper allergy diagnosis has been shown to require extensive testing #4 J. Expert, Allergy on the Net, 5 New Eng. J. Med. 9, 10 (2002), at http://www.nejm.org/expert/v5/allergy.html.

#4 Keep as is/Change

The medical staff could not accommodate all incoming requests for allergy testing, leading to agitation of prisoners and strain on medical resources. (Brubaker Aff. 9, 10.) Additionally, the prison cafeteria received an influx of complaints, as well as special requests and disorderly conduct, requiring additional guards for security. (Brubaker Aff. 11.) Based on these events, Brubaker, the longtime warden of the prison, rejected certain publications addressed to Ossining as detrimental to the security and resources of the prison, an action authorized by federal regulation 28 C.F.R. § 540.71(b) (2009). #5 I.M. Tough, Warden Power, 15 N.Y.Law Sch. L. Rev. 12, 15-17 (1983).

#5 Keep as is/Change

In March, a blood test revealed Ossining was borderline anemic; he was prescribed iron supplements to combat this condition. (Ossining Aff. 12.) In April, Ossining diagnosed himself as suffering from celiac disease, an extremely rare infection, and claimed he needed an endoscopy to confirm his diagnosis. (Flowers Aff. 6.) Celiac disease can be fatal if not treated properly. #6 Adam Gourna, Celiac Disease: A Killer, New York Times, December 12, 1994, at F3, available at 1994 WL 2321843. Reviewing his blood test results, Dr. Gerta Flowers, a specialist in internal medicine and resident physician at the prison, determined that Ossining did

#6 Keep as is/Change

not exhibit such severe symptoms warranting further investigation and rejected his request for an endoscopy. (Flowers Aff. 7.) In July, Ossining requested a gluten-free diet, claiming only this diet could treat celiac disease. (Ossining Aff. 21.) Dr. Flowers informed the prison that sufficient alternatives in the prison cafeteria were available to Ossining should he prefer to eat a gluten-free diet. (Flowers Aff. 8.) The prison has promised that should Ossining present severe symptoms in the future, it would treat him appropriately. (Brubaker Aff. 15.)

STANDARD OF REVIEW

The issue before this Court is whether the trial court properly applied the law to the facts in granting summary judgment. The court's review of the district court's ruling on a motion for summary judgment is de novo. #7 Pope v. Hightower, 101 F.3d 1382, 1383 (11ᵗʰ Cir. 1996).

#7 Keep as is/Change

SUMMARY OF ARGUMENT

Ossining's First and Eighth Amendment claims fail based on the established facts in the record. With regard to the Eighth Amendment, Ossining shows no evidence of a serious medical need, his treatment by the prison did not violate contemporary standards of decency, and the medical staff was not deliberately indifferent to his condition. #8 U.S. CONST. amend. VIII. As for the First Amendment, because assertion of his rights posed a threat to the security of the prison and created an unreasonable burden on prison resources, Warden Brubaker's rejection of particular publications was justified. #9 Amend. I.

#8 Keep as is/Change

#9 Keep as is/Change

ARGUMENT

The prisoner, Dr. Charles Ossining, is currently serving a five-year sentence for defrauding the federal government. Ossining alleges the prison violated his First Amendment rights by denying him access to professional journals and his Eighth Amendment rights by denying him a gluten-free diet and further testing for a rare disease for which he made a self-diagnosis. While detainees are accorded protections of the Constitution, prisoner's rights are inherently restricted, and some constitutional violations may be acceptable if they serve "legitimate penological interests," such as order, security, and safety. #10 See Thornburgh v. Abbott, 490 U.S. 407-408 (1989). Moreover, as operation of a prison falls under the province of the legislative and executive branches of government, deference should be paid by the courts to appropriate prison authorities regulating this delicate balance between prison security and legitimate rights of prisoners. #11 Turner v. Safley, 482 U.S. 78, 84-85 (1987)

#10 Keep as is/Change

#11 Keep as is/Change

I. PLAINTIFF'S EIGHTH AMENDMENT CLAIM OF CRUEL AND UNUSUAL PUNISHMENT IS WITHOUT MERIT BECAUSE THE PRISONER EXHIBITED NO MEDICAL CONDITION WARRANTING SPECIAL TREATMENT

Ossining fails to present sufficient evidence of a serious medical problem related to being denied a gluten-free diet or evidence that the prison was "deliberately indifferent" to his symptoms, as required for claims under the Eighth Amendment. See #12 Helling, 509 U.S. 25, 29 (1993). In #13 Helling, the Supreme Court established

#12 Keep as is/Change

#13 Keep as is/Change

a two-prong test for proving Eighth Amendment violations. Under the subjective prong (A), the prisoner must show deliberate indifference by the prison toward a serious risk posed to the prisoner. Under the objective prong (B), the prisoner must show that the unreasonable risk of harm he faces is contrary to contemporary standards of decency. #14 Id. at 35-36. Because Ossining received adequate treatment for his ailments and exhibited no medical condition warranting special treatment, he fails both prongs of the Eighth Amendment test.

#14 Keep as is/Change

A. The prison was not deliberately indifferent to prisoner's medical condition when the prison physician reviewed prisoner's blood test results to find no severe symptoms of celiac disease warranting further treatment and the prison menu offered adequate gluten-free alternatives

Under the subjective prong, the prisoner must show (1) the prison had knowledge of a serious risk of harm to him and (2) deliberate indifference by the prison toward this risk. #15 Id. at 35.

#15 Keep as is/Change

1. The prison had no subjective knowledge of any serious risk of harm to the prisoner in denying him a gluten-free diet or in rejecting his request for an endoscopy to further test for celiac disease

Ossining fails to show prison officials knew of and disregarded "an excessive risk to his health or safety." #16 See Farmer v. Brennan, 511 U.S. 825, 837 (1994); 42 U.S.C. § 1983 (2003). As serious complications from celiac disease are rare and Dr. Flowers determined that the prisoner did not present such severe symptoms to warrant further investigation, Ossining fails to show the prison's subjective knowledge of a serious risk of harm when denying him a gluten-free diet and further testing. In #17 Campbell et al. v. Sikes, the plaintiff inmate alleged cruel and unusual punishment when the defendant prison psychiatrist misdiagnosed her with poly-substance abuse disorder when in fact she had a bipolar disorder, a diagnosis unreported in jail records or prior hospitalization records. The court affirmed the grant of summary judgment for the prison because there was no evidence that the psychiatrist knew the prisoner had bipolar disorder, that he knew he misdiagnosed her, or that he knew of a substantial risk of serious harm to the inmate as a result of his treatment. #18 Campbell v. Sikes, 169 F.3d 1353, 1366-68 (1999). Similarly, Ossining fails to present evidence from which a reasonable jury could infer that Dr. Flowers or other prison officials knew he had celiac disease, or knew they were misdiagnosing him, or knew their treatment was grossly inadequate but proceeded with the treatment anyway. As in #19 Campbell, Ossining's medical records did not indicate a prior history of celiac disease and a professional review of his blood did not give Dr. Flowers reason for concern. Therefore, Ossining fails the first part of the subjective prong of the Helling test because the prison exhibits no subjective knowledge of his mistreatment.

#16 Keep as is/Change

#17 Keep as is/Change

#18 Keep as is/Change

#19 Keep as is/Change

2. The prison was not deliberately indifferent toward the medical concerns of the prisoner

Ossining fails to demonstrate his medical treatment by the prison constituted the "unnecessary and wanton infliction of pain," as required to show deliberate indiffer-

#20 Keep as is/Change

#21 Keep as is/Change

#22 Keep as is/Change

#23 Keep as is/Change

#24 Keep as is/Change

#25 Keep as is/Change

#26 Keep as is/Change

#27 Keep as is/Change

#28 Keep as is/Change

ence. #20 Mustave Hurt, Unimaginable Pain, 742 Geo. L.J. 801, 831-32 (2003) (discussing the requirements to show deliberate indifference). In Estelle, the prisoner injured his back while engaged in prison work, claiming deliberate indifference by the prison for failure to perform an X-ray to treat him. The court held that questions concerning forms of treatment are matters of medical judgment, and that failure by prison medical staff to use additional diagnostic techniques beyond ordinary treatment does not constitute deliberate indifference or cruel and usual punishment. #21 Estelle v. Gamble, 429 S. Ct. 97, 107 (1976). Similarly, Dr. Flowers's refusal to order an endoscopy to confirm Ossining's self-diagnosis of celiac disease following her professional review of his blood test results does not constitute deliberate indifference to his medical needs. Ossining offers no evidence that prison medical staff failed to meet appropriate professional standards in determining that his symptoms did not warrant further testing. Moreover, Ossining's difference in opinion from prison officials concerning diagnosis and recommended treatment does not constitute cruel and unusual punishment. #22 See id. at 100; but see Harris v. Thigpen, 941 F.2d 1495, 1505 (11th Cir. 1991)(holding that difference of opinion does constitute cruel and unusual punishment). While an endoscopy may have led to an appropriate diagnosis and treatment for his condition, Ossining fails to show deliberate indifference as medical decisions concerning forms of treatment beyond ordinary care do not constitute cruel and unusual punishment. #23 See Estelle, 429 U.S. 97 at 107.

Denial of Ossining's request for a special gluten-free diet does not constitute deliberate indifference because the prisoner lacks convincing symptoms requiring special treatment. See 25 Op. Off. Leg. Counsel 370, 381-82 (1995). #24 In McElligot v. Goley, 182 F.3d 1248, 1256-1258 (11th Cir. 1999), an inmate with a history of stomach problems was treated by prison doctors with Tylenol, Pepto-Bismol, and an anti-gas medication when experiencing severe intestinal pains, even after it was evident these treatments were not responding to his deteriorating condition. The court held that while prison doctors could not be held liable for failing to diagnose the inmate's colon cancer, the failure to further diagnose and treat severe pain experienced by a prisoner was evidence of deliberate indifference. #25 See McElligot v. Foley, 182 F.3d 1248, 1256-58 (11th Cir. 1999); Noah Lee, Deliberate Indifference: What's It All About? 31 (3d ed. 2001). Unlike the inmate in McElligot, Ossining exhibits no severe symptoms of celiac disease. The prison staff examined Ossining, conducted a blood test, prescribed him iron supplements to overcome his weight loss and psychological depression, and professionally reviewed his blood work to conclude there was nothing seriously wrong with him. Therefore, as the prison exercised professional standards of care in evaluating his health, and as the inmate exhibits no severe symptoms warranting special treatment, Ossining fails to show deliberate indifference to his medical needs. #26 See United States Sent. G.L. Man. §5D2.1(f) (2001).

B. The prison's denial of prisoner's requests for a special gluten-free diet and additional testing for a rare disease do not violate contemporary standards of decency

Under the objective prong, Ossining fails to show his exposure to an unreasonable risk of harm contrary to "contemporary standards of decency." #27 Helling, 509 United States at 36. The objective standard requires showing treatment rising to the level of "serious" deprivation. #28 Campbell, 169 F.3d at 1363. In Rhodes, the

Court held confining two inmates to a single cell did not constitute the "unnecessary and wanton infliction of pain" that violates the Eighth Amendment because inmates suffered only minor deprivations of privileges, not necessities such as essential food, medical care, or sanitation. Only when these "minimal civilized measure of life's necessities" are denied is there basis for an Eighth Amendment violation. #29 Rhodes v. Chapman, 452 U.S 337, 346, 349 (1981). Similarly, Wellville's denial of additional testing and special diet to Ossining when trained medical professionals fail to recognize symptoms requiring such treatment does not constitute deprivation of life's minimal necessities. #30 RESTATEMENT (SECOND) OF TORTS § 931 (1994). Ossining was not denied adequate medical care when he was examined by prison medical staff, had his blood tested and reviewed by Dr. Flowers, and was prescribed iron supplements to combat weight loss and fatigue. Moreover, Ossining was never denied essential food as adequate alternatives remained available in the cafeteria should Ossining prefer a gluten-free diet. Therefore, life's minimal necessities were not denied, and Ossining fails the objective standard as his treatment did not violate contemporary standards of decency.

II. PRISONER'S FIRST AMENDMENT CLAIM IS WITHOUT MERIT BECAUSE WARDEN BRUBAKER REVIEWED AND DENIED PRISONER'S PUBLICATIONS IN RESPONSE TO THE UNREASONABLE BURDEN PLACED UPON THE PRISON'S RESOURCES AS AUTHORIZED UNDER 28 C.F.R. §540.71

As authorized under 28 C.F.R. § 540.71(b), Warden Brubaker legitimately restricted Ossining's right to receive publications deemed "detrimental to the security, good order, or discipline of the institution..." 28 C.F.R. § 540.71. Exercise of constitutional rights within the prison must pay due regard to the order and security of the prison environment. #31 See Turner Railroad v. Safley, 482 U.S. 78, 84-85 (1987). Ossining fails to show Wellville's restrictions on his First Amendment rights were not "reasonably related to legitimate penological interests" as required under the four-part Turner-Thornburgh test. #32 See Id. at 89; See Thornburgh, 490 U.S. at 401. Under Turner-Thornburgh, the Court must consider the following factors: (A) the impact that accommodation of the asserted constitutional right will have on others in the prison; (B) whether the governmental objective underlying the regulations at issue is legitimate and neutral, and whether the regulations are rationally related to that objective; (C) whether the regulation represents an exaggerated response to prison concerns; and (D) whether there are alternative means of exercising the right that remain open to prison inmates at de minimis cost to penological interests. #33 Owen v. Wille, 117 F.3d at 1235 (11th Cir. 1997). As Ossining's exercise of his First Amendment right created an unreasonable burden on resources of the prison and put prison security in jeopardy, restricting his access to medical publications was constitutional because it was reasonably related to a legitimate penological interest.

A. Accommodation of prisoner's asserted First Amendment right would be detrimental to the order and security of the prison, placing an unreasonable burden on the resources of the prison medical facility and cafeteria

The Court should be particularly deferential to the informed discretion of Warden Brubaker given interests in security when Ossining's assertion of his

#29   Keep as is/Change

#30   Keep as is/Change

#31   Keep as is/Change

#32   Keep as is/Change

#33   Keep as is/Change

constitutional right created a "ripple effect" among fellow inmates and prison staff. **#34** See U.S. v. White, 490 U.S. 84, 87 (1990). In Turner, a class of inmates challenged prison regulations restricting correspondence between inmates as violations of their First Amendment rights. The court deferred to judgment of correction officials and upheld the regulation as reasonably related to legitimate security interests given the potential for coordinating criminal activity by inmate-to-inmate correspondence, and given the probability of material circulating within the prison in a "ripple effect." **#35** See Turner, 482 U.S. at 84-85.

Like Turner, Warden Brubaker determined that Ossining created a "ripple effect," threatening the order and security of the prison while placing an unreasonable burden on prison resources, by circulating publications among prisoners to encourage them to believe they were sick. According to Brubaker, the temporal relationship between Ossining's receipt of medical publications and increased inmate complaints indicates a correlation between the assertion of his constitutional rights and the riling up of prisoners, overtaxing of prison personnel, and additional expenditure of prison resources. **#36** Ossining v. Brubaker, No. CIV.A.02-2332, 2003 WL 66432 at *6 (Jan. 6, 2003). Dramatic increases in infirmary visits and requests for allergy testing among inmates, many of whom showed no symptoms warranting testing, support Brubaker's hypothesis. Given the threat to order and cost of additional resources required to accommodate Ossining's assertion of his rights, deference should be given to Brubaker's informed discretion in rejecting these publications.

B. Governmental objective in maintaining prison security is legitimate and neutral, and prison regulations governing the availability of publications to inmates rationally relate to this objective by reducing frivolous medical complaints and special requests

Under the second factor of the Turner-Thornburgh test, the Court must determine whether (1) the governmental objective underlying the regulation at issue is legitimate and neutral, and whether (2) the regulation is rationally related to that objective. **#37** State of Alabama v. Carter, 507 U.S. 411, 418 (1992).

1. Protecting prison security is a legitimate and neutral governmental objective

In rejecting Ossining's publications, Warden Brubaker acted pursuant to 28 C.F.R. § 540.71, whose "underlying objective of protecting prison security is undoubtedly legitimate and is neutral with regard to the content of the expression regulated." **#38** North West Electric Company v. University of Colorado, 211 U.S. 415, 417 (1991). In Thornburgh, inmates filed a class action against the prison challenging regulations excluding incoming sexually explicit publications. The Court upheld the regulations as maintenance of prison order and security is a legitimate governmental purpose, and because the prison's ban on sexually explicit material was neutrally based on security interests. **#39** See cf. Thornburgh, 490 U.S. at 414-15. Like Thornburgh, Ossining's publications were rejected because they created obstacles to the legitimate governmental objective of maintaining prison security. Warden Brubaker's rejection of only those publications deemed a threat to prison security remained "neutral" to the legitimate governmental interest in maintaining security and order. Therefore, Brubaker's exercise of authority under 28 C.F.R. § 540.71 was consistent with the legitimate and neutral objectives underlying the regulation.

#34 Keep as is/Change
#35 Keep as is/Change
#36 Keep as is/Change
#37 Keep as is/Change
#38 Keep as is/Change
#39 Keep as is/Change

2. Application of prison regulation governing the availability of publications to inmates is rationally related to the governmental objective

There is a "valid, rational connection" between the rejection of various publications addressed to Ossining and the legitimate government interests in security and preservation of resources. #40 See Turner, 482 U.S. at 89; see also 28 C.F.R. § 540.71 (2002) (establishing security as legitimate government interest). In Onishea, inmates with HIV brought a class action challenging the prison's segregation of recreational, religious, and educational programs based on prisoners' HIV status. The prison justified its actions claiming the cost of hiring additional guards to monitor the threat of "high-risk" behavior in integrated programs would create an undue financial burden on resources. The Court upheld the segregated programs as rationally related to governmental objectives because "penological concerns such as security and cost are legitimate, and...these are in fact the concerns behind the program requirements that participating prisoners neither create a threat of disorder or unreasonable costs." #41 Onishea v. Hopper, 171 F.3d 1289, 1300 (11th Cir. 1999). Similarly, Brubaker's rejection of certain items addressed to Ossining was rationally related to legitimate governmental interests because of the Warden's concern that these publications created threat of disorder and unreasonable costs for the prison. By rejecting these publications, Warden Brubaker intended to remove obstacles to maintaining security by reducing the agitation of prisoners, easing the burden placed on the prison medical staff, and removing the need for additional guards to maintain order in the cafeteria. Therefore, as security was the underlying concern behind Brubaker's actions, his rejection of Ossining's publications was rationally related to legitimate governmental objectives. #42 See H.R. 81, 108th Cong. (2003) (establishing security as legitimate governmental objective), available at http://thomas.-%20loc.gov/bss/d108/d108laws.html.

C. The prison regulation is not an exaggerated response to prison concerns because alternatives accommodating prisoner's rights at de minimus cost to penological interests are not immediately obvious or feasible

Rejection of prisoner's publications is not an exaggerated response to the threat these items posed to prison resources and security because there are no "obvious, easy alternatives." #43 See Jeremy Stevens, Taking Control 41-42 (Amanda Bradley ed., Scholastic Press 3d ed. 2001). In Spellman, inmates challenged the prison's blanket ban on publications sent to prisoners in administrative segregation on the grounds that the regulation was an exaggerated response to security and safety concerns. The Court held the prison's actions unconstitutional, recognizing alternatives to the blanket ban, such as placing reasonable limits on the quantity of publications permitted in confinement, which still addressed the concerns of security, fire, and sanitation. #44 See Spellman v. Hopper, 95 F.supp.2d 1267, 1286 (M.D. Ala. 1999). Unlike Spellman, Brubaker rejected only Ossining's medical publications, items deemed a threat to prison security; Brubaker did not blanket ban all publications sent to Ossining. Moreover, unlike Spellman, less restrictive alternatives can be rejected because of reasonably grounded fears they will lead to greater harm or administrative inconvenience. #45 See Alabama Constitution article V, § 9. The resources required to read through every allergy magazine received to eliminate publications

#40 Keep as is/Change

#41 Keep as is/Change

#42 Keep as is/Change

#43 Keep as is/Change

#44 Keep as is/Change

#45 Keep as is/Change

Citation—Study Aid Material

deemed a threat would be too expansive as prisoners have complained of a wide variety of allergies. Also, allowing Ossining to read magazines while in confinement would not come at a de minimus cost to the prison as additional resources would be required to fund such an arrangement. #46 <u>See</u> James King, <u>Costs of Confinement</u>, 28 N. Ill. U. L. Rev. 609, 621-22 (2001). Thus, as less restrictive alternatives are not readily available or feasible, the Warden's actions do not represent an exaggerated response to legitimate penological concerns.

#46 Keep as is/Change

D. <u>The prison restrictions on prisoner's receipt of publications are reasonable as prisoner has alternative means of exercising his First Amendment rights to keep up with developments in his field of work.</u>

Ossining fails the fourth factor of the <u>Turner-Thornburgh</u> test because other means of expression remain available to the prisoner despite imposition of prison regulations restricting his access to certain publications. See Stevens, <u>Taking Control</u> at 45. In <u>Turner</u>, the prison restricted inmate-to-inmate correspondence between prisons to prevent future criminal behavior, a legitimate security concern. The Court held the fourth factor satisfied if any other means of expression remained open to the prisoners, not necessarily other means of communicating with inmates in other prisons. <u>Turner</u>, 482 U.S. at 90, 92. Similarly, Brubaker's application of the regulation merely prohibits publications of particular kind, and does not deprive the prisoner of all means of expression. The prison is not prohibiting Ossining from gaining access to allergy information as he can still receive phone calls and visits from colleagues who can keep him up to date. Moreover, the prisoner is still free to receive a variety of other publications. Alternative means of exercising his First Amendment rights are still available to the prisoner, and therefore, Ossining fails to satisfy the fourth factor.

CONCLUSION

For the above stated reasons, the judgment of the District Court should be affirmed.

Respectfully submitted,

_____

Attorney for Respondents

CERTIFICATE OF SERVICE

I swear on this day, the 28th of February, 2003, that I have served Respondent's brief on Appellant's counsel.

_____

Attorney for Respondents

Answer Key on page 316

IV.   STRATEGIES FOR USING THE BLUEBOOK

The Bluebook is not as intimidating as it appears at first glance. The trick for using it is to learn these three things:

1. the purpose of citation;
2. the design, layout, and basic citation rules of the Bluebook; and
3. some of the often-used rules.

A.   *The Purpose of Bluebook Citation*

Lawyers use citation to provide authority in legal documents and to find the law referenced in legal documents. The Bluebook, officially titled, *The Bluebook: A Uniform System of Citation,* is designed to provide a uniform system of citation rules so that lawyers can easily find and reference legal sources. Eventually, when electronic filings are required with links to each cited source, citation might become obsolete. But until that time, lawyers are required to use citation that permits other lawyers easy access to their references. The Bluebook and ALWD (discussed above) are the most commonly used citation systems. Using correct citation adds credibility to your writing; if a judge can trust your citations, she can also trust your analysis.

B.   *Design, Layout, and Basic Citation Rules of the Bluebook*

1.   Bluebook Design

The introduction in the Bluebook explains the purpose and function of the book. The Bluebook, in general, provides citation formats for scholarly documents, such as law review articles. The "quick reference" on the front inside cover is a cheat sheet for most-often used citations for law reviews. In addition to the rules laid out in the main section of the Bluebook, there are a number of important tables toward the end of the book. There are also an index and a table of contents to help in locating rules.

Most practicing lawyers cite to the law in legal documents, not scholarly articles. The Bluebook section, called the **Bluepages,** provides additional citation rules for court documents and legal memoranda. The Bluepages are organized by legal source (cases, statutes, constitutions, and so on) and provide easy-to-understand formatting and examples. In addition, the Bluepages contain two tables: BT1 for abbreviations in court documents and BT2 for local and jurisdiction-specific citation rules. The "quick reference" on the inside back cover of the Bluebook provides a cheat sheet for most-often used citations for legal documents. (The rules and examples in this book follow the citation rules for court documents unless otherwise noted.)

2. Bluebook Layout

The main highlights of the Bluebook contain the following:

1. The Bluepages, for practicing lawyers, are organized by category:
    - Cases (Rule B4)
    - Statutes, Rules, and Regulations (Rule B5)
    - Constitutions (Rule B6)
    - Court and Litigation Documents (Rule B7)
    - Books and Other Nonperiodic Materials (Rule B8)
    - Journals, Magazine, and Newspaper Articles (Rule B9)
2. **Citation rules,** which are organized by category:
    - Cases (Rule 10)
    - Constitutions (Rule 11)
    - Statutes (Rule 12)
    - Administrative and Executive Materials, including Rules and Regulations (Rule 14)
    - Books, Reports, and Other Nonperiodic Materials (Rule 15)
    - Periodical Materials (Rule 16)
3. **Tables** (on white pages with a blue edge), which lay out specific requirements of:
    - United States Jurisdictions (T1)
      - Federal Judicial and Legislative Materials (T1.1)
      - Federal Administrative and Executive Materials (T1.2)
      - States and the District of Columbia (T1.3)
      - Other United States Jurisdictions (T1.4)
    - Foreign Jurisdictions (T2)
    - Intergovernmental Organizations and Treaty Sources (T3 - T4)
    - Abbreviations for Arbitral Reporter Sources (T5)
    - Abbreviations for Case Names and Court Names (T6 - T7)
    - Abbreviations for Explanatory Phrases and Legislative Documents (T8 - T9)
    - Abbreviations for Geographical Terms (T10)
    - Abbreviations for Judges and Officials and Months (T11 - T12)
    - Abbreviations for Periodicals (T13)
    - Abbreviations for Publishing Terms and Services (T14 - T15)
    - Abbreviations for Document Subdivisions (T16)

In addition, the Bluebook contains a table of contents, which is helpful for finding rules on broad topics, such as law reviews, and an index, which is helpful for finding rules on specific subjects such as pinpoint cites.

3. Bluebook Basic Citation Rules

a. Cases (Rule 10)

Citation of a U.S. Supreme Court Case:

Lakeside v. Oregon, 435 U.S. 333, 345 (1978).

> Lakeside = plaintiff
> Oregon = defendant
> 435 = reporter volume #
> U.S. = reporter abbreviation
> 333 = first page
> 345 = specific page
> (1978) = date case decided

NOTE: Be sure to include both the first page of the cited case and a specific page if one is referenced.

Citation of a case decided by the U.S. Court of Appeals for the Eleventh Circuit:

Campbell v. Sikes,169 F.3d 1353, 1366-68 (11th Cir. 1999).

> Campbell = plaintiff
> Sikes = defendant
> 169 = reporter volume #
> F.3d = reporter abbreviation
> 1353 = first page
> 1366-68 = specific pages
> 11th Cir. = court—this is necessary if it's not clear from reporter abbreviation
> 1999 = date case decided

Short form for cases:

Campbell, 169 F.3d at 1369.

> Campbell = plaintiff; use defendant's name in short cite if plaintiff's name is a
>   common litigant (i.e., United States)
> 169 = reporter volume #
> F.3d = reporter abbreviation
> 1369 = specific page

b. *Constitutions (Rule 11)*

Citation of Section 2 of the Eighteenth Amendment to the U.S. Constitution:

U.S. Const. amend. XVIII, §2.

> U.S. Const. = abbreviation of Constitution
> amend. = abbreviation of amendment
> XVIII = # of amendment
> § 2 = # of section if applicable

c. *Statutes (Rule 12)*

Citation of an entire statute, the Federal Trademark Dilution Act of 1995, as codified in the United States Code:

Federal Trademark Dilution Act, 15 U.S.C. § 1125 (2000).

> Federal Trademark Dilution Act = official name
> 15 = title #
> U.S.C. = abbreviation of code
> § 1125 = section #
> 2000 = date of code edition

Citation of an individual provision of the United States Code:

15 U.S.C. § 1125 (2000).

> 15 = title #
> U.S.C. = abbreviation of code
> § 1125 = section #
> 2000 = date of code edition

Short citation of provision of the United States Code:

15 U.S.C. § 1125 or § 1125.

> 15 = title #
> U.S.C. = abbreviation of code
> § 1125 = section #
> or § 1125 = section #

d.   Rules and Regulations (Rule 14)

Citation of a particular provision of a regulation in the Code of Federal Regulations:

49 C.F.R. § 172.101 (2005).

> 49 = title #
> C.F.R. = abbreviation of regulations
> § 172.101 = section #
> 2005 = date of C.F.R. edition

NOTE: Whenever possible, cite all federal rules and regulations to the Code of Federal Regulations (C.F.R.) by title, section, and year.

Short citation of particular provision of a regulation in the C.F.R.:

49 C.F.R. § 172.101 or § 172.101.

> 49 = title #
> C.F.R. = abbreviation of regulations
> § 172.101 = section #
> or § 172.101 = section #

e.   Books (Rule 15)

Citation of treatise:

William L. Prosser & W. Page Keeton, <u>Prosser and Keeton on the Law of Torts</u> § 3.65 (5th ed. 1984).

> William L. Prosser & W. Page Keeton = full name of 1st and 2nd authors
> <u>Prosser and Keeton on the Law of Torts</u> = title of treatise
> § 3.65 = section #
> 5th ed. 1984—edition—if there is more than one—and date of edition

Citation of a particular page in a novel:

J. K. Rowling, <u>Harry Potter and the Sorcerer's Stone</u> 125 (1997).

> J.K. Rowling—use full name of author unless author uses initials only
> <u>Harry Potter and the Sorcerer's Stone</u> = title of book
> 125 = section or page #
> 1997 = year published

f. Periodical Materials (Rule 16)

Citation of particular pages within a law review article:

Mustave Hurt, <u>Unimaginable Pain</u>, 742 Geo. L.J. 801, 831-32 (2003) (discussing the requirements to show deliverage indifference).

> Mustave Hurt = full name of author
> <u>Unimaginable Pain</u> = title of article
> 742 = journal volume #
> Geo. L.J. = abbreviation of journal
> 801 = first page of article
> 831-32 = specific pages
> 2003 = year published
> (discussing the requirements to show deliberate indifference)—parenthetical describes article or point from article

Citation of an entire magazine article:

J. Madeleine Nash, <u>Fertile Minds</u>, Time, Feb. 3, 1997, at 18.

> J. Madeline Nash = author's full name
> Fertile Minds = title of article
> Time = name of magazine
> Feb. 3, 1997 = cover date
> at 18 = first page

Citation of a newspaper article:

Adam Gourna, <u>Celiac Disease: A Killer</u>, N.Y. Times, Dec. 12, 1994, at F3.

> Adam Gourna = author's full name
> <u>Celiac Disease: A Killer</u> = headline
> N.Y. Times = abbreviation of newspaper
> Dec. 12, 1994 = date
> at F3 = page #

C. Often-Used Bluebook Rules

The following are some of the most-often used rules in the Bluebook citation format. They are provided for practitioners' use in court documents and legal memoranda.

- Typefaces, p. 255
- Basic Structure and Signals, p. 256
- Subdivisions and Pinpoint Cites, p. 258
- Short Citations, p. 258
- Abbreviations, p. 259

Bluebook Typefaces (Bluepages 1, 2, 7, 8, 9, 13 and Rule 2)

BLUEBOOK RULE	KEY POINTS

B2: Citation Sentences and Clauses: Bluepages Tip
 	
Underscoring or italics may be appropriate in court documents or legal memoranda. However, check your local rules for the court's preference (Table BT2).
 	
    Example: <u>Pope v. Hightower</u>
 	
Rule 2: Typefaces for Law Reviews
	• Practitioners underscore or italicize all case names, including the "v."
	• Where the Bluepages indicates to use underscoring, italics may be substituted. Be consistent with underscoring or italics throughout the document.
	• In law reviews, three typefaces are commonly used:
	  1. Ordinary Roman (plain text)
	  2. Italics
	  3. Large and small capitals
	
	See Rule 2 for specifics.

B8: Books and Other Nonperiodic Materials B9: Journal and Newspaper Articles Example: <u>Killer Tornado</u>, Newsweek, Mar. 3, 1991, at 39.	Underscore or italicize the title of a book or the title of an article appearing in a periodical.

B1: Typeface Conventions
 	
This rule tries to clarify the distinction between the Bluepages typeface and law review typeface. It provides an exclusive list of underscored (or italicized) sources for practitioners.
 	
Words and Phrases Introducing Related Authority
 	
    Example: <u>Red Sox Say Manager's Contract Won't Be Renewed</u>, N.Y. Times, Oct. 27, 2003, <u>available at</u> http://www.nytimes.com/aponline/sports/AP-BBA-Red-Sox-Little.html.
 	
If not specified as underscored or italicized, practitioners print everything else in ordinary Roman type.
 	
    Example: U.S. Const. amend. XVIII, § 2
	• Underscore or italicize subsequent case history.
	• Underscore or italicize "<u>available at</u>" and other similar words and phrases referring to related authority.
	• Underscore or italicize <u>id.</u> and <u>supra</u>.
	
	Print reporters, services, constitutions, statutes, Restatements, model codes, rules, executive orders, administrative materials, unpublished sources, and treaties in ordinary Roman type.

B7.3: Capitalization in Textual Sentences	• Capitalize "Court" in the following circumstances:

Examples: The Court of Appeals for the First Circuit held ...
 	
The Supreme Court held ...
 	
This Court should hold ...
	1. When naming any court in full;
	   2. When referring to the U.S. Supreme Court;
	   3. When referring to the court that will be receiving that document.
	• Capitalize party designations: Plaintiff, Defendant, Appellant, etc., when referring to those actual parties in your case only.

Bluebook Basic Structure and Signals (Bluepages 2, 3, 11 and Rule 1)

BLUEBOOK RULE	KEY POINTS
B2: Citation Sentences and Clauses Examples: <u>See</u> <u>Jones v. Smith</u>, 345 U.S. 322 (1985). <u>Jones v. Smith</u>, 345 U.S. 322 (1985); <u>see also</u> <u>Cambridge v. Boston</u>, 235 U.S. 412 (1977). Rule 1.1: Citation Sentences and Clauses in Law Reviews Example: [Footnote]2. Other authors have made similar assertions. <u>Cf.</u> Mustave Hurt, <u>Unimaginable Pain</u>, 742 Geo. L.J. 801, 831-32 (2003).	• Citations in court documents and legal memoranda traditionally appear within the text rather than in footnotes or endnotes. A citation within the text can appear in a stand-alone sentence or in a citation clause. • A citation sentence begins with a capital and ends with a period. If it contains multiple citations, it will include semicolons to separate each citation. • A citation clause is set off from the text with commas. • In law reviews, citations appear in footnotes. At times, an author might make an assertion within a footnote; here, a citation should appear in the footnote after the assertion.
B3: Introductory Signals Rule 1.2: Introductory Signals Example: <u>See generally</u> Killer Tornado, Newsweek, Mar. 3, 1991, at 39.	A signal is a sign to the reader indicating the type of authority about to be cited. • Signals that indicate support are no signal, <u>e.g.</u>, <u>accord</u>, <u>see</u>, <u>see also</u>, <u>cf.</u> • A signal that suggests a useful comparison is compare ... with .... • Signals that indicate contradiction are <u>contra</u>, <u>but see</u>, <u>but cf</u>. • A signal that indicates background material is see generally.
B3.5: Order of Signals Rule 1.3: Order of Signals Example: <u>See</u> Mustave Hurt, <u>Unimaginable Pain</u>, 742 Geo. L.J. 801, 831-32 (2003); <u>see also</u> <u>Killer Tornado</u>, Newsweek, Mar. 3, 1991, at 39. <u>But see</u> Adam Gourna, <u>Celiac Disease: A Killer</u>, N.Y. Times, Dec. 12, 1994, at F3.	• Signals of different types must be grouped in different citation sentences. • When more than one signal is used in a citation, the signals should appear in the order listed in Rule 1.2. • Signals of the same type must be strung together with a single citation sentence and separated by semicolons.

B3.5: Order of Signals Rule 1.4: Order of Authorities Within Each Signal Example: <u>See</u> <u>Turner</u>, 482 U.S. at 89; <u>see also</u> 28 C.F.R. § 540.71 (2002) (establishing security as legitimate government interest).	• Authorities within each signal are separated by semicolons. • General order: constitutions; statutes; treaties; cases; legislative materials; administrative and executive materials; resolutions, decisions, and regulations of intergovernmental organizations; records, briefs, and petitions; secondary materials; cross references. • In addition, the Bluebook has rules regarding the order within each one of these categories. • However, if one authority is more helpful, it should precede the others.
B11: Explanatory Parentheticals Rule 1.5: Parenthetical Information Example: 28 C.F.R. § 540.71 (2002) (establishing legitimate government interest).	• Additional information about a citation is added in a parenthetical at the end of the citation sentence or clause. • The text in a parenthetical need not be a full sentence; omit extraneous words such as "the." • Often, parentheticals begin with a present participle; however, a quotation or short phrase is also appropriate. • Parenthetical information is recommended when the relevance of the cited authority might not otherwise be clear to the reader. • Explanatory parenthetical phrases that do not directly quote the authority often begin with a present participle and usually do not begin with a capital letter. • If the parenthetical information includes one or more full sentences, it should start with a capital letter and end with the correct punctuation. • Explanatory parenthetical phrases come before any citations concerning subsequent history or other related authority. Rule 1.5(b) explains the order in which to present multiple parentheticals within a citation.

Bluebook Subdivisions and Pinpoint Cites
(Bluepages 4.1.2 and Rule 3)

BLUEBOOK RULE	KEY POINTS

B4.1.2: Reporter and Pinpoint Citation
 	
Rule 3.2(a): Pages, Footnotes, Endnotes, and Graphical Materials
 	
    Example: <u>Campbell v. Sikes</u>, 169 F.3d 53, 66 (1999).
 	
    Example: <u>McElligot v. Foley</u>, 182 F.3d 1248, 1256-58 (11th Cir. 1999).
 	
    Example: <u>Rhodes v. Chapman</u>, 452 U.S. 337, 346, 349 (1981).
	• When referring to specific material within a source, include both the page on which the source begins and the page on which the specific materials appear, separated by a comma.
	• When citing material that spans more than one page, give the inclusive page numbers, separated by a hyphen or dash. Always retain the last two digits, but drop other repetitious digits.
	• Cite nonconsecutive pages by giving the individual page numbers separated by commas.
	• Give page number or numbers before the date parenthetical, without any introductory abbreviation.
	• Use "at" if page number may be confused with another part of the citation.
	• Use a comma to set off the "at."
	• If you are referring specifically to material on the first page of a source, repeat the page number.
	• When citing material within a concurring or dissenting opinion, give only the initial page of the case and the page on which the specific material appears. See B4.1.2.

Bluebook Short Citations (Rule 4)

BLUEBOOK RULE	KEY POINTS

In Bluepages, see specific sections for each appropriate short form (e.g., cases, statutes, and so on).
 	
Rule 4.1: "<u>Id.</u>"
 	
    Example:
 	
    1. <u>Helling</u>, 509 U.S. 25, 29 (1993).
    2. <u>Id.</u> at 35-36.
    3. <u>See</u> <u>id.</u>
	• Only use short citation format after an authority has been cited once in full citation format and when the reader will not be confused as to which source is being referenced.
	• Use <u>id.</u> when citing the immediately preceding authority. Capitalize <u>id.</u> when it appears in the beginning of a citation sentence; do not capitalize <u>id.</u> when it is not the beginning of a sentence.
	• <u>Id.</u> may not be used to refer to one authority in a preceding footnote if the preceding footnote cites more than one source.

Rule 4.2: "Supra" and "Hereinafter" Example: Hurt, supra note 3, at 8.	• Used to refer to legislative hearings, books, pamphlets, unpublished materials, nonprint resources, periodicals, services, treaties, international agreements, regulations, directives, and decisions of intergovernmental organizations. • Do not use to refer to cases, statutes, constitutions, legislative materials, Restatements, model codes, or regulations. • Supra form consists of the last name of the author, followed by a comma and the word "supra," then the footnote in which the full citation can be found, and the specific volume, paragraph, section, or page numbers cited.

Bluebook Abbreviations (Rule 6, Rule 10, BT1, Tables 1-6)

BLUEBOOK RULE	KEY POINTS
Rule 6.1: Abbreviations	• Abbreviations not found within the Bluebook should be avoided unless they are unambiguous and save substantial space. • Generally, close up adjacent capitals (N.W.), but do not close up single capitals with longer abbreviations (D. Mass.). See Rule 6.1.
Rule 6.2(a) Rule 6.2(c): Section (§) and Paragraph (¶) Symbols	• Spell out numbers zero to ninety-nine, but use numerals for larger numbers. Exceptions to this rule are laid out in Rule 6.2(a). • Spell out the words "section" and "paragraph" in the text. • In citations, the symbols should be used with a space between § or ¶ and the numeral.
Rule 10: Abbreviating Case Names	• Rule 10.2.1(c) addresses abbreviations of all case names whether they appear in text or in citations. • Rule 10.2.2 addresses further abbreviations for case names that appear in citations. • Rule 10.3.2: Reporters

BT1: Abbreviations in Court Documents	• The tables in the back of the Bluebook contain abbreviations for specific jurisdictions as well as for specific terms.
T1: Abbreviations for Specific Jurisdictions	• Rules within the Bluebook will also have specific requirements for that rule.
T6: Case Names and Institutional Authors in Citations	
T7: Court Names	• Example: Rule 10.2 for abbreviating case names.
T8: Explanatory Phrases	
T9: Legislative Documents: T9	
T10: Geographical Terms	
T11: Judges and Officials	
T12: Months	
T13, Periodicals	
T14: Publishing Terms	
T15: Services	
T16: Subdivisions	

Bluebook Cases (Bluepages 4 and Rule 10)

BLUEBOOK RULE	KEY POINTS

B4.1: Full Citation
 	
Rule 10.1: Basic Citation Forms
	• U.S. Supreme Court case:
	  • Example: <u>Thornburgh v. Abbott</u>, 490 U.S. 401, 407-08 (1989).
	• U.S. Court of Appeals case:
	  • Example: <u>Pope v. Hightower</u>, 101 F.3d 1382, 1383 (11th Cir. 1996).
	• Do not use superscripts when abbreviating words like "11th."

B4.1.1: Case Name Rule 10.2: Case Names	• Include only the necessary information in a case name and underline the entire case name up until the comma (do not underline the comma). • Use only the surname. • Omit words indicating multiple parties. Look up the abbreviations required in B4.1.1 and 10.2. Note that 10.2.2 provides extra rules for case names in citation sentences and clauses (as opposed to references to case names in text). 1. When a case name is used in a textual sentence (in text or footnotes), you should follow 10.2.1 (see below). 2. When a case name is used in a citation sentence or clause, you should refer to rules 10.2.1 and 10.2.2 (see below).

Rule 10.2.1: General Rules for Case Names
 	
Example: <u>Harris v. Thigpen</u>
 	
Not: <u>Harris et al. v. Thigpen, Kramer & Levin</u>.
 	
Example: <u>Alabama v. Carter</u>, 507 U.S. 411, 418 (1992).
 	
Example: <u>Commonwealth v. Robertson</u>
 	
Not: <u>Commonwealth of Virginia v. Robertson</u>
 	
Example: <u>Montana Moving Co. v. Rhode Island Storage, Inc.</u>
 	
Not: <u>Montana Moving Co., Inc. v. Rhode Island Storage, Inc.</u>
	• Omit words indicating multiple parties, such as "et al.," and all parties other than the first listed on each side.
	• Abbreviate only widely known acronyms and the following eight words unless the word begins a party's name:
	  1. &
	  2. Ass'n
	  3. Bros.
	  4. Co.
	  5. Corp.
	  6. Inc.
	  7. Ltd.
	  8. No.
	• Usually omit "The" as the first word of a party's name.
	• Geographical terms: Omit "State of," "Commonwealth of," and "People of," except when citing decisions of the courts of that state. When citing decisions of the courts of that state, use "State," "Commonwealth," or "People."
	• Business firms: Omit "Inc.," "Ltd.," "L.L.C.," "N.A.," "F.S.B.," and similar terms if the name also contains a word such as "Ass'n," "Bros.," "Co.," and "R.R."

Rule 10.2.2: Additional Rules for Case Names That Appear in Citations Example: <u>Turner R.R. v. Safley</u> *Not:* <u>Turner Railroad v. Safley</u>. <u>Not:</u> <u>U.S. v. White</u>	• Always abbreviate any word listed in Table 6 (T6) and any geographic term in Table 10 (T10), unless the geographical unit is a named party. • Abbreviate other words of eight letters or more if the result is unambiguous and substantial space is saved. • Do not abbreviate "United States" in the case name when the United States is the actual party. (However, abbreviate United States when it is part of the party's name—e.g., U.S. Steel.)
Rule 10.3.3: Public Domain Format	• United States Court of Appeals for numbered circuits: 2d Cir., 4th Cir. • State Courts: Indicate state and court of decision, but do not include the name of the court if the court of decision is the highest court in the state. Omit jurisdiction if it is unambiguously conveyed by the reporter. • See Table T7 for court abbreviations.
B4.1.2: Reporter and Pinpoint Citation Example: <u>Jones v. Smith</u>, 230 U.S. 432, 434 (1986).	• When providing reporter information, you should provide the volume and abbreviation for the reporter as well as the page on which the opinion begins. • A pinpoint cite or jump cite is a reference to the specific page(s) for your proposition.

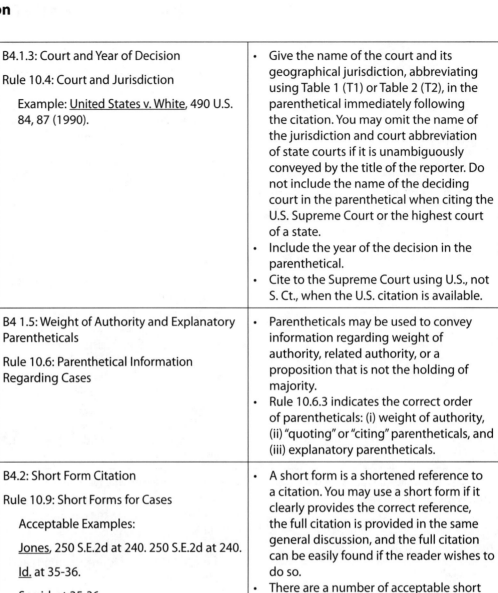

B4.1.3: Court and Year of Decision	• Give the name of the court and its geographical jurisdiction, abbreviating using Table 1 (T1) or Table 2 (T2), in the parenthetical immediately following the citation. You may omit the name of the jurisdiction and court abbreviation of state courts if it is unambiguously conveyed by the title of the reporter. Do not include the name of the deciding court in the parenthetical when citing the U.S. Supreme Court or the highest court of a state.
Rule 10.4: Court and Jurisdiction	
Example: <u>United States v. White</u>, 490 U.S. 84, 87 (1990).	
	• Include the year of the decision in the parenthetical.
	• Cite to the Supreme Court using U.S., not S. Ct., when the U.S. citation is available.
B4 1.5: Weight of Authority and Explanatory Parentheticals	• Parentheticals may be used to convey information regarding weight of authority, related authority, or a proposition that is not the holding of majority.
Rule 10.6: Parenthetical Information Regarding Cases	
	• Rule 10.6.3 indicates the correct order of parentheticals: (i) weight of authority, (ii) "quoting" or "citing" parentheticals, and (iii) explanatory parentheticals.
B4.2: Short Form Citation	• A short form is a shortened reference to a citation. You may use a short form if it clearly provides the correct reference, the full citation is provided in the same general discussion, and the full citation can be easily found if the reader wishes to do so.
Rule 10.9: Short Forms for Cases	
Acceptable Examples:	
<u>Jones</u>, 250 S.E.2d at 240. 250 S.E.2d at 240.	
<u>Id.</u> at 35-36.	• There are a number of acceptable short forms; most of them include "at" with a pinpoint cite.
<u>See id.</u> at 35-36.	• When using a name for a short form, use the first party's name unless it is a geographical term or government name.
	• "<u>Id.</u>" may be used in court documents and legal memoranda to refer to a case cited in the previous citation. When used at the beginning of a citation sentence, capitalize the "i." However, when used in the middle of a citation sentence, do not capitalize the "i." Do not use "<u>supra</u>" to refer to previously cited cases in a court document or legal memorandum.

Bluebook Constitutions (Bluepages 6 and Rule 11)

BLUEBOOK RULE	KEY POINTS

B6: Constitutions
 	
Rule 11: Constitutions
 	
   Example: U.S. Const. amend. XVIII, § 2.
	• Abbreviate United States (U.S.).
	• Abbreviate United States (U.S.) if referring to the federal Constitution, or refer to Table T10 for the appropriate abbreviation if citing a state constitution.
	• Use Const., not CONST.
	• If the constitutional provision has been repealed, amended, or superseded, refer to Rule 11 for appropriate citation format.
	• Short form: Do not use short citation form (other than id.) for constitutions.
	• Cite state constitutions by the abbreviated name of the state and the word "Const."
	• Abbreviate subdivisions of constitutions according to Table 16 (T16).
	    • Example: Ala. Const. art. V, § 9.

Bluebook Statutes (Bluepages 5 and Rule 12)

BLUEBOOK RULE	KEY POINTS

B5: Statutes, Rules, and Regulations
 	
Rule 12.1: Basic Citation Forms for Statutes.
 	
   Example: 42 U.S.C. § 1983 (1994).
 	
   Example: 42 U.S.C. §§ 8401-8405 (2000).
	• Cite current statutes to the official code. (Cite U.S.C., not U.S.C.A. or U.S.C.S.)
	• Place periods in between "U.S.C."
	• Do not underline statute citations.
	• Leave a space between "§" and the cited section numbers.
	• When citing multiple sections, use "§§."
	• Include the year the code was published in a parenthetical.
	• Include the official name of the act when available.

Example for Law Review: IND. CODE § 35-42-5-1 (1998). Example for Practitioner: Mo. Ann. Stat. §565.225(3) (West 2010). Example: 18 U.S.C.A. § 1028 (West 2000 & Supp. 2010)	• Cite to the official federal and state codes whenever possible. The official federal code is the United States Code, "U.S.C." To determine the official code for a particular state, see Table T1. • If citing to a code that is published, edited, or compiled by someone other than state officials, give the name of the publisher, editor, or compiler in the parenthetical phrase (Rule 12.3.1(d)). For example: West (2006). • According to Rule 12.3.1(a), if the statute is commonly cited using a different name or is known by a popular name, give that name and the original section number preceding the normal citation format. • If the statute appears in a supplement or pocket part, cite the statute according to Rule 3.1(c). See Rule 12.3.1(e) for examples of the proper citation format. • If a statute has been invalidated, repealed, or amended, cite it in accordance with Rule 12.7. When citing a current version of a statute that has prior history, you may give the prior history in an explanatory parenthetical phrase according to Rule 12.8. • Some statutes require special citation forms. Rule 12.9 indicates that these include the Internal Revenue Code (12.9.1), ordinances (12.9.2), model codes, restatements, standards, and sentencing guidelines (12.9.5).
B5.1.3: Rules of Evidence and Procedure; Restatements; Uniform Acts	Do not include dates.

Rule 12.9.3: Rules of Evidence and Procedure
 	
Rule 12.9.5: Model Codes, Restatements, Standards, and Sentencing Guidelines
 	
    Examples: Fed. R. Evid. 213 Fed. R. Crim. P. 11.
 	
    Restatement (Second) of Torts § 84 (1989).
 	
    Example: U.S. Sentencing Guidelines Manual § 5D2.1(f) (2001).	

B5.2: Short Forms (for Statutes) Rule 12.10: Short Forms for Statutes Example: 42 U.S.C. § 1221 or § 1221.	• _Id._ may be used in court documents and legal memoranda to refer to the previously cited statute or to a statute within the same title previously cited. • Use chart from 12.10(b) to determine proper format for named statutes, U.S. Code provisions, state code provisions, and session laws.

Bluebook Administrative and Executive Materials (Bluepages 5.1.4 and Rule 14)

BLUEBOOK RULE	KEY POINTS
B5.1.4: Administrative Rules and Regulations Rule 14.2: Rules, Regulations, and Other Publications Example: 28 C.F.R. § 540.71 (2003).	Whenever possible, cite all federal rules and regulations to the Code of Federal Regulations (C.F.R.) by title, section or part, and year.
	• Be sure to cite the most recent edition of C.F.R., according to Rule 14.2(a). • Do not leave spaces between the letters of "C.F.R." • If a federal rule or regulation is known by a common name or is typically cited using a name, indicate that name before the title number, using the format specified in Rule 14.2(a).
Example: Numismatic Products Pricing, 76 FR 417 (Dec 29, 2010).	• According to Rule 14.2(a), if a rule or regulation has not yet been published in C.F.R., cite to the Federal Register. Administrative notices should be cited to the Federal Register.
Example: Flexsteel Industries, Inc., 311 N.L.R.B. 257 (1993).	• Cite to arbitrations and administrative adjudications using the same format for cases in Rule 10. However, according to Rule 14.3.1, case names or administrative adjudications are identified by the first-listed private party, or by the official subject-matter title. Case names of arbitrations are cited according to Rule 10 or, if adversary parties are not named, like administrative adjudications according to Rule 14.3.1(a).
Example: Attorney-General—Secretary of War, 20 Op. Att'y Gen. 740 (1894).	• Advisory opinions from the United States Attorney General or any other government entity are cited according to the "Department of Justice" section in Table T1.2. • Federal tax statutes are cited according to Rule 12.8.1, but other federal taxation materials, including Treasury regulations, determinations, and cases, are cited according to Table T1.2.
Example: Exec. Order No. 12,356, 3 C.F.R. 166 (1983). Example: Proclamation No. 13526, 75 Fed. Reg. 707 (Dec. 29, 2009).	• Presidential executive orders are found in title 3 of C.F.R. and should be cited to C.F.R. according to Rule 14.2, with a parallel citation to the United States Code if therein. However, if an executive order is not found in C.F.R., cite according to the Federal Register. Examples of each citation format can be found under the heading "Executive Office of the President" in Table T1.2. • Patents should be cited according to the patent number and the data the patent was filed, using the format specified in "Department of Commerce, Patent and Trademark Office (USPTO)" in Table T1.2.

B5.2: Short Form Citation	• Use chart in Rule 14.4(c) to determine proper format for regulations.
Rule 14.4: Short Forms for Regulations	• <u>Id.</u> may be used in court documents and legal memoranda to refer to the previously cited regulation or to a regulation within the same title previously cited.
Example: 28 C.F.R. § 540.71 or § 540.71.	

Bluebook Books, Reports, and Other Nonperiodic Materials (Bluepages 8 and Rule 15)

BLUEBOOK RULE	KEY POINTS

B8: Books and Other Nonperiodic Materials
 	
Rule 15: Books, Reports, and Other Nonperiodic Materials
 	
    Example: <u>Noah Lee, Deliberate Indifference: What's It All About?</u> 31 (3d ed. 2001).
 	
    Example: Emily Noel et al., <u>The Costs and Benefits of Negligence</u> 56-72 (2d ed, 1988).
 	
    Example: Jeremy Stevens, <u>Taking Control</u> 41-42 (Amanda Bradley ed., Scholastic Press 3d. ed. 2001).
	• Cite books, reports, and other nonperiodic materials by author, title (underlined), pinpoint page, section or paragraph, edition (if more than one), and date (in parenthetical).
	• When citing a publication for the first time, give the author's full name as it appears on the publication. However, do not include designations indicating academic degrees such as "Dr." See Rule 15.1.
	• For works with two authors, give their names in the order in which they are listed on the title page, separated by "&" (Rule 15.1(a)).
	• For works with more than two authors, you may use the name of the first author listed followed by "et al." or, where it is important to include all the authors' names and space is not an issue, you may list all of their names, separating the final name with "&"(Rule 15.1(b)).
	• Rule 15.2 specifies the format for works with editors or translators. Give the full name of the editor in a parenthetical as it appears in the publication. In the same parenthetical, after the full name of the editor, indicate the editor's title with "ed.," the name of the publisher (if other than the original publisher), and the year of publication.
	• According to Rule 15.3, give the name of the work according to how it appears on the title page. Refer to Rule 8 to determine which words in a title to capitalize. Do not omit articles from the title.

Example: John T. Smith, Jr., <u>Morality and Law</u> 67 (1965). Example: <u>Blacks Law Dictionary</u> (9th ed. 2009).	• For works that have been published in only one edition, give the year of publication in parentheses (Rule 15.4(a)(i)). For works that have been published in multiple editions, cite the latest edition according to Rule 15.4(a) unless an earlier edition is more relevant • Some works are cited so frequently that they have special citation forms in Rule 15.8. These works include Black's Law Dictionary, American Jurisprudence, and Corpus Juris Secundum.
B8.2: Short Form Citation Rule 15.9: Short Citation Forms Example: Stevens, <u>supra</u>, at 45.	• If the work was cited as the immediately preceding authority, use <u>id.</u> • If the work has been cited in full, but not as the immediately preceding authority, use <u>supra</u>.

Bluebook Periodicals (Bluepages 9 and Rule 16)

BLUEBOOK RULE	**KEY POINTS**
B9.1.1: Consecutively Paginated Journals Rule 16.4: Consecutively Paginated Journals Example: Mustave Hurt, <u>Unimaginable Pain</u>, 742 Geo. L.J. 801, 831-32 (2003).	• Include author, title of work, volume number, periodical name, first page of work, pages on which cited material appears, and year. • Use Table 13 (T.13) to abbreviate the names of periodicals. • Cite the author's full name as it appears in the publication according to Rule 15.1. • Cite the full title of the article as it appears on the title page of the publication, but refer to Rule 8 for capitalization. • Cite the volume number, followed by the abbreviation of the journal name according to Table T13, and the page number on which the cited material begins. • Indicate the date of publication in a parenthetical.
B9.1.2: Nonconsecutively Paginated Journals and Magazines Rule 16.5: Nonconsecutively Paginated Journals and Magazines Example: <u>Killer Tornado</u>, Newsweek, Mar. 3, 1991, at 39, 40.	• Cite works appearing within periodicals that are separately paginated within each issue by author, title, periodical name, date of issue, and first page of work and/or pages on which material appears. • Use Table 13 (T13) to abbreviate names of periodicals.

B9.1.4: Newspaper Articles Rule 16.6: Newspapers Example: <u>Celiac Disease: A Killer</u>, N.Y. Times, Dec. 12, 1994, at F3.	• Use Table 13 (T13) to abbreviate names of newspapers. • Cite the same as for nonconsecutively paginated periodicals (Rule 16.4), but only the first page of the work need be cited.
Rule 16.7: Student Written Law Review Materials	• If the piece you are citing is student-written, follow Rule 16.7.1(a) if it is signed or 16.7.1(b) if it is unsigned. Be sure to indicate the type of piece you are citing, either a "Note" or "Comment" or some other type of work. • For book reviews by nonstudents, reference Rule 16.7.2. • For book reviews written by students, reference Rule 16.7.1(c). • If the work under review is unclear from the surrounding text, include a second parenthetical following the date of publication identifying the work.

Bluebook Electronic Media (Rule 18)

BLUEBOOK RULE	KEY POINTS
Rule 18.2.1: General Internet Principles	• When an authenticated, official, or exact copy of a source can be found online, citation can be made as if to the original print source (without URL information). Some states have started to discontinue printed official legal sources and instead rely on online versions as the official resource, but the federal government continues to publish official print versions.
(a) Sources that can be cited as if to original print source	• Note the Bluebook's definitions of and distinctions among "Authenticated Documents," "Official Versions," and "Exact Copies."
(b) Sources to which the URL should be appended	• When a cited source is available in print but is so obscure as to be practically unavailable, citation should be as if to the printed source, but append the URL directly to the end of citation to indicate online location of the copy.
(c) Sources using "available at" to indicate when access is available online	• If a printed source is available, a parallel citation to an electronic source may be appropriate where it would substantially improve access to the information. Citation should be made to the printed source first and then separately to the electronic source, introduced with the explanation phrase *"available at."*

Rule 18.2.2: Direct Citation to Internet Sources Include: Author, Title, Date (and Time When Relevant), URL	• Cite to an Internet source when the material does not exist in a traditional printed format or when the printed source exists but cannot be found or is practically unavailable because it is so obscure. • Cite to the most stable electronic location. • Include information to facilitate the clearest path of access, including title page, pagination, and publication date as they appear on the website. The URL should be separated by a comma and appended to the end of the citation.
Rule 18.2.3: Parallel Citations to Internet Sources Example: Diana Donahoe, *Strip Searches of Students: Addressing the Undressing of Children in Schools and Redressing the Fourth Amendment Violations,* 75 Mo. L. Rev. (forthcoming 2010), available at http://ssrn.com/abstract=444455.	• When a source is available in a traditional printed medium, you may provide a parallel cite to an Internet source with identical content if it will substantially improve access to the source. • The parallel Internet cite should be introduced with the explanatory phrase *"available at."* Rule 18.2.3(a). • The author, title, pagination, and publication date of the original printed source should be used even when the Internet provides slightly different information. But if the information on the Internet differs materially from the information in the traditional printed source, a parallel citation should not be used. Rule 18.2.3(b). • A parallel citation does not affect the order of authorities. Rule 18.2.3(c).

Rule 18.3.1: Commercial Electronic Databases: Cases	• When case is unreported, but available on widely used electronic database, it may be cited to the database.

Example: <u>Ossining v. Brubaker</u>, No. CIV.A.02-2332, 2003 U.S. Dist. LEXIS 5130, at *1 (S.D. Ala. Jan. 6, 2003).	• Provide the case name, docket number, database identifier, court name, and full date of most recent major disposition.
	
	   • Example: Westlaw: WL
	       Lexis: LEXIS
	
	• Screen or page numbers, if assigned, should be preceded by an asterisk. Paragraph numbers, if assigned, should be preceded by a paragraph symbol.
	• If the electronic database provides a unique identifying number for the case, remember to provide it following the case name, preceded by "No."
	• If citing to a specific page or screen of an opinion, indicate the page number preceded by an asterisk. If citing to a particular paragraph, indicate the paragraph number preceded by "¶."
	• For addresses, books, periodicals, and other secondary material, refer to Rule 18.3.4.

Rule 18.3.2: Constitutions and Statutes	• Cite statutes according to Rules 12.3 and 12.4.
Example: Mich. Comp. Laws § 22.33 (West, Westlaw through 2003 Sess.). Example: Mich. Comp. Laws Ann. § 22.33 (Michie, LEXIS through 2003 Legislation).	• In addition, when citing statutes from an electronic database (such as Lexis or Westlaw), give within a parenthetical the name of the database and information about the currency of the database, as provided by the database itself, instead of the year of the code according to Rule 12.3.2. • Also give the name of the publisher, editor, or compiler unless the code is published, edited, compiled, by or under the supervision of federal or state officials (see Rule 12.3.1(d)).

V. STUDY AIDS—BLUEBOOK CITATION

A. *Bluebook Quick References and Checklists*

📝 1. The Bluebook in General: Quick Reference

To use the Bluebook effectively, you should understand the following:

- The purpose of citation
- The design, layout, and basic rules of the Bluebook
- Some often-used rules of the Bluebook

Purpose of Citation

The purpose of citation is to allow lawyers to easily find and reference legal sources.

Design, Layout, and Basic Bluebook Citation Rules

Bluebook Design

- In general, provides citation formats for scholarly documents.
- "Quick Reference" on front inside cover provides most-often used citations for law reviews.
- Bluepages provide citation rules for court documents and legal memoranda.
- "Quick Reference" on back inside cover provides most-often used citations for court documents and legal memoranda.

Bluebook Layout

Citations

- Cases: Rule 10
- Constitutions: Rule 11
- Statutes: Rule 12
- Administrative and Executive Materials, including Rules and Regulations: Rule 14
- Books, Reports, and Other Nonperiodic Materials: Rule 15
- Periodical Materials: Rule 16

Tables

- United States Jurisdictions: T1
  - Federal Judicial and Legislative Materials: T1.1
  - Federal Administrative and Executive Materials: T1.2
  - States and the District of Columbia: T1.3
  - Other Untied States Jurisdictions: T1.4
- Foreign Jurisdictions: T2
- Intergovernmental Organizations and Treaty Sources: T3 and T4
- Abbreviations for Arbitral Reporter Sources: T5

- Abbreviations for Case Names and Court Names: T6 and T7
- Abbreviations for Explanatory Phrases and Legislative Documents: T8 and T9
- Abbreviations for Publishing Terms and Services: T14 and T15
- Abbreviations for Document Subdivisions: T16
- Table of Contents
- Index

Basic Bluebook Citation Rules

- Cases: Rule 10
- Constitutions: Rule 11
- Statutes: Rule 12
- Rules and Regulations: Rule 14
- Books: Rule 15
- Periodical Materials: Rule 16

Often-Used Bluebook Citation Rules

- Typefaces: Bluepages 1, 2, 7, 8, 9, and Rule 2
- Basic Structure and Signals: Bluepages 2, 3, 11 and Rule 1
- Subdivisions and Pinpoint Cites: Bluepages 4.1.2 and Rule 3
- Short Citations: Rule 4
- Abbreviations: Rule 6
- Cases: Bluepages 4 and Rule 10
- Constitutions: Bluepages 6 and Rule 11
- Statutes: Bluepages 5 and Rule 12
- Administrative and Executive Materials: Bluepages 5.1.4 and Rule 14
- Books, Reports, and Other Nonperiodic Materials: Bluepages 8 and Rule 15
- Periodicals: Bluepages 9 and Rule 16
- Electronic Media: Rule 18

---

2. Bluebook Typeface Conventions: Checklist

✓ Bluepages B1 addresses typeface conventions for court documents. In court documents, underline (or italicize) the following:
  - Case names
  - Titles of books and articles
  - Titles of legislative materials
  - Introductory signals
  - Explanatory phrases introducing subsequent case history
  - Words and phrases introducing related authority (such as "quoted in" or "citing")
  - Cross-references (such as "id." and "supra")

✓ Remember to underline the "v." in case names.
✓ Note that citations in law review articles have different typeface conventions than court documents. Bluepages B1 and Rule 2 address these differences.

 ### 3. Basic Structure and Signals for Bluebook Citations: Checklist

✓ Types of Signals: See Rule 1.2.
- Signals that show support: <u>E.g.</u>, <u>Accord</u>, <u>See</u>, <u>See also</u>, <u>Cf.</u>
- Signals that suggest a useful comparison: <u>Compare</u> ... <u>with</u> ...
- Signals that indicate contradiction: <u>Contra</u>, <u>But see</u>, <u>But cf.</u>
- Signals that indicate background material: <u>See generally</u>

✓ Order of Signals: See Rule 1.3. Signals of the same basic type are strung together within one citation sentence and are separated from each other by semicolons. If there are signals of different types then they must be grouped in separate citation sentences. Follow order in Rule 1.2 (Support, Comparison, Contradiction, and Background).

✓ Order of Authorities Within Each Signal: See Rule 1.4 for more details within each category. Constitutions; Statutes; Treaties and other International Agreements; Cases; Legislative Materials; Administrative and Executive Materials; Resolutions, Decisions, and Regulations of Intergovernmental Organizations; Records, Briefs, and Petitions; Secondary Materials. Cases decided by the same court are arranged in reverse chronological order.

✓ Parenthetical Information explains the relevance of a particular authority to proposition given in the text. See Rule 1.5.
- Explanatory parenthetical phrases that do not directly quote the authority usually begin with a present participle and usually do not begin with a capital letter.
- If the parenthetical information includes one or more full sentences, it should start with a capital letter and end with the correct punctuation.
- Explanatory parenthetical phrases come before any citations concerning subsequent history or other related authority. Rule 1.5(b) explains the order in which to present multiple parentheticals within a citation.

---

4.   Bluebook Citation Signals: Checklist

Signals in Text	Proposition	Cited Authority and Meaning
SUPPORT		
[No signal]		Directly <u>states</u> proposition.
<u>See</u>; <u>see also</u>		Clearly <u>supports</u>; obviously follows from proposition.
<u>Cf.</u>		Analogous proposition.
<u>E.g.</u>; <u>see, e.g.,</u>		Multiple authorities clearly <u>state</u> the proposition.
CONTRADICTION		
<u>Contra</u>		Directly <u>states</u> contrary proposition.
BACKGROUND		
<u>See generally</u>		Helpful, related background material.
COMPARISON		
<u>Compare</u> … <u>with</u> …		Comparison of cited authorities supports proposition.

5. **Bluebook Rules for Citing Subdivisions and Pinpoint Cites: Checklist**

Rule 3.2(a) address the proper format for citations to specific page numbers:

- Give page number or numbers before the date parenthetical, without any introductory abbreviation.
- Use "at" if page number may be confused with another part of the citation.
- Use a comma to set off the "at."
- If you are referring specifically to material on the first page of a source, repeat the page number.
- When citing material within a concurring or dissenting opinion, give only the initial page of the case and the page on which the specific material appears. See B4.1.2.
- When citing material that spans more than one page, give the inclusive page numbers separated by the en dash (–). Always retain the last two digits but drop other repetitious digits.
- Cite nonconsecutive pages by giving the individual page numbers separated by commas.

---

 6. **Bluebook Rules for Short Form Citations: Checklist**

✓ According to Bluepages B4.2 and Rule 4, once you have provided one full citation to an authority, you are free to use a "short form" in later citations to the same authority, so long as (i) it will be clear to the reader from the short form what is being referenced, (ii) the earlier full citation falls in the same general discussion, and (iii) the reader will have little more trouble quickly locating the full citation. General rule: Avoid confusion.

✓ For short form citations to cases, refer to Rule 10.9. Use one party's name, the volume number, reporter designation, and page number.
  - Example: <u>Youngstown</u>, 343 U.S. at 585.
  - Party Name: When using only one party name in a short form citation, use the name of the first party, unless that party is a geographical or governmental unit or other common litigant.

✓ B5.2 and Rule 12.10 gives the short form citation rules for statutes, rules, and regulations.

✓ <u>Id.</u>: Use to refer to the immediately preceding authority (B4.2 and Rules 4.1, 10.9).
  - The "i" in "<u>id.</u>" is capitalized only when it begins a citation sentence.
  - To refer to a different page within the immediately preceding authority, add "at" and the new pinpoint cite.

- <u>Id.</u> may be used only when the preceding citation cites to only one source.
- ✓ <u>Supra</u>: See Rule 4.2. Once a work in a periodical, book, legislative hearing, report, unpublished work, or nonprint resource has been fully cited, use <u>id.</u> to refer to material cited in the immediately preceding citation. Otherwise, use <u>Supra</u> for legislative hearings, reports, unpublished materials, nonprint resources, periodicals, regulations, etc. that have previously been cited fully. <u>Supra</u> form generally consists of the last name of the author of the work, followed by a comma and the word "<u>Supra</u>." Indicate any manner the citation differs from the former (B9.2, Rule 16.9). Example: Reich, <u>Supra</u> note 18, at 6.

---

 7.   **Bluebook Abbreviations: Checklist**

- ✓ Rule 6.1 is the general rule on abbreviations. Tables at the end of the Bluebook contain lists of specific abbreviations:
  - Arbitral Reporters: T5
  - Case Names: T6, Rule 10.2
    - Rule 10.2.1(c) addresses abbreviations of all case names whether they appear in text or in citations.
    - Rule 10.2.2 addresses further abbreviations for case names that appear in citations.
  - Court Names: T7
  - Reporters: T1, Rule 10.3.2
  - Explanatory Phrases: T8
  - Legislative Documents: T9
  - Current Official and Unofficial Codes: T1, Rule 12.3
  - Ordinances: 12.9.2
  - Rules of Evidence and Procedure: 12.9.3
  - Geographical Terms: T10
  - Judges and Officials: T11
  - Months: T12
  - Periodicals: T13, Rules 16.3-16.6
  - Publishing Terms: T14
  - Services: T15
  - Subdivisions: T16
- ✓ Spacing: Generally, close up adjacent single capitals (e.g., N.W.), but do not close up single capitals with longer abbreviations (e.g., D. Mass.). See Rule 6.1.

---

8.   **Bluebook Rules for Citing Cases: Checklist**

- ✓ According to Rule 10.1 and Bluepages B4.1, the general citation form for cases includes: Case Name, reporter volume number + reporter abbreviations + first page of case, page # (deciding court + date of decision).
- ✓ Case Names: Rule 10.2

a. For case names that appear in textual sentences and citation sentences, refer to Rule 10.2.1:
   - Omit all parties other than the first one on each side. Omit words indicating multiple parties, such as "et al." See Rule 10.2.1(a) and B4.1.1.
   - Abbreviate only widely known acronyms that appear in Rule 6.1(b) and these eight words: &, Ass'n, Bros., Co., Corp., Inc., Ltd., and No. See Rule 10.2.1(c).
   - Omit "The" as the first word of a party's name. See Rule 10.2.1(d).
   - Omit "State of," "Commonwealth of," and "People of" unless citing decisions of the courts of that state, in which case only "State," "Commonwealth," or "People" should be retained. See Rule 10.2.1(f).
   - Generally, omit given names or initials of individuals, but not in names or businesses of firms. See Rule 10.2.1(g).
   - Omit business firm designations such as "Inc." if the name of the firm also contains a word that clearly indicates its status as a business firm, such as "Ass'n." See Rule 10.2.1(h).

b. For case names that appear in citations, also refer to Rule 10.2.2. Note that case names in citations generally follow the rules detailed in Rule 10.2.1, with the following modifications:
   - Abbreviate any word that appears in Table T6.
   - Abbreviate states, countries, and other geographical units as they appear in Table T10. However, do not abbreviate geographical units if they are the entire name of a party (including "United States").
   - Abbreviate words of eight letters or more if doing so saves substantial space and the abbreviations are unambiguous.

✓ Reporters: see Rule 10.3.2, B4.1.2, and Table T1. A citation to a reporter should include the volume number of the reporter, the abbreviated name of the reporter as found in Table T1, and the page on which the case begins.

✓ Public Domain Format: see Rule 10.3.3. See Table T7 for court abbreviations.
   - United States Court of Appeals for numbered circuits: 2d Cir., 4th Cir.
   - State Courts: Indicate state and court of decision, but do not include the name of the court if the court of decision is the highest court in the state. Omit jurisdiction if it is unambiguously conveyed by reporter title.

✓ Use dates of decisions according to Rule 10.5 and B4.1.3.

✓ According to Rule 10.6 and B4.1.5, parentheticals may be used to convey information regarding weight of authority, related authority, or a proposition that is not the holding of majority. Rule 10.6.3 indicates the correct order of parentheticals: (i) weight of authority, (ii) "quoting" or "citing" parentheticals, and (iii) explanatory parentheticals.

✓ If a case is unreported but available on electronic media, cite it according to Rules 10.8.1 and 18.

✓ Appropriate short form citations for cases are listed in Rule 10.9 and B4.2.

---

 9. Bluebook Rules for Citing Constitutions: Checklist

✓ Abbreviate United States (U.S.) if referring to the federal Constitution, or refer to Table T10 for the appropriate abbreviation if citing a state constitution (Rule 11).

✓ Abbreviate "Constitution" as "Const." (Rule 11).

✓ Refer to Table T16 for the appropriate abbreviations of article (art.), amendment (amend.), section (§), and clause (cl.).

✓ If the constitutional provision has been repealed, amended, or superseded, refer to Rule 11 for the appropriate citation format.

✓ <u>Id.</u> is the only acceptable format for short citations to constitutions (Rule 11).

---

 10. Bluebook Rules for Citing Statutes: Checklist

✓ Cite to the official federal and state codes whenever possible. The official federal code is the United States Code, "U.S.C." To determine the official code for a particular state, see Table T1.

✓ Make sure that the abbreviations of code names are properly formatted. There should be periods and no spaces between the letters "U.S.C." See Table T1 to determine the proper abbreviation formats for state codes.

✓ Use "§" to denote the section number of the code that you are citing. Leave a space between "§" and the section number, and use "§§" if you are citing multiple sections.

✓ Include the date of the code edition cited in a parenthetical following the section number (Rules 12.3.2 and 12.4(e)). If citing to a code that is published, edited, or compiled by someone other than state officials, give the name of the publisher, editor, or compiler in the parenthetical phrase (Rule 12.3.1(d)). For example: (West 2006).

✓ According to Rule 12.3.1(a), if the statute is commonly cited using a different name or is known by a popular name, give that name and the original section number preceding the normal citation format.

✓ If a statute appears in a supplement or pocket part, cite the statute according to Rule 3.1(c). See Rule 12.3.1(e) for examples of the proper citation format.

✓ If a statute has been invalidated, repealed, or amended, cite it in accordance with Rule 12.7. When citing a current version of a statute that has prior history, you may give the prior history in an explanatory parenthetical phrase according to Rule 12.8.

✓ Some statutes require special citation forms. Rule 12.9 indicates that these include the Internal Revenue Code (12.9.1), ordinances (12.9.2), rules of evidence and procedure (12.9.3), uniform acts (12.9.4), and model codes, restatements, standards, and sentencing guidelines (12.9.5).

✓ If a statute is previously cited, you may use a short form of the statute according to Rule 12.10(c). Id. may be used in court documents and legal memoranda if the same statute is previously cited or the statute is within the same title as a previously cited statute.

 ## 11. Bluebook Citations for Administrative and Executive Materials: Checklist

✓ Cite federal rules and regulations (except Treasury materials) to the Code of Federal Regulations (C.F.R.). Rules and regulations found in C.F.R. should be identified by title, section number or part, and year of the code edition cited, using the format specified in Rule 14.2.

   a. Be sure to cite the most recent edition of C.F.R., according to Rule 14.2(a).

   b. Do not leave spaces between the letters of "C.F.R."

✓ If a federal rule or regulation is known by a common name or is typically cited using a name, indicate that name before the title number, using the format specified in Rule 14.2(a).

✓ According to Rule 14.2(a), if a rule or regulation has not yet been published in C.F.R., cite to the Federal Register. Administrative notices should also be cited to the Federal Register.

✓ To use a short citation to identify a rule or regulation, use one of the formats listed in Rule 14.4(c).

✓ Cite to arbitrations and administrative adjudications using the same format for cases in Rule 10. However, according to Rule 14.3.1, case names of administrative adjudications are identified by the first-listed private party, or by the official subject-matter title. Case names of arbitrations are cited according to Rule 10 or, if adversary parties are not named, like administrative adjudications according to Rule 14.3.1(a).

✓ Advisory opinions from the United States Attorney General or any other government entity are cited according to the "Department of Justice" section in Table T1.2.

✓ Federal tax statutes are cited according to Rule 12.9.1, but other federal taxation materials, including Treasury regulations, determinations, and cases, are cited according to Table T1.2.

✓ Presidential executive orders are found in title 3 of C.F.R. and should be cited to C.F.R. according to Rule 14.2, with a parallel citation to the United States Code if therein. However, if an executive order is not found in C.F.R., cite according to the Federal Register. Examples of each citation format can be found under the heading "Executive Office of the President" in Table T1.2.

✓ Patents should be cited according to the patent number and the date the patent was filed, using the format specified in "Department of Commerce, Patent and Trademark Office (USPTO)" in Table T1.2.

 ## 12. Bluebook Citations for Books, Reports, and Other Nonperiodic Materials: Checklist

✓ According to Rule 15.1, when citing a publication for the first time, give the author's full name as it appears on the publication. However, do not include designations indicating academic degrees such as "Dr."

    a. For works with two authors, give their names in the order in which they are listed on the title page, separated by "&" (Rule 15.1(a)).

    b. For works with more than two authors, you may use the name of the first author listed followed by "et al." or, where it is important to include all the authors' names and space is not an issue, you may list all of their names, separating the final name with "&" (Rule 15.1(b)).

✓ Rule 15.2 specifies the format for works with editors or translators. Give the full name of the editor in a parenthetical as it appears in the publication. In the same parenthetical, after the full name of the editor, indicate the editor's title with "ed.," the name of the publisher (if other than the original publisher), and the year of publication.

✓ According to Rule 15.3, give the name of the work according to how it appears on the title page. Refer to Rule 8 to determine which words in a title to capitalize. Do not omit articles from the title.

✓ For works that have been published in only one edition, give the year of publication in parentheses (Rule 15.4(a)(i)). For works that have been published in multiple editions, cite the latest edition according to Rule 15.4(a) unless an earlier edition is more relevant.

✓ Some works are cited so frequently that they have special citation forms in Rule 15.8. These works include Black's Law Dictionary, American Jurisprudence, and Corpus Juris Secundum.

 ## 13. Bluebook Rules for Citing Periodical Materials: Checklist

✓ For consecutively paginated journals (Rule 16.4):

    a. Cite the author's full name as it appears in the publication according to Rule 15.1.

    b. Cite the full title of the article as it appears on the title page of the publication, but refer to Rule 8 for capitalization.

    c. Cite the volume number, followed by the abbreviation of the journal name according to Table T13, and the page number on which the cited material begins.

    d. Indicate the date of publication in a parenthetical.

e. If the piece you are citing is student-written, follow Rule 16.7.1(a) if it is signed or 16.7.1(b) if it is unsigned. Be sure to indicate the type of piece you are citing, either a "Note" or "Comment" or some other type of work.

f. For book reviews written by nonstudents, reference Rule 16.7.2. For book reviews written by students, reference Rule 16.7.1(c). If the work under review is unclear from the surrounding text, include a second parenthetical following the date of publication identifying the work.

✓ For newspaper articles (Rule 16.6):

a. Cite the author's full name as it appears in the publication according to Rule 15.1.

b. Cite the full title of the article as it appears on the title page of the publication, but refer to Rule 8 for capitalization.

c. Abbreviate the title of the newspaper according to Table T13.

d. Indicate the date of the article, abbreviating the month according to Table T12.

e. Indicate the page on which the article appears. Note that only the first page need be identified.

  ## 14. Bluebook Rules for Citing Electronic Media: Checklist

✓ Rule 18 addresses citation to the internet in general.

a. Rule 18.1 provides basic citation forms.

b. Rule 18.2 discusses citation to the internet and general principles. Cite to an internet source when it does not exist in a traditional printed format or when the printed source exists but cannot be found or is practically unavailable because it is so obscure. For a citation to an internet source, include: Authors' names, title of the specific web page (underlined), title of main website page, date (and perhaps time if updated multiple times per day), and the URL. Parallel citations to internet sources (Rule 18.2.3) should be given if doing so will substantially improve access to the document. Give the citation to the primary source, followed by the words "available at" and the URL.

✓ Rule 18.3 addresses case citation formats for documents found on widely used electronic databases.

a. Unreported cases that are available on a widely used electronic database such as LexisNexis or Westlaw can be cited to that database according to Rule 18.3.1.

b. If the electronic database provides a unique identifying number for the case, remember to provide it following the case name, preceded by "No."

c. If citing to a specific page or screen of an opinion, indicate the page number preceded by an asterisk. If citing to a particular paragraph, indicate the paragraph number preceded by "¶."

✓ Rule 18.3.2 addresses constitutions and statutes found on commercial electronic databases.
   a. Cite codes according to Rules 12.3 and 12.4.
   b. When citing a code contained in an electronic database, remember to include a parenthetical that gives information regarding the currency of the statute or constitution as indicated in the database.
✓ Rule 18.3.4 addresses books, periodicals, and other secondary materials.

B. Bluebook Quizzes

⚇? 1. Bluebook Typeface Conventions: Quiz

Assume the following citations appear in court documents.

1. Choose the correct citation for <u>Missouri v. Holland</u>.

   A. <u>Missouri</u> v. <u>Holland</u>, 252 U.S. 416 (1922).
   B. <u>Missouri v. Holland</u>, 252 U.S. 416 (1922).
   C. <u>Missouri v. Holland,</u> 252 U.S. 416 (1922).
   D. Missouri v. Holland, 252 U.S. 416 (1922).

2. Which citation does NOT have an error?

   A. See <u>Brown v. Board of Education</u>, 347 U.S. 438 (1954).
   B. <u>Brown</u>, 347 U.S. at 440.
   C. <u>Clark v. Davis</u>, 533 U.S. 678, 719 (2001) (citing <u>Evanson v. United States</u>, 345 U.S. 206 (1953)).
   D. Matt Corney, Red House (Oxford ed., Penguin Books 1979) (1899).

3. Which citation does NOT have an error?

   A. <u>See id.</u> at 348.
   B. <u>Id. at 348.</u>
   C. <u>See id.</u> at 348.
   D. See <u>id.</u> at 348.

4. Which citation does NOT have an error?

   A. Gretel C. Kovach, Use of False Hiring Data Found in Dallas Schools, N.Y. Times, Nov. 15, 2 A10.
   B. Greg Gelpi, Attorney Still Loves Fighting for Little Guys, <u>Augusta Chron.</u>, Dec. 8, 2008, at B.
   C. David Rudovsky, Police Abuse: Can the Violence Be Contained?, 27 Harv. C.R.-C.L. L. Rev 500 (1992).
   D. Andrew Rosenthal, <u>Medicine and the Law</u>, N.Y. Times, June 15, 1990, at A1.

5. Which citation does NOT have an error?

    A. <u>Sciolino v. City of Newport News</u>, 480 F.3d 642, 647 (4th Cir. 2007) (<u>Wilkinson, J., dissenting.</u>

    B. Id. at 735.

    C. <u>Codd v. Velger</u>, 429 U.S. 624, 627 (1977).

    D. <u>U.S. Const</u>. amend XIV, § 1.

Answer Key on page 320

 2. Basic Structure and Signals for Bluebook Citations: Quiz

Assume the following citations appear in court documents.

1. Choose the string citation without an error.

    A. <u>See</u> <u>Edwards v. Arizona</u>, 451 U.S. 477 (1981). <u>But see</u> <u>Berkemer v. Mac-Carty</u>, 468 U.S. 420 <u>Compare</u> <u>Orozco v. Texas</u>, 394 U.S. 324 (1969).

    B. <u>See</u> <u>Edwards v. Arizona</u>, 451 U.S. 477 (1981); <u>but see</u> <u>Berkemer v. McCarty</u>, 468 U.S. 420 (1984).

    C. <u>Edwards v. Arizona</u>, 451 U.S. 466 (1981). <u>See</u> <u>Berkemer v. McCarty</u>, 468 U.S. 420 (1984).

    D. <u>See</u> <u>Edwards v. Arizona</u>, 451 U.S. 477 (1981). <u>But see</u> <u>Berkemer v. Mac-Carty</u>, 468 U.S. 420 (1984).

2. Choose the string citation without an error.

    A. <u>See</u> <u>Edwards v. Arizona</u>, 451 U.S. 477 (1981); <u>State v. Bradshaw</u>, 457 S.E.2d 456 (W. Va. 2 <u>Orozco v. Texas</u>, 394 U.S. 324 (1969).

    B. <u>See</u> <u>Edwards v. Arizona</u>, 451 U.S. 477 (1981); <u>Orozco v. Texas</u>, 394 U.S. 324 (1969).

    C. <u>See</u> <u>State v. Bradshaw</u>, 457 S.E.2d 456 (W. Va. 1995); <u>State v. Singleton</u>, 624 S.E.2d 527 (2005).

    D. <u>See</u> <u>Edwards v. Arizona</u>, 451 U.S. 477 (1981); U.S. Const. amend V.

3. Choose the string citation without an error.

    A. <u>See</u> Greg Gelpi, <u>Attorney Still Loves Fighting for Little Guys</u>, Augusta Chron., Dec. 8, 2008, a <u>Swilley v. Alexander</u>, 629 F.2d 1018, 1020 (5th Cir. 1980).

    B. <u>See</u> 42 U.S.C.A. § 1983 (2009); <u>Swilley v. Alexander</u>, 629 F.2d 1018, 1020 (5th Cir. 1980).

    C. <u>See</u> 42 U.S.C.A. § 1983 (2009); U.S. Const. amend XIV, § 1.

    D. <u>See</u> <u>Cox v. Roskelley</u>, 359 F.3d 1105, 1110 (9th Cir. 2002); <u>Codd v. Velger</u>, 429 U.S. 624, 62 (1977).

4. Choose the citation without an error.

   A. <u>Cox v. Roskelley</u>, 359 F.3d 1105, 1110 (9th Cir. 2002) (holding once stigmatizing information placed into Cox's personnel file, it became public record under Washington law).
   B. ("Nor shall any State deprive person of life, liberty, or property, without due process of the law Const. amend XIV, §1.
   C. Gretel C. Kovach, <u>Use of False Hiring Data Found in Dallas Schools</u> (newspaper ran article after obtaining report, marked highly confidential, through a records request), N.Y. Times, Nov. 15, A10.
   D. U.S. Const. ("Nor shall any State deprive person of life, liberty, or property, without due process law") amend XIV, § 1.

5. Choose the string citation without an error.

   A. <u>See also</u> <u>Miranda v. Arizona</u>, 384 U.S. 436 (1966); <u>see</u> <u>Edwards v. Arizona</u>, 451 U.S. 477 (1984).
   B. <u>See</u> S.C. Const. art. I, § 12; U.S. Const. art. IV, § 1.
   C. <u>See</u> <u>Miranda v. Arizona</u>, 384 U.S. 436 (1966); <u>see</u> <u>Edwards v. Arizona</u>, 451 U.S. 477 (1981).
   D. <u>See</u> <u>State v. Jameson</u>, 461 S.E.2d 67 (W. Va. 1995). <u>But see</u> <u>State v. Green</u>, 310 S.E.2d 48 Va. 1983).

Answer Key on page 321

⬤? 3.   Bluebook Citation Signals: Quiz

You are researching a state water quality issue for a partner at your firm, and you have uncovered a number of authorities that support, contradict, or supplement the following excerpt from a Maryland statute: Factories may not dispose of hazardous materials in the Chesapeake Bay. What signal would you use to best cite each authority described below?

1. A case decided by the Maryland Court of Appeals (the highest court in Maryland) that holds that factories cannot dispose of hazardous materials in Maryland rivers.

   A. No signal
   B. <u>But see</u>
   C. <u>See, e.g.,</u>
   D. <u>Cf.</u>
   E. <u>Contra</u>

2. A law review article that discusses hazardous waste disposal laws in several states on the eastern seaboard, including Maryland.

   A. No signal
   B. <u>See generally</u>
   C. <u>See</u>
   D. <u>Cf.</u>
   E. <u>Contra</u>

3. A Delaware statute that prohibits dumping of hazardous materials in the Chesapeake Bay.

    A. No signal
    B. <u>See generally</u>
    C. <u>Accord</u>
    D. <u>Cf.</u>
    E. <u>See</u>

4. One of several Maryland cases holding that factories may not dispose of hazardous waste in Maryland waters.

    A. No signal
    B. <u>See, e.g.,</u>
    C. <u>See</u>
    D. <u>See generally</u>
    E. <u>Compare</u> … <u>with</u> …

5. A Maryland Court of Appeals case holding that factories may not dispose of hazardous materials in the Chesapeake Bay.

    A. No signal
    B. <u>See</u>
    C. <u>But see</u>
    D. <u>Contra</u>
    E. <u>Cf.</u>

6. A Maryland Court of Appeals case holding that no individual or organization may dispose of polluting materials in the bays or other marshland areas of the state of Maryland.

    A. No signal
    B. <u>Cf.</u>
    C. <u>See</u>
    D. <u>But see</u>
    E. <u>See, e.g.,</u>

Answer Key on page 322

⚇? 4. Bluebook Order and Punctuation of Signals and Citations: Quiz

1. Select the correct citation sentence:

    A. <u>See</u> Matthews v. Potter, 19 P.2d 368 (Cal. 1999). <u>See also</u> Morrison v. Perkins, 56 P.2d 247 (Cal. 2000). <u>But see</u> Smith v. Jennings, 85 P.2d 465 (Cal. 2001).
    B. <u>See</u> Matthews v. Potter, 19 P.2d 368 (Cal. 1999); <u>see also</u> Morrison v. Perkins, 56 P.2d 247 (Cal. 2000); <u>but see</u> Smith v. Jennings, 85 P.2d 465 (Cal. 2001).

    C. See also Morrison v. Perkins, 56 P.2d 247 (Cal. 2000); see Matthews v. Potter, 19 P.2d 368 (Cal. 1999). But see Smith v. Jennings, 85 P.2d 465 (Cal. 2001).

    D. See Matthews v. Potter, 19 P.2d 368 (Cal. 1999); see also Morrison v. Perkins, 56 P.2d 247 (Cal. 2000). But see Smith v. Jennings, 85 P.2d 465 (Cal. 2001).

2. Which of the following is the correct order and punctuation of signals when more than one signal is used?

    A. See; cf.; but see; see generally.
    B. See; cf. But see. See generally.
    C. See. But see. Cf. See generally.
    D. See; cf. But see; see generally.
    E. See. Cf. But see. See generally.

3. A partner at your firm has asked you to revise a draft office memorandum containing the following sentence: See, e.g., 18 U.S.C. § 588 (1998); 13 U.S.C. § 12 (1994); Lineman v. Fawcett, 689 U.S. 214 (1991); Hingel v. Brown, 855 U.S. 114 (1987); Smith v. Tenorman, 255 F.2d 2087 (2d Cir. 1997), aff'd, 225 U.S. 3 (1999); Dohr v. Abrams, 255 F. Supp. 2d 651 (D.D.C. 1989); Masters v. Perlman, 23 F.3d 785 (7th Cir. 1986). How would you revise this citation sentence?

    A. The ordering of citations is correct; no changes are necessary.
    B. The citations should be in the following order: See, e.g., 18 U.S.C. § 588 (1998); 13 U.S.C. § 12 (1994); Lineman; Smith; Hingel; Masters; Dohr.
    C. The citations should be in the following order: See, e.g., 13 U.S.C. § 12 (1994); 18 U.S.C. § 588 (1998); Lineman; Hingel; Smith; Masters; Dohr.
    D. The citations should be in the following order: See, e.g., 18 U.S.C. § 588 (1998); 13 U.S.C. § 12 (1994); Lineman; Hingel; Dohr; Masters; Smith.
    E. The citations should be in the following order: See, e.g., 18 U.S.C. § 588 (1998); 13 U.S.C. § 12 (1994); Lineman; Hingel; Masters; Smith; Dohr.

Answer Key on page 323

---

 5. **Bluebook Rules for Citing Subdivisions and Pinpoint Cites: Quiz**

Assume the following citations appear in court documents.

1. Choose the correct citation for information on page 347 of Beckwith v. United States.

    A. Beckwith v. United States, 425 U.S. 341, 347 (1976).
    B. Beckwith v. United States, 425 U.S. 341, at 347 (1976).
    C. Beckwith v. United States, 425 U.S. 341, p. 347 (1976).
    D. Beckwith v. United States, 425 U.S. 341-47 (1976).

2. Choose the citation without an error.

   A. Christina M. Fernandez, <u>A Case-by-Case Approach to Pleading Scienter Under the Private Securities Litigation Reform Act of 1995</u>, 97 Mich. L. Rev 2265, p. 2271 (1978).
   B. <u>Sciolino v. City of Newport News</u>, 480 F.3d 642 (4th Cir. 2007) (Wilkinson, J., dissenting, 654).
   C. <u>State v. Bradshaw</u>, 457 S.E.2d 456, 457, 459 (W. Va. 1995).
   D. <u>Codd v. Velger</u>, 429 U.S. 624 to 626 (1977).

3. Choose the citation without an error.

   A. 459 <u>State v. Bradshaw</u>, 457 S.E.2d 456 (W. Va. 1995).
   B. <u>Miranda v. Arizona</u>, 384 U.S. 436, 440 (1966).
   C. <u>Bishop v. Wood</u>, 426 U.S. 341 (1976) ("Fourteenth Amendment is not a guarantee against in or ill-advised personnel decisions") 349.
   D. <u>State v. Mullens</u>, 172, 650 S.E.2d 169 (W. Va. 2007).

4. Choose the correct citation for information on page 2082 of the Michigan Law Review.

   A. Kim Scheppele, <u>Foreword: Telling Stories</u>, 87 Mich. L. Rev. 2073 (1989), 2082.
   B. Kim Scheppele, <u>Foreword: Telling Stories</u>, 2082, 87 Mich. L. Rev. 2073 (1989).
   C. Kim Scheppele, <u>Foreword: Telling Stories</u>, 87 Mich. L. Rev. 2073, 2082 (1989).
   D. Kim Scheppele, <u>Foreword: Telling Stories</u>, 87 Mich. L. Rev. 2073 at 2082 (1989).

5. Choose the correct citation for information on pages 479, 481, 485 in Edwards v. Arizona.

   A. <u>Edwards v. Arizona</u>, 451 U.S. 477, 479, 481, and 485 (1981).
   B. <u>Edwards v. Arizona</u>, 451 U.S. 477-85 (1981).
   C. <u>Edwards v. Arizona</u>, 451 U.S. 477 (1981) 479, 481, 485.
   D. <u>Edwards v. Arizona</u>, 451 U.S. 477, 479, 481, 485 (1981).

Answer Key on page 324

6. Bluebook Rules for Short Form Citations: Quiz

Assume the following citations appear in court documents.

1. Choose the correct short citation for <u>Orozco v. Texas</u>, 394 U.S. 324, 327 (1969), if it is the only source in immediately preceding citation and cited page 327.

   A. <u>Id.</u> at 327.
   B. <u>Orozco v. Texas</u>, at 327.
   C. <u>Id.</u> 394 U.S. 324, 327.
   D. <u>Orozco</u>, at 327.

2. Choose the correct short citation for <u>Orozco v. Texas</u>, 394 U.S. 324, 327 (1969), if the same cite was used three citations earlier.

    A. <u>Orozco v. Texas</u>, 394 U.S. at 327
    B. <u>Orozco</u>, 394 U.S. 324, 327.
    C. <u>Id.</u> at 327.
    D. <u>Orozco</u>, 394 U.S. at 327.

3. Choose the correct short citation for <u>Sciolino v. City of Newport News</u>, 480 F.3d 642, 654 (4th Cir. 2007), Judge Wilkinson's dissenting opinion if the previous citation is from the same case but cites the majority.

    A. <u>Id.</u> at 654 (Wilkinson, J., dissenting).
    B. <u>Sciolino v. City of Newport News</u>, 480 F.3d 642, 654 (4th Cir. 2007) (Wilkinson, J., dissenting).
    C. Sciolino, 480 F.3d 642 at 654 (Wilkinson, J., dissenting).
    D. <u>Id.</u> (Wilkinson, J., dissenting) at 654.

4. Choose the correct short citation for 30 U.S.C. § 1330(a)(1) if the previous citation is 30 U.S.C. § 1331 (2000).

    A. 30 U.S.C. § 1330(a)(1) (2000).
    B. <u>Id.</u> (a)(1).
    C. <u>Id.</u> § 1330(a)(1).
    D. <u>Id.</u> at § 1330(a)(1).

5. Choose the correct short cite for Katherine Crystzer, <u>You're Fired!</u> Bishop v. Wood: <u>When Does a Letter in Former Public Employee's Personnel File Deny a Due Process Liberty Right?</u>, 16 Geo. Mason L. Rev 44 (2009), if it was used three citations earlier.

    A. Crystzer, <u>You're Fired!</u>, at 450.
    B. Crystzer, <u>supra</u>, at 450.
    C. Crystzer, <u>You're Fired!</u> Bishop v. Wood: <u>When Does a Letter in a Former Public Employee's Personnel File Deny a Due Process Liberty Right?</u>, 16 Geo. Mason L. Rev 447, 450 (2009)
    D. <u>Id.</u> at 450.

6. Choose the correct short cite for Deborah L. Rhode, <u>Justice and Gender</u> 56, 70-71 (1989), if the immediately preceding cite is for the same source on page 60.

    A. <u>Id.</u> at 70-71.
    B. Rhode, <u>id.</u> at 70-71.
    C. Rhode, <u>Justice and Gender</u>, at 70-71.
    D. Rhode, <u>supra</u>, at 70-71.

7. Choose the correct short citation for <u>Orozco v. Texas</u>, 394 U.S. 324, 327 (1969), if it is one of three sources in the immediately preceding citation and cited on page 329.

    A. <u>Id.</u> at 327.
    B. <u>Orozco v. Texas</u>, at 327.
    C. <u>Id.</u> 394 U.S. 324, 327.
    D. <u>Orozco</u>, 394 U.S. at 327.

Answer Key on page 325

⚇? 7.   Bluebook Abbreviations: Quiz

Assume the following citations appear in court documents.

1. The following case appears in a textual sentence. Choose the answer that abbreviates the case name correctly.

    A. <u>NLRB v. General Hospital, Inc.</u>, 61 U.S. 3 (1951).
    B. <u>NLRB v. General Hosp.</u>, Inc., 61 U.S. 3 (1951).
    C. <u>N.L.R.B. v. General Hospital, Inc.</u>, 61 U.S. 3 (1951).
    D. <u>NLRB v. General Hospital, Incorporated</u>, 61 U.S. 3 (1951).

2. The following Ninth Circuit Court case appears in a citation sentence. Choose the answer that abbreviates the case name correctly.

    A. <u>Sunnyside Memorial School v. County Housing Department</u>, 537 F.2d 361, 366 (9th Cir. 1976).
    B. <u>Sunnyside Mem'l. Sch. v. County Hous. Dep't.</u>, 537 F.2d 361, 366 (9th Cir. 1976).
    C. <u>Sunnyside Mem'l Sch. v. County Hous. Dep't</u>, 537 F.2d 361, 366 (9th Cir. 1976).
    D. <u>Sunnyside v. Mem'l Sch. v. County Hous. Dep't</u>, 537 F.2d 361, 366 (9th Circuit 1976).

3. Choose the correct citation for the Federal Register.

    A. Importation of Dairy Products, 60 Federal Register 50,379 (Sept. 29, 1995).
    B. Importation of Dairy Products, 60 F.R. 50,379 (September 29, 1995).
    C. Importation of Dairy Products, 60 Fed. Reg. 50,379 (Sept. 29, 1995).
    D. Importation of Dairy Products, 60 Fed.Reg 50,379 (September 29, 1995).

4. Choose the correct citation for Rule 12(b)(2) of the Federal Rules of Civil Procedure.

    A. Fed. Rule Civ. P. 12(b)(2).
    B. Fed. R. Civ. P. 12(b)(2).
    C. Fed R Civ P 12(b)(2).
    D. Federal Rule of Civil Procedure 12(b)(2).

5. Choose the correct citation for an article in the George Mason Law Review.

    A. Kathy Crytzer, <u>Meeting of the Minds</u>, 16 Geo. Mason L. Rev. 447, 450 (2000).

    B. Kathy Crytzer, <u>Meeting of the Minds</u>, 15 G.M. L. Rev. 447, 450 (2000).

    C. Kathy Crytzer, <u>Meeting of the Minds</u>, 15 Geo. Mason L.R. 447, 450 (2000).

    D. Kathy Crytzer, <u>Meeting of the Minds</u>, 16 Geo Mason L Rev 447, 450 (2000).

Answer Key on page 326

8? 8. Bluebook Rules for Citing Cases: Quiz

Assume the following citations appear in court documents.

1. Choose the correct citation for <u>United States v. MacDonald</u>, decided in the Fourth Circuit Court of Appeals in 1976.

    A. 531 F.2d 196, 199, <u>United States v. MacDonald</u>, (4th Cir. 1976).

    B. <u>United States v. MacDonald</u>, 531 F.2d 196, 199 (4th Cir. 1976).

    C. United States v. MacDonald. 531 F.2d 196. 199 (4th Cir. 1976)

    D. <u>U.S. v. MacDonald</u>, 531 F.2d 196, 199 (4th Cir. 1976).

2. Choose the correct citation for <u>Commonwealth of Pennsylvania v. Ferrone</u>, decided in the Pennsylvania Superior Court in 1982. (Assume this citation appears in a court document submitted to a Pennsylvania court.)

    A. <u>Commonwealth v. Ferrone</u>, 448 A.2d 637 (Pa. Super. Ct. 1982).

    B. <u>Commonwealth of Pennsylvania v. Ferrone</u>, 448 A.2d 637 (Pa. Super. Ct. 1982).

    C. <u>Commonwealth of Penn. v. Ferrone</u>, 448 A.2d 637 (Pa. Super. Ct. 1982).

    D. <u>Penn. v. Ferrone</u>, 448 A.2d 637 (Pa. Super. Ct. 1982).

3. Choose the correct citation for <u>Miranda v. Arizona</u> in the United States Reports.

    A. <u>Miranda v. Arizona</u>, 384 S. Ct. 436 (1966).

    B. <u>Miranda v. Arizona</u>, 384 U.S. 436 (S. Ct. 1966).

    C. <u>Miranda v. Arizona</u>, 384 U.S. 436 (1966).

    D. <u>Miranda v. Arizona</u>, 384 U.S. 436 (U.S. 1966).

4. Choose the correct citation for <u>Johnson v. Seiler</u> decided by the Fourth Circuit Court of Appeals and reported in the Second Edition Federal Reporter.

    A. <u>Johnson v. Seiler</u>, 225 F.2d 308 (4th Cir. 1998).

    B. <u>Johnson v. Seiler</u>, 225 F.2d 308 (4th Cir. 1998).

    C. <u>Johnson v. Seiler</u>, 225 F.2d 308 (4th Circuit 1998).

    D. <u>Johnson v. Seiler</u>, 225 S.E.2d 308 (4th Cir. 1998).

5. Choose the correct citation for Justice Scalia's dissenting opinion in <u>Jamison v. Blueline Railroad</u>.

    A. <u>Jamison v. Blueline R.R.</u>, 338 U.S. 25, 47 (2004) (Scalia, J., dissenting) (rejecting Court's conception of the exclusionary rule).

    B. <u>Jamison v. Blueline R.R.</u>, 338 U.S. 25, 47 (2004). (Scalia, J., dissenting) (rejecting Court's conception of the exclusionary rule).

    C. <u>Jamison v. Blueline R.R.</u>, 338 U.S. 25, 47 (2004) (rejecting Court's conception of the exclusionary rule) (Scalia, J., dissenting).

    D. Jamison v. Blueline R.R., 338 U.S. 25, 47 (2004 Scalia J., dissenting) (rejecting Court's conception of the exclusionary rule).

6. Choose the correct citation for the unreported case of <u>Chavez v. Norton</u>, available on Lexis.

    A. <u>Chavez v. Norton</u>, No. 02-3924, 2004 U.S. App. LEXIS 2598713, 220 (3d Cir. Oct. 14, 2004).

    B. <u>Chavez v. Norton</u>, No. 02-3924, No. 02-3924, 2004 U.S. App. LEXIS 2598713, at *220 (3d 2004).

    C. <u>Chavez v. Norton</u>, No. 02-3924, 2004 U.S. App. LEXIS 2598713, *220 (3d Cir. Oct. 14, 2004).

    D. <u>Chavez v. Norton</u>, No. 02-3924, 2004 U.S. App. LEXIS 2598713, at *220 (3d Cir. Oct. 14, 2004).

Answer Key on page 327

⚇? 9. Bluebook Rules for Citing Constitutions: Quiz

Assume that the following citations appear in court documents.

1. Choose the correct citation format for the Fifth Amendment to the U.S. Constitution.

    A. U.S. Const. Amend. V.
    B. United States Constitution, amendment V.
    C. U.S. Const. amend. V.
    D. U.S. Const. amend V.

2. Which one of these citations to Article I, Section 1, of the Kansas Constitution is correct?

    A. Kan. Const. art. I, § 1.
    B. Kan. Const. art. I, sec. 1.
    C. Ka. Const. art. I, § 1,
    D. Kansas Constitution, art. 1, § 1.

3. What is the correct short citation format for Article II of the U.S. Constitution if it was cited in the immediately preceding section?

    A. Art. II.
    B. U.S. Const. II.
    C. II.
    D. Id.

4. Choose the correct format for citing the Eighteenth Amendment to the U.S. Constitution (repealed in 1993).

    A. U.S. Const. Amend. XVIII (repealed 1933).
    B. U.S. Const. amend. XVIII (repealed 1933).
    C. U.S. Const. amend. XVIII (*repealed* 1933).
    D. U.S. Const. amend. XVIII, repealed 1933.

5. What is the correct citation format for Article II, Section 3 of the Pennsylvania Constitution?

    A. Pa. Const. art. II, § 3.
    B. Pen. Const. art. II, § 3.
    C. Pa. Const. Art. II, § 3.
    D. Pen. Const. art 2, § 3.

Answer Key on page 328

⊗? 10. Bluebook Rules for Citing Statutes: Quiz

Assume that the following citations appear in court documents.

1. In the citation 28 U.S.C. § 585 (2000), what does the "28" signify?

    A. The section number of the statute
    B. The title number of the statute in the United States Code
    C. The session of Congress that enacted the statute
    D. The number of provisions in the cited statute

2. Choose the correct *full* citation for Title 42, Section 1975 of the United States Code.

    A. 42 USC § 1975 (2000).
    B. 42 U.S.C. § 1975.
    C. 42 U.S.C. § 1975 (2000).
    D. 42 U.S.C. §1975 (2000).

3. If using a short citation to refer to the statute from question 2, which one of the following options is an acceptable format?

    A. § 1975.
    B. 42 U.S.C.
    C. U.S.C. § 1975.
    D. 42.

4. Which of the following citations to the Internal Revenue Code is NOT correctly formatted?

   A. 26 U.S.C. § 153 (2000).
   B. I.R.C. § 153 (2000).
   C. 26 U.S.C. § 291 (2000).
   D. Int. Rev. Code § 291 (2000).

5. Choose the preferred citation format for the Indiana Code.

   A. Ind. Code § 3-5-1-1 (2008).
   B. Ind. Code Ann. § 3-5-1-1 (West 2006).
   C. Ind. Code Ann. § 3-5-1-1 (LexisNexis 2006).
   D. In. Code § 3-5-1-1 (2008).

6. Choose the correct citation for Federal Rule of Civil Procedure 11(a)(5).

   A. F.R.C.P. 11(a)(5).
   B. Fed R Civ P 11(a)(5).
   C. Fed. R. Civ. P. 11(a)(5).
   D. F.R.C.P. § 11(a)(5).

Answer Key on page 329

8? 11. Bluebook Citations for Administrative and Executive Materials: Quiz

Assume that the following citations appear in court documents.

1. Which of the following citations to title 40, section 49.9861 of the Code of Federal Regulations is correct?

   A. 40 Code Fed. Reg. § 49.9861 (1999).
   B. 40 Code Fed. Reg. §49.9861 (1999).
   C. 40 C.F.R. § 49.9861 (1999).
   D. 40 C. F. R. § 49.9861 (1999).

2. Choose the correct short form citation to title 40, section 49.9861 of the Code of Federal Regulations.

   A. 40 C.F.R. § 49.9861 (1999)
   B. 40 C.F.R. § 49.9861
   C. 40 C.F.R.
   D. 49.9861.

3. A rule is published on page 25,684 of volume 74 of the Federal Register, but it has not yet been entered into the Code of Federal Regulations. Choose the correct citation for that rule.

    A. Airworthiness Directives, 74 Fed. Reg. 25,684 (May 30, 2009) (to be codified at 14 C.F.R. pt. 39).

    B. Airworthiness Directives, 74 F.R. 25,684 (May 30, 2009) (to be codified at 14 C.F.R. pt. 39).

    C. Airworthiness Directives, 74 Fed. Reg. 25,684 (to be codified at 14 C.F.R. pt. 39).

    D. Airworthiness Directives, 74 Fed.Reg. 25684 (May 30, 2009) (to be codified at 14 C.F.R. pt. 39).

4. Which of the following citations to volume 24, page 2,834 of the Virginia Register of Regulations (dated June 9, 2008) is correct?

    A. 24 Va. Reg. Regs. 2,834 (June 9, 2008).

    B. 24 V.R.R. 2834 (June 9, 2008).

    C. 24 Va. Reg. Regs. 2834.

    D. 24 Va. Reg. Regs. 2834 (June 9, 2008).

5. Choose the correct citation for a 1982 advisory opinion from the United States Attorney General, volume page 369.

    A. 43 Op. Attorney General 369 (1982).

    B. 43 Op. Att'y Gen. 369 (1982).

    C. 43 Op. Att'y. Gen. 369 (1982).

    D. 43 Op. Atty. Gen. 369 (1982).

6. Presidential Executive Order 12001 is not in the Code of Federal Regulations, but it is found in volume 4 page 33,709 of the Federal Register. Which of the following citations is correct?

    A. Exec. Order No. 12,001, 42 Fed. Reg. 33,709 (June 29, 1977).

    B. E.O. No. 12,001, 42 Fed. Reg. 33,709 (June 29, 1977).

    C. E.O. No. 12,001, 42 F.R. 33,709 (June 29, 1977).

    D. Exec. Order No. 12001, 42 Fed. Reg. 33709 (June 29, 1977).

Answer Key on page 330

---

12. Bluebook Citations for Books, Reports, and Other Nonperiodic Materials: Quiz

Assume that the following citations appear in court documents.

1. Choose the correct citation to page 171 of <u>The Nine: Inside the Secret World of the Supreme Court</u>, by Jeffrey Toobin.

    A. <u>The Nine: Inside the Secret World of the Supreme Court</u> 171 (Anchor Books, 2007) (2007) J Toobin.

    B. Toobin, J., <u>The Nine: Inside the Secret World of the Supreme Court</u> 171 (2007).

    C. Jeffrey Toobin, <u>The Nine: Inside the Secret World of the Supreme Court</u>, 171 (2007).

    D. Jeffrey Toobin, <u>The Nine: Inside the Secret World of the Supreme Court</u> 171 (2007).

2. Which of the following citations to the tenth edition of <u>A History of the Modern World to 1815</u>, by R.R. Palmer, Joel Colton, and Lloyd Kramer (listed in this order on the title page), is correct?

    A. R.R. Palmer et al., <u>A History of the Modern World</u> to 1815 (10th ed. 2006).

    B. R.R. Palmer et al <u>A History of the Modern World to 1815</u> (10th ed. 2006).

    C. R.R. Palmer, Joel Colton and Lloyd Kramer, <u>A History of the Modern World to 1815</u> (10th ed.).

    D. Joel Colton, Lloyd Kramer & R.R. Palmer, <u>A History of the Modern World to 1815</u> (10th ed.).

3. Choose the correct citation to volume 2 of <u>Michael Burlingame's Abraham Lincoln: A Life</u>, published in 2008.

    A. Michael Burlingame, <u>Abraham Lincoln: A Life</u> vol. 2 (2008).

    B. Michael Burlingame, <u>Abraham Lincoln: A Life</u> 2 (2008).

    C. 2 Michael Burlingame, <u>Abraham Lincoln: A Life</u> (2008).

    D. Vol. 2 Michael Burlingame, <u>Abraham Lincoln: A Life</u> (2008).

4. Choose the correct citation for an originally unpublished letter from Alexander Hamilton to John Jay dated November 26, 1775, published on page 43 of <u>Alexander Hamilton: Writings</u>.

    A. Letter from Alexander Hamilton to John Jay (Nov. 26, 1775), in <u>Alexander Hamilton: Writing</u> 43 (2001).

    B. Letter to John Jay (Nov. 26, 1775), *in* <u>Alexander Hamilton: Writings</u> 43 (2001).

    C. Letter from Alexander Hamilton to John Jay (November 26, 1775), *in* <u>Alexander Hamilton: Writings</u> 43 (2001).

    D. Letter from Alexander Hamilton to John Jay (Nov. 26, 1775) <u>Alexander Hamilton: Writings</u> 43 (2001).

5. Which citation to the ninth edition of <u>Black's Law Dictionary</u>, published in 2009, is correct?

    A. <u>Black's Law Dictionary</u> (9th ed. 2009).

    B. <u>Black's Law Dictionary</u> (9th ed. 2009).

    C. <u>Black's Law Dictionary</u> (9th edition 2009).

    D. <u>Black's Law Dictionary</u> (9th ed., 2009).

Answer Key on page 331

🖥? 13. Bluebook Rules for Citing Periodicals: Quiz

Assume that the following citations appear in court documents.

1. Which of the following citations to a June 1, 2009, article on page E2 of the *San Francisco Chronicle* is correct?

   A. Peter Hartlaub, SFJazz Show Gets to the Roots, S.F. Chron., June 1, 2009, at E2.
   B. Peter Hartlaub, <u>SFJazz Show Gets to the Roots</u>, S.F. Chron., June 1, 2009, at E2.
   C. Hartlaub, Peter, <u>SFJazz Show Gets to the Roots</u>, S.F. Chron., June 1, 2009, at E2.
   D. Peter Hartlaub, <u>SFJazz Show Gets to the Roots</u>, <u>S.F. Chron.</u>, June 1, 2009, at E2.

2. Choose the correct citation to a June 1, 2009, Op-Ed article by Paul Krugman on page A21 of the New York Times.

   A. Paul Krugman, Op-Ed., <u>Reagan Did It</u>, N.Y. Times, June 1, 2009, at A21.
   B. Paul Krugman, Op-Ed., Reagan Did It, N.Y. Times, June 1, 2009, at A21.
   C. Paul Krugman, <u>Reagan Did It</u>, N.Y. Times, June 1, 2009, at A21.
   D. Paul Krugman, Op-Ed., <u>Reagan Did It</u>, New York Times, June 1, 2009, at A21.

3. Choose the correct citation to an April 2009 article by Eugene Volokh that appeared in volume 97 of the *Georgetown Law Journal*.

   A. Eugene Volokh, <u>Symbolic Expression and the Original Meaning of the First Amendment</u>, 97 Georgetown Law Journal 1057 (2009).
   B. Eugene Volokh, <u>Symbolic Expression and the Original Meaning of the First Amendment</u>, 97 Law J. 1057 (2009).
   C. Eugene Volokh, <u>Symbolic Expression and the Original Meaning of the First Amendment</u>, 97 L.J. 1057 (2009).
   D. Eugene Volokh, <u>Symbolic Expression and the Original Meaning of the First Amendment</u>, 97 J. 1057 (2009).

4. Which citation to a March 2007 student-written note, signed by Adrian Barnes and published in volume 1 the *Columbia Law Review*, is correct?

   A. Note, <u>Do They Have to Buy from Burma? A Preemption Analysis of Local Antisweatshop Procurement Laws</u>, 107 Colum. L. Rev. 426 (2007).
   B. Adrian Barnes, Note, <u>Do They Have to Buy from Burma? A Preemption Analysis of Local Antisweatshop Procurement Laws</u>, 107 Col. L.R. 426 (2007).

C. Adrian Barnes, note, <u>Do They Have to Buy from Burma? A Preemption Analysis of Local Antisweatshop Procurement Laws</u>, 107 Colum. L. Rev. 426 (2007).

D. Adrian Barnes, Note, <u>Do They Have to Buy from Burma? A Preemption Analysis of Local Antisweatshop Procurement Laws</u>, 107 Colum. L. Rev. 426 (2007).

5. Choose the correct citation to a nonstudent-written book review by Derrick A. Bell, Jr., reviewing <u>Just Schools: The Idea of Racial Equality in American Education</u> by David L. Kirp. The review appeared in the Texas L Review in August 1983.

A. Derrick A. Bell, Jr., <u>School Desegregation Postmortem</u>, 62 Tex. L. Rev. 175 (1983) (reviewing David L. Kirp, <u>Just Schools: The Idea of Racial Equality in American Education</u> (1982)).

B. Derrick A. Bell, <u>School Desegregation Postmortem</u>, 62 Tex. L. Rev. 175 (1983) (reviewing David L. Kirp, <u>Just Schools: The Idea of Racial Equality in American Education</u> (1982)).

C. Derrick A. Bell, Jr., <u>School Desegregation Postmortem</u>, 62 Tex. L. Rev. 175 (1983) (reviewing David L. Kirp, Just Schools: The Idea of Racial Equality in American Education (1982)).

D. Derrick A. Bell, Jr., <u>School Desegregation Postmortem</u>, 62 Texas L.R. 175 (1983) (reviewing David L. Kirp, <u>Just Schools: The Idea of Racial Equality in American Education</u> (1982)).

Answer Key on page 332

? 14. Bluebook Rules for Citing Electronic Media: Quiz

Assume that the following citations appear in court documents.

1. Choose the correct citation format for a case that is unreported but is available on Westlaw and has been assigned a unique database identifier. There are no page numbers assigned to this case, but cite to screen two of the case.

A. <u>Fenstermacher v. Telelect, Inc.</u>, No. 90-2159-O, 1992 WL 175114, at *2 (D. Kan. July 17, 1992).

B. <u>Fenstermacher v. Telelect, Inc.</u>, 1992 WL 175114, at *2 (D. Kan. July 17, 1992).

C. <u>Fenstermacher v. Telelect, Inc.</u>, No. 90-2159-O, 1992 WL 175114, at 2 (D. Kan. July 17, 1992).

D. <u>Fenstermacher v. Telelect, Inc.</u>, No. 90-2159-O, 1992 WL 175114, at *2 (D. Kan. 1992).

2. Which of the following citations to Baldwin's Kentucky Revised Statutes Annotated, as found on Westlaw correct? Note that the Kentucky Statutes are current on Westlaw through the end of the 2008 legislation.

    A. Ky. Rev. Stat. Ann. § 38.100 (West, 2008).

    B. Ken. Stat. Ann. § 38.100 (West, Westlaw through 2008 legislation).

    C. Ky. Rev. Stat. Ann. § 38.100 (West, Westlaw through 2008 legislation).

    D. Ky. Rev. Stat. Ann. 38.100 (West, Westlaw through 2008 legislation).

3. The following *New York Times* article is available only on the Internet and is not available in traditional print format. Choose the correct citation format.

    A. Matthew Saltmarsh, Interest Rates Held Steady in Europe, N.Y. Times, June 4, 2009, http://www.nytimes.com/2009/06/05/business/global/05euro.html?hpw.

    B. Matthew Saltmarsh, <u>Interest Rates Held Steady in Europe</u>, N.Y. Times, June 4, 2009, http://www.nytimes.com/2009/06/05/business/global/05euro.html?hpw.

    C. Matthew Saltmarsh, Interest Rates Held Steady in Europe, N.Y. Times, June 4, 2009, *available* http://www.nytimes.com/2009/06/05/business/global/05euro.html?hpw.

    D. Matthew Saltmarsh, <u>Interest Rates Held Steady in Europe</u>, New York Times, June 4, 2009, http://www.nytimes.com/2009/06/05/business/global/05euro.html?hpw.

4. The following article is available both in the print version of the New York Times and online. Choose the correct parallel citation.

    A. David Jolly, <u>Despite Devaluation Fear, Latvia Stands by Currency</u>, N.Y. Times, June 4, 2009, at B4, http://www.nytimes.com/2009/06/05/business/global/05latvia.html?hpw.

    B. David Jolly, <u>Despite Devaluation Fear, Latvia Stands by Currency</u>, N.Y. Times, at B4, *available* http://www.nytimes.com/2009/06/05/business/global/05latvia.html?hpw (June 4, 2009).

    C. David Jolly, <u>Despite Devaluation Fear, Latvia Stands by Currency</u>, N.Y. Times, June 4, 2009, at http://www.nytimes.com/2009/06/05/business/global/05latvia.html?hpw.

    D. David Jolly, <u>Despite Devaluation Fear, Latvia Stands by Currency</u>, N.Y. Times, June 4, 2009, available at http://www.nytimes.com/2009/06/05/business/global/05latvia.html?hpw.

5. Choose the correct citation to a fictional e-mail from George Ferman, Assistant Dean at Georgetown Law to Alex Aleinikoff, Dean of Georgetown Law.

    A. E-mail from George Ferman, Assistant Dean, Georgetown Law, to Alex Aleinikoff, Dean, Georgetown Law (Oct. 1, 2009, 08:15:01 EST) (on file with author).

    B. E-mail from George Ferman, Georgetown Law, Assistant Dean, to Alex Aleinikoff, Georgetown Law, Dean (Oct. 1, 2009, 08:15:01 EST) (on file with author).

    C. George Ferman, Assistant Dean, Georgetown Law, to Alex Aleinikoff, Dean, Georgetown Law (Oct. 1, 2009, 08:15:01 EST) (on file with author).

    D. E-mail from George Ferman to Alex Aleinikoff (Oct. 1, 2009, 08:15:01 EST) (on file with author).

6.   Which of the following citations to a commercial audio recording is correct?

    A. U2, <u>The Joshua Tree</u> (1987).

    B. U2, <u>The Joshua Tree</u> (Island Records).

    C. U2, <u>The Joshua Tree</u> (Island Records 1987).

    D. U2, <u>The Joshua Tree</u> (1987) (Island Records).

Answer Key on page 333

C. *Bluebook Citation Self-Assessment*

INSTRUCTIONS: **This self-assessment is designed to test your knowledge of the basic Bluebook citation rules covered in chapter 4. Read through the document, taking note of the numbered and highlighted passages. Each number and highlighted passage represents a question about which you should decide whether the citation is correct as is or whether a change is needed. If a change is needed, please make the correct change in citation format. When you are finished, check your work against the answer key on pages 334-338. The answer key also indicates for each item the applicable citation rule or form. This review will help you to assess your understanding of the Bluebook citation forms and to more quickly and accurately provide citations for your own documents.**

Civil Action No. 02-2332

UNITED STATES COURT OF APPEALS FOR THE ELEVENTH CIRCUIT

DR. CHARLES OSSINING, Appellant, v.

HARRISON BRUBAKER, ET AL., APPELLEES

ON APPEAL FROM UNITED STATES DISTRICT COURT FOR THE SOUTHERN DISTRICT OF ALABAMA

BRIEF OF RESPONDENT

STATEMENT OF ISSUES PRESENTED FOR REVIEW

    I. Whether an inmate, exhibiting no medical condition warranting special treatment, and having received adequate care for all documented symptoms, has an Eighth Amendment claim when, following self-diagnosis of a rare condition, the prison declined his request for a special diet and further unnecessary testing.

    II. Whether the trial court correctly found an inmate's First Amendment rights were not violated when the Warden reviewed and denied individual publications according to prison regulations in response to the unreasonable burden placed upon the prison's resources.

STATEMENT OF THE CASE

<u>Nature of the Case</u>

    This is an appeal of summary judgment in a prisoner's rights case. Respondents request that summary judgment be affirmed as there are no genuine issues of fact in dispute, and that appellant's 42 U.S.C. § 1983 complaint be dismissed as treatment did not violate prisoner's constitutional rights. Appellant brings his claims under the First and Eighth Amendments #1 U.S. Const. Amend. I; #2 U.S. Const. amend. VIII.

#1 Keep as is/Change

#2 Keep as is/Change

Procedural History

Ossining alleges violations of his First and Eighth Amendment rights by the prison. The United States District Court for the Southern District of Alabama granted the defendant's motion for summary judgment. The District Court concluded that plaintiff's receiving of publications caused unreasonable burdens on the resources of the prison and that the prison was not deliberately indifferent to any serious medical needs of the plaintiff. #3 Ossining v. Brubaker, No. CIV.A.02-2332, 2003 U.S. Dist. LEXIS 5130, at *1 (S.D. Ala. Jan. 6, 2003).

#3 Keep as is/Change

STATEMENT OF FACTS

The prisoner, Dr. Charles Ossining, was convicted of Medicare fraud, mail fraud, and making false claims to the government. At the time of Ossining's incarceration in January 2002, a routine medical examination revealed he was in good health, without any notations of medical problems. (Brubaker Aff. 7.) After his arrival, Ossining received a considerable number of medical journals and newsletters pertaining to allergies. (Brubaker Aff. 8.) Ossining specifically ordered informational brochures concerning various types of allergies and treatments for the purpose of disseminating this information to other prisoners. (Ossining Aff. 4.) By the end of March, the infirmary reported a significant increase in prisoner visits: 15% higher than the same quarter a year before, and requests for allergy testing increased 100%. More than half of these requests were declined as these prisoners showed no symptoms warranting testing. Many inmates requesting allergy testing indicated Ossining had suggested they be tested for various allergies. (Brubaker Aff. 9.) Proper allergy diagnosis has been shown to require extensive testing. #4 J. Expert, Allergy on the Net, 5 New Eng. J. Med. 9, 10 (2002), at http://www.nejm.org/expert/v5/allergy.html.

#4 Keep as is/Change

The medical staff could not accommodate all incoming requests for allergy testing, leading to agitation of prisoners and strain on medical resources. (Brubaker Aff. 9, 10.) Additionally, the prison cafeteria received an influx of complaints, as well as special requests and disorderly conduct, requiring additional guards for security. (Brubaker Aff. 11.) Based on these events, Brubaker, the long-time warden of the prison, rejected certain publications addressed to Ossining as detrimental to the security and resources of the prison, an action authorized by federal regulation 28 C.F.R. §540.71(b). #5 I.M. Tough, Warden Power, 15 N.Y.Law Sch. L. Rev. 12, 15-17 (1983).

#5 Keep as is/Change

In March, a blood test revealed Ossining was borderline anemic; he was prescribed iron supplements to combat this condition. (Ossining Aff. 12.) In April, Ossining self-diagnosed himself as suffering from celiac disease, an extremely rare infection, and claimed he needed an endoscopy to confirm his diagnosis. (Flowers Aff. 6.) Celiac disease can be fatal if not treated properly. #6 Adam Gourna, Celiac Disease: A Killer, New York Times, December 12, 1994, at F3, available at 1994 WL 2321843. Reviewing his blood test results, Dr. Gerta Flowers, a specialist in internal medicine and resident physician at the prison, determined that Ossining did not exhibit such severe symptoms warranting further investigation and rejected his request for an endoscopy. (Flowers Aff. 7.) In July, Ossining requested a gluten-free diet, claiming only this diet could treat celiac disease. (Ossining Aff. 21.) Dr. Flowers

#6 Keep as is/Change

informed the prison that sufficient alternatives in the prison cafeteria were available to Ossining should he prefer to eat a gluten-free diet. (Flowers Aff. 8.) The prison has promised that should Ossining present severe symptoms in the future, it would treat him appropriately. (Brubaker Aff. 15.)

STANDARD OF REVIEW

The issue before this Court is whether the trial court properly applied the law to the facts in granting summary judgment. The court's review of the district court's ruling on a motion for summary judgment is de novo. #7 <u>Pope v. Hightower</u>, 101 F.3d 1382, 1383 (11th Cir. 1996).

#7 Keep as is/Change

SUMMARY OF ARGUMENT

Ossining's First and Eighth Amendment claims fail based on the established facts in the record. With regard to the Eighth Amendment, Ossining shows no evidence of a serious medical need, his treatment by the prison did not violate contemporary standards of decency, and the medical staff was not deliberately indifferent to his condition. #8 U.S. CONST. amend. VIII. As for the First Amendment, because assertion of his rights posed a threat to the security of the prison and created an unreasonable burden on prison resources, Warden Brubaker's rejection of particular publications was justified. #9 Amend. I.

#8 Keep as is/Change

#9 Keep as is/Change

ARGUMENT

The prisoner, Dr. Charles Ossining, is currently serving a five-year sentence for defrauding the federal government. Ossining alleges the prison violated his First Amendment rights by denying him access to professional journals and his Eighth Amendment rights by denying him a gluten-free diet and further testing for a rare disease for which he made a self-diagnosis. While detainees are accorded protections of the Constitution, prisoner's rights are inherently restricted, and some constitutional violations may be acceptable if they serve "legitimate penological interests," such as order, security, and safety. #10 <u>See Thornburgh v. Abbott</u>, 490 U.S. 407-408 (1989). Moreover, as operation of a prison falls under the province of the legislative and executive branches of government, deference should be paid by the courts to appropriate prison authorities regulating this delicate balance between prison security and legitimate rights of prisoners. #11 <u>Turner v. Safley</u>, 482 U.S. 78, 84-85 (1987)

#10 Keep as is/Change

#11 Keep as is/Change

I. PLAINTIFF'S EIGHTH AMENDMENT CLAIM OF CRUEL AND UNUSUAL PUNISHMENT IS WITHOUT MERIT BECAUSE THE PRISONER EXHIBITED NO MEDICAL CONDITION WARRANTING SPECIAL TREATMENT

Ossining fails to present sufficient evidence of a serious medical problem related to being denied a gluten-free diet or evidence that the prison was "deliberately indifferent" to his symptoms, as required for claims under the Eighth Amendment. <u>See</u> #12 <u>Helling</u>, 509 U.S. 25, 29 (1993). In #13 <u>Helling</u>, the Supreme Court established a two prong test for proving Eighth Amendment violations. Under the subjective prong (A), the prisoner must show deliberate indifference by the prison toward a

#12 Keep as is/Change
#13 Keep as is/Change

serious risk posed to the prisoner. Under the objective prong (B), the prisoner must show that the unreasonable risk of harm he faces is contrary to contemporary standards of decency. #14 Id. at 35-36. Because Ossining received adequate treatment for his ailments and exhibited no medical condition warranting special treatment, he fails both prongs of the Eighth Amendment test.

A. The prison was not deliberately indifferent to prisoner's medical condition when the prison physician reviewed prisoner's blood test results to find no severe symptoms of celiac disease warranting further treatment and the prison menu offered adequate gluten-free alternatives

Under the subjective prong, the prisoner must show 1) the prison had knowledge of a serious risk of harm to him and 2) deliberate indifference by the prison toward this risk. #15 Id. at 35.

1. The prison had no subjective knowledge of any serious risk of harm to the prisoner in denying him a gluten-free diet or in rejecting his request for an endoscopy to further test for celiac disease

Ossining fails to show prison officials knew of and disregarded "an excessive risk to his health or safety." #16 See Farmer v. Brennan, 511 U.S. 825, 837 (1994); 42 U.S.C. § 1983 (2003). As serious complications from celiac disease are rare and Dr. Flowers determined that the prisoner did not present such severe symptoms to warrant further investigation, Ossining fails to show the prison's subjective knowledge of a serious risk of harm when denying him a gluten-free diet and further testing. In #17 Campbell et al. v. Sikes, the plaintiff inmate alleged cruel and unusual punishment when the defendant prison psychiatrist misdiagnosed her with poly-substance abuse disorder when in fact she had a bipolar disorder, a diagnosis unreported in jail records or prior hospitalization records. The court affirmed the grant of summary judgment for the prison because there was no evidence that the psychiatrist knew the prisoner had bipolar disorder, that he knew he misdiagnosed her, or that he knew of a substantial risk of serious harm to the inmate as a result of his treatment. #18 Campbell v. Sikes, 169 F.3d 1353, 1366-1368 (1999). Similarly, Ossining fails to present evidence from which a reasonable jury could infer that Dr. Flowers or other prison officials knew he had celiac disease, or knew they were misdiagnosing him, or knew their treatment was grossly inadequate but proceeded with the treatment anyway. Like #19 Campbell, Ossining's medical records did not indicate a prior history of celiac disease and a professional review of his blood did not give Dr. Flowers reason for concern. Therefore, Ossining fails the first part of the subjective prong of the Helling test because the prison exhibits no subjective knowledge of his mistreatment.

2. The prison was not deliberately indifferent toward the medical concerns of the prisoner

Ossining fails to demonstrate his medical treatment by the prison constituted the "unnecessary and wanton infliction of pain," as required to show deliberate indifference. #20 Mustave Hurt, Unimaginable Pain, 742 Geo. L.J. 801, 831-32 (2003) (discussing the requirements to show deliberate indifference). In Estelle, the prisoner

#14 Keep as is/Change

#15 Keep as is/Change

#16 Keep as is/Change

#17 Keep as is/Change

#18 Keep as is/Change

#19 Keep as is/Change

#20 Keep as is/Change

injured his back while engaged in prison work, claiming deliberate indifference by the prison for failure to perform an X-ray to treat him. The court held that questions concerning forms of treatment are matters of medical judgment, and that failure by prison medical staff to use additional diagnostic techniques beyond ordinary treatment does not constitute deliberate indifference or cruel and usual punishment.

#21 Keep as is/Change

#21 Estelle v. Gamble, 429 S. Ct. 97, 107 (1976). Similarly, Dr. Flowers' refusal to order an endoscopy to confirm Ossining's self diagnosis of celiac disease following her professional review of his blood test results does not constitute deliberate indifference to his medical needs. Ossining offers no evidence that prison medical staff failed to meet appropriate professional standards in determining that his symptoms did not warrant further testing. Moreover, Ossining's difference in opinion from prison officials concerning diagnosis and recommended treatment does not constitute cruel and unusual punishment.

#22 Keep as is/Change

#22 See id. at 100; but see Harris v. Thigpen, 941 F.2d 1495, 1505 (11th Cir. 1991)(holding that difference of opinion does constitute cruel and unusual punishment). While an endoscopy may have led to an appropriate diagnosis and treatment for his condition, Ossining fails to show deliberate indifference as medical decisions concerning forms of treatment beyond ordinary care do not constitute cruel and unusual punishment.

#23 Keep as is/Change

#23 See Estelle, 429 U.S. 97 at 107.

Denial of Ossining's request for a special gluten-free diet does not constitute deliberate indifference because the prisoner lacks convincing symptoms requiring special treatment. See 25 Op. Off. Legal Counsel 370, 381-82 (1995).

#24 Keep as is/Change

#24 In McElligot v. Goley, 182 F.3d 1248, 1256-1258 (11th Cir. 1999), an inmate with a history of stomach problems was treated by prison doctors with Tylenol, Pepto-Bismol, and an anti-gas medication when experiencing severe intestinal pains, even after it was evident these treatments were not responding to his deteriorating condition. The court held that while prison doctors could not be held liable for failing to diagnose the inmate's colon cancer, the failure to further diagnose and treat severe pain experienced by a prisoner was evidence of deliberate indifference.

#25 Keep as is/Change

#25 See McElligot v. Foley, 182 F.3d 1248, 1256-58 (11th Cir. 1999); Noah Lee, Deliberate Indifference: What's It All About? 31 (3d ed. 2001). Unlike McElligot, Ossining exhibits no severe symptoms of celiac disease. The prison staff examined Ossining, conducted a blood test, prescribed him iron supplements to overcome his weight loss and psychological depression, and professionally reviewed his blood work to conclude there was nothing seriously wrong with him. Therefore, as the prison exercised professional standards of care in evaluating his health, and as the inmate exhibits no severe symptoms warranting special treatment, Ossining fails to show deliberate indifference to his medical needs.

#26 Keep as is/Change

#26 See United States Sent. G.L. Man. §5D2.1(f) (2001).

B. The prison's denial of prisoner's requests for a special gluten-free diet and additional testing for a rare disease do not violate contemporary standards of decency

Under the objective prong, Ossining fails to show his exposure to an unreasonable risk of harm contrary to "contemporary standards of decency."

#27 Keep as is/Change

#27 Helling, 509 United States at 36. The objective standard requires showing treatment rising to the level of "serious" deprivation.

#28 Keep as is/Change

#28 Campbell, 169 F.3d at 1363. In Rhodes, the Court held confining two inmates to a single cell did not constitute the "unnecessary and wanton infliction of pain" that violates the Eighth Amendment because inmates suffered only minor deprivations of privileges, not necessities such as essential food, medical care, or sanitation. Only when these "minimal civilized measure of life's necessities" are denied is there basis for an Eighth Amendment violation. #29 Rhodes v. Chapman, 452 U.S 337, 346, 349 (1981). Similarly, Wellville's denial of additional testing and special diet to Ossining when trained medical professionals fail to recognize symptoms requiring such treatment does not constitute deprivation of life's minimal necessities. #30 RESTATEMENT (SECOND) OF TORTS § 931 (1994). Ossining was not denied adequate medical care when he was examined by prison medical staff, had his blood tested and reviewed by Dr. Flowers, and was prescribed iron supplements to combat weight loss and fatigue. Moreover, Ossining was never denied essential food as adequate alternatives remained available in the cafeteria should Ossining prefer a gluten-free diet. Therefore, life's minimal necessities were not denied, and Ossining fails the objective standard as his treatment did not violate contemporary standards of decency.

#29 Keep as is/Change

#30 Keep as is/Change

II. PRISONER'S FIRST AMENDMENT CLAIM IS WITHOUT MERIT BECAUSE WARDEN BRUBAKER REVIEWED AND DENIED PRISONER'S PUBLICATIONS IN RESPONSE TO THE UNREASONABLE BURDEN PLACED UPON THE PRISON'S RESOURCES AS AUTHORIZED UNDER 28 C.F.R § 540.71

As authorized under 28 C.F.R. § 540.71 (b), Warden Brubaker legitimately restricted Ossining's right to receive publications deemed "detrimental to the security, good order, or discipline of the institution..." 28 C.F.R. § 540.71. Exercise of constitutional rights within the prison must pay due regard to the order and security of the prison environment. #31 See Turner Railroad v. Safley, 482 U.S. 78, 84-85 (1987). Ossining fails to show Wellville's restrictions on his First Amendment rights were not "reasonably related to legitimate penological interests" as required under the four-part Turner-Thornburgh test. #32 See Id. at 89; See Thornburgh, 490 U.S. at 401. Under Turner-Thornburgh, the court must consider the following factors: A) the impact that accommodation of the asserted constitutional right will have on others in the prison; B) whether the governmental objective underlying the regulations at issue is legitimate and neutral, and whether the regulations are rationally related to that objective; C) whether the regulation represents an exaggerated response to prison concerns; and D) whether there are alternative means of exercising the right that remain open to prison inmates at de minimis cost to penological interests. #33 Owen v. Wille, 117 F.3d at 1235 (11th Cir. 1997). As Ossining's exercise of his First Amendment right created an unreasonable burden on resources of the prison and put prison security in jeopardy, restricting his access to medical publications was constitutional because it was reasonably related to a legitimate penological interest.

#31 Keep as is/Change

#32 Keep as is/Change

#33 Keep as is/Change

A. Accommodation of prisoner's asserted First Amendment right would be detrimental to the order and security of the prison, placing an unreasonable burden on the resources of the prison medical facility and cafeteria

The Court should be particularly deferential to the informed discretion of Warden Brubaker given interests in security when Ossining's assertion of his constitutional right created a "ripple effect" among fellow inmates and prison staff.

#34 Keep as is/Change

#35 Keep as is/Change

#36 Keep as is/Change

#37 Keep as is/Change

#38 Keep as is/Change

#39 Keep as is/Change

#34 See <u>U.S. v. White</u>, 490 U.S. 84, 87 (1990). In <u>Turner</u>, a class of inmates challenged prison regulations restricting correspondence between inmates as violations of their First Amendment rights. The court deferred to judgment of correction officials and upheld the regulation as reasonably related to legitimate security interests given the potential for coordinating criminal activity by inmate-to-inmate correspondence, and given the probability of material circulating within the prison in a "ripple effect." #35 <u>See</u> <u>Turner</u>, 482 U.S. at 84-85.

Like <u>Turner</u>, Warden Brubaker determined that Ossining created a "ripple effect," threatening the order and security of the prison while placing an unreasonable burden on prison resources, by circulating publications among prisoners to encourage them to believe they were sick. According to Brubaker, the temporal relationship between Ossining's receipt of medical publications and increased inmate complaints indicates a correlation between the assertion of his constitutional rights and the riling up of prisoners, over taxing of prison personnel, and additional expenditure of prison resources. #36 <u>Ossining v. Brubaker</u>, No. CIV.A.02-2332, 2003 WL 66432, at *6 (Jan. 6, 2003). Dramatic increases in infirmary visits and requests for allergy testing among inmates, many of whom showed no symptoms warranting testing, support Brubaker's hypothesis. Given the threat to order and cost of additional resources required to accommodate Ossining's assertion of his rights, deference should be given to Brubaker's informed discretion in rejecting these publications.

B. <u>Governmental objective in maintaining prison security is legitimate and neutral, and prison regulations governing the availability of publications to inmates rationally relate to this objective by reducing frivolous medical complaints and special requests</u>

Under the second factor of the <u>Turner-Thornburgh</u> test, the Court must determine whether 1) the governmental objective underlying the regulation at issue is legitimate and neutral, and whether 2) the regulation is rationally related to that objective. #37 <u>State of Alabama v. Carter</u>, 507 U.S. 411, 418 (1992).

1. <u>Protecting prison security is a legitimate and neutral governmental objective</u>

In rejecting Ossining's publications, Warden Brubaker acted pursuant to 28 C.F.R. § 540.71, whose "underlying objective of protecting prison security is undoubtedly legitimate and is neutral with regard to the content of the expression regulated." #38 <u>North West Electric Company v. University of Colorado</u>, 211 U.S. 415, 417 (1991). In <u>Thornburgh</u>, inmates filed a class action against the prison challenging regulations excluding incoming sexually explicit publications. The Court upheld the regulations as maintenance of prison order and security is a legitimate governmental purpose, and because the prison's ban on sexually explicit material was neutrally based on security interests. #39 <u>See</u> <u>cf.</u> <u>Thornburgh</u>, 490 U.S. at 414-15. Like <u>Thornburgh</u>, Ossining's publications were rejected because they created obstacles to the legitimate governmental objective of maintaining prison security. Warden Brubaker's rejection of only those publications deemed a threat to prison security remained "neutral" to the legitimate governmental interest in maintaining security and order. Therefore, Brubaker's exercise of authority under 28 C.F.R. § 540.71 was consistent with the legitimate and neutral objectives underlying the regulation.

2. <u>Application of prison regulation governing the availability of publications to inmates is rationally related to the governmental objective</u>

There is a "valid, rational connection" between the rejection of various publications addressed to Ossining and the legitimate government interests in security and preservation of resources. #40 <u>See</u> <u>Turner</u>, 482 U.S. at 89; see also 28 C.F.R. § 540.71 (2002) (establishing security as legitimate government interest). In <u>Onishea</u>, inmates with HIV brought a class action challenging the prison's segregation of recreational, religious, and educational programs based on prisoners' HIV status. The prison justified its actions claiming the cost of hiring additional guards to monitor the threat of "high-risk" behavior in integrated programs would create an undue financial burden on resources. The Court upheld the segregated programs as rationally related to governmental objectives because "penological concerns such as security and cost are legitimate, and...these are in fact the concerns behind the program requirements that participating prisoners neither create a threat of disorder or unreasonable costs." #41 <u>Onishea v. Hopper</u>, 171 F.3d 1289, 1300 (11th Cir. 1999). Similarly, Brubaker's rejection of certain items addressed to Ossining was rationally related to legitimate governmental interests because of the Warden's concern that these publications created threat of disorder and unreasonable costs for the prison. By rejecting these publications, Warden Brubaker intended to remove obstacles to maintaining security by reducing the agitation of prisoners, easing the burden placed on the prison medical staff, and removing the need for additional guards to maintain order in the cafeteria. Therefore, as security was the underlying concern behind Brubaker's actions, his rejection of Ossining's publications was rationally related to legitimate governmental objectives. #42 <u>See</u> H.R. 81, 108th Cong. (2003) (establishing security as legitimate governmental objective), available at http://thomas.-20loc.gov/bss/d108/d108laws.html.

C. <u>The prison regulation is not an exaggerated response to prison concerns because alternatives accommodating prisoner's rights at de minimus cost to penological interests are not immediately obvious or feasible</u>

Rejection of prisoner's publications is not an exaggerated response to the threat these items posed to prison resources and security because there are no "obvious, easy alternatives." #43 <u>See</u> Jeremy Stevens, <u>Taking Control</u> 41-42 (Amanda Bradley ed., 3d ed. Scholastic Press 2001). In <u>Spellman</u>, inmates challenged the prison's blanket ban on publications sent to prisoners in administrative segregation on the grounds that the regulation was an exaggerated response to security and safety concerns. The Court held the prison's actions unconstitutional, recognizing alternatives to the blanket ban, such as placing reasonable limits on the quantity of publications permitted in confinement, which still addressed the concerns of security, fire, and sanitation. #44 <u>See</u> <u>Spellman v. Hopper</u>, 95 F.supp.2d 1267, 1286 (M.D. Ala. 1999). Unlike <u>Spellman</u>, Brubaker rejected only Ossining's medical publications, items deemed a threat to prison security; Brubaker did not blanket ban all publications sent to Ossining. Moreover, <u>unlike</u> Spellman, less restrictive alternatives can be rejected because of reasonably grounded fears they will lead to greater harm or administrative inconvenience. #45 <u>See</u> Alabama Constitution article V, § 9. The resources

#40 Keep as is/Change

#41 Keep as is/Change

#42 Keep as is/Change

#43 Keep as is/Change

#44 Keep as is/Change

#45 Keep as is/Change

required to read through every allergy magazine received to eliminate publications deemed a threat would be too expansive as prisoners have complained of a wide variety of allergies. Also, allowing Ossining to read magazines while in confinement would not come at a de minimus cost to the prison as additional resources would be required to fund such an arrangement. #46 <u>See</u> James King, <u>Costs of Confinement</u>, 28 N. Ill. U. L. Rev. 609, 621-22 (2001). Thus, as less restrictive alternatives are not readily available or feasible, the Warden's actions do not represent an exaggerated response to legitimate penological concerns.

#46 Keep as is/Change

D. <u>The prison restrictions on prisoner's receipt of publications are reasonable as prisoner has alternative means of exercising his First Amendment rights to keep up with developments in his field of work</u>

Ossining fails the fourth factor of the <u>Turner-Thornburgh</u> test because other means of expression remain available to the prisoner despite imposition of prison regulations restricting his access to certain publications. <u>See</u> Stevens, <u>Taking Control</u> at 45. In Turner, the prison restricted inmate-to-inmate correspondence between prisons to prevent future criminal behavior, a legitimate security concern. The Court held the fourth factor satisfied if any other means of expression remained open to the prisoners, not necessarily other means of communicating with inmates in other prisons. <u>Turner</u>, 482 S.Ct. at 90, 92. Similarly, Brubaker's application of the regulation merely prohibits publications of particular kind, and does not deprive the prisoner of all means of expression. The prison is not prohibiting Ossining from gaining access to allergy information as he can still receive phone calls and visits from colleagues who can keep him up to date. Moreover, the prisoner is still free to receive a variety of other publications. Alternative means of exercising his First Amendment rights are still available to the prisoner, and therefore, Ossining fails to satisfy the fourth factor.

CONCLUSION

For the above stated reasons, the judgment of the District Court should be affirmed.

Respectfully submitted,

_____

Attorney for Respondents

CERTIFICATE OF SERVICE

I swear on this day, the 28th of February, 2003, that I have served Respondent's brief on Appellant's counsel.

_____

Attorney for Respondents

Answer Key on page 334

Appendix A: Answer Keys

I. RESEARCH SOURCES ANSWER KEYS

A. Quizzes

1. Research Sources (in General) (page 94)

1. C
2. E
3. C
4. B
5. A

6. C
7. D
8. D
9. B
10. A

2. Congress and Federal Statutes (page 96)

1. D
2. A

3. B
4. B

3. Federal Courts and Federal Cases (page 97)

1. A
2. B

3. D
4. D

4. Federal Administrative Law (page 97)

1. B
2. D

3. D
4. C

5. State Legislatures and State Statutes (page 98)

1. A
2. C

3. B
4. C

6. State Courts and State Cases (page 99)

1. C
2. B
3. D

4. A
5. B

7. Legislative History (page 100)

1.	F	5.		F
2.	T	6.	a.	T
3.	T		b.	T
4.	F		c.	T

8. Looseleaf Services (page 100)

1.	F	4.	F
2.	F	5.	T
3.	T	6.	T

9. Secondary Sources (page 101)

1.	C	3.	A
2.	B	4.	B

II.   RESEARCH STRATEGIES ANSWER KEYS

A. Quizzes

1. Research Strategy (in General) (p. 181)

1.	G	7.	A
2.	C	8.	B
3.	B	9.	E
4.	D	10.	B
5.	C	11.	E
6.	B	12.	E

2. Binding vs. Persuasive Law (p. 185)

1.	D	4.	A
2.	B	5.	E
3.	C		

3. Finding Statutes (p. 187)

1.	B	3.	C
2.	A	4.	E

4. Finding Cases (p. 188)

1.	A	4.	B
2.	E	5.	D
3.	B		

5. Updating (p. 189)

1. D
2. C
3. D
4. C

III. CITATION ANSWER KEYS

A. *ALWD Quizzes*

1. ALWD Typeface Conventions (page 223)

1. B - The comma that follows the case name should not be italicized or underlined (Rule 12.0).

2. B - This is the correct citation according to Rules 12.0 and 12.20(b). The comma that follows the case name should not be italicized or underlined.

3. A - The introductory signal and "id." are properly underlined according to Rule 44.6(b).

4. D - This is the correct typeface format according to Rule 23.1(d).

5. C - This is the correct typeface format according to Rule 12.2(a).

2. Basic Structure and Signals for ALWD Citations (page 224)

1. B - This citation uses the proper format for signals according to Rules 44.8(a) and 44.3. Authorities should be separated with a semi-colon and one space (Rule 45.2).

2. B - This citation uses the correct order of authorities according to Rule 44.8(a). For cases from the same court, cases should be cited in reverse chronological order (Rule 45.3(h)).

3. B - This citation uses the correct order of authorities according to Rule 45.4(a). Statutes should be cited before cases (Rule 45.4(a)).

4. A - The explanatory parenthetical is correctly placed and formatted according to Rules 46.2(a) and 46.3.

5. D - This citation uses signals correctly according to Rules 44.8(a), (c), 44.3, and 45.2. For cases from the same court, cases should be cited in reverse chronological order (Rule 45.3(h)).

3. ALWD Citation Signals (page 225)

1. D - This is the correct signal according to Rule 44.3.

2. B - This is the correct signal according to Rule 44.3.

3. C - This is the correct signal according to Rule 44.3. The Maryland statute is in accord with the Delaware statute (Rule 44.3).

4. B - This is the correct signal according to Rule 44.3.

5. A - This is the correct signal according to Rule 44.3. Signals should not be used when the cited authority directly supports the stated proposition.

6. C - This is the correct signal according to Rule 44.3.

4. ALWD Order and Punctuation of Signals and Citations (page 227)

1. B - This is the correct citation sentence according to Rule 44.8(a).

2. A - This is the correct citation sentence according to Rules 44.8(a) and 44.3.

3. C - This is the correct citation sentence according to Rules 45.4(a) and 44.3. Federal statutes should be cited sequentially by title number and section number.

5. ALWD Rules for Citing Subdivisions and Pinpoint Cites (page 228)

1. A - According to Rules 12.1 and 12.5(b), this is the correct format for a citation to specific material within a case.

2. C - According to Rules 5.4, 12.1, and 12.5(b), this is the correct citation.

3. B - According to Rules 5.4, 12.1, and 12.5(b), this is the correct citation.

4. C - According to Rule 5.2(b)(2), this is the correct format to a citation to specific material from a law review article.

5. D - According to Rule 5.4, this is the proper format for a citation to nonconsecutive pages.

6. ALWD Rules for Short Form Citations (page 229)

1. A - According to Rules 12.20(a) and 11.3(b)(1) and (e), this is the correct short form citation to a case that is the only source in the immediately preceding citation and that cites the same page number.

2. D - According to Rule 12.20(b), this is the correct short form citation to a case that was not in the immediately preceding citation.

3. A - According to Rules 12.11(a) and 11.3(e), this is the correct short form citation.

4. D - According to Rule 14.6, this is the correct short form citation.

5. C - According to Rule 23.2(b), this is the correct short form citation.

6. A - According to Rules 23.2(a) and 11.3(b)(1), this is the correct short citation.

7. D - <u>Id.</u> should not be used if there is more than one source in the immediately preceding citation. See Rules 11.3(b)(1) and (4)(a).

7. ALWD Abbreviations (page 230)

1. A - The abbreviations in this citation are correct according to Rule 12.2(e)(7).

2. E - The abbreviations in this citation are correct according to Appendix 3, Part E, General Abbreviations.

3. C - "Fed. Reg." is the proper abbreviation for the Federal Register according to Rule 19.3.

4. B - This is the correct abbreviation for the Federal Rules of Civil Procedure according to Rule 17.1.

5. A - "Geo. Mason L. Rev." is the proper abbreviation for the George Mason Law Review according to Appendix 5, Abbreviations for Legal Periodicals.

8. ALWD Rules for Citing Cases (page 231)

1. B - The reporter is correctly cited according to Rule 12.4(a)(1) and the Fourth Circuit is correctly abbreviated according to Appendix 4(B), Federal Courts.

2. A - This is the correct citation according to Rule 12.4(b), Appendix 1 (under Pennsylvania), and Appendix 1B, State Appellate Court Decisions.

3. C - "U.S." is the correct abbreviation for the United States Reports and is the official reporter for United States Supreme Court decisions according to Rule 12.4(c) and Appendix 1, Federal Materials.

4. B - The reporter is correctly cited according to Rule 12.4(a)(1) and Appendix 1, Federal Materials. The Fourth Circuit is correctly abbreviated according to Appendix 4(B), Federal Courts.

5. A - The parenthetical information in this citation is properly formatted according to Rules 12.11(a), 46.2(a), and 46.3.

6. A - The parenthetical information in this citation is properly formatted according to Rules 12.12(a), (b), and (d).

9. ALWD Rules for Citing Constitutions (page 232)

1. C - This is the correct citation format according to Rule 13.2. "Const." and "amend." are correctly abbreviated according to Appendix 3, General Abbreviations, C and E.

2. A - This is the correct citation format according to Rule 13.2(a), and "Kan." is correctly abbreviated according to Appendix 3, General Abbreviations, B.

3. D - This is the correct citation format according to Rules 11.3(b) and 13.4.

4. B - This is the correct citation format according to Rules 13.2, 13.3, and Appendix, 3 General Abbreviations, C and E.

5. A - This is the correct citation format according to Rule 13.2(a), and "Pa." is correctly abbreviated according to Appendix 3, General Abbreviations, B.

10. ALWD Rules for Citing Statutes (page 233)

1. B - According to Rule 14.2, the number preceding the abbreviation of the relevant code signifies the title number of the statute.

2. C - This is the correct citation format according to Rule 14.2.

3. A - This is an acceptable short form citation according to Rule 14.6.

4. D - This citation format is not correct.

5. A - This is the correct citation format according to Appendix 1, Primary Sources by Jurisdiction.

6. C - This is the correct citation format according to Rule 17.1.

11. ALWD Citations for Administrative and Executive Materials (page 234)

1. C - This is the correct citation format for C.F.R. provisions according to Rule 19.1.

2. B - According to Rule 19.2, this is the correct alternate short form citation.

3. A - According to Rule 19.3(e), this is the correct citation format for a regulation that has not yet been entered into the Code of Federal Regulations.

4. A - According to Rule 20.3 and Appendix 1, Primary Sources by Jurisdiction, this is the correct format for a citation in the Virginia Register of Regulations.

5. D - This is the proper citation format for an advisory opinion according to Rule 19.7.

6. D - This is the proper citation format for an Executive Order according to Rule 19.9.

12. ALWD Citations for Books, Reports, and Other Nonperiodic Materials (page 235)

1. D - The author's name is correctly formatted (Rule 22.1), the title is correctly formatted (Rule 22.1), the page number is correctly formatted (22.1(c). The publisher information should also be included (Rule 22.1(i)).

2. A - In citing books with more than two authors, use the author's name followed by "et al." according to 22.1(a), and include a comma and one space after the edition and before the publisher's name (Rules 22.1(f), (i)).

3. A - This is the correct citation format according to Rule 22.1. The volume number appears after the book title (Rule 22.1 (c)).

4. D - In citing an originally unpublished letter, begin the citation with the phrase "Ltr. from," (Rule 32.1(a)). Cite the rest of the letter according to Rule 32.3, 22.1(l), or 22.1(m). The publisher information should also be included (Rule 22.1(i)).

5. D - This is the correct citation according to Rule 25.1.

13. ALWD Rules for Citing Periodical Materials (page 237)

1. B - This is the correct citation for a newspaper according to Rule 23.1(d).

2. C - This is the correct citation for a journal article according to Rule 23.1 and Appendix 5, Abbreviations for Legal Periodicals.

3. D - This is the correct citation for a journal article according to Rule 23.1(a) and Appendix 5, Abbreviations for Legal Periodicals.

4. A - This is the correct citation for a nonstudent-written book review according to Rule 23.1(b)(2).

14. ALWD Rules for Citing Electronic Media (page 238)

1. E - This is the correct citation format for unreported cases available on Westlaw according to Rule 12.12(b). According to Rule 12.12(d), the docket number is not a required element for cases published on Lexis-Nexis or Westlaw.

2. C - This is the correct citation format according to Appendix 1, Primary Sources by Jurisdiction, and Rule 14.5.

3. B - This is the correct citation format for an article found on the Internet according to Rules 23.1(d), 38.2, and 40.1.

4. D - This is the correct citation format for a parallel citation according to Rules 23.1(d), 38.2, and 40.1.

5. A - This is the correct citation format for a personal e-mail message according to Rule 41.1(d).

6. C - This is the correct citation format for a commercial recording according to Rule 34.1.

B. *ALWD Self-Assessment*

1. ALWD Citation Self-Assessment (page 240)

1. Change. Answer: U.S. Const. amend. I;. Explanation: Rule 13.2, abbreviate and use lowercase letters for designations such as "article" or "amendment."

2. Keep as is. Answer: U.S. Const. amend. VIII. Explanation: Rule 13.2, abbreviate and use lowercase letters for designations such as "article" or "amendment."

3. Keep as is. Answer: <u>Ossining v. Brubaker</u>, No. CIV.A.02-2332, 2003 U.S. Dist. LEXIS 5130 at *1 (S.D. Ala. Jan. 6, 2003). Explanation: Rules 12.12(a), (b), and (d). The docket number is optional in citing cases from Lexis or Westlaw. Careful: Many jurisdictions do not allow citations to unpublished cases.

4. Change. Answer: Judith Expert, <u>Allergy on the Net</u>, 6 New Eng. J. Med. 9, 10 (2002) (available at http://www.nejm.org/expert/v5/allergy.html). Explanation: Rule 23.1(a), use the author's full name. Rule 38.1(b), include electronic source information in a parenthetical after the print source.

5. Change. Answer: Irving M. Tough, <u>Warden Power</u>, 16 N.Y. L. Sch. L. Rev. 12, 15-17 (1983). Explanation: Rule 23.1(a), use the author's full name. Abbreviate the name of the periodical using Appendix 5.

6. Change. Answer: Adam Gourna, <u>Celiac Disease: A Killer</u>, N.Y. Times F3 (Dec. 12, 1994) (available at 1994 WL 2321843). Explanation: Rule 23.1(d), abbreviate newspaper names using Appendix 3 or 5. Rule 23.1(e), after the abbreviated newspaper name, give the page on which the article starts. Rule 23.1(f), place the abbreviated date in a parenthetical. Rule 38.1(b), include electronic source information in a parenthetical after the print source.

7. Change. Answer: <u>Pope v. Hightower</u>, 101 F.3d 1382, 1383 (11th Cir. 1996). Explanation: Rule 12.6(a), no superscript in court name.

8. Change. Answer: U.S. Const. amend. VIII. Explanation: Rule 13.2, do not use all capitals in citing amendments.

9. Change. Answer: <u>Id.</u> Explanation: Rule 13.4, use <u>id.</u> as a short form citation for constitution provisions when appropriate.

10. Change. Answer: <u>See</u> <u>Thornburgh v. Abbott</u>, 490 U.S. 401, 407-08 (1989). Explanation: Rule 12.5(a), after the reporter abbreviation, give the page on which the case begins. Any pinpoint references follow, separated by a comma.

11. Change. Answer: <u>Turner v. Safley</u>, 482 U.S. 78, 84-85 (1987). Explanation: Rule 43.1(a), a citation sentence begins with a capital letter and ends with a period.

12. Change. Answer: <u>Helling v. McKinney</u>, 509 U.S. 25, 29 (1993). Explanation: Rule 12.20, use a short citation form only if you have previously cited the case in full.

13. Keep as is. Answer: <u>Helling</u>. Explanation: Rule 12.20, case that has been cited in full in the same general discussion may be referred to by one of the parties' names without further citation.

14. Change. Answer: <u>Id.</u> at 35-36. Explanation: Rule 11.3, italicize or underline <u>id.</u> Rule 12.20, generally, the case name may be omitted if the reader will have no doubt about the case to which the citation refers.

15. Keep as is. Answer: <u>Id.</u> at 35. Explanation: Rule 12.20, generally, the case name may be omitted if the reader will have no doubt about the case to which the citation refers.

16. Change. Answer: <u>See</u> 42 U.S.C. § 1983 (2003); <u>Farmer v. Brennan</u>, 511 U.S. 825, 837 (1994). Explanation: Rule 45.4(a), cite statutes before cases within the same signal. Rule 12.2(a), italicize or underline case names.

17. Change. Answer: <u>Campbell v. Sikes</u>. Explanation: Rule 12.2(c), omit words indicating multiple parties, such as "et al."

18. Change. Answer: <u>Campbell v. Sikes</u>, 169 F.3d 1353, 1366-68 (11th Cir. 1999). Explanation: Rule 12.6, include the name of the court within the parenthetical, unless the name of the reporter clearly indicates which court decided the case.

19. Change. Answer: <u>Campbell</u>,. Explanation: Rules 12.2(a) and 12.20, italicize short case names.

20. Keep as is. Answer: Mustave Hurt, <u>Unimaginable Pain</u>, 742 Geo. L.J. 801, 831-32 (2003) (discussing the requirements to show deliberate indifference). Explanation: Rule 23.1.

21. Change. Answer: <u>Estelle v. Gamble</u>, 439 U.S. 97, 107 (1976). Explanation: Rule 12.4(c), cite to U.S., if therein; otherwise cite to S. Ct., L. Ed., or U.S.L.W., in that order of preference.

22. Keep as is. Answer: <u>See</u> <u>id.</u> at 100, <u>but see</u> <u>Harris v. Thigpen</u>, 941 F.2d 1495, 1505 (11th Cir. 1991) (holding that difference of opinion does constitute cruel and unusual punishment). Explanation: Rule 44.8(c), separate different signals and their citations with a semicolon.

23. Change. Answer: <u>See</u> <u>Estelle</u>, 429 U.S. at 107. Explanation: Rule 12.20, use only the pinpoint page number in short form case citations.

24. Keep as is. Answer: <u>McElligot v. Goley</u>, 182 F.3d 1248, 1256-1258 (11th Cir. 1999), OR <u>McElligot v. Goley</u>, 182 F.3d 1248, 1256-58 (11th Cir. 1999). Explanation: According to Rule 5.3, you may drop the last two digits of page numbers or keep them.

25. Change. Answer: <u>See</u> <u>id.</u>; Noah Lee, <u>Deliberate Indifference: What's It All About?</u> 31 (3d ed., Biking 2001). Explanation: Rule 22.1(i), in citing books, include the publisher's name within the parenthetical. Rule 45.4(a), cite primary sources such as cases before secondary sources such as books. A short cite would be appropriate for the case assuming it was correctly referenced in the immediate previous citation (the full citation would also be correct).

26. Change. Answer: <u>See</u> <u>U.S. Sentencing Guidelines Manual</u> § 5D2.1(f) (2001). Explanation: Rule 27.5, cite U.S. sentencing guidelines as shown in the examples in Rule 27.5. Rule 6.2, use a space after a section symbol.

27. Change. Answer: <u>Helling</u>, 509 U.S. at 36. Explanation: Rule 12.4, abbreviate case reporters as shown in Appendix 1.

28. Keep as is. Answer: <u>Campbell</u>, 169 F.3d at 1363. Explanation: Rule 12.20, a short form is used after the first time a case is cited in full in the document.

29. Keep as is. <u>Rhodes v. Chapman</u>, 452 U.S. 337, 346, 349 (1981). Explanation: Rule 12.5(b), cite nonconsecutive pages by giving the individual page numbers separated by commas.

30. Change. Answer: <u>Restatement (Second) of Torts</u> § 931 (1994). Explanation: Rule 27.1(a), use upper- and lowercase letters and italic type when citing the title of a Restatement.

31. Change. <u>See</u> <u>Turner R.R. v. Safley</u>, 482 U.S. 78, 84-85 (1987). Explanation: Rule 12.2, abbreviate words in case names according to Appendix 3, unless doing so would cause confusion for the reader.

32. Change. Answer: <u>See</u> <u>id.</u> at 89; <u>Thornburgh</u>, 490 U.S. at 401. Explanation: Rule 45.1, signals of the same basic type must be strung together within a single citation sentence and separated by semicolons. Rule 11.3(d), when <u>id.</u> does not start a new sentence, use a lowercase "i." Rule 12.20, italicize or underscore short case names.

33. Change. Answer: <u>Owen v. Wille</u>, 117 F.3d 1235, 1235 (11th Cir. 1997). Explanation: Rule 12.5(b), when referring specifically to the first page of a source, repeat that page number.

34. Keep as is. Answer: <u>See</u> <u>U.S. v. White</u>, 490 U.S. 84, 87 (1990). Explanation: Rule 12.2(g) now permits the use of "U.S." or "United States" when referring to the name of a party in a case citation.

35. Keep as is. Answer: <u>See</u> <u>Turner</u>, 482 U.S. at 84-85. Explanation: Rule 12.20, a short form is used after the first time a case is cited in full in the document.

36. Change. Answer: <u>Ossining v. Brubaker</u>, No. CIV.A.02-2332, 2003 WL 66432 at *6 (S.D. Ala. Jan 6, 2003). Explanation: Rule 12.12(a)(2), if the database identifier does not clearly indicate which court decided the case, add the court's abbreviation before the date within the parenthetical. Careful: Many jurisdictions do not allow citation to unpublished cases.

37. Change. Answer: <u>Ala. v. Carter</u>, 507 U.S. 411, 418 (1992). Explanation: Rule 12.2(h)(2), omit "State of" in case names except when citing decisions of the courts of that state. Abbreviate state names according to Appendix 3.

38. Change. Answer: <u>N.W. Elec. Co. v. Univ. of Colo.</u>, 211 U.S. 415, 417 (1991). Explanation: Rule 12.2, abbreviate words in case names according to Appendix 3, unless doing so would cause confusion for the reader.

39. Change. Answer: <u>Thornburgh</u>, 490 U.S. at 414-15. Explanation: Rule 44.3, introductory signals. <u>See cf.</u> is not a signal in any circumstance.

40. Change <u>See</u> <u>Turner</u>, 482 U.S. at 89; <u>see also</u> 28 C.F.R. § 540.71 (2002) (establishing security as legitimate government interest). Explanation: Rule 44.6(b), italicize or underline signals.

41. Keep as is. Answer: <u>Onishea v. Hopper</u>, 171 F.3d 1289, 1300 (11th Cir. 1999). Explanation: Rule 12.1.

42. Change. Answer: <u>See</u> H.R. 81, 108th Cong. (Jan. 4, 2003) (available at http://thomas.-%20oc.gov/bss/d108/d108laws.html) (establishing security as legitimate governmental objective). Explanation: Rule 38.1.

43. Change. Answer: <u>See</u> Jeremy Stevens, <u>Taking Control</u> 41-42 (Amanda Bradley ed., 3d ed., Scholastic Press 2001). Explanation: Rule 22.1(d) and (f), place the editor's name first, the edition second, the publisher's name third, and the year of publication last.

44. Change. Answer: <u>See</u> <u>Spellman v. Hopper</u>, 95 F. Supp. 2d 1267, 1286 (M.D. Ala. 1999). Explanation: Rule 12.4, abbreviate reporter names according to Appendix 1.

45. Change. Answer: <u>See</u> Ala. Const. art. V, § 9. Explanation: Rule 13.2, abbreviate the name of the constitution and designations such as "article" or "amendment."

46. Keep as is. Answer: <u>See</u> James King, <u>Costs of Confinement</u>, 28 N. Ill. U. L. Rev. 609, 621-22 (2001). Explanation: Rule 23.1(d), abbreviate periodical names according to Appendix 5.

C. *Bluebook Quizzes*

1. Bluebook Typefaces Conventions (page 282)

1. B - Correct.
   A is incorrect. The entire case name, including the "v." is underlined. See Rules B2 and B1.
   C is incorrect. The comma after the case name should not be underlined. See Rules B2 and B1.
   D is incorrect. The case name should be underlined. See Rules B2 and B1.

2. B - Correct.
   A is incorrect. Introductory signals are underlined. See Rules B1 and B3.3.
   C is incorrect. The word "citing" should be underlined. Words and phrases introducing related authority are underlined. See Rule B1.
   D is incorrect. The title of the book, "Red House" should be underlined. See Rule B1.

3. A - Correct.
   B is incorrect. Only the "id." is underlined, not the page reference. See Rules 10.9 and B1.
   C is incorrect. The space between "See" and "Id." should not be underlined. See Rules 10.9, B2, and B7.
   D is incorrect. Introductory signals are underlined according to Rule B1.

4. D - Correct.
   A is incorrect. The title of the article should be underlined. See Rules 16.6, B9.1.4, and B1.
   B is incorrect. The newspaper's name should not be underlined, but the title of the article should be. See Rules 16.6, B9.1.4, and B1.
   C is incorrect. The name of the author should not be underlined, but the title of the article should be. See Rules 16.6, B9.1.1, and B1.

5. C - Correct.
   A is incorrect. The parenthetical information should not be underlined. See Rules B4.1.5 and B11.
   B is incorrect. "Id." should be underlined. See Rules 10.9 and B1.

D is incorrect. "U.S. Const." should not be underlined. See Rules 11, B6, and B1.

2. Basic Structure and Signals for Bluebook Citations (page 283)

1. D - Correct.
   A is incorrect. The citation with "Compare" should come before "But see." See Rule 1.3 and B3. Compare should also be used with "with."
   B is incorrect. There should be a period between the two citations and the "b" in "but see" should be capitalized. See Rule 1.3 and B3.
   C is incorrect. The two citations should not be separate sentences but part of the same citation sentence separated by a semicolon. See Rule 1.3 and B3.

2. B - Correct.
   A is incorrect. Orozco should come before Bradshaw because Supreme Court cases come before state cases. See Rules 1.4 and B3.
   C is incorrect. Singleton should come before Bradshaw because the citations should be in reverse chronological order. See Rules 1.4 and B3.
   D is incorrect. Constitutions come before cases in citation sentences. See Rules 1.4 and B3.

3. B - Correct.
   A is incorrect. Cases come before secondary sources. See Rules 1.4 and B3.
   C is incorrect. Constitutions come before cases. See Rules 1.4 and B3.
   D is incorrect. Supreme Court cases should come before court of appeals cases. See Rules 1.4 and B3.

4. A - Correct.
   B is incorrect. Parenthetical information does not come before the citation. See Rules 1.5, B3, and B11.
   C is incorrect. Parenthetical information comes at the end of the citation. See Rules 1.5, B3, and B11.
   D is incorrect. Parenthetical information comes at the end of the citation. See Rules 1.5, B3, and B11.

5. D - Correct.
   A is incorrect. The "See" citation should come before "See also." See Rules 1.2, 1.3, and B3.
   B is incorrect. The U.S. Constitution comes before state constitutions. See Rules 1.4 and B3.
   C is incorrect. This citation string needs only the first "see." See Rules 1.2 and B3.

3. Bluebook Citation Signals (page 284)

1. D - Correct. (<u>See</u> would also be correct.)
   A is incorrect. Use no signal when directly quoting an authority (see Rule 1.2(a)).
   B is incorrect. "<u>But see</u>" is used when contradicting an authority (see Rule 1.2(a)).
   C is incorrect. Use "<u>See, e.g.,</u>" when the cited authority states the proposition (see Rule 1.2(a)).
   E is incorrect. Cited authority is not contrary to the proposition (see Rule 1.2(c)).

2. B - Correct.
   A is incorrect. Use no signal when directly quoting an authority (see Rules 1.2(a) and B3.1).
   C is incorrect. Cited authority does not clearly support the proposition (see Rules 1.2(a)).
   D is incorrect. Use this signal when the cited authority is different from the proposition but analogous to it (see Rules 1.2(a)).
   E is incorrect. Cited authority is not contrary to the proposition (see Rule 1.2(c)).

3. C - Correct.
   A is incorrect. Use no signal when directly quoting an authority (see Rule 1.2(a)).
   B is incorrect. Use "<u>See, e.g.,</u>" when the cited authority states the proposition (see Rule 1.2(a)).
   D is incorrect. Use this signal when the cited authority is different from the proposition but analogous to it (see Rule 1.2(a)).
   E is incorrect. Cited authority does not clearly support the proposition (see Rule 1.2(a)).

4. B - Correct.
   A is incorrect. Use no signal when directly quoting an authority (see Rule 1.2(a)).
   C is incorrect. Use e.g. when you want to tell the reader there are several cases even if you do not cite all of them.
   D is incorrect. Use "<u>See, e.g.,</u>" when the cited authority states the proposition (see Rule 1.2(a)).
   E is incorrect. <u>Compare</u> ... <u>with</u> ... is used when comparison of the authorities will offer support for a proposition (see Rule 1.2(a)).

5. A - Correct.
   B is incorrect. Cited authority directly states the proposition. It does not offer support for the proposition (see Rule 1.2(a)).
   C is incorrect. Use "<u>But see.,</u>" when cited authority supports a proposition contrary to the main proposition (see Rule 1.2(c)).
   D is incorrect. Cited authority is not contrary to the proposition (see Rule 1.2(c)).

E is incorrect. Cited authority is not analogous to the proposition. It directly states it (see Rule 1.2(a)).

6. C - Correct.

A is incorrect. Use no signal when directly quoting an authority (see Rule 1.2(a)).

B is incorrect. Cited authority is not analogous to the proposition. It directly states it (see Rule 1.2(a)).

D is incorrect. Use "<u>But see.</u>," when cited authority supports a proposition contrary to the main proposition (see Rule 1.2(c)).

E is incorrect. Use "<u>See, e.g.,</u>" when the cited authority states the proposition (see Rule 1.2(a)).

4. Bluebook Order and Punctuation of Signals and Citations (page 285)

1. D - Correct.

A is incorrect. Signals of the same basic type—supportive—must be strung together within a single citation sentence and separated by semi-colons according to Rule 1.3.

B is incorrect. Signals of different must be grouped in different citation sentences according to Rule 1.3.

C is incorrect. When "<u>See</u>" is used, it should appear before "<u>See also</u>" in a citation sentence according to Rules 1.3 and Rule 1.2.

2. B - Correct.

A is incorrect. According to Rule 1.3, signals of different types must be grouped in different citation sentences. Only signals of the same basic type are strung together within a single citation sentence and separated by semi-colons.

C is incorrect. According to Rule 1.3, signals of the same basic type—supportive and comparative—are strung together within a single citation sentence and separated by semi-colons.

D is incorrect. According to Rule 1.2, "<u>Cf</u>" should be before "<u>But see</u>".

E is incorrect. According to Rule 1.3, signals of the same basic type—supportive and comparative—are strung together within a single citation sentence and separated by semi-colons. In addition signals should be in lower case when used to begin a citation clause.

3. C - Correct.

A is incorrect. The ordering of citations should be changed.

B is incorrect. 13 U.S.C. § 12 (1994) should be cited before 18 U.S.C. § 588 (1998) according to Rule 1.4 (b). Statues in U.S.C. should be in progressive order of U.S.C. title.

D is incorrect. 13 U.S.C. § 12 (1994) should be cited before 18 U.S.C. § 588 (1998). Statues in U.S.C. should be in progressive order of U.S.C. title (Rule 1.4 (b)).

E is incorrect. 13 U.S.C. § 12 (1994) should be cited before 18 U.S.C. § 588 (1998). Statues in U.S.C. should be in progressive order of U.S.C. title (Rule 1.4 (b)).

5. Bluebook Rules for Citing Subdivisions and Pinpoint Cites (page 286)

1. A - Correct.
   B is incorrect. Do not use "at" unless the page number may be confused with another part of the citation. See Rules 3.2 and B4.1.2.
   C is incorrect. Use "p." or "pp." only in internal cross-references. See Rules 3.2 and B4.1.2.
   D is incorrect. Use a comma between the first page of the case and the pinpoint cite: 341, 347. See Rules 3.2 and B4.1.2.

2. C - Correct.
   A is incorrect. Do not use "p." See Rules 3.2 and B9.1.1.
   B is incorrect. The page number does not go in the parenthetical information but after "642." See Rules 3.2 and B4.1.2.
   D is incorrect. See Rules 3.2 and B4.1.2.

3. B - Correct.
   A is incorrect. The page number does not go at the beginning of the citation. See Rules 3.2 and B4.1.2.
   C is incorrect. The page number does not go at the end of the citation but is separated by a comma after "341." See Rules 3.2 and B4.1.2.
   D is incorrect. The page number does not come before the reporter abbreviation. See Rules B4.1.2 and 3.2.

4. C - Correct.
   A is incorrect. The page number does not go at the end of the citation but follows a comma after "2073." See Rules 3.2 and B9.1.1.
   B is incorrect. The page number follows a comma after "2073." See Rules 3.2 and B9.1.1.
   D is incorrect. There is no need to use "at," and the page number should be separated by a comma. See Rules 3.2 and B9.1.1.

5. D - Correct.
   A is incorrect. Do not use "and." See Rules 3.2 and B4.1.2.
   B is incorrect. Cite nonconsecutive page numbers by giving individual page numbers separated by commas. See Rules 3.2 and B4.1.2.
   C is incorrect. The page numbers should be separated by commas and appear after "477." See Rules 3.2 and B4.1.2.

6.   Bluebook Rules for Short Form Citations (page 287)

1.   A - Correct.

B is incorrect. Do not repeat the case name if the same case is cited in the preceding citation. Use Id. instead. See Rules 4.1, Rules 10.9, and B4.2.

C is incorrect. See Rules 4.1, Rules 10.9, and B4.2.

D is incorrect. See Rules 4.1, Rules 10.9, and B4.2.

2.   D - Correct.

A is incorrect. Do not repeat the full case name if the case is cited in one of the preceding five footnotes. See Rules 10.9 and B4.2.

B is incorrect. There is no need to put "324" after "U.S."; instead use "U.S. at 327." See Rules 10.9 and B4.2.

C is incorrect. Do not use Id. unless the case is the only source in the preceding citation. See Rules 10.9 and B4.2.

3.   A - Correct.

B is incorrect. Do not use the full citation if the same case is the only source in the previous citation. See Rules 10.9(b) and B4.2.

C is incorrect. See Rules 10.9(b) and B4.2.

D is incorrect. The page number comes before the parenthetical information. See Rules 10.9(b) and B4.2.

4.   C - Correct.

A is incorrect. Do not use the full citation for different provisions within the same title. See Rules 12.10 and B5.2.

B is incorrect. The citation needs to include the different provision. See Rules 12.10 and B5.2.

D is incorrect. Do not use "at." See Rules 12.10 and B5.2.

5.   B - Correct.

A is incorrect. Use "supra" instead of the title. See Rules 16.9 and B9.2.

C is incorrect. Do not use the entire citation but instead use supra. See Rules 16.9 and B9.2.

D is incorrect. Do not use Id. unless the work is in the immediately preceding authority. See Rules 16.9 and B9.2.

6.   A - Correct.

B is incorrect. Do not repeat the author's name if the same source appears in the immediately preceding citation. See Rules 15.10 and B8.2.

C is incorrect. There is no need to give the book title. See Rules 15.10 and B8.2.

D is incorrect. Do not use supra if the source is in the immediately preceding citation. See Rules 15.10 and B8.2.

7.   D - Correct.

A is incorrect. Do not use Id. if there is more than one source in the immediately preceding citation.

B is incorrect. Do not cite both party names in a short citation unless the reference to only one party's name would be ambiguous. See Rules 10.9 and B4.2.

C is incorrect. See Rules 10.9 and B4.2

7. Bluebook Abbreviations (page 289)

1. A - Correct.

    B is incorrect. In a textual sentence, "Hospital" should not be abbreviated according to Rule 10.2.1(c).

    C is incorrect. According to Rule 6.1(b), omit the periods between letters of entities with widely recognized initials, such as NLRB, in text, in case names, and as institutional authors.

    D is incorrect. Incorporated should be abbreviated "Inc" according to Rule 10.2.1 (c).

2. C - Correct.

    A is incorrect. In a citation sentence, "Memorial" should be abbreviated "Mem'l," "School" should be abbreviated "Sch.," "Housing" should be abbreviated "Hous.," and "Department" should be abbreviated "Dep't." See Rules 6.1 and 10.2.2, and Table T.6.

    B is incorrect. There should not be periods after "Mem'l" and "Dep't." See Rules 6.1 and 10.2.2, and Table T.6.

    D is incorrect. "Circuit" should be abbreviated "Cir." See Rule 6.1 and Table T.7.

3. C - Correct.

    A is incorrect. Do not fully spell out "Federal Register. See Rules 14.1 and 14.2, and Table T.9.

    B is incorrect. "F.R." is not the correct abbreviation for "Federal Register," and "September." should be abbreviated. See Rules 14.1 and 14.2, and Tables T.9 and T.12.

    D is incorrect. There is a space between "Fed." and "Reg.," and September is abbreviated "Sept." See Rules 6 and 14.1, and Tables T.9 and T.12.

4. B - Correct.

    A is incorrect. "Rule" should be abbreviated. See Rule 12.9.3 and Table T.9.

    C is incorrect. Each abbreviated word should have a period after it. See Rule 12.9.3 and Table T.9.

    D is incorrect. "Federal," "Rule," "Civil," and "Procedure" all need to be abbreviated. See Rule 12.9.3 and Table T.9.

5. A - Correct.

    B is incorrect. "George Mason" is improperly abbreviated. See Table T.13 and Rule 16.4.

    C is incorrect. "Law Review" is improperly abbreviated. See Table T.13 and Rule 16.4.

D is incorrect. The periods after "Geo," "L," and "Rev" are missing. See Table T.13 and Rule 16.4.

8. Bluebook Rules for Citing Cases (page 290)

1. B - Correct.
   A is incorrect. The reporter information comes after the case name. See Rule 10.3.
   C is incorrect. Do not use periods except for at the end of the citation. See Rule 10.
   D is incorrect. Do not abbreviate "United States" when it stands alone as a named party. See Rules 10.2.2 and B4.1.1.

2. A - Correct.
   B is incorrect. Omit "of Pennsylvania." See Rule 10.2.1(f).
   C is incorrect. Omit "of Penn." See Rule 10.2.1(f).
   D is incorrect. Use "Commonwealth" instead of "Penn." See Rule 10.2.1(f).

3. C - Correct.
   A is incorrect. "S. Ct." is not the correct reporter abbreviation for the United States Reports nor is the Supreme Court Reporter the official reporter. See Rule 10.4 and Table T1.
   B is incorrect. Remove "S. Ct." See Rule 10.4 and Table T1.
   D is incorrect. Remove "U.S." before the date. See Rule 10.4 and Table T1.

4. B - Correct.
   A is incorrect. The letters "th" should not be in superscript. See Rule 10.4 and Table T1.
   C is incorrect. Abbreviate "Circuit." See Rule 10.4 and Tables T1 and T7.
   D is incorrect. "S.E.2d" stands for "South Eastern Reporter, Second Edition," not "Federal Reporter, Second Edition." See Rule 10.4 and Table T1.

5. A - Correct.
   B is incorrect. The parenthetical information is part of the citation sentence and thus should not be separated by a period. See Rule 10.6.
   C is incorrect. The parenthetical information is the incorrect order. See Rule 10.6.2.
   D is incorrect. Weight of authority goes in a separate parenthetical than the date. See Rule 10.6.1.

6. D - Correct.
   A is incorrect. Screen or page numbers, if assigned, should be preceded by an asterisk. See Rules 10.8.1 and 18.3.1.
   B is incorrect. Give the full date of the decision. See Rules 10.8.1 and 18.3.1.

C is incorrect. Citation is missing "at" before the page number. See Rules 10.8.1 and 18.3.1.

9. Bluebook Rules for Citing Constitutions (page 291)

1. C - Correct.
   A is incorrect. The first letter of "Amend." should not be capitalized according to Rules B6 and 11.
   B is incorrect. United States" and "Constitution" should be abbreviated according to Rules B6 and 11, and "amendment" should be abbreviated according to Table T16.
   D is incorrect. This choice is incorrect because there should be a period following the abbreviation of "amendment," according to Table T16.

2. A - Correct.
   B is incorrect. According to Table T16, in this context, the correct abbreviation for section is the symbol "§."
   C is incorrect. According to Table T10, "Kan." is the correct abbreviation for "Kansas."
   D is incorrect. "Kansas" should be abbreviated "Kan." according to Table T10, and "Constitution" should be abbreviated "Const." according to Rules B6 and 11.

3. D - Correct.
   A is incorrect. Id. is the correct short citation format for constitutions according to Rule 11.
   B is incorrect. Id. is the correct short citation format for constitutions according to Rule 11.
   C is incorrect. Id. is the correct short citation format for constitutions according to Rule 11.

4. B - Correct.
   A is incorrect. According to Rules B6 and 11, "Amend." should not be capitalized.
   C is incorrect. According to Rule 11, "repealed" should not be italicized in this citation format.
   D is incorrect. According to Rule 11, there must be parentheses around "repealed 1933."

5. A - Correct.
   B is incorrect. "Pa." is the correct abbreviation of "Pennsylvania" according to Table T10.
   C is incorrect. "Art." should not be capitalized according to Rules B6 and 11.
   D is incorrect. "Pa." is the correct abbreviation of "Pennsylvania" according to Table T10, and the Roman numeral II should be used rather than the Arabic number 2 according to Rules B6 and 11.

10. Bluebook Rules for Citing Statutes (page 292)

1. B - Correct.
   A is incorrect. The "28" refers to the title number of the statute. The number following the abbreviation of the statute is the section number.
   C is incorrect. The "28" refers to the title number of the statute.
   D is incorrect. The "28" refers to the title number of the statute.

2. C - Correct.
   A is incorrect. There should be periods in between the letters "U.S.C."
   B is incorrect. A short form citation for a statute may omit the date of the code edition cited according to Rule 12.10, but a full citation must include the date of the code edition.
   D is incorrect. There should be a space between "§" and the cited section number.

3. A - Correct.
   B is incorrect. This option omits the section number of the statute, which must always be included in a short citation.
   C is incorrect. Two acceptable short form citations are 42 U.S.C. § 1975 or § 1975.
   D is incorrect. This is an incomplete short form citation. Instead, according to Rule 12.10, the short form citation could read 42 U.S.C. § 1975.

4. D - Correct.
   A is incorrect. This citation is properly formatted. The Internal Revenue Code can be cited as Title 26 of the United States Code.
   B is incorrect. This citation is properly formatted. According to Rule 12.9.1, in citations to the Internal Revenue Code, "26 U.S.C." may be replaced with "I.R.C."
   C is incorrect. This citation is properly formatted.

5. A - Correct.
   B is incorrect. This is the correct citation form for West's Annotated Indiana Code, but it is not the preferred statutory compilation for the Indiana Code.
   C is incorrect. This is the correct citation form for Burns Indiana Statutes Annotated on LexisNexis, but it is not the preferred statutory compilation for the Indiana Code.
   D is incorrect. The correct abbreviation for "Indiana Code" is "Ind. Code."

6. C - Correct.
   A is incorrect. According to Rule 12.9.3, the correct abbreviation for a Federal Rule of Civil Procedure is "Fed. R. Civ. P."
   B is incorrect. There should be periods following each of the terms in the abbreviation of the Federal Rules of Civil Procedure.

D is incorrect. According to Rule 12.9.3, the correct abbreviation for a Federal Rule of Civil Procedure is "Fed. R. Civ. P." In addition, there should be no "§" before the rule number

11. Bluebook Citations for Administrative and Executive Materials (page 293)

1. C - Correct.
   A is incorrect. According to Rules B5.1.4 and 14.2, the correct abbreviation for the Code of Federal Regulations is "C.F.R."
   B is incorrect. According to Rules B5.1.4 and 14.2, the correct abbreviation for the Code of Federal Regulations is "C.F.R.," and there should be a space between "§" and the section number.
   D is incorrect. There should be no spaces between the letters in "C.F.R."

2. B - Correct.
   A is incorrect. This citation is properly formatted. However, it is not an acceptable short form citation according to Rule 14.4.
   C is incorrect. The section number must be included in any short form citation (Rule 14.4).
   D is incorrect. There must be a "§" before the section number (Rule 14.4).

3. A - Correct.
   B is incorrect. As indicated in Rule 14.2(a), the correct abbreviation for the Federal Register is "Fed. Reg."
   C is incorrect. You must include the date of the Federal Register that you are referencing, according to Rule 14.2(a).
   D is incorrect. There must be a space between "Fed." and "Reg." and a comma in the page number "25,684" (Rule 14.2(a)).

4. D - Correct.
   A is incorrect. According to Rule 6.2, there should not be a comma in numbers with fewer than five digits.
   B is incorrect. According to Table T.1, the correct abbreviation for the Virginia Register of Regulations is "Va. Reg. Regs."
   C is incorrect. When citing to an administrative register, you must include the month, day, and year of its publication.

5. B - Correct.
   A is incorrect. According to Table T1.2, "Attorney General" should be abbreviated to read "Att'y Gen."
   C is incorrect. According to Table T1.2, there should not be a period following the abbreviation "Att'y."
   D is incorrect. There should be an apostrophe in the abbreviation "Att'y" as indicated in Table T1.2.

6. A - Correct.

B is incorrect. The correct abbreviation for a presidential executive order is "Exec. Order," according to Table T1.2.

C is incorrect. The correct abbreviation for a presidential executive order is "Exec. Order," according to Table T1.2, and the correct abbreviation for the Federal Register is "Fed. Reg."

D is incorrect. According to Rule 6.2, numbers with five or more digits require commas.

12. Bluebook Citations for Books, Reports, and Other Nonperiodic Materials (page 294)

1. D - Correct.

A is incorrect. The name of the author is misplaced. According to Rules B8.1 and 15.1, the author's name should precede the title of the book.

B is incorrect. Include the author's full name as it appears on the publication, according to Rules B8.1 and 15.1.

C is incorrect. There should not be a comma separating the title of the publication and the page cited).

2. A - Correct.

B is incorrect. There should be a period following "al." and a comma separating "et al." and the title of the book.

C is incorrect. While it is acceptable to list all three authors' names according to Rules B8.1 and 15.1(b), use an ampersand (&) instead of "and" between the second and third authors' names.

D is incorrect. The authors should be listed in the order in which their names appear on the title page of the publication, according to Rules B8.1 and 15.1(b).

3. C - Correct.

A is incorrect. The volume number is incorrectly placed. It should precede the author's name, according to Rules B8.1 and 15.3.

B is incorrect. The volume number is incorrectly placed. It should precede the author's name, according to Rules B8.1 and 15.3.

D is incorrect. According to Rules B8.1 and 15.3, the volume number should be indicated by "2." Omit the abbreviation "vol." before the "2."

4. A - Correct.

B is incorrect. According to Rule 15.5.2(b), a letter should be identified both by the sending party and the receiving party.

C is incorrect. November should be abbreviated "Nov."

D is incorrect. According to Rule 15.5.2(b), identify the letter as included in a collection of works by using the term "in."

5. B - Correct.

A is incorrect. Do not use superscript in referencing a numbered edition of a publication.

C is incorrect. Edition should be abbreviated to read "ed." according to Rules B8.1 and 15.8.

D is incorrect. There should not be a comma between "ed." and "2009" according to Rules B8.1 and 15.8.

13. Bluebook Rules for Citing Periodicals (page 296)

1. B - Correct.

   A is incorrect. The title of the article should be underlined according to Rules B9.1.4 and 16.3.

   C is incorrect. The author's name should be cited as it appears in the newspaper, according to Rule 15.1.

   D is incorrect. According to Rule B1, the title of a publication should be underlined in the text of a document, but not in a citation.

2. A - Correct.

   B is incorrect. The title of the article should be underlined according to Rules B9.1.4 and 16.3.

   C is incorrect. According to Rule 16.6(a), designate Op-Ed articles with "Op-Ed." between the name of the author and the title of the article.

   D is incorrect. Abbreviate the name of periodicals according to Table T.13 for periodicals and Table T.10 for geographic locations.

3. C - Correct.

   A is incorrect. Abbreviate the title of the periodical according to Table T.13.

   B is incorrect. Abbreviate the title of the periodical according to Table T.13.

   D is incorrect. According to Table T.13, there should not be a space between the letters "L." and "J."

4. D - Correct.

   A is incorrect. If a student-written note or comment is signed, Rules B9.1.3 and 16.7.1(a) indicate that you must list the author's full name before the designation of the work as a "note" or "comment."

   B is incorrect. According to Table T.13, the correct abbreviation for the Columbia Law Review is "Colum. L. Rev."

   C is incorrect. The designation of the piece, "Note," should be capitalized according to Rules B9.1.3 and 16.7.1.

5. A - Correct.

   B is incorrect. According to Rule 15.1, include designations such as "Jr." when citing an author's full name.

   C is incorrect. Titles of books should be either underscored or italicized in citations according to Rule B1.

   D is incorrect. According to Table T.13, the correct abbreviation for the Texas Law Review is "Tex. L. Rev."

14. Bluebook Rules for Citing Electronic Media (page 297)

1. A - Correct.

   B is incorrect. If a case in LexisNexis or Westlaw has been assigned a unique database identifier, include that number following the case name (Rule 18.3.1).

   C is incorrect. Screen or page numbers in unreported opinions should be preceded by an asterisk according to Rule 18.3.1.

   D is incorrect. When citing unreported opinions, give the full date of the opinion as it appears in Westlaw or LexisNexis, including month, day, and year (Rule 18.3.1).

2. C - Correct.

   A is incorrect. According to Rule 18.3.2, when citing a code contained in an electronic database, give a short description regarding the currency of the database as provided by the database itself, rather than just the year of publication.

   B is incorrect. According to Table T.1, the correct abbreviation to Baldwin's Kentucky Revised Statutes Annotated is "Ky. Rev. Stat. Ann."

   D is incorrect. See Rules 3.2 and B4.1.2.

3. B - Correct.

   A is incorrect. The title of the article should be underlined.

   C is incorrect. According to Rule 18.2.2, the Internet URL should be appended directly to the end of the citation, not preceded by "available at."

   D is incorrect. The name of the publication should be abbreviated to "N.Y. Times."

4. D - Correct.

   A is incorrect. Include the phrase "available at" before the parallel internet citation according to Rule 18.3.2.

   B is incorrect. The date of the article should go after the name of the publication but before the page number on which the article is found.

   C is incorrect. The phrase "available at" should be italicized.

5. A - Correct.

   B is incorrect. According to Rule 17.2.4, the respective titles of the sender and recipient should precede the organization or institution that each one works for.

   C is incorrect. According to Rule 17.2.4, e-mails should be identified by the words "E-mail from" preceding the name of the sender.

   D is incorrect. Identify the sender and recipient of an e-mail using the title and employer of each (Rule 17.2.4).

6. C - Correct

   A is incorrect. Include the name of the recording company in a parenthetical following the name of the album, according to Rule 18.7.1.

B is incorrect. According to Rule 18.7.1, include the date of release in a parenthetical, along with the name of the recording company.
D is incorrect. According to Rule 18.7.1, the name of the recording company should precede the date of release, and both should be included in one parenthetical.

D. *Bluebook Self-Assessment*

1. Bluebook Citation Self-Assessment (page 300)

1. Change: Answer: U.S. Const. amend. I;. Explanation: Rule 11.

2. Keep as is. Answer: U.S. Const. amend. VIII. Explanation: Rule 11.

3. Keep as is. Answer: <u>Ossining v. Brubaker,</u> No. CIV.A.02-2332, 2003 U.S. Dist. LEXIS 5130, at *1 (S.D. Ala. Jan. 6, 2003). Explanation: Rule 18.3.1, Commercial Electronic Databases, cases; when a case is reported but unavailable on a widely used electronic database, then it may be cited to that database.

4. Change. Answer: Judith Expert, <u>Allergy on the Net</u>, 5 New Eng. J. Med. 9, 10 (2002), <u>available at</u> http://www.nejm.org/expert/v5/allergy.html. Explanation: Rule 18.2, Author; use the author's full name. Bluepages B2; you may substitute underscoring for italics.

5. Change. Answer: Irving M. Tough, <u>Warden Power</u>, 15 N.Y.L. Sch. L. Rev. 12, 15-17 (1983). Explanation: Rule 16.1, Author; use the author's full name. Bluepages B2; you may substitute underscoring for italics. Rule 16, Periodical Materials; abbreviate journal names using Table T13: Periodicals.

6. Change. Answer: Adam Gourna, <u>Celiac Disease: A Killer</u>, N.Y. Times, Dec. 12, 1994, at F3, <u>available at</u> 1994 WL 2321843. Explanation: Rule 16.6, Newspapers. Rule 16.6(e), Commercial electronic databases. T13 Months.

7. Change. Answer: <u>Pope v. Hightower</u>, 101 F.3d 1382, 1383 (11th Cir. 1996). Explanation: Rule 10, Cases No Superscript.

8. Change. Answer: U.S. Const. amend. VIII. Explanation: Rule 11, Constitutions.

9. Change. Answer: U.S. Const. amend. VIII. Explanation: Rule 11, constitutions do not use a short citation form (other than <u>id.</u>) for constitutions.

10. Change. Answer: <u>See</u> <u>Thornburgh v. Abbott</u>, 490 U.S. 401, 407-08 (1989). Explanation: Rule 10, Cases. Rule 3.2(a), when referring to specific material within a source, include both the page on which the source begins and the page on which the specific materials appear, separated by a comma.

11. Change. Answer: <u>Turner v. Safley</u>, 482 U.S. 78, 84-85 (1987). Explanation: Rule 1.1(b)(i); citation sentences start with a capital letter and end with a period.

12. Change. Answer: <u>Helling v. McKinney</u>, 509 U.S. 25, 29 (1993). Explanation: Rule 10.9, Short Forms for Cases; only use a short form if you have previously cited the case.

13. Keep as is. Answer: <u>Helling</u>. Explanation: Rule 10.9(c), Short Forms for Cases in Text; a case that has been cited in full in the same general discussion may be referred to by one of the parties' names without further citation.

14. Change. Answer: <u>Id.</u> at 35-36. Explanation: Rule 4.1, "Id." Use <u>id.</u> when referring to immediate prior reference. Always underscore <u>id.</u> (including the period).

15. Keep as is. Answer: <u>Id.</u> at 35. Explanation: Rule 10.9, Short forms for cases. Rule 4.1, use <u>id.</u> when referring to immediate preceding authority. Bluepages, always underscore <u>id.</u> (including the period).

16. Change. Answer: <u>See</u> 42 U.S.C. § 1983 (2003); <u>Farmer v. Brennan,</u> 511 U.S. 825, 837 (1994). Explanation: Rule 1.4, Order of Authorities Within Each Signal.

17. Change. Answer: <u>Campbell v. Sikes</u>. Explanation: Rule 10.2.1(a), Case Names in textual Sentences; omit words indicating multiple parties, such as "et al."

18. Change. Answer: <u>Campbell v. Sikes</u>, 169 F. 3e 1353, 1366-68 (11th Cir. 1999). Explanation: Rule 10.4, Court and Jurisdiction. Rule 3.2(a), Page numbers.

19. Change. Answer: <u>Campbell</u>. Explanation: Bluepages, Case names; underscore or italicize all case names.

20. Keep as is. Answer: Mustave Hurt, <u>Unimaginable Pain</u>, 742 Geo. L.J. 801, 831-32 (2003) (discussing the requirements to show deliberate indifference). Explanation: Introductory Rule I.4 (g), Typical Legal Citations Analyzed; Periodical materials. Rule 16, Periodical Materials. Table T13, Periodicals; journal abbreviations.

21. Change. Answer: <u>Estelle v. Gamble</u>, 429 U.S. 97, 107 (1976). Explanation: Rule 10, Cases. Table T1, cite to U.S., if therein; otherwise cite to S. Ct., L. Ed., or U.S.L.W. in that order of preference.

22. Change. Answer: <u>See id.</u> at 100. <u>But see</u> <u>Harris v. Thigpen</u>, 941 F.2d 1495, 1505 (11th cir. 1991) (holding that difference of opinion does constitute cruel and unusual punishment). Explanation: Rule 1.3, Order of Signals; signals of different types must be grouped in different citation sentences.

23. Change. <u>See</u> <u>Estelle</u>, 429 U.S. at 107. Explanation: Rule 10.9, Short Forms for Cases. Bluepages, Short Forms in Court Documents and Legal Memoranda.

24. Change. Answer: <u>McElligot v. Foley</u>, 182 F.3d 1248, 1256-58 (11th Cir. 1999), Explanation: Rule 3.2. When citing material that spans more than one page, retain the last two numbers, but drop any other repeating digits.

25. Keep as is. Answer: <u>See id.</u>; Noah Lee, <u>Deliberate Indifference: What's It All About?</u> 31 (3d ed. 2001). Explanation: Rule 15, Books, Reports, and Other Nonperiodic Materials. Rule 15.4, Edition, Publisher, Date. Rule 1.4, Order of Authorities Within Each Signal; authorities within each signal are separated by semicolons; cases before books. Bluepages, B8, Sources and Authorities: Books and Other Nonperiodic Materials. A short cite for McElligot would be appropriate if the full citation was correctly given in previous sentence (the full citation would also be correct).

26. Change. Answer: <u>See</u> U.S. Sentencing Guidelines Manual § 5D2.1(f) (2001). Explanation: Rule 12.9.5, Model Codes, Restatements, Standards, and Sentencing Guidelines. Rule 6.2(c), Sections & Paragraph Symbols; when the symbols are used, there should be a space between § and the numeral.

27. Change. Answer: <u>Helling</u>, 509 U.S. at 36. Explanation: Rule 10.9, Short Forms for Cases. Table T1: United States Jurisdictions; for Supreme Court, cite to U.S.

28. Keep as is. Answer: <u>Campbell</u>, 169 F.3d at 1363. Explanation: Rule 10.9, Short Forms for Cases. Rule B4.2, Short Forms.

29. Keep as is. Answer: <u>Rhodes v. Chapman</u>, 452 U.S. 337, 346, 349 (1981). Explanation: Rule 3.3(d), Multiple Pages, Footnotes, and Endnotes; cite non-consecutive pages by giving the individual page numbers separated by commas.

30. Change. Answer: Restatement (Second) of Torts § 931 (1994). Explanation: Rule 12.9.5, Model Codes, Restatements, Standards, and Sentencing Guidelines. Bluepages, see B1 for typefaces in legal documents vs. journals.

31. Change. Answer: <u>See</u> <u>Turner R.R. v. Safley</u>, 482 U.S. 78, 84-85 (1987). Explanation: Rule 20.2.2, Case Names in Citations; always abbreviate any word listed in Table T.6.

32. Change. Answer: <u>See id.</u> at 89; <u>Thornburgh</u>, 490 U.S. at 401. Explanation: Bluepages B2, Citation Sentences and Clauses in Court Documents. Rule 1.3, Order of Signals; signals of the same basic type must be strung together within a single citation sentence and separated by semicolons.

33. Change. Answer: <u>Owen v. Wille</u>, 117 F.3d 1235, 1235 (11th Cir. 1997). Explanation: Rule 3.3(a), Pages, Footnotes, Endnotes, and Graphical Materials; when referring specifically to the first page of a source, repeat the page number.

34. Change. Answer: <u>See</u> <u>United States v. White</u>, 490 U.S. 84, 87 (1990). Explanation: Rule 10.2.2, Case Names in Citations; do not abbreviate "United States."

35. Keep as is. Answer: <u>See</u> <u>Turner</u>, 482 U.S. at 84-85. Explanation: Rule 10.9, Short Forms for Cases. Rule 3.3(d), Multiple pages, Footnotes, Endnotes; when citing material that spans more than one page, give the inclusive page numbers, separated by a hyphen or dash. Always retain the last two digits, but drop other repetitious digits.

36. Change. Answer: <u>Ossining v. Brubaker</u>, No. CIV.A.02-2332, 2003 WL 66432, at *6 (S.D. Ala. Jan. 6, 2003). Explanation: Rule 18.3.1, Commercial Electronic Databases, cases; provide the case name, docket number, database identifier, court name, and full date of the most recent major disposition of the case.

37. Change. Answer: <u>Alabama v. Carter</u>, 507 U.S. 411, 418 (1992). Explanation: Rule 10.2.1(f), Geographical Terms; omit "state of" except when citing decisions of the courts of that state, in which case only "State" should be retained.

38. Change. Answer: <u>N.W. Elec. Co. v. Univ. of Colo.</u>, 211 U.S. 415, 417 (1991). Explanation: Rule 10.2.2, Case Names in Citations; always abbreviate any word listed in Table T6; abbreviate states, countries, and other geographical units as indicated in Table T10, unless the geographical unit is a named party.

39. Change. Answer: <u>Thornburgh</u>, 490U.S. at 414-15. Explanation: Rule 1.2, Introductory Signals. <u>See</u> <u>cf.</u> is not a signal in any circumstance.

40. Change. <u>See</u> <u>Turner</u>, 482 U.S. at 89; <u>see also</u> 28 C.F.R. § 540.71 (2002) (establishing security as legitimate government interest). Explanation: Rule 1.2, Introductory Signals. Rule 1.3, Order of Signals. Rule 1.4, Order of Authorities Within Each Signal. Rule 1.5, Parenthetical Information.

41. Keep as is. Answer: <u>Onishea v. Hopper</u>, 171 F.3d 1289, 1300 (11th Cir. 1999). Explanation: Rule 10, Cases. Bluepages B2, Citation Sentences and Clauses; citation sentences begin with capital letters and end with periods. Rule 1.1, Citation Sentences and Clauses in Law Review Footnotes.

42. Change. Answer: <u>See</u> H.R. 81, 108th Cong. (2003) (establishing security as legitimate governmental objective), <u>available at</u> http://thomas.-%20loc.gov/bss/d108/d108laws.html. Explanation: Rule 18.2, The Internet. Rule 18.2.3(c), Parenthetical Information; explanatory and other parentheticals should be placed after the date information

for that aspect of the citation to which the parenthetical pertains. Rule 13.2(a), Unenacted federal bills and resolutions.

43. Change. Answer: <u>See</u> Jeremy Stevens, <u>Taking Control</u> 41-42 (Amanda Bradley ed., Scholastic Press, 3d ed. 2001). Explanation: Rule 15, Books, Reports, and Other Non-periodic Materials; cite books by author, editor and/or translator. Rule 15.2, Editor or Translator; give the full name of the editor/ translator, publisher, edition, and date of publication in that order. Separate the editor/ translator from other publication information with a comma.

44. Change. Answer: <u>See</u> <u>Spellman v. Hopper</u>, 95 F. Supp. 2d 1267, 1286 (M.D. Ala. 1999). Explanation: T.1F., Supp 2d has spaces.

45. Change. Answer: <u>See</u> Ala. Const. art. V, § 9. Explanation: Rule 11, Constitutions; cite state constitutions by the abbreviated name of the state and the word "Const." Abbreviate subdivisions of constitutions according to Table T.17.

46. Keep as is. Answer: James King. <u>Costs of Confinement</u>, 28 N. Ill. U. S. Rev. 609, 621-622 (2001). Explanation: Rule 16, Periodical Materials. Rule 16.4, Consecutively Paginated Journals; cite works found within periodicals that are consecutively paginated throughout an entire volume by author, title of work, volume number, periodical name, first page of the work and page or pages on which specific material appears, and year enclosed in parenthesis at the end of the citation. Table T13: Periodicals.

Appendix B

TABLE OF CONTENTS WITH SCREEN NUMBERS

Note: The first column indicates the print book page number, and the second column indicates the ebook screen number.